The Fragmented World

COMPETING PERSPECTIVES ON TRADE, MONEY AND CRISIS

Chris Edwards

Methuen
LONDON and NEW YORK

First published in 1985 by
Methuen & Co. Ltd
11 New Fetter Lane, London EC4P 4EE

Published in the USA by
Methuen & Co.
in association with Methuen, Inc.
733 Third Avenue, New York, NY 10017

Typeset by Scarborough Typesetting Services
and printed in Great Britain by
Richard Clay (The Chaucer Press) Ltd
Bungay, Suffolk

British Library Cataloguing in Publication Data
Edwards, Chris, 1939–
    The fragmented world: competing perspectives
    on trade, money and crisis. –
    (Development and underdevelopment)
    1. Economics
    I. Title.   II. Series
    330.1   HB171

    ISBN 0–416–73390–5
    ISBN 0–416–73400–6 (pbk.)

Library of Congress Cataloging in Publication Data
Edwards, Chris.
    The fragmented world.

    (Development and underdevelopment)
    Bibliography: p.
    Includes index.
    1. International economic relations.
    2. Economic development.
    I. Title.   II. Series.
    HF1411.E3 1985   337   84–20782

    ISBN 0–416–73390–5
    ISBN 0–416–73400–6 (pbk.)

Contents

List of tables

List of figures

Series editors' preface

Development studies is a complex and diverse field of academic research and policy analysis. Concerned with the development process in all the comparatively poor nations of the world, it covers an enormous geographical area and a large part of the modern history of the world. Such a large subject area has generated a varied body of literature in a growing number of journals and other specialist publications, encompassing such diverse issues as the nature and feasibility of industrialization, the problem of small-scale agriculture and rural development in the Third World, the trade and other links between developed and developing countries and their effects on the development prospects of the poor, the nature and causes of poverty and inequality, and the record and future prospects of 'development planning' as a method of accelerating development. The nature of the subject matter has forced both scholars and practitioners to transcend the boundaries of their own disciplines whether these be social sciences, like economics, human geography or sociology, or applied sciences such as agronomy, plant biology or civil engineering. It is now a conventional wisdom of development studies that development problems are so multi-faceted and complex that *no* single discipline can hope to encompass them, let alone offer solutions.

This large and interdisciplinary area and the complex and rapidly changing literature pose particular problems for students, practitioners and specialists seeking a simple introduction to the field or some part of the field with which they are unfamiliar. The Development and Underdevelopment series attempts to rectify these problems by providing a number of brief, readable introductions to important issues in development studies written by an international range of specialists. All the texts are designed to be readily comprehensible to students meeting the issues for the first time, as well as to practitioners in developing countries, international agencies and voluntary bodies. We hope that, taken together, these books will bring to the reader a sense of the main preoccupations and problems in this rich and stimulating field of study and practice.
RAY BROMLEY
GAVIN KITCHING

Preface and acknowledgements

Originally the motivation for this book was provided by the need for a text which presents the unequal exchange theories of Emmanuel, Amin and others in terms which are intelligible to first- and second-year university undergraduates. In teaching courses on international economics over the past six years I have discovered that students have found difficulty with (1) Emmanuel's own book (because it is so long-winded); and (2) the writings of the other 'neo-Ricardian' theorists such as Mainwaring, Metcalfe and Steedman (because of their complex algebraic presentation).

Thus, in explaining Emmanuel to students, I have had to use articles in journals, but these suffer from two defects. First, they are not easily accessible to students; but secondly, and more important, they do not put the theories of unequal exchange in their historical context, nor do they show the relationships between unequal exchange theories on the one hand, and neo-classical and Marxist theories on the other. This book aims to do both these things. It attempts to place unequal exchange in the context of other theories about the world division of labour. It does this because I have found economic theories much easier to understand if they are placed in a comparative framework. The book also explicitly examines the political implications of each of the schools of thought. Looking at them in this light will, I think, add to the excitement of the book as well as helping the reader to understand the theories.

Thus the nature of this book changed substantially during the period of writing. Originally intended as a presentation of Emmanuel's unequal exchange and the associated controversy, it developed into a full-scale textbook on comparative international economics. It is, then, much more than a text on unequal exchange: indeed, because of its comparative approach, it is broader in coverage than most of the widely used textbooks on international economics. I attempt not only to compare a wide range of theories from Milton Friedman to Marx, but also to integrate theories about money with theories about trade.

Yet, at the same time, it is shorter than many of the textbooks on international economics. Thus readers may find understanding easier if the book is read in conjunction with other references. To encourage and assist this, each chapter ends with a section headed 'Notes on further reading'. These are not bibliographies, as such, and are not intended to be exhaustive lists of the books and articles on each topic. (They cannot be exhaustive, because there are, of course, many texts on international economics that I have not read.) The notes refer to texts or sections of texts, be they articles or books, which I have found helpful, as have many of the students that I have taught. If read alongside the chapters, they should be of interest; teachers of international economics are likely to find them particularly useful. A full bibliography will be found in the References at the end of the book.

The book also contains a further aid to understanding the flow of ideas. Each chapter ends with a flow-diagram summary which should serve as a quick check on the contents of the chapter after reading it.

This book emerges from courses on economic principles and international economic relations given in the School of Development Studies at the University of East Anglia (UEA). I have been influenced by those who taught and attended those courses. I thank all those students, sympathetic colleagues, and constructive critics in UEA and elsewhere who have helped, but particular thanks go to: Simon Bell and Barbara Dewing, for patient and long-suffering help with typing references and diagrams; John Cameron and Ken Cole, with whom I have developed a comparative approach to economic theory – such an approach is adopted in our book, *Why Economists Disagree* (Cole, Cameron and Edwards, 1983); Frank Ellis, Rhys Jenkins and especially David Evans, who have helped my understanding of particular trade theories; Howard Nicholas, who has helped my understanding of theories of money, particularly Marx's theories; Howard White, Jerry Coakley and Diane Elson, for making many valuable suggestions for improvement; and finally, thanks go to Gavin Kitching, a patient editor, to Tidings Ndhlovu for careful indexing, and to Rosalind Malt for invaluable support and friendship. All of these have given me much encouragement even though they might not agree with all that is written; the style and content are, of course, my responsibility.

1

The world division of labour and economic theories

1.1 THE WORLD DIVISION OF LABOUR — WHAT DO WE HAVE TO EXPLAIN?

If we look at international exchange — or intercountry production and trade or the world division of labour and property — what do we have to explain? What do we want to explain? These questions are, I claim, inextricably linked. Concepts, classifications, or 'facts' are not independent of theory — indeed they follow from as well as inform the theory. A presentation is part of a particular theoretical perspective. For example, if the world is presented in map form using Mercator's projection, it appears as something quite different from a world presented through Peters's projection — as shown in Figure 1.1. The projection of Mercator (the adopted Latinized name of the sixteenth-century Flemish cartographer Gerhard Kremer) is one of the most widely used projections. It is accurate in terms of direction and is, therefore, useful for navigation — but if you want it for some other purpose than sailing around the world, it may be less than useful. As a Christian Aid poster puts it: 'His [Mercator's] cartographic representation distorts the earth in favour of countries inhabited by white people' (Christian Aid, 1977).

As shown in Figure 1.1, Scandinavia appears in Mercator's projection to be equal in area to India, and yet India's 3.3 million square kilometres is three times as great as Scandinavia's 1.1 million square kilometres. This area relationship is shown accurately in the 1977 projection of the German historian Arno Peters. But as with any attempt to project the almost spherical world on a two-dimensional piece of paper, Peters's projection must also distort. In this case accuracy of direction has been maintained only for the principal points of the compass — north, south, east and west. Thus both Mercator's and Peters's projections distort the world in attempting to abstract it on to a two-dimensional plane.

Similarly, any attempt at abstraction is likely to be selective in the 'facts' that it selects to represent 'reality'. If we wish to summarize the world in statistics, we face a similar problem. What sort of classification or grouping do we use? We could, for example, summarize the world statistically as shown in Table 1.1.

A comparison of Peters' "Equal Area" projection...

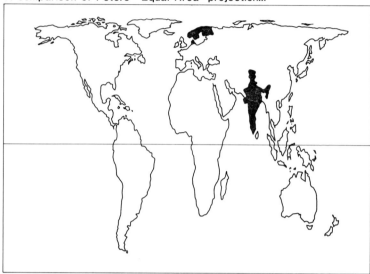

...with Mercator's projection

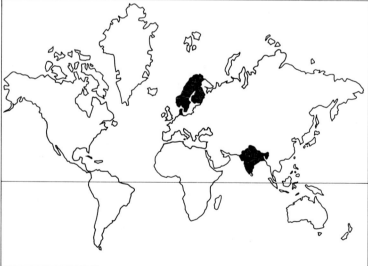

Figure 1.1 Perspectives on the world.

Table 1.1 The world in statistics – one perspective

	Population (1981)		National income (GNP) (1981)			Land area	
	Million	% of world	Per person ($ US)	Total (bn $ US)	% of world	Million sq. kilometres	% of world
Low-income oil importers	1,164	26	244	284	2	21	16
Middle-income oil importers	622	14	1,670	1,039	9	26	20
Oil exporters	507	11	1,250	634	5	15	12
All developing countries	2,293	51	853	1,957	16	62	48
Capital-surplus oil exporters	15	—	13,460	202	2	4	3
Industrialized countries	720	16	11,120	8,006	66	31	24
Centrally planned economies (including China)	1,428	32	1,384	1,977	16	33	25
Total	4,456	100[1]	2,725	12,142	100	130	100

Source: World Bank, 1983, table 1 (annex). For a country-by-country list, see ibid.; and for a map showing the countries, see World Bank, 1983, 142, 143.

Note:
1 Does not sum due to rounding.

In the table the world is split into groups of countries using a mixture of criteria. The countries are grouped primarily according to whether they are 'developing' or 'developed'. After this initial classification, they are grouped according to whether they are oil importing or oil exporting (if they are 'developing' countries) or whether they are industrialized, centrally planned, or capital-surplus oil exporters if they are not 'developing'. Thus the emphasis seems to be on relative income (GNP per person), the need or otherwise for a particular source of energy (oil), the type of technology used (industrialization), or the potential access to high technology (capital surplus) and the type of institutional structure in existence (centrally planned or otherwise). And so, using this mix of criteria, the world's population (4.556 billion), its annual income ($12,142 billion) and any other attribute (for example, land area is shown in Table 1.1) can be divided into groups. These are the categories used by the International Bank for Reconstruction and Development (IBRD, but more generally known as the World Bank) in some of the tables of its 1983 *World Development Report* (World Bank, 1983).

Is this sort of classification objective? Is it value-free? Why call some countries 'developed' and others 'developing'? Why are the latter group sometimes called 'less developed' or even 'under developed'? Clearly classifications are not as innocuous on closer examination as they seem to be at first sight. Indeed, the argument here is that classifications follow from particular economic theories. Thus in looking at the classifications of the world's population used in Table 1.1 we need to ask: why emphasize relative income, technology and industrialization, capital availability and the institutional structure for planning?

Why not put a much greater stress on the role of and scope for a free market whether it be in a 'poor' or 'rich' country? Indeed, the definition of 'developed' or 'underdeveloped' may be based on whether the individuals in a country can or cannot contract and recontract in a free market. The latter emphasis is, for example, quite marked in the writings of the famous (or infamous) American economist, Milton Friedman and his followers. As Friedman put it in an article first published in 1958, 'it thus seems clear that a free-market without central planning has, at least to date, been not only the most effective route to economic development but the *only* effective route to a rising standard of life for the masses of the people' (see Friedman, in Bhagwati and Eckaus, 1970, 72; emphasis in original).

Yet another definition of development is that adopted by a group of economists who are often referred to as the 'underdevelopment' or 'dependency' theorists. These economists reflect, to some extent at least, the rising nationalism of that group of countries which became newly independent, politically, in the 1950s and 1960s. Most of these 'new' nation-states were in Africa and Asia (see Figure 8.1 for more details), but together with the Latin American countries, they are often collectively referred to as the Third World, and they suffer, the dependency theorists argue, not from 'less development' but from '*under*development'.

This use of the term Third World to refer to the 'developing', 'less developed', or 'underdeveloped' countries was common by the mid-1950s – at about the time of the first meeting of the 'non-aligned' countries at Bandung in Indonesia. The Third World is generally understood to refer to the countries of Latin America, Asia (including China but excluding the USSR) and Africa (excluding the Republic of South Africa). In the context of Table 1.1 this includes 'all developing countries' and 'capital-surplus oil exporters', as well as the People's Republic of China.

The use of the term Third World seems to have been developed from the political left in France in the late 1940s. At that time some of the French left were using terms such as 'third force' or 'third way' to indicate their independence from the Communist Party, and the capitalist parties of the right. Similarly, by the mid-1950s three countries in particular (India, Egypt and Yugoslavia) began to refer to themselves as the 'Third World' to indicate their non-alignment or independence of the superpowers of the First and Second Worlds.

Although the Third World has been a more or less unambiguous term since the 1950s, the terms First and Second Worlds have been used in various senses since the 1970s. Until then it was generally accepted that:

the First World referred to the capitalist west (broadly the countries now belonging to the Organization of Economic Cooperation and Development – the OECD – namely Japan, Australia, New Zealand, Canada and the USA, and those in western Europe);

the Second World referred to the richer of the centrally planned or 'socialist' economies (namely the USSR and those in eastern Europe).

But then, in the mid-1970s, different categories were used in the foreign policy discussions of the Communist Party of China (CCP). The CCP, in its 'Three Worlds' policy, referred to the First World as consisting of the superpowers of the USA and the USSR, with the Second World consisting of the other developed countries (Japan and the richer countries in western Europe). (For further discussions of these concepts, see Open University, 1983, section 2, block 1; Worsley, 1978, especially the foreword; *Peking Review*, no. 44; 1974; Horowitz, 1966, chapter 1).

In this book where the terms First, Second and Third Worlds are used at all, they are used in the most commonly accepted sense: that is the First World refers to the 'capitalist west', the Second World to the 'socialist east' and the Third World to the 'less or underdeveloped south'.

Having said this it immediately must be pointed out that those economists writing within a Marxist framework are highly critical of this primary focus on *countries*. They prefer to move away from a classification based on national boundaries towards an emphasis on *classes* within countries, with classes being defined in respect to the ownership and control of the means of production (land, factories, etc.).

Thus we already have three different bases of classification and analysis. The argument of this introductory chapter is that each of these classifications is likely to follow from, or be predicated on, a separable body of economic theory, and that it is useful to identify, analyse, and understand each of these sets of theory. The question that is likely to be in the impatient reader's mind is: why not select one theory which is correct, which embodies 'reality' and present only that?

My brief answer is that there is not one indisputable 'social reality', in which case the next response may be, why don't I make my mind up, and present only the body of theory that I find the most convincing? This time my answer is that the comparative approach adopted in this book, in which each theory is explained and contrasted, better enables those theories to be understood as well as the policies which follow from them. In the same way as theories lurk behind the policies advocated and the classifications used, so are crucial assumptions hidden within the theories. The purpose of this book is *not* to explain the origin of these theories, since this is not a book on the history of economic thought. Nor is it the purpose to look in detail at the assumptions and components of each of the theories. (The reader who is interested in these more general and fundamental aspects of economic theory and policy is encouraged to refer to Cole *et al.*, 1983.) The scope of this book is more limited, namely to examine those arms of each of the economic theories which attend to the aspects of international trade and the world division of labour.

1.2 ECONOMIC THEORIES – THE COMPETING EXPLANATIONS AND THEIR SOURCES

Here I identify three main sets of economic theories, the subjective preference, cost-of-production and abstract labour. These schools of economics are founded on three theories of value – that is theories of how value comes into existence, and why things have the 'worth' or 'value'

they have. These competing theories had effectively established themselves by the end of the nineteenth century. Figure 1.2 suggests that the
father-figure of economics is Adam Smith, inasmuch as it is in the
writings of this late-eighteenth-century philosopher–economist from
Scotland that a dual theory of value can be found. It was from this theory
of value that, on the one hand, the writings of Jevons, Walras and
Menger (writers in the subjective preference school) developed and, on
the other hand, that Ricardo developed his theories.

It is in turn, in the writings of David Ricardo in the first quarter of the
nineteenth century, that traces of both of the other two schools of
economic thought can be found. And so by the end of the nineteenth
century with the development of the joint-stock company and the
separation of capitalist control and ownership, three schools of economic
thought were identifiable. This is not to say that there have not been
later developments, refinements and modifications of these sets of
theory, but by the end of the nineteenth century there existed three
interest groups – owners, managers and direct producers – for which a
particular body of economic thought was, ideologically, most appropriate.

But to say that three schools of economic thought were and still are
identifiable is not the same as saying that every economist can be neatly
pigeon-holed into one of the three boxes. There are some who clearly do
not fit into any one box. The theories of value identified here are 'ideal
types', in the sense that not only are the sets of assumptions, theories and
policy conclusions embraced by each of these types internally consistent,
but the policies can also, as argued above, be identified as ideologically
appropriate to specific interest groups. As one might expect, there have
been some attempts at 'cross-breeding' or 'synthesis' between these ideal
types giving rise to 'neo-classical' and 'neo-Marxist' theories, as shown
in Figure 1.2.

Generally, but not exclusively, in this book I refer to the three main or
'ideal' theories of value. The obvious question that then arises is: why
not categorize theories into a larger number of groups, and why use only
three? My answer is that the research of my colleagues (Ken Cole and
John Cameron) and myself has identified these three schools as having
assumptions, theories and policies which are logically consistent. In
addition, they all link description to prescription, and thus all appeal to
rationalism, to realism and to activism. This, then, is my brief answer.
Put in this way, it may sound arrogant. But by the end of the book I hope
that you will agree that this approach illuminates rather than obfuscates.
It is, however, beyond the scope of this book to trace the development of
each of these three schools of economic thought (for more detail, see Cole

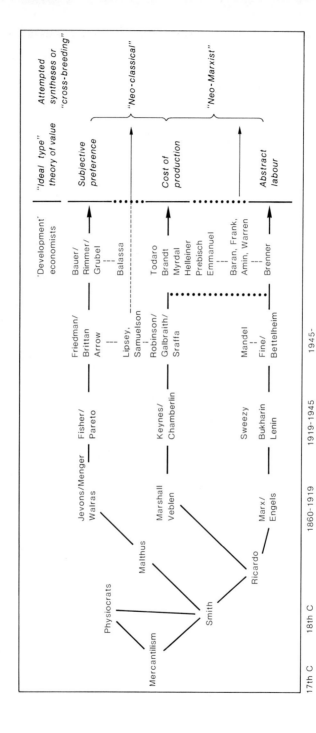

Figure 1.2 The historical development of economic thought.

et al., 1983). Here I have restricted myself to summarizing the major writers, politicians, interest groups, and the assumptions, theories and policies of each of the schools (see Tables 1.2 and 1.3). Table 1.3 presents a summary of the international 'policies' espoused by each of the three schools.

For the *subjective preference* body of economic thought (associated with Milton Friedman and Grubel in the USA, the German economist von Hayek, and Peter Bauer and Alan Walters in the UK), the promotion of free markets, unfettered by state economic intervention, is an indispensable prerequisite for economic growth and political freedom. Thus the present British government, led by Margaret Thatcher, whose policies lean on this theory, has cast doubt (see FCO, 1980) on many of the interventionist arguments put forward by the Brandt Commission. The latter, the Independent Commission on International Development Issues under the chairmanship of Willy Brandt, ex-head of the West German government, held its opening session in Germany in December 1977. By the end of 1979 the commission had produced a report under the title *North–South: A Programme for Survival* (Brandt, 1980). The report made a number of recommendations to deal with north–south relations, 'the great social challenge of our time', and to 'suggest ways of promoting adequate solutions to the problems involved in development' (ibid., 7, 8). In its terms of reference the Brandt Commission said that it would keep the call for a new international economic order (NIEO) at the centre of its concerns. The call for a NIEO had come formally from the United Nations in 1974. It will be examined in more detail in Chapter 8 but, briefly, it is the demand by the south (the less developed countries or the Third World) for a more equal distribution of the world's income.

In the view of the Brandt Commission and other advocates of the NIEO reforms are needed in international institutions to bring about this redistribution. The assumptions and theories which lie behind these policy recommendations are common to the *cost-of-production* school of economic thought. This school, associated with the American John Kenneth Galbraith, and in the realm of international economics with the Canadian Gerry Helleiner, the Swedish Gunnar Myrdal, and the British Paul Streeten and Frances Stewart, cast doubt on the efficacy of the present world market to achieve rapid development, particularly in the less developed countries (LDCs).

Writers within this school argue that the world's monetary and aid institutions need to be overhauled in line with changing technology. In addition, they argue that markets can be made to work more efficiently in the complex industrial world of today if they are regulated by national and international institutions which are being adapted continually to the

Table 1.2 The theories of the three schools of economic thought – a comparative summary

The origins of the theories	The theories (their theory of value)	Major writers	Leading politicians and interest groups	Starting-point (nature of society)	Theory of social change – society develops through	
Adam Smith (late eighteenth century) →	Subjective preference (neo-classical)	Friedman Bauer	Thatcher (UK) Reagan (USA) capitalists	The (rational) individual (universal human behaviour)	Free expression of individuals through markets	Leading
Ricardo (early nineteenth century) →	Cost-of-production (neo-Ricardian)	Galbraith Brandt	Jenkins, Owen (UK) Brandt, Schmidt (Germany) bureaucracy/ technocracy	Physical environment (requires appropriate institutions)	Linking institutions and changing technology	
Marx (late nineteenth century) →	Abstract labour (Marxist)	Fine Bettelheim	None 'working classes'	Power (control over production determines social relationships)	The revolutionary transformation of modes of production	

	society changed by	*leading to a higher civilization*	*paradoxes*
Subjective preference theory	rationalist revolution (revolution of ideas)	escape from work– economic liberty a necessary condition of political liberty	Oppression of individuals (communists) required to protect liberty of individuals (who decides where the threats come from?)
Cost-of-production theory	industrial revolution (revolution of technology)	control over nature; institutional control over physical environment removes constraints from freedom	'It is to the educational and scientific estate . . . that we must turn for the requisite political initiative' (Galbraith, 1977, 373). (Who decides who are in the educational and scientific estate?)
Abstract labour theory	social revolution (through class struggle)	work as a creative force; conscious control over *social* environment	'Between capitalist and communist society . . . the state can only take the form of a revolutionary dictatorship of the proletariat' (Marx, 1974, 355). (Who defines the proletariat?)

Table 1.3 The policies of the three schools of economic thought – a comparative summary

School of economic thought	Assumptions and theory of value				
	Necessitate policies of	With objective of	Requiring	Because crisis due to:	Determinants of international trade
Subjective preference (neo-classical)	Non-interference of state with exchange relationships	Ensuring smooth operations of free markets without uncertainty caused by inflation	Restrictions on money supply	Irresponsible governments (excess money supply)	Different national factor endowments
Cost-of-production (neo-Ricardian)	Planning by 'responsible élite'	Promoting fair distribution and full employment	New institutions to regulate the economy	Rigidities in economy and conflicts over distribution	Different national production conditions and bargaining powers over distribution
Abstract labour (Marxist)	Class struggle	Overthrowing capitalism and promoting socialism	Organization of working class	Contradictions of capitalism – tendency for rate of profit to fall	Expansion of capital through worldwide competition

thus

	International policy should	Theory (translation) of theory at international level		Refer to
Subject preference (neo-classical)	Promote free flow of factors and commodities; abolish protectionism; oppose official, non-military aid	Free market countries have developed fastest (Friedman: compare post-Meiji Japan and post-independence India)	→	Grubel, 1977; Little et al., 1970; Friedman and Friedman, 1980; FCO, 1980; Bauer, 1981
Cost-of-production (neo-Ricardian)	Adapt international institutions to correct distributional inequalities and to promote technology; promote the NIEO	Unregulated markets promote development for the few	→	Brandt Report, 1980; Helleiner, 1976 — — → Emmanuel, 1972
	Countries most isolated from 'capitalism' have developed fastest (Baran: compare Japan and India; Frank: look at Latin America)	But look at expansion of 'capitalism' and the development of forces of production world-wide (Warren and Schiffer)	→	Baran, 1957; Frank, 1967; Warren, 1980; Schiffer, 1981
Abstract labour (Marxist)	Promote international solidarity of workers (and peasants?)	Experience of social crises and revolutions; internationalization of production by capital accumulation	→	Brenner, 1977

needs of the world economy. Thus the cost-of-production theorist is the
enthusiastic advocate of a NIEO. Changes are needed to prevent arguments over income distribution from blocking the introduction of the
advanced technology necessary for economic growth.

By contrast, writers within the third school of economic thought,
associated with and deriving from the ideas of Karl Marx, are more
sceptical about the extent to which mere institutional reforms are likely
to achieve one of the Brandt Commission's objectives, namely to 'shape
the world's future in peace and welfare, in solidarity and dignity'. The
writers within this school such as the Belgian Ernest Mandel, the American Paul Sweezy, the French Charles Bettelheim and the British Ben
Fine, place more stress on the control of wealth and power *within*
countries than on the distribution of income *between* countries. They
question whether a redistribution of income between nation-states is the
most important objective; it is at best a means towards the end of
enabling the mass of people in the world to gain control over production,
the basis of their lives. They agree with the cost-of-production school
that the end in sight is a more fundamental freedom than the subjective
preference school's mere liberty of free exchange in the market-place.
But when the Marxists argue that the achievement of freedom for all is
likely to require more than just institutional reforms and may well
require more or less continuous revolutions, they are in clear disagreement with the cost-of-production school.

For the Marxist school, the appearance of market freedoms and prices
within capitalism conceals the fundamental realities of power relationships. Similarly, the average or 'socially necessary' labour time used to
produce a commodity is separated or 'abstracted' from the commodity's
price; hence the term *abstract labour theory of value* can be applied to this
school. This approach enables them, the Marxists claim, to rip the veil
from the apparently equal relationships in the market to reveal the
historically specific capitalist system or 'mode of production'. And the
purpose of revealing and of analysing this mode is to bring about its
destruction.

The four chapters that follow look at the ways in which the three
schools analyse the world economy; and examine both the theories and
the policies of these three sets of economic theory. But before setting out
on this task, it is important at this point to repeat an earlier word of warn-
ing. In categorizing economic theories into three groups I am not
arguing that every economist falls neatly into a particular group. First,
not all economists are consistent; and secondly, there are different points
of emphasis by writers *within* each school. Thus the division of economic
theories into three schools is itself an abstraction.

On ways of viewing the world in map form look at Mazrui, 1980; *New Internationalist*, June 1983, 2, 3; Open University, 1983, Third World Atlas, 4–7; and more generally, Kidron and Segal, 1981. The latter's stimulating *State of the World Atlas* not only compares the Mercator and Peters projections (as I have done in Figure 1.1), but also attempts to present major topics of public concern in map form. It contains sixty-five maps showing aspects of world government, business, labour, health, housing, and so on. For further 'images, definitions, and connotations' of the Third World and 'development', see Open University, 1983, Atlas, 8–9, and block 1.

In this chapter Table 1.1 presents the statistical world in one form; variations on this theme can be found in World Bank, 1983, the same source from which the table was constructed. As far as the grouping into three schools is concerned, this is not the only book to use such a threefold classification: reference has already been made to Cole *et al.*, 1983; and for a briefer introduction by the same three authors, see Cameron *et al.*, 1980. For other references to the three schools of economists, see the article, written in 1974, in Rowthorn, 1980, and the introduction in Smith and Toye, 1979. Smith and Toye refer only to international trade, while Rowthorn's article is of a more general nature. Neither of these uses exactly the same classification as adopted here, but close likenesses with this classification are discernible; this is particularly true of Rowthorn's piece. For a similar threefold classification within sociology, see Benton, 1977.

SUMMARY

1.1 To explain/understand world division of labour/world economy

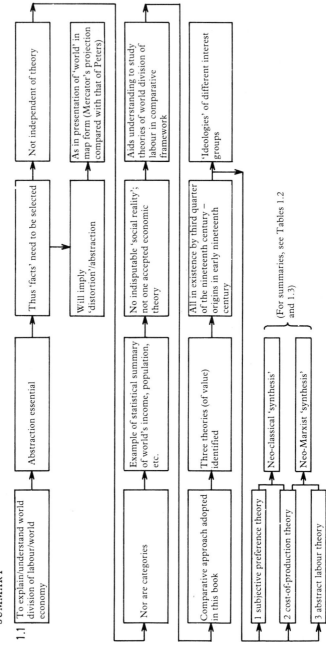

Abstraction essential

Thus 'facts' need to be selected

Not independent of theory

Will imply 'distortion'/abstraction

As in presentation of 'world' in map form (Mercator's projection compared with that of Peters)

Nor are categories

Example of statistical summary of world's income, population, etc.

No indisputable 'social reality'; not one accepted economic theory

Aids understanding to study theories of world division of labour in comparative framework

Comparative approach adopted in this book

Three theories (of value) identified

All in existence by third quarter of the nineteenth century – origins in early nineteenth century

'Ideologies' of different interest groups

1 subjective preference theory

2 cost-of-production theory

3 abstract labour theory

Neo-classical 'synthesis'

Neo-Marxist 'synthesis'

(For summaries, see Tables 1.2 and 1.3)

2

The free-marketeers and the rise and fall of the Heckscher–Ohlin theory

2.1 FREE TO CHOOSE – THE ESSENCE OF SUBJECTIVE THEORY

Free to Choose is the title of a recent book by Milton Friedman, written jointly with Rose Friedman (1980). It is the clearest expression of the case for the free market in capitalism, or more formally of the subjective preference theory of value. For Friedman, as for others within this school, the *end* as well as the *means* of development is the free expression of individuals in exchange. In an earlier article, Friedman had argued, 'what is required in the underdeveloped countries . . . is . . . an atmosphere of freedom, of maximum opportunity for individuals to experiment, and incentive for them to do so in an environment in which there are objective tests of success and failure – in short, a vigorous, free capitalistic market' (Friedman, in Bhagwati and Eckaus, 1970, 71). This atmosphere of freedom in the market will 'release the energies of millions of able, active and vigorous people who have been chained by ignorance, custom and tradition' (ibid.).

For Friedman, the energy release in the west came from the rationalist revolution of the Enlightenment, the period in which people began to be free of the dictates of lords and sovereigns, and in which a free market began to flourish. With the progressive destruction of the divine rule of kings in the seventeenth and eighteenth centuries, individuals became free to express their tastes and talents. This free expression of individuals in the market-place suffices for development. It is all that is required: the behaviour of individuals is rational and unchanging, therefore it is universal.

This rational individual, endowed with tastes and talents, is assumed to act so as to maximize his or her personal welfare or utility. Two problems arise from this statement.

First, because utility cannot be measured in any absolute sense, individuals' preferences, as revealed in the market-place, have to be assumed to reflect the maximization of utility. This assumption must remain just that, since there is no way in which it can be empirically tested. This gives rise to the temptation to cross the line between saying 'the world acts *as if* it were composed of independent individuals' and 'the world *is* composed of independent individuals'. As the Cambridge economist Joan Robinson put it, 'utility is a metaphysical concept of impregnable circularity' (Robinson, 1968, 48).

The second problem is: who is the individual? Do all individuals, regardless of age, maximize utility – or just adult individuals, or the 'heads' of households? This is a problem which is posed in a textbook by Lancaster only to be assumed away (see Lancaster, 1974, 217). But clearly, although it is a problem, it is a less serious one than that of the nature of assumptions about independent individuals, whoever they are.

The assumption that the world is composed of independent individuals is the essence of subjective preference theory. Once we accept this, we can accept a whole corpus of theory which has both rigour and elegance. And in a world of assumed possessive individuals, what more could we want? If we accept that social behaviour consists of relating to others through the exchange of different tastes and talents, then we will be able to enjoy all sorts of neat theorems dressed in pretty mathematical clothing! These tell us that there is no contradiction between the individual interest and the 'social' interest, since no one has to enter into a contract if it is not in his/her interest to do so. An attractive equilibrium (entirely voluntary) can be shown to exist, where individuals sacrifice their self-contained utility in supplying labour and capital. The costs of this sacrificed leisure and of postponed consumption are matched by the rational individual against the utility derived from consuming the products purchased in the market. And if we rebut or, more likely, conveniently ignore the argument that an extra dollar's income is worth less to a rich person than to a poor one, we can safely say that the free market will give us the best of all possible worlds – a situation of 'Pareto optimality' ('no one can be made better off without someone else being made worse off').

Having become a member of this school, we then find ourselves objecting to active government intervention in the economy. We shall argue for the role of the state being limited to providing law and order – to ensure a framework for enforcing voluntary contracts and thereby maintaining incentives. We shall want to promote competitive markets for the sale of outputs and the purchase of inputs. Trade unions will be discouraged as unnecessary and undesirable, as will restrictive practices by companies. The special talents of entrepreneurs who, motivated by profit maximization, play the crucial role of combining production inputs, must not be inhibited by 'non-economic' constraints or discouraged by high taxation.

We shall be sceptical of aggregate relationships expressed in national accounts, since such measures do not always reflect the values as expressed in the markets. Some goods and services will not have been the subject of exchange in a free market and will have been included in the national accounts at their 'cost of production'. Who can say, then, what is their real worth? And so (in the context of the USSR) Friedman has argued 'the ordinary man is by no means better off now than before the communists took over. . . . The achievements of which Russia justifiably boasts are . . . [ones] that from the point of view of the consumer classify strictly as monument building' (Friedman, in Bhagwati and Eckaus, 1970, 72).

Thus we will be sceptical of national accounts aggregates, such as gross national product (GNP), as measures of welfare or standards of living. We will beware of what Douglas Rimmer has referred to as 'macromancy', the elevation of macroeconomic aggregates to a form of incantation (see Rimmer, 1973, 51). Rimmer argues that 'conceptually as well as statistically the growth of GNP is a worthless indicator of social progress' and that 'national accounts . . . reflect the expanding ambitions of governments' (ibid., 14, 30).

In so far as national accounts are used at all the aggregates that will be stressed are those relating to personal consumption expressed in the free market. The higher is 'free' consumption, the better. And the lower the level of state expenditure, in general the more healthy the economy. But things are not quite so simply correlated as this. A government's share of gross domestic product and a country's share of world incomes are correlated. The richer the country, the greater the share of the government in national expenditure (see Kidron and Segal, 1981, table 26).

Presumably the response of subjective preference theorists to this would be to say that the income of the richer countries would be even higher if state expenditure were lower. In any case, they might say, state intervention in the economy may be considerable even though the government's share of national expenditure is small. For example, the government's share of gross domestic product in India is similar to that in Japan; but, as the Friedmans in *Free to Choose* argue, the 'tyranny of controls' was greater in India thirty years after independence, in 1947, than it was in Japan in the thirty years after the Meiji Restoration of 1867. Despite the eighty-year difference, the Friedmans claim that a valid comparison of the situations of the two countries can be made. The 'resource' differences that did exist should have favoured India, they say, rather than Japan. And yet despite this, 'the outcome was vastly different

. . . [in Japan] the lot of the ordinary man improved rapidly', whereas in India 'the standard of life of the poorest third of the population has probably declined' (Friedman and Friedman, 1980, 83).

The explanation of the difference, they claim, lies not in different human characteristics but in the relative freedom for initiative and enterprise in post-Meiji Japan as compared with post-independence India. In the latter case, they imply, the deadening hand of government control has stifled the initiative of enterprising Indians:

> The explanation is the same as for the difference between West and East Germany, Israel and Egypt, Taiwan and Red China. Japan relied primarily on voluntary cooperation and free-markets – on the model of the Britain of its time. India relied on central economic planning – [again] on the model of the Britain of its time.   (ibid., 85)

The rapid recovery of the Japanese economy after the Second World War, they also imply, was due to the relatively free market. Some may, and do, disagree with this Friedmanite interpretation of history – contrast, for example, the fifth chapter of Baran, 1957, with the Friedmans' second chapter. Baran argues that Japan's relative wealth compared to India's is the result of their differing histories in the colonial period, with Japan being isolated while India was plundered by the British.

But for the Friedmans, the message is clear: the state must not impede the free market. For they claim that

> there is, as it were, an invisible hand in politics that operates in precisely the opposite direction to Adam Smith's invisible hand. Individuals who intend only to promote the *general interest* are led by the invisible political hand to promote a *special interest* that they had no intention to promote.   (Friedman and Friedman, 1980, 340)

Consistent with this, any flows of resources between countries which are not subjected to the 'discipline' of the market should be opposed, unless they are initiated to preserve the operations of the free markets. Thus non-military, government-to-government aid must be opposed, but military aid, if designed to keep out totalitarianism and to preserve the 'free world', is acceptable, as is economic aid channelled through charitable agencies (see Bauer, 1976; Friedman, in Bhagwati and Eckaus, 1970). Government-to-government economic aid is likely to be adverse to economic development, because it strengthens the government sector at the expense of the private sector, and encourages monument building. The strictures on government non-military aid are consistent with the rest of the theoretical structure, but the advocacy of military aid has an awkward edge. The argument is: military aid (and the coercion it implies) is necessary to ensure economic freedom; thus coercion is necessary to ensure liberty. This is something of a paradox, but as Table 1.2 indicates, the other schools are not free of similarly fundamental paradoxes.

Thus, for subjective preference theory, freedom is all-important, whether that freedom be exercised in national or international markets. Individuals should be able to exercise their talents wherever they choose, and should be free to buy goods from any source in the world without impediment. The free exercise of talents implies, then, that there should be no 'closed shops' within workplaces and no controls on international migration. In the piece referred to earlier, Rimmer bemoans the 'fictitious' national boundaries and the controls on immigration and ends with a somewhat defeatist sentiment: 'to recommend that enterprising strangers of alien race and religion be allowed to immigrate would not be telling government what it wants to know in Uganda, Indonesia, Egypt and Burma – and not even in Britain' (Rimmer, 1973, 60).

Fortunately for the subjective preference theorists, such political constraints are not as important as they might seem. Although national controls on migration impede individual liberty, their effects on welfare are not too harmful. For, the subjective preference theorists argue, free trade in goods and money-capital will tend to compensate for any international restrictions on labour mobility. Thus it is, perhaps, not surprising that it was with the tightening of restrictions on international labour migration after the First World War that a neo-classical theory of international trade was developed by two Swedish economists, Eli Heckscher and Bertil Ohlin. It is the development of this Heckscher—Ohlin theory which is discussed in Section 2.2.

2.2 THE RISE OF THE HECKSCHER—OHLIN THEORY

A student taking a course in international economics will be confronted at an early stage with the theory of *comparative advantage* (see, for example, Sodersten, 1980, chapter 1). The principle of comparative advantage is usually presented in something like the following terms:

	prices (in terms of international money – say, ounces of gold)	
	UK	*India*
cloth	40	60
corn	45	50

The argument runs that the UK would gain by producing nothing but cloth in spite of the fact that it produces *both* goods (corn and cloth) more cheaply. People in the UK would gain by exchanging cloth for India's corn, because the latter (India) has a *comparative* or relative advantage in the production of corn. That is to say, in producing an additional unit of corn, India gives up less than a unit of cloth – to be precise, 50/60ths – whereas the UK, in producing an additional unit of corn, has to sacrifice *more* than a unit – to be precise, 45/40ths of a unit – of cloth. Thus the UK has a comparative advantage in the production of cloth and should specialize in its production. If the UK does specialize in cloth production, and India specializes in the production of corn, then it is argued that there will be a gain from such specialization represented in an increase in total world production.

Two issues should then follow from such a presentation, but usually only one is discussed in the textbooks on international trade. The one which is usually discussed is: what determines these comparative costs? The second, not usually discussed, is: by what mechanism does it become profitable for traders to buy corn from India and sell it in the UK when the Indian price of corn is, initially, higher (in gold or international money) than that in the UK? I defer discussion of this second question until Section 6.1, when I move on to the connection between theories of international trade and international money. In this chapter I confine the discussion to the first issue: what are the determinants of comparative costs?

Usually the principle of comparative advantage is traced back to the beginning of the nineteenth century, to the writings of Robert Torrens and particularly David Ricardo. Both these economists were living and writing on political economy in Britain at the close of the Napoleonic Wars. Ricardo's analysis, contained in his *Principles of Political Economy and Taxation*, is discussed in some detail in Chapter 3. Here it is sufficient to point out that Ricardo's cost differences were based on differences in technology or production conditions. Thus the UK might have a comparative advantage in the production of cloth because of superior technology. As we shall see later (in Chapters 3 and 4), those economists whose theories derive from Ricardo (the neo-Ricardians) have developed theories of trade based not only on differences in technology, but also on differences in distribution and, in particular, on differences in wage bargaining.

By contrast with Ricardo, and about a century after him, the Heckscher–Ohlin theory emphasized differences in factor endowments as the basis of comparative advantage. This theory assumes that technology *is* equally available in all parts of the world. The central argument is that relatively labour-abundant countries will tend to specialize in relatively labour-intensive goods. More precisely, a country which has a high ratio of labour relative to other factors (such as land or capital) will tend to specialize in the production of goods which are relatively *labour*-intensive. And so, in our earlier example, if corn is a labour-intensive good relative to cloth, and if labour is relatively abundant in India, then India will tend to specialize in corn production. It will have, according to the Heckscher—Ohlin theory, a comparative advantage in the production of corn, and there will be gains from trade for people in both India and the UK.

But the Heckscher—Ohlin theory went further than this. Not only did it argue that there will be gains from trade, but also that there will be a tendency for wage rates (and other factor prices) to be equalized, following the development of trade. The reasoning behind this 'factor price equalization', as it came to be called, is as follows: as India specializes in the production of corn, thus switching production away from cloth, its pattern of production becomes more labour-intensive. As a result, India's relative abundance of labour is reduced, the marginal productivity of labour in India rises and wages also rise. Conversely, in the UK, as cloth production replaces corn production, labour becomes less scarce, the marginal productivity of labour falls and wages also fall. Thus with free trade in goods encouraging specialization, wages in India rise; wages in the UK fall; and the primary question posed by Heckscher in 1919, namely: 'under what conditions, how, and to what extent, foreign trade evens out the scarcity of factors of production among countries' (Heckscher, 1919, 285), begins to be answered.

If these conditions for evening out the relative scarcity of factors are not too restrictive, we can, as free-traders, advocate the liberalization of trade secure in the knowledge that not only will there be gains to the trading nations, but that there will be a tendency to world equity, inasmuch as labour will be paid at the same rate for the same effort and skill across the world. Some economists have found the conditions too restrictive and the logic untenable, but others still cling to the Heckscher—Ohlin theory with considerable faith. It is still the talisman for many in the citadels of free trade, having considerable ideological importance, but in 1919 when Heckscher first put it forward, it was particularly opportune. To understand why, we need to look in more detail at the historical context in which it was developed; and then, after taking a brief historical look, return to the assumptions and logic of the theory.

Heckscher wrote his article setting out the theory soon after the First World War. His pupil, Ohlin, developed the theory in a book first published in 1933 (though the reference used here is Ohlin 1967). The Heckscher–Ohlin model was further extended and developed, most notably by the American Paul Samuelson, so that the theory is often referred to as the Heckscher–Ohlin–Samuelson (HOS) theory. But it was in 1919 that the core of the HOS theory was initiated with the publication of Heckscher's article entitled 'The effect of foreign trade on the distribution of income' (see Heckscher, 1919).

In the half-century or so prior to its publication there had been two developments in the world which, in this context, are important to note. First, there was massive international labour migration, mostly between Europe and North America. Between the middle of the nineteenth century and the 1930s almost 60 million people were known to have migrated overseas, while many more went unrecorded. Immigration into the USA reached its peak between 1880 and the outbreak of the First World War, and in the fifteen years between 1900 and 1915 about 12 million people immigrated into the USA (see Open University, 1976, 58–60). But soon after the end of the First World War, restrictions on immigration were introduced by the US government, rendering obsolete the inscription on the Statue of Liberty at the entrance to New York Harbor: 'Give me your tired, your poor; Your huddled masses yearning to breathe free; The wretched refuse of your teeming shore; Send these, the homeless, tempest-tossed to me; I lift my lamp beside the golden door.' Thus ended a period of mass migration huge even by the standards of those movements of labour in the 1960s and 1970s from southern to northern Europe, from Central to North America, from south to west Asia and within West Africa.

The second point to note about the historical context of Heckscher's article is the growing strength of *protectionist* movements towards the end of the nineteenth and the beginning of the twentieth century. For between the middle of the nineteenth and the beginning of the twentieth century the great powers of the period – Britain, France, Germany and Russia – had carved up the world. The population of the territories annexed, as colonies, by these powers grew from around 150 million in the mid-nineteenth century to more than 500 million by the end of the century (Brown, 1974, 185). This was a period of intense competition between these colonizing countries and the USA. By 1970 German and American capital was emerging into the world market to challenge Britain as the 'workshop of the world'. Their industries, particularly those linked to military needs, were being developed behind protective tariffs. Indeed, this seems to have been the case not only for German and American industries, but also for French and others. As Michael Barratt Brown puts it: 'after Britain all countries that successfully industrialized their economies did so behind the protection of tariff walls' (ibid., 149).

In 1844 Robert Torrens had referred to the 'hostile tariffs of foreign rivals', and in nineteenth-century Britain a campaign grew for increased defences against these hostile tariffs. At the beginning of the twentieth century Joseph Chamberlain, an ex-Colonial Secretary with interests in the Midlands engineering industry, led a campaign for imperial trade preference, a system of preferential tariffs linking Britain and its colonies.

But there was also opposition to the protectionists. Chamberlain's campaign was opposed by the stronger traders and producers who could benefit from a trading system unconstrained by imperial preferences or other restrictions.

Thus at the beginning of this century there was a substantial continuing interest in free trade not only in Britain, but also in the new industrialized countries (NICs). With this interest under threat, the argument for free trade needed to be restated. And if it could be restated in such a way as to show that free trade was not only desirable, but that it might compensate for the restrictions on labour migration introduced after the First World War, then so much the better. The Heckscher theory offered just such a prospect. Certainly it was directed at such a problem. Whether it provided a satisfactory answer has been doubted by many economists who have questioned both its assumptions and its logic; but others still find it convincing.

The Heckscher–Ohlin theory in detail

As stated earlier, the Heckscher theory, as developed, is usually presented in a highly abstract form of two countries (in my example Britain and India), producing two goods (cloth and corn) using two factors (say, labour and capital). We are presented, in other words, with a $2 \times 2 \times 2$ model. As the widely used textbook by Caves and Jones points out, the HOS 'two by two model . . . has proven to be immensely popular not only in the area of international trade, but also in other fields' (Caves and Jones, 1977, 108), even though in the 1973 edition of their book they had admitted that 'in practice, Nature persistently presents us with at least 3 factors of production and more commodities and countries'.

Note, in the above, that it is nature that provides us with at least three factors of production, and many more commodities and countries. Caves and Jones thus assume a model in which the countries of the world are simply endowed with different quantities of factors of production. The countries exist – we don't ask how. The factors of production are distributed between these countries – again, no questions are asked. Of course, this is only the 'basic trade model' and we can modify it later, but this approach has set the tone and has established the methodology. The establishment of nation-states and the wars between them have to be explained, like so many other things, by 'non-economic factors'. I come back to this issue in Chapter 9.

Thus in the neo-classical writings on international trade of, for example, Caves and Jones we are presented with an endowment model. If we assume, in this $2 \times 2 \times 2$ model, that the two goods (corn and cloth) are produced using different quantities of the factors of production (capital and labour), and that the two countries (the UK and India) are endowed with different amounts of capital and labour, then we have the potential for factor price equalization following trade between the countries. Assume that the UK is relatively well endowed with capital and that India is well endowed with labour. The blueprints for producing the two goods, corn and cloth, are available equally freely in both countries, but cloth is *always* the more capital-intensive good.

From such assumptions the Heckscher–Ohlin theory then goes on to argue that 'capital' will be relatively cheap in the UK, because it is relatively abundant. Conversely, in India labour, being abundant, will be cheap. And because corn is assumed to be the relatively labour-intensive good, it will be cheaper, relative to cloth, in India than in the UK. India will then have a comparative advantage in the production of corn. It is at this point that the argument usually skips a crucial stage. Refer back to the table of prices given on p. 21: one question is immediately raised – how will merchants find it profitable to sell Indian corn in the UK when a unit of corn costs 50 ounces of gold in India and only 45 ounces in the UK? The answer is, of course, that at these prices trade *from* India *to* the UK will be unprofitable. Before two-way trade can take place, prices will have to change to reveal the comparative advantage as a competitive or profitable advantage. Such an adjustment is often assumed without being made explicit. For the moment I will do the same. But be warned! We shall return to this second issue in Chapter 6.

But now let us follow the orthodox textbooks in assuming that a two-way trade does take place in accordance with revealed comparative advantage, with Indian corn exchanging for British cloth. Thus the production of corn will increase in India, substituting for cloth production, and production in the UK will tend to switch from corn to cloth. As a result of an increased production of the 'capital-intensive' cloth in the UK, more 'capital' will be used, and British 'capital' will become, relative to labour, less abundant. Its marginal productivity and price, according to the HOS theory, will tend to rise. Conversely, in India more labour will be absorbed as the production of corn, the relatively labour-intensive good, expands. Thus labour will become increasingly scarce in India, raising its price relative to capital. Therefore, the factor price ratios in Britain and India will tend to converge, and if the tendency to specialization and the resulting substitution of labour and capital go far enough, they will be identical. This is what Heckscher not surprisingly referred to as a 'harmonious state of equilibrium' (Heckscher, 1919, 290).

Thus trade continues to expand until an equalization of the relative scarcity of the factors of production among countries has occurred. The argument can be presented more formally (see, for example, Shone, 1972, chapter 3) by saying that if both countries produce *both* cloth and corn and share the same technology, their pre-trade points must lie on the same curve relating goods price ratios and factor price ratios. Therefore, in Figure 2.1 the factor endowment in India gives rise to a pre-trade goods price ratio OP_I, whereas the factor endowment in the UK gives rise to a pre-trade price ratio of OP_{UK}. Thus, before trade, the price of corn *relative* to cloth is higher in the UK than it is in India. The mix of production in India is then assumed to move from point I_0 in Figure 2.1 towards the production of more corn (as indicated by the arrow). In the UK, on the other hand, specialization moves in the direction of cloth from point UK_0.

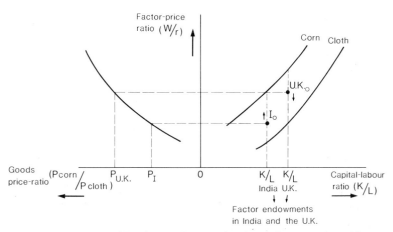

Figure 2.1 Factor intensities, factor prices, goods prices – the pre-trade position.

Note: I_0 and U.K.$_0$ are the assumed pre-trade production mixes in the two countries; other terms and notation should be clear from the text.

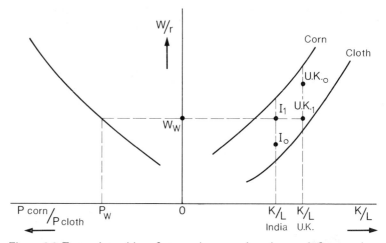

Figure 2.2 Factor intensities, factor prices, goods prices and factor price equalization after trade.

Note: I_0, U.K.$_0$ are the pre-trade production mixes (see Figure 2.1); I_1, U.K.$_1$ are the production mixes following trade.

If the tendency to specialization can go far enough, then a common goods price ratio in the two countries (allowing for transport costs between them) will be consistent with the same factor price ratio. This is shown in Figure 2.2, the common, or world, price ratio of goods being denoted as OP_w with factor price ratios being equalized at OW_w. Eureka! Trade is not only advantageous, it actually evens out differences in wages between the two countries. Thus, to quote Heckscher, 'differences in the prices of factors of production . . . nullify themselves even in the absence of movements of the factors' (Heckscher, 1919, 286) and 'under the assumption of the same technique in all countries, it follows that nothing is lost either in the individual country or in the world as a whole by the fact that the factors of production remain where they are . . . [showing] that mobility of factors of production between countries would not necessarily mean a gain for the transferred factors' (ibid., 289).

Thus Heckscher's article gave the politicians the theoretical ammunition to argue that not only would free trade provide gains to trading countries, but it would also lead to world equity. The politicians could now cite 'respectable, professional sources' in support of both restrictions on labour migration (in the name of 'cultural stability' or whatever) and free trade in goods. Unfortunately for them, however, the Heckscher–Ohlin–Samuelson (HOS) theory was to come under severe attack from a variety of directions. Section 2.3 briefly discusses the most important of these attacks on Heckscher's 'harmonious state of equilibrium'.

2.3 THE FALL OF THE HECKSCHER—OHLIN THEORY

Already I am sure you will have had some doubts about the assumptions of the original factor price equalization version of the Heckscher—Ohlin theory and its validity. Clearly wage rates have not been equalized across the world. Is this because free trade has not been practised, and therefore the theory of factor price equalization has had no chance of operating, or is the theory itself of doubtful validity?

Certainly in this century, as in the nineteenth, there never has been completely free trade in goods across national boundaries and, in that sense, the theory of factor price equalization has never had a fair trial. But there are many economists who have questioned the realism of the assumptions, and some who have questioned the logic of the HOS. Even in his 1919 article Heckscher questioned whether the production patterns in countries could be changed sufficiently to even out the relative scarcities of factors. He argued that before the massive migration of labour from Europe to the USA in the second half of the nineteenth century, there was such a scarcity of labour to land in the USA that changes in production were unlikely to be sufficient to equalize factor price ratios. Indeed this, Heckscher argued, was a major explanation of the emigration of Europeans to the USA (see Heckscher, 1919, 291). In the American case the factor endowment before the migration was *so* different from that of the countries with which the USA traded that the relative scarcity of factors could not be evened out sufficiently, by changes in patterns of production, to bring about factor price equalization.

This is illustrated in Figure 2.3 by reference to the previous India—UK example. Compare this with Figure 2.2, in which there is one world commodity price equivalent to *one* set of wage rates in the world economy. But in Figure 2.3 the specialization of production has not been able to even out wage rates. In this case there will be strong pressure on labour to migrate, or for technology to change.

For factor price equalization to take place, that is for wage rates to be equalized without international labour migration or changes in technology, the two countries need to have factor endowment ratios which are not too dissimilar. This is particularly the case if the internal labour-force changes with changes in the wage rates. Thus it is reasonable to suppose that as wages in India rise with the relatively abundant labour

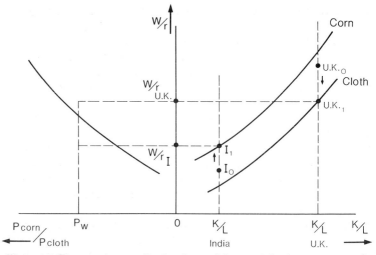

Figure 2.3 Factor price equalization impossible, specialization cannot go far enough.

being soaked up by the expanding production of labour-intensive corn, then the supply of Indian labour will itself expand. In other words, we should assume that trade may provide an 'outlet' or 'vent for surplus labour', as leisure becomes less attractive relative to work with the rising wage rate in India. Conversely, in the UK as the wage rate falls with the reduced scarcity of labour, then the labour supply itself is likely to contract. Thus, as Heckscher realized, the factor endowments may not be fixed regardless of factor prices and we may get the 'rather paradoxical result that when supply reactions are taken into account, foreign trade tends to increase the relative differences in the supply of factors of production in different countries' (ibid., 293). These changes in the *domestic* labour forces will at the very least reduce, and may even offset, the tendency for relative factor endowments to be equalized by changes in production patterns. In terms of Figures 2.1–2.3 instead of the factor endowments of India and the UK being fixed at all factor price (w/r) ratios, they would themselves vary with those factor price ratios.

The likelihood of factor prices being equalized may be further reduced when we allow for the existence of non-traded goods. So far it has been assumed that there are two produced goods, corn and cloth, both of which are traded. But if it is assumed that there are some goods (for example, cement), the transport costs for which are so great that they are never traded, the possibility is raised of a significant wedge being driven between the factor price ratios in India and the UK, even after trade has taken place.

Thus we already have two arguments which challenge the theory that trade will even out the scarcities of factors and equalize their 'rewards'. But other, more fundamental doubts have been cast on the theory. One relates to the availability of technology; the other to the more complex issue of factor intensity.

Many economists have questioned the assumption that the same techniques of production are available in all countries. For example, Raymond Vernon has argued that there is a hierarchy of production between the rich and poor countries, so that the most technologically advanced products are first produced in the rich countries and only later get transferred to poor countries. This 'product cycle' approach could of course be explained by the Heckscher–Ohlin free market theory, with the 'new' products being capital-intensive ones, but instead Vernon emphasized the role of market 'imperfections'. He argued that production techniques are *not* equally available in all countries precisely because of differences in the technologies already in use. Thus we may have to 'take a long detour away from comparative cost analysis into areas which fall under the rubrics of communication and external economies' (Vernon, 1966, 309). However, other economists such as Ivor Pearce (1970, 326) have defended the assumption of 'equal blueprint availability'. Certainly this is a central assumption of factor price equalization theory.

But even when production techniques are assumed to be equally available in all trading countries, a fundamental problem still arises. For one crucial assumption of the HOS theory is that one good (corn in the earlier example) is always, at *all* wage rates and rates of profit (or 'factor price ratios'), more labour-intensive than the other (cloth in the example). But if this assumption is dropped and we allow for what is usually called *factor intensity reversal*, then factor price equalization may not occur. If you cut through the jargon, this is obvious: see Figure 2.4 for an example. At some factor price ratios corn is more labour-intensive, and at others it is more capital-intensive. Thus, again, we can have *two* factor price ratios (w/r_{UK} and w/r_{India}) consistent with *one* world price ratio (p_w) for the goods. In such a case wages in India will never be equal to those in the UK, however free the trade. At this point you might find it helpful to compare Figure 2.4 with Figure 2.2.

But how likely is the factor intensity reversal shown in Figure 2.4? Unfortunately for the supporters of the HOS, highly likely, particularly when we move away from the unrealistic world of just two factors of production (say, labour and one specific machine). Ivor Pearce has pointed to the difficulty of establishing whether one country is more

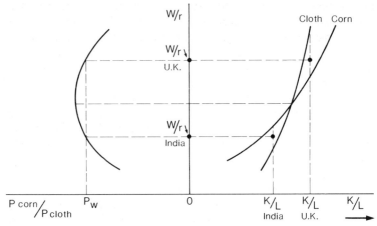

Figure 2.4 Factor intensity reversal: factor prices unequal.

abundant in labour than another when there are three or more factors of production (ibid., 521). Thus, in our earlier example, we may assume that labour, weaving machines and land are used to produce corn and cloth in India and the UK. Even such a simplified world as this may cause problems when we try to define relative labour abundance. For we may find that whereas the ratio of labour to weaving machines is *higher* in India than in the UK, the ratio of labour to land may be *lower*. To talk unambiguously of labour abundance we must aggregate the factors into two categories, say, labour and 'capital'. But then, as Pearce points out, when we do that, we might easily have factor intensity reversal, depending on the units (acres, hours, etc.) that we use to aggregate the factors (ibid., 488–9).

The logical objections – the capital controversy

This problem of aggregation is obviously a serious one, once we consider any reasonably 'realistic' picture of the world in which a number of different machines (weaving, spinning, ploughing, etc.) are used as well as land to produce even just two goods. Indeed, this aggregation problem constitutes a most important basis for an attack on the HOS theory, because it strikes at the fundamental *logic* of the theory. The aggregation problem was highlighted in Pierro Sraffa's *The Production of Commodities by Means of Commodities* (1960). For many years previously Sraffa had worked at Cambridge University on a fifteen-volume collection of David Ricardo's writings. It was this work which provided the stimulus for the 1960 book and, to some extent, the controversy that emerged from the book stimulated the development of a neo-Ricardian analysis of international trade. For despite the somewhat unexciting title, Sraffa's book provided the basis not only for an attack on the HOS theory, but more generally an attack on the aggregative neo-classical economics. Thus its basic idea deserves closer scrutiny.

The basic problem arises because the Heckscher–Ohlin theory never sticks to one definition of 'capital'. Capital is sometimes used in the physical sense to refer to machines, sometimes to a fund of savings or money to be invested. It conflates and confuses the two with rather serious consequences.

The theory had argued that if 'capital' was abundant, it would be cheap. Thus we need some unambiguous way of saying whether or not 'capital' is abundant. Surely we can do this, it might be argued, by looking at the number of machines? But clearly with many different types of machine (that is with 'heterogeneous' capital), we will need to aggregate them in money terms. Thus to talk of aggregated capital in, for example, the production of cloth, we need to add spinning machines to weaving machines to balers, and so on. Such an aggregation will be ambiguous unless it is done in money terms. But surely (the next reply might be) we can simply add their market values together? But – and this is where we again confront the problem of aggregation – the market values are likely to change with the rate of interest, that is with the factor price ratio. The problem is not simply that capital is heterogeneous – the same could be said of labour – but that machines are commodities produced by commodities, and those commodities themselves command interest.

Thus the Heckscher–Ohlin theory is now faced with a logical problem. It wants to say that if capital is abundant, it will be cheap, that is the rate of interest (or profit) will be low. And yet it seems that we cannot define whether capital is abundant without first specifying the rate of interest. We are in a nasty vicious circle! To understand, in simple terms, this complex capital valuation problem which is at the heart of the so-called 'capital controversy', assume that you find yourself in the unfortunate position of being unemployed. You may, in desperation, decide to sink your principles by sinking your principal, that is invest, in a business producing plastic replicas of the American President. You may calculate that a machine can be bought for $200 which, after all living expenses, will give you a cash surplus of $110 in the first year and $121 in the second year – but which will be obsolete and worthless at the end of the second year (maybe, in this case, because of the short-lived appeal of the product, but more usually because the machinery is worn

Table 2.1 The profitability of the presidential plastic-replica producing machine

	Year 1 ($)	Year 2 ($)
Amount owing to the bank	200	110
Interest at 10% p.a.	20	11
Cumulative amount outstanding	220	121
Year's cash surplus	(110)	(121)
Amount owing at the end of the year	110	nil

out). Is the machine worth buying? If you can borrow the money from the bank at an interest rate of 10 per cent a year, you may decide that it is worth it, since at the end of the second year you will just be able to pay off the interest and the bank loan (see Table 2.1 for the calculations).

But now suppose that just before you buy the machine, the interest rate changes to 20 per cent a year. If your estimate of the revenue is unchanged, the machine will be worth much less to you, as you will now be unable to meet your debt and living expenses without incurring further debt. You may decide that producing plastic replicas of presidents wasn't going to be much fun anyway. This heart-rending but simple example has been used to show that if the interest rate ('factor price ratio') changes, the value of capital is also likely to change. It is illegitimate, then, to talk of the value of capital independently of distribution – that is of relative factor prices. Yet this is exactly what the HOS theory does. A central argument of the theory is that if capital is scarce, the rate of interest will be high. The value of capital is assumed to be measurable independently of the rate of interest or factor price ratio.

This assumption of independence is crucial to the marginal productivity theory of income distribution, developed by an American economist, J. B. Clark, at the turn of the century (see Clark, 1965). Clark compared his theory with Milton's *Paradise Lost*, inasmuch as it justified the ways of God to man. The argument of the marginal productivity theory of distribution was, simply, that each factor of production received the value of its own contribution to production: we get what we deserve. Clark pointed out that entrepreneurs employ factors (labour, capital, land, etc.) until the value of what these factors contribute at the margin (their marginal revenue product) is equal to their marginal cost to the entrepreneur. And since each individual entrepreneur is assumed to be too small to influence the price of factors, the marginal unit cost of each factor is the same as its price. Thus it would seem that the price of a factor must be equal to the value of what it produces. Eureka! We get what we deserve and goods prices tend to determine factor prices.

Another way of reaching the same conclusion is through the use of algebra. Assume that there are just two factors of production, labour and 'capital'. Then the value of output must be equal to the wage bill plus the cost of 'capital', or:

$$QP = wL + rK$$

where: Q = quantity produced;
      P = price of product per unit;
      w = wage rate per hour;
      L = number of hours worked;
      r = the annual rate of interest;
      K = the value of capital.

If, then, labour (L) is held constant, but capital is increased slightly (dK), we find that:

$$d(QP) = r(dK); \text{ or } \frac{d(QP)}{d(K)} = r.$$

That is the rate of interest (r) is equal to the marginal productivity of capital, or $d(QP)/d(K)$.

Again we have arrived at the same conclusion as before, but this time through the use of the seemingly 'more objective' use of mathematics. The provider of capital has received exactly what he/she has produced and thus what he/she deserves. Distribution is 'natural' and the ways of God are justified to man! And so, by extension, if a good is produced under the same technical conditions in two countries (so that the marginal productivity of capital is the same in both), and if the price of the good is equalized through trade, then the marginal productivity of capital will be equalized. With this being the same in both countries, the factor prices (equal to the value of marginal productivity by assumption) will be equalized.

The argument seems to be deceptively simple. It is, but it is also simply deceptive. It suffers from *misplaced aggregation*. For although the individual entrepreneur faces given factor prices, the economy as a whole does not. This was clearly shown by Sraffa using a two-factor, two-good model similar to that used to illustrate the HOS theory. Sraffa presented an example of an economy producing a surplus (over what is required for immediate consumption) from the production of two goods (say, corn and cloth) and in which the surplus was divisible between two factors of production, labour and capital. He showed quite simply that in such an economy the price ratio of corn to cloth is indeterminate until the price ratio of labour to capital (the 'distribution') is specified. (The argument can be easily summarized using some simple algebra, but if you have already grasped the problem intuitively, you may want to skip the next three paragraphs.)

It is clear that the production (input–output) equations for corn and cloth (our 'economy') could be specified as follows:

$$(a_{11}p_1 + a_{21}p_2)(1 + r) + wa_1 = p_1$$
$$(a_{12}p_1 + a_{22}p_2)(1 + r) + wa_2 = p_2.$$

Here it is assumed that:

corn and cloth (the two goods, 1 and 2) are produced and are each used in the production of the other, so that a_{12} is, for example, the quantity of good 1 used in the production of good 2 (cloth);

p_1 and p_2 are the prices of corn and cloth respectively;
the net output (surplus) is distributed between capital and labour;

r is the rate of interest on the goods advanced for production;

w is the wage rate paid at the end of the production period;
the labour inputs (say, hours) per unit (of corn and cloth) are specified as a_1 and a_2.

Now the algebra may look forbidding, but the argument is simple, for even if we assume that the physical coefficients for the goods and labour inputs (the as) are assumed to be fixed (by technology and working practices), we are still left with four variables (p_1, p_2, r and w) in two equations. And even if we get rid of one of the goods' prices by using it as a numeraire and setting it equal to one, so that the price of one good (say, corn) is expressed in terms of the other, we are still left with three variables in two equations. And it is a mathematical fact that one needs as many equations as variables in order to find a solution.

Thus Sraffa's book showed that the relative prices of our two goods (corn and cloth) cannot be determined until the distribution of the surplus – technologically fixed in Sraffa's model – between capital and labour has been resolved. In other words, Sraffa suggested that instead of profits and wages being dependent on prices, the direction of causation tended to go the other way. Thus the HOS was shown to be logically flawed and unable to deal with the production of commodities by means of commodities.

When we look, therefore, at the real world in which there are a variety of goods in the production of other goods – that is when we allow for heterogeneous capital goods – the whole basis of aggregated neo-classical economics crumbles. It is no longer possible to say that $d(QP)/d(K)$ – the value of the marginal productivity of capital – determines r (the rate of interest). Thus labour and capital do not necessarily get what they deserve, and once we allow for goods' prices changing as factor prices change, then we can quite easily get the same effect as that produced by factor intensity reversal (refer to Figure 2.4). As a British economist, Ian Steedman, put it in an introduction to a recent collection of 'neo-Ricardian' essays on trade theory: 'the HOS tradition is flawed by an inadequate treatment of "capital", which confuses capital as a fluid fund of finance with capital as a specified list of produced means of production' (Steedman, 1979a, 6). Once we distinguish between these two different concepts of capital (capital as a physical collection of machines, and capital as a fluid fund of money), we can have one goods price consistent with two factor price ratios, and factor price equalization will not hold.

But not only is the basis of factor price equalization destroyed by the capital valuation problem. In addition, the predictive aspects of the Heckscher–Ohlin theory are questioned. For how can we argue with any conviction that a capital-abundant country will produce capital-intensive goods more cheaply than other countries, and therefore export them, when we cannot define capital abundance in isolation from the cost of capital? And since we cannot unambiguously measure capital in physical terms, we *have* to resort to a measurement in price terms. But then we are in grave danger, to say the least, of arguing in a circle. It is not very useful to say that countries have an abundance of labour if most of their exports have a low value added per employee. We surely need an independent measure of labour abundance. In other words, we do not say anything useful when we say that labour is abundant if it is cheap, when at the same time we say that it is cheap if it is abundant.

Thus what the capital controversy did, among other things, was to reveal that the distribution between capital and labour is not a 'natural' process. Sraffa's book shows that distribution between groups such as capital and labour cannot be said to be determined by their respective contributions to production. Neither labour nor capital gets what it deserves. And neither the wage rate nor the rate of profit is fixed; the division of the technologically fixed surplus is clearly determined outside the model or set of equations.

Thus, returning to the earlier example, even if corn production increases in India, there is no certainty that unemployment in India will fall; but even if it does, wage rages will not necessarily rise. Conversely, real wage rates might be maintained in the UK even when unemployment increases. Thus comparative advantage does not appear 'naturally' from the economic system, but can be created by what the neo-classicists consider to be 'extraeconomic' action. What the capital controversy shows is that logically this bargaining over distribution must be part of the model and, therefore, not 'extraeconomic'.

Now it might be suggested that the equalization of factor prices has become more likely with the massive growth in international capital mobility which has occurred in the half-century since the development of the Heckscher–Ohlin theory. Certainly it is likely that the international rate of profit has tended to be equalized, with the internationalization of capital that has taken place. We shall return to this issue in later chapters, but for the moment it is important to emphasize that comparative advantage is not a 'natural' process in the way that free-marketeers often suggest. With the destruction of the marginal productivity theory of distribution, it is clear that each factor does not get paid what it deserves, and that comparative advantage can be 'created'.

It is not surprising that with the publication of Sraffa's book a flood of articles on the 'aggregation problem' was unleashed. The logic of neo-classical economics, and with it the HOS theory, was swept away. The paradoxes which had been suggested by empirical work on trade in the 1950s and the early 1960s were not paradoxes at all. The most famous of these so-called paradoxes was the 1953 study by an American-based economist, Wassily Leontief (for concise summaries of this and other similar studies, see Magee, 1980, 22–3), Leontief, in a study of American trade based on 1947 data, had found that exports from the USA were more labour-intensive than imports (Leontief, 1953). This seemed to be contrary to the HOS model which predicted that a capital-abundant country like the USA would export relatively capital-intensive goods.

Explanations for this apparent 'paradox' were not slow in coming. Some resorted to a relaxation of the HOS assumptions either by arguing that the exports were new products in which the USA had an advantage because other countries lacked the technology (see, for example, Vernon, 1966); or by arguing that the US tariff structure distorted trade in such a way as to encourage the export of labour-intensive goods (see Travis, 1964). Others resorted to a 'neo-factor proportions' approach in which 'human capital' or 'research and development expenditure' was simply added to other 'capital'. But a more fundamental objection came from those economists who argued with the flowering of the 'capital controversy' in the 1960s that once the capital aggregation problem was recognized, there was no longer a 'paradox' to be explained. As Metcalfe

and Steedman put it: 'It is sufficient to recognize that when the endowment of capital means the value of capital, the HOS analysis gives no
prediction whatever concerning the pattern of trade and thus neither
Leontief's findings nor any other empirical findings relating to the
pattern of trade can be regarded as "paradoxical"' (Steedman, 1979a, 73).

Nevertheless, many economists still carry on as though the controversy had never occurred. The Leontief paradox is still alive, if a bit
sickly, and there are some, like Caves and Jones, whose commitment to
the ailing neo-classical world is so strong that we find them saying in the
small print of a footnote: 'Economists recognise many difficulties in the
concept of "capital" – its homogeneity, the difficulties of measurement,
etc. Here we ignore these problems and assume capital is in the form of
homogeneous machines useful in producing clothing' (Caves and Jones,
1977, 94).

Other economists on the right of the political spectrum are more
honest. Some might be tempted to change the aggregated categories and
replace capital by land, so that the HOS model is unflawed, but as
pointed out by Steedman (1979a, p. 5), a model without capital is hardly
convincing. An alternative is to deny the relevance of aggregates. Indeed,
Frank Hahn, the Cambridge economist, has argued that:

> This [neo-classical] theory has nothing simple to offer in answer to the
> question why is the share of wages, or of profits, what it is? The ques-
> tion is prompted by our interest in the distribution of income between
> social classes, and social class is not an explanatory variable of neo-
> classical theory.   (Hahn, 1972, 2)

The response of purists on the political right is to retreat into a dis-
aggregated world consisting of millions of separate individuals choosing
between millions of goods and attempting to maximize their individual
utilities. We are back, in other words, to the world of pure subjective
preference theory in which society is simply a summation of many
different activities. In such a world migration controls are regretted for
preventing individuals from freely exercising their talents in their own
interests and, indirectly, in the interest of others. Thus factor mobility is
simply a matter of a response to prices, without consideration of the
general social conditions which have given rise to those factors and
prices. Of course, historically, there were price incentives to move slaves
or indentured labour from one area of the world to another, but such
movements were accompanied by specific sets of social conditions which
made them profitable. The ahistorical approach of subjective preference
theory and its relegation of social conditions to a 'non-economic' status

sweep such problems away. Individuals have fixed tastes and talents, and the fewer questions asked about how these are derived, the better.

In the summation society of subjective preference theorists, in which the state and other 'social conditions' are non-economic factors, we can still argue for free trade and free movement of money-capital on the ground that, even if factor prices are not equalized, there will at least be welfare gains for individuals within the trading nations. These individuals will still have an opportunity to express their tastes by buying foreign and domestic goods under more or less similar conditions even if, regrettably, they are unable to move freely across international boundaries to exercise their talents. The resulting international and intranational income distributions are not of much concern to them. For as the Friedmans argue, in a world which is full of gambles, some are bound to win and others to lose (Friedman and Friedman, 1980, chapter 5). What matters is equality of opportunity, not equality of outcome. In the words of Margaret Thatcher, 'opportunity means nothing unless it includes the right to be equal' (quoted in Labour Research Department, 1977, 31).

But there are a substantial number of economists who are not quite so indifferent to inequality of outcome. Nor are they quite so ready to relegate institutional factors to the status of the 'non-economic'. Indeed, there is a whole school of economists who argue that distribution and institutional considerations must be at the forefront of any analysis of the international economy. This is the 'cost-of-production' school. And it is to their ideas that we turn in Chapter 3.

NOTES ON FURTHER READING

For a clear expression of the principles and policies of the subjective preference theory, one can do little better than refer to the Friedmans' *Free to Choose* of 1980. For a systematic interpretation of that world, look at Cole *et al.*, 1983, chapters 3 and 4. More specifically, in the world of aid, see Friedman, in Bhagwati and Eckaus, 1970; Bauer, 1976; and for trade, see Little *et al.*, 1970, or Milner and Greenaway, 1979. (Later in this book we return to the issues of trade and protection, so more references will follow.) In the more general context of 'development and the Third World', see Friedman and Friedman, 1980, or Bauer, 1981.

The section in this chapter on the rise of the HOS theory is original but, for the historical context, Brown, 1974, is stimulating, if a little rambling, see especially chapters 6–8. There are many sources in which an exposition of the HOS theory can be found; in my experience students have found most of them difficult or dull. The original sources should be consulted, namely Heckscher, 1919; Ohlin, 1967; but of the presentations in textbooks, the clearest are probably those in Caves and Jones, 1977, chapters 7 and 8 – consult the 1980 edition; Findlay, 1970; Shone, 1972, chapter 3; Sodersten, 1980. For a discussion of the HOS theory within the broader context of international trade theories, refer to the survey in Chipman, 1965–6, though it is long (in three parts). For discussions of the so-called Leontief paradox, see Findlay, 1970; Sodersten, 1980; Yeats, 1981. For the capital controversy, the easiest texts to start with are probably Meek, 1961; Robinson, 1971. Most students find Sraffa, 1960, difficult; but Harcourt, 1972, is more accessible. For more specific criticisms of the HOS theory, see the introduction in Smith and Toye, 1979; Stewart, in Streeten, 1973; Magee, 1980, chapter 2. Also refer to Steedman, 1979a, 1979b, confining yourself to the first chapter in each, and then, once confidence is gained or curiosity aroused, look at readings 5 and 6 in Steedman, 1979a.

For the Friedmans' interpretation of the histories of India and Japan, see Friedman and Friedman, 1980, chapter 2. You may find it stimulating to read this alongside Baran, 1957, chapter 5, and J. B. Moore's *Social Origins of Dictatorship and Democracy* (Moore, 1966, chapters 5 and 6).

SUMMARY

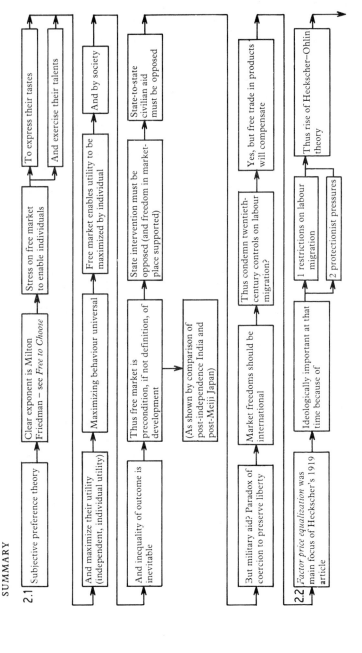

2.1 Subjective preference theory → Clear exponent is Milton Friedman – see *Free to Choose* → Stress on free market to enable individuals → To express their tastes / And exercise their talents

And maximize their utility (independent, individual utility) → Maximizing behaviour universal → Free market enables utility to be maximized by individual → And by society

And inequality of outcome is inevitable → Thus free market is precondition, if not definition, of development → (As shown by comparison of post-independence India and post-Meiji Japan)

State intervention must be opposed (and freedom in market-place supported) → State-to-state civilian aid must be opposed

But military aid? Paradox of coercion to preserve liberty → Market freedoms should be international → Thus condemn twentieth-century controls on labour migration? → Yes, but free trade in products will compensate

2.2 *Factor price equalization* was main focus of Heckscher's 1919 article → Ideologically important at that time because of → 1 restrictions on labour migration / 2 protectionist pressures → Thus rise of Heckscher–Ohlin theory

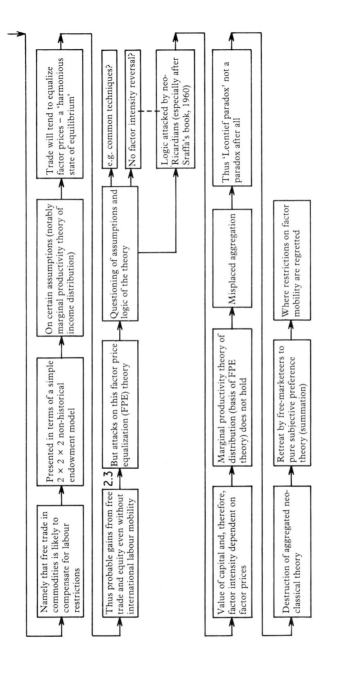

Trade will tend to equalize factor prices – a 'harmonious state of equilibrium'

On certain assumptions (notably marginal productivity theory of income distribution)

Presented in terms of a simple 2 × 2 × 2 non-historical endowment model

Namely that free trade in commodities is likely to compensate for labour restrictions

e.g. common techniques?

No factor intensity reversal?

Logic attacked by neo-Ricardians (especially after Sraffa's book, 1960)

Questioning of assumptions and logic of the theory

Thus 'Leontief paradox' not a paradox after all

2.3 But attacks on this factor price equalization (FPE) theory

Thus probable gains from free trade and equity even without international labour mobility

Misplaced aggregation

Value of capital and, therefore, factor intensity dependent on factor prices

Marginal productivity theory of distribution (basis of FPE theory) does not hold

Where restrictions on factor mobility are regretted

Destruction of aggregated neo-classical theory

Retreat by free-marketeers to pure subjective preference theory (summation)

3

The rise of cost-of-production theory

3.1 PLURALISM AND DISTRIBUTION

In Sraffa's *Production of Commodities by Means of Commodities* there is a strong emphasis on the separation of distribution from production. But somewhat paradoxically, as was pointed out in Chapter 2, this means that the prices of production depend on the wage–profit distribution. Sraffa's book was not published until 1960, but he was developing the ideas in it as early as the 1930s. At about the same time, also in Cambridge, John Maynard Keynes was writing *The General Theory of Employment, Interest and Money*. In this Keynes emphasizes the conflict between 'speculation' and 'enterprise' as an ultimate cause of stagnation in a monetized, industrial economy in which the role of finance-provider (or rentier) is separated from that of production decision-maker (or entrepreneur). Thus Keynes emphasized the possibility of a distributional conflict interfering with production and investment decisions, with the solution being euthanasia for the rentier and the state taking over the financing of investment (see Keynes, 1976, chapter 24).

But just as the separation of distribution from production did not originate with Sraffa, the idea of distributional conflicts producing stagnation did not originate with Keynes's concern with the role of the rentier. Both these ideas can be traced back to the early nineteenth century, more than a century before the appearance of Keynes's *General Theory*. They trace to an economist-stockbroker MP, David Ricardo – with the thread running through the writings of John Stuart Mill (in the middle of the nineteenth century), Alfred Marshall (in the late nineteenth century) and on through the twentieth-century writings of Veblen, Sraffa, Keynes and Galbraith. All these writers have common ideas which can be traced back to Ricardo, and may be referred to as the 'cost-of-production' school inasmuch as their starting-point for economic analysis is the cost of production derived from a production

technology and distribution, both of which are assumed to be determined outside the immediate production or labour process.

But it was following the publication of Sraffa's book in the 1960s that
cost-of-production theory (COP) experienced a resurgence. This can be
explained by the power of Sraffa's ideas; and by the emergence in the
1970s of an economic crisis especially in the advanced economies of the
west, and the political polarization generated by this crisis. Since in
essence Sraffa's ideas were not new, I prefer to emphasize this political
polarization as an explanation of the COP rebirth. Certainly, in British
politics at least, the ideas of the COP theorists have been clearly reflected
in the ideas of the newly emergent Social Democratic alliance. And at the
international level the Brandt Report is a clear reflection of COP theory.
But more about these policy expressions later in this chapter and the
next; first, I take a brief look at the origins of COP theory – the arguments of David Ricardo.

David Ricardo and the foundations of cost-of-production theory

In his *Principles of Political Economy and Taxation* Ricardo developed a
theory of stagnation or 'crisis', which provided the basis of his call for the
abolition of restrictions on wheat imports into Britain, restrictions better
known as the Corn Laws. His theory of stagnation was based on a
number of assumptions. In agriculture diminishing returns were
assumed, so that as previously uncultivated land was brought into use, so
the output per acre and per labour-day fell. But in Ricardo's model there
was no possibility of a fall in wages compensating for this fall in productivity. Wages were assumed to be at subsistence level, an assumption
derived from Ricardo's clergyman contemporary, Thomas Malthus. It
was this gloomy assumption which gave rise to the labelling of economics as the 'dismal science'. Thus the wage was always tending to be
driven to subsistence level by population pressures.

From these assumptions of diminishing returns in agriculture and a
subsistence wage Ricardo developed a theory of a declining rate of profit
leading to stagnation, which, he argued, applied to the Britain of his
time. Restrictions on wheat imports into England (Corn Laws) had been
tightened in 1815 to protect domestic agriculture following a series of
good harvests. These restrictions meant that the extra food demanded by
the soldiers and sailors returning from the Anglo-French (Napoleonic)
wars had to be grown domestically. With diminishing returns in agriculture, recourse had to be had to less fertile land, but with wages fixed, the
surplus on this less fertile 'marginal' land was lower than on the more

fertile 'intramarginal' land. Ricardo argued that the landlords would cream off the differential surplus on the land of higher productivity in the form of rent. A more detailed exposition can be found in Cole *et al.* (1983, chapter 5).

In the section on crisis theory, and more generally in Ricardo's *Principles*, technology, the surplus and distribution are all given from outside the model by assumption. The same theoretical structure provides the basis of the cost-of-production models, in which there is a separation of the process of production from that of surplus distribution. These models are used not only in the valuable critique of the HOS theory (as shown in Chapter 2), but they also provide the basis for a body of economic theory in its own right (as we shall see later and in Chapter 4). For the separation of production conditions from distribution raises the possibility of distributional conflicts interfering with the production decision, and in turn generating further distributional conflicts. It is this central concern with the distribution of a technologically fixed surplus, and the tendency to stagnation if free market forces are allowed to operate, that distinguishes the cost-of-production approach from the other economic camps.

Some cost-of-production theorists are referred to as neo-Ricardians because their theory is even more directly derived from Ricardo (through Sraffa) than COP theory in general. These neo-Ricardian (or Sraffian) writers have been particularly involved in international trade theory – examples of such writers are Ian Steedman, Lyn Mainwaring and David Metcalfe. We shall look specifically at their theories in Section 3.2. The controversial suggestion of this book is that Emmanuel's *unequal exchange* theory also falls within this neo-Ricardian category – this point is developed in Chapter 4, but for the moment we return briefly to COP theory in general.

Cost-of-production theory today

In general, in COP theory social relations are largely determined by the needs of technology and conditioned by the pattern of distribution; but both technology and distribution are determined outside the model. This is not to say that technology is unchanging; it is simply assumed to be a function of institutions. Thus it changes as people learn more about the physical world. In turn these changes in technology bring about changes in distribution and generate the potential for new distributional conflicts. If the latter are to be avoided, new institutional structures will be required. Otherwise disproportionate power is likely to accrue to particular groups in society. For Ricardo, such disproportionate power accrued to landlords; for Keynes, it accrued to the rentier; and for Galbraith, it accrues to big business. The common link is not the enemy, it is the scepticism about prices as a measure of social worth. At the same time, there is faith in a representative 'pluralist' state rising above sectional interests. Alongside and complementing the 'cost-of-production' theory of value are the pluralist theory of politics and the sociological theories of bureaucracy. Capitalism does not need to be smashed; it can be reformed.

But who identifies the Galbraithian disinterested élite which will form the 'representative pluralist state'? This is a paradox parallel to that faced by Friedman in his advocacy of unfreedom for some to protect the freedom of the market, and, Friedman argues, of the many. The COP problem arises from the theory's assertion that increasingly complex societies require highly trained élites to run them. The need for strong pluralist institutions is paramount. An argument of the Swedish economist, Gunnar Myrdal, typifies this approach: in his opinion much of the stagnation in the less developed world is due to the lack of a 'strong state' (see Myrdal, in Streeten, 1969). And at the international level successive reports (Pearson, 1969; Brandt, 1980, 1983), calling for new institutional initiatives, have been theoretically based within the COP school. Thus the first Brandt Report argued that 'a country will only be able to benefit from additional technology if it can absorb and adapt what it has already received, and if it can provide the "welcoming structure" which can connect up new technology to old societies' (Brandt, 1980, 194).

Thus the emphasis is on an institutional structure suited to an outside technology. There is nothing particularly new in this; as the ex-secretary-general of the Economic Commission for Latin America (ECLA), Raul Prebisch, has argued, the Brandt Report contains 'Nothing new – just what we had been saying all along' (*South*, January 1981, 33).

Nevertheless, although there is a foundation common to the COP theorists, there are some differences of emphasis within this group of economists in their approach to international trade. In the remainder of this chapter, and in the next, the theories of two identifiably separate groups are examined. The first group is referred to as the *Sraffian* group, simply because they present their ideas in an explicitly formal, Sraffian framework, derived from Ricardo. This group places an emphasis on the choice of technique and on the implications of that choice for inter-country gains and losses from trade. The theories of this Sraffian wing will be examined briefly in Section 3.2.

The other wing within the neo-Ricardian school I have labelled the *unequal exchange* wing. By contrast with the Sraffian group, the unequal exchange wing explicitly focuses on particular groups of countries. In general, their world is divided into a dominating 'core' and a dominated 'periphery'. The dominating core is the developed north; the dominated periphery is the less developed south. When reference is made to the north, it is usually to the western industrial economies – the so-called First World – rather than the socialist countries of the east – the Second World. Thus the less developed south becomes the Third World. This wing of neo-Ricardianism emphasizes imperfections in markets between the First and Third Worlds and their implications for world income distribution and, more generally, for world development. We shall look at the theories of this wing and the different versions of unequal exchange in Chapter 4.

The informed reader may be surprised that some of the unequal exchange theories are discussed here within the context of neo-Ricardianism and not under a Marxist or neo-Marxist heading, as they are in Smith and Toye (1979, 9–11). I hope that by the end of Chapter 5 – in which the contrasting methodology of the Marxist school is set out – the reasons will be convincing; but for the moment, I plead patience from the reader.

3.2 THE 'SRAFFIAN' APPROACH TO TRADE THEORY

The Sraffian approach to trade theory has been developed in recent years by four economists in particular – namely Lyn Mainwaring, Ian Metcalfe, Sergio Parinello and Ian Steedman. The last has edited a collection of writings by the four (Steedman, 1979a) as well as producing a book of his own, entitled, *Trade amongst Growing Economies* (1979b). As was pointed out in Chapter 2, this wing has provided the basis for an effective attack on the HOS theory by bringing to the fore the role of produced means of production, and by distinguishing between capital as a physical good and capital as a fund of finance on which a rate of profit or interest is calculated. Thus neo-classical theory has been unable to say much about growth and trade, whereas Steedman argues that the alternative neo-Ricardian approach places 'capital' goods, profits and accumulation at the centre of the analysis (see Steedman, 1979a, 7) and is, therefore, crucially concerned with growth.

The writings of these authors are developed within a specifically Sraffian approach. Their formal, rigorous method systematically looks at the intercountry gains and losses from trade which arise from switches in production techniques as distribution between labour and capital and, therefore, goods prices change. These switches in production techniques as factor prices change are at the heart of the Sraffian approach to international trade theory.

This problem of techniques changing as factor prices change is somewhat similar to the 'transformation' problem faced by Ricardo. The latter, in his *Principles*, showed that he was well aware that prices were unlikely to be proportional to the hours of labour directly and indirectly spent in producing goods, but this was a problem that he could not solve.

The Ricardian 'transformation' problem

It may be easier to understand Ricardo's problem by looking at a simple example. Assume that in 1980 a plough was used, together with 300 hours of labour, to produce 1 ton of corn, while 400 hours of labour were used to produce a bale of cloth. In comparing the total labour-hours directly and indirectly embodied in corn and cloth we should clearly include those used in producing the plough in, say, 1979. Assume that these totalled 200 hours and that the plough was completely used up in 1980 and worthless at the end of the season. Thus a total of 300 (1980) hours + 200 (1979) hours = 500 hours of labour will have been used to produce 1 ton of corn, while 400 (1980) hours will have been used in the production of a bale of cloth. We might expect the price ratio between a ton of corn and a bale of cloth to be 500/400 or 1.25. But if profits were 'earned' in the production of ploughs in 1979, the plough will have cost more than the equivalent of 200 labour-hours. Thus there will be an additional 'profit weight' attached to the 1979 labour carried forward into 1980, and embodied in the plough. This additional weight will in turn become embodied in the corn. Thus the price ratio of corn to cloth is likely to be greater than 1.25; how much greater will depend on the rate of profit.

Thus the ratios of labourtimes of goods will, in general, be different from their price ratios; the labourtimes will have been 'transformed' by the profit structure into a different set of prices. Although Ricardo was aware of this 'transformation problem', he assumed it away by arguing that the effects on prices of changes in labour productivity over time would be far more important than the effects of deviations of prices from labour inputs due to differing 'capital intensities' of goods. By contrast, the Sraffian approach emphasizes these 'revaluation' effects – that is the effect on the price or value of a capital good of a change in the rate of profit and vice versa. As one can imagine, these 'feedback' effects can be quite complex when an example is used that incorporates a number of goods which can be produced with differing 'capital intensities'. Thus it is not surprising that the Sraffian trade theory has been developed using what, for most students, is a difficult, algebraic analysis.

But what the Sraffians show is important. In opposition to the free-traders they argue that with a choice of techniques and in a growing economy, a country may suffer a *loss* from trade when its without-trade, or autarkic, situation is compared with its with-trade situation. Their presentation is, for most students, difficult, but some of the flavour of the argument may be understood by looking at a relatively simple presentation of possible gains from trade.

The possible gains from trade

The gains from trade may be split into two parts, with the gain from exchange (arising from a change in the pattern of *consumption*) being separated from the gain from specialization (arising from a change in the pattern of *production*). Some students may find it easier to understand this split (and the possibility of losses from free trade) by looking at the graphical presentation in Keith Griffin's *Underdevelopment in Spanish America* (1971, 93–6). But for those who find graphical presentations confusing, I will attempt to present the Sraffian or neo-Ricardian losses-from-trade argument without using graphs.

Let us start with the simplest possible example, in which India produces two goods (say, 100 tons of corn and 100 bales of cloth) using all the resources (say, labour and land) at its disposal. Now, in a situation of autarky (that is in a situation in which India does no trade whatsoever with any other country), India must consume exactly what it produces. Thus 1 ton of corn must exchange for 1 bale of cloth. This will be the price ratio (or 'barter terms of trade') of corn and cloth.

But now suppose that we make a Ricardian assumption that available production techniques are different in the rest of the world (ROW), and that the price ratio of corn to cloth in the ROW is different from that in India. Assume that 1 ton of corn exchanges for 2 bales of cloth – that is cloth in the ROW is cheaper than in India. If India and the ROW trade, India and the ROW are likely to gain from *exchange*, even if production patterns remain unchanged. Thus, even if India continues to produce 100 tons of corn and 100 bales of cloth, it will gain from exchanging some of its relatively cheap corn for the ROW's relatively cheap cloth.

For example, assume, for simplicity, that India is a 'small country', so that the world corn–cloth price ratio remains at, say, 2:1 (cloth being relatively cheap) even when India trades with the ROW. At that price ratio India could consume: 90 tons of corn and 120 bales of cloth *after* trade, compared with 100 tons of corn and 100 bales of cloth *before* trade.

Thus India would export 10 tons of corn and import 20 bales of cloth. If its 'new' (after-trade) pattern of consumption is valued at the 'old' (before-trade) prices, India has clearly gained from exchange. How big this gain will be depends on demand preferences in India, given that we have assumed the Indian production pattern remains unchanged.

But now assume that the production pattern in India changes. This is, of course, highly likely, since the change in the corn–cloth price ratio from 1:1 to 2:1 will have increased profits and/or wages in corn and reduced them in cloth production. It is likely that Indian resources (labour and land) will move out of cloth production, either into the production of the more profitable corn or into unemployment. Where the resources end up will depend on how flexible they are in terms of prices and/or production possibilities.

The free-marketeers tend to argue for flexibility, so that resources are assumed to be fully employed. Thus, in the example, the assumption would be that either the resources continue to be employed in cloth production (implying that they are willing to take a cut in wages, rents, profits, etc.) or that they switch into the production of corn (implying that they are sufficiently flexible to switch into other 'industries' without extensive retraining, modification, etc.). If the latter is the case, so that Indian corn production increases, then there is likely to be a *specialization* gain to India in addition to the *exchange* gain already realized from trade. This 'specialization' gain is usually assumed to occur by the free-marketeers, for they generally assume that resources are flexible and that there are few, if any, 'factor market price distortions'.

The possible losses from trade

But if resources are assumed to be inflexible both in technical and in price terms, then the resources previously employed in cloth production are likely to become unemployed. If the resources employed in cloth production are technically specialized, they will not be switched into corn production. And if the workers employed in cloth production refuse to take a cut in wages or the employers stop producing cloth because of the fall in the rate of profit on cloth, then Indian cloth production will fall. Cloth workers will be underemployed and cloth machinery will lie idle. Then instead of the 'trade winds' being warm and harmonious, they will be cold and harsh. Indeed, there may well be a loss from trade, with the gain from exchange being more than counter-balanced by the loss from specialization as a result of the increase in unemployment. In which case India will tend to be living on bread alone.

The nature of this loss is easy to understand. But the Sraffians raise the possibility of trade losses occurring in a somewhat less obvious form. Their contribution has been to point to the possibility of trade losses resulting not from a factor price inflexibility or 'distortion', but from a situation in which prices are flexible. Nevertheless, the effect is the same: there is, as they put it, a 'similarity in the effects on the economy of a positive rate of interest and a factor market distortion' (Steedman, 1979a, 55).

The Metcalfe–Steedman approach was original in showing that a net loss from trade (similar to that arising from a 'factor market distortion') might result from changes in the choice of technique. They showed that, on realistic assumptions, the change in goods prices resulting from the exposure to international trade may induce a change or 'switch' in the production techniques used. Such a change may involve the 'scrapping or "junking" of the old equipment whose value cannot be realised on any market' (ibid., 9, and essay 12).

The Metcalfe–Steedman argument is a very difficult one to follow in detail without using mathematics, but it goes through the following stages:

with the exposure to trade, the price ratios of goods change;

with the change in the price ratios of goods, there may well be a switch in the production techniques used to produce the goods;

with a switch in production techniques, some machinery previously used to produce goods is 'devalued' and is no longer profitable to use;

the loss from this devaluation and scrapping needs to be taken into account in calculating the net gain or loss from trade.

It is somewhat misleading to present this in terms of the earlier example of cloth and corn, since Metcalfe and Steedman's analysis is in terms of two commodities produced by the same two commodities as well as by two primary inputs (say, labour and land). But crudely, in the earlier example, assume that India switches into the production of corn from cloth and expands the production of corn, but that it does so only by using a different technique from that previously used in the no-trade situation. The change in technique may itself be induced by the different goods prices faced in the international market, in which case the old corn-producing equipment becomes redundant. As Metcalfe and Steedman put it: 'By producing and exchanging one more unit of commodity 1, the capitalists must, in such a situation, reduce the domestic net output of commodity 2 by more than the amount of commodity 2 which they will obtain through trade for the unit of commodity 1' (ibid., 54).

Thus assuming profit maximization, Metcalfe and Steedman show that net productive capacity might be reduced following trade, and that this loss might be large enough to outweigh any gains from exchange.

Thus the criticisms of the Heckscher–Ohlin trade theory which stemmed from the Sraffian-inspired neo-Ricardian revival not only destroyed the 'strong' factor price equalization case for free trade, but also questioned whether there are any gains to be had at all from 'unmanaged' trade. This doubt arises even without raising further questions about interpersonal income distribution – that is whether losses to some Indians (in, say, cloth production) are counterbalanced by the gains to others (in the more profitable corn production).

Furthermore, as Steedman points out in his introduction to the *Fundamental Issues in Trade Theory* collection, the Sraffians do not have to rely on 'imperfections' in competition or 'price distortions' in demonstrating that trade losses can result (ibid., 12). This is in contrast to the approach of the unequal exchange wing, where differences between countries in wage bargaining and access to technology are stressed. It is on these unequal exchange theories that Chapter 4 focuses its attention.

NOTES ON FURTHER READING

To get the flavour of the cost-of-production view of the world, see David Owen's *Face the Future*, 1981; or the Brandt Commission's reports: *North–South: A Programme for Survival*, 1980, and *Common Crisis*, 1983. See also Open University, 1983, part B, block 4. For a systematic and historical treatment of the cost-of-production school, look at Cole *et al.*, 1983, chapters 5–7. In the field of international trade the writings of the Canadian economist Gerald Helleiner are fairly representative of this school: see Helleiner, 1972, 1976. In the context of both this chapter and the next it may be helpful to read, or even reread, the pieces on 'three schools' in Rowthorn, 1980; Cameron *et al.*, 1980; or Cole *et al.*, 1983, chapter 1. Also refer to Evans, 1979.

For Ricardo's ideas, his *Principles of Political Economy and Taxation*, 1971, chapter VI, is likely to be the most useful, despite the dry style. A little more lively are the third chapters of Barber, 1967, and of Dobb, 1973; or see Deane, 1978, chapter 5.

It is difficult to recommend introductory texts for the Sraffian wing of neo-Ricardian trade theory. Beginners are likely to find Steedman difficult, but the introductory essay in Steedman, 1979a, gives a reasonably clear overview of the collection. For a critical review of this collection, see Ethier, in *Economica*, May 1981, 207–8.

SUMMARY

3.1

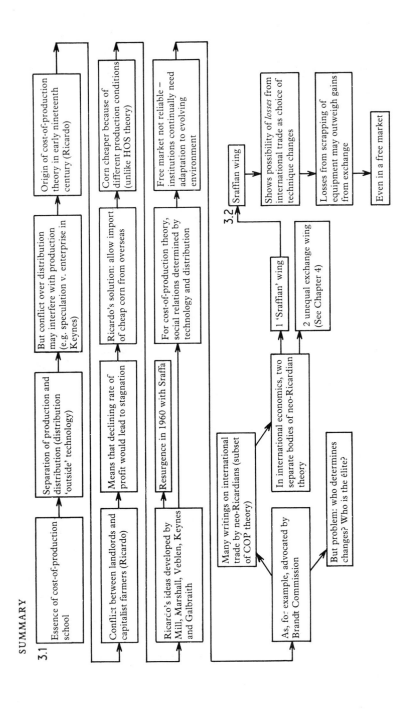

Essence of cost-of-production school → Separation of production and distribution (distribution 'outside' technology) → But conflict over distribution may interfere with production (e.g. speculation v. enterprise in Keynes) → Origin of cost-of-production theory in early nineteenth century (Ricardo)

Conflict between landlords and capitalist farmers (Ricardo) → Means that declining rate of profit would lead to stagnation → Ricardo's solution: allow import of cheap corn from overseas → Corn cheaper because of different production conditions (unlike HOS theory)

Ricardo's ideas developed by Mill, Marshall, Veblen, Keynes and Galbraith → Resurgence in 1960 with Sraffa → For cost-of-production theory, social relations determined by technology and distribution → Free market not reliable – institutions continually need adaptation to evolving environment

Many writings on international trade by neo-Ricardians (subset of COP theory) → In international economics, two separate bodies of neo-Ricardian theory → 1 'Sraffian' wing / 2 unequal exchange wing (See Chapter 4)

As, for example, advocated by Brandt Commission → But problem: who determines changes? Who is the élite?

3.2

Sraffian wing → Shows possibility of *losses* from international trade as choice of technique changes → Losses from scrapping of equipment may outweigh gains from exchange → Even in a free market

4

Neo-Ricardianism and unequal exchange

Prebisch and declining terms of trade

The writings of Raul Prebisch, when he was secretary-general of the Economic Commission for Latin America, can be said to have founded both the unequal exchange wing of neo-Ricardian trade theory as well as the neo-Marxist 'dependency' school. In an article first published in 1950 Prebisch claimed that 'while the centres kept the whole benefit of the technical development of their industries, the peripheral countries transferred to them a share of the fruits of their own technical progress' (Prebisch, 1962, 5). This division of the world into north and south is central, as we shall see, to the *unequal exchange* of Arghiri Emmanuel, but the centre–periphery division is also a main focus of the neo-Marxist 'dependency' writings of Paul Baran, Osvaldo Sunkel, Samir Amin, Immanuel Wallerstein and Gunder Frank. The latter (the dependency school) is discussed in Chapter 5 because its analysis depends heavily on 'non-economic' factors, by contrast with the approach of Prebisch and Emmanuel for whom imperialism is associated with relatively free trade.

The above quotation is a succinct summary of Prebisch's theory. He has argued that because the industrialized centre, by contrast with the periphery, has retained the whole benefit of the technical development of their industries, the terms of trade have turned steadily against primary producers from the 1870s to the Second World War. In this context Prebisch was referring to the barter terms of trade, calculated by dividing the price index of exports by the price index of imports. Prebisch's claim was based on the experience of the UK over that period. He pointed out that the prices of British exports had risen relative to imports, arguing that British imports and exports were representative of

Table 4.1 World exports by commodity and area 1960–80 ($ billion)

From	1960			1980		
	DCs	LDCs	Total[1]	DCs	LDCs	Total[1]
Primary commodities						
oil[2]	3	8	11	84	348	432
others[3]	24	18	42	237	118	355
Total	27	26	53	321	466	787
Manufactures and others[4]	55	4	59	885	142	1,027
Total	82	30	112	1,206	608	1,814

Source: World Bank, 1981a, table 1.

Notes:
1 Excludes centrally planned economies (including China).
2 SITC 3.
3 SITC 0–2, 4 and 68.
4 SITC 5–8 (excluding 68) and 9.

raw materials and manufactures respectively, so that the improvement in the British 'commodity' or barter terms of trade represented a general deterioration in the terms of trade of primary products relative to manufactures. Taking the relative prices in 1876–80 as a base of 100, the terms of trade index was shown to have dropped to 64 by the 1936–8 period. Thus in the late 1930s a peso or rupee of primary product exports would buy only 64 per cent of the volume of manufactures that they would have bought sixty years earlier. Conversely, 'an average of 58.6 per cent more primary products was needed to buy the same amount of finished manufactures' (ibid., 4). Furthermore, since Prebisch implied that the peripheral countries were more heavily dependent on primary products for their exports – they still are, relatively, as is shown in Table 4.1 – the deterioration in the terms of trade for primary products also meant a deterioration in the terms of trade of the less developed countries (LDCs).

Thus the argument was that the terms of trade tended to move against the peripheral countries in favour of the industrialized centre. Prebisch claimed that this movement had to be understood in the context of cyclical movements in trade, because 'the prices of primary products rise more rapidly than industrial prices in the upswing, but also they fall more in the downswing, so that in the course of the cycles the gap between the prices of the two is progressively widened' (ibid., 6). The widening gap was explained by 'the greater ability of the masses in the . . . centres to obtain rises in wages during the upswing and to maintain the higher level during the downswing' (ibid.). Thus the relatively weak bargaining power of the workers in the primary *sector* was likely to lead to a secular deterioration in the terms of trade for peripheral countries.

These arguments were first put forward by Prebisch in 1950; similar arguments were later put forward by Arthur Lewis in 1954, by Gunnar Myrdal in 1956 and by Staffan Linder in 1961. More particularly, Hans Singer advanced arguments so close to those of Prebisch that reference is often made to the Prebisch–Singer thesis (see, for example, Evans, 1979, 266; Sodersten, 1980, chapter 12). Lewis argued that the less developed countries possessed unlimited reserves of labour in the subsistence sector, and that these reserves prevented wages from rising in the production of primary products, even when productivity rose. For example, the output of sugar per acre had trebled over the past seventy-five years and yet 'workers in the sugar industry continue to walk barefooted and live in shacks' (Lewis, 1954, 183). The reason, Lewis argued, lay in the fact 'that the subsistence sectors of tropical economies are able to release however many workers the sugar industry may want, at wages which are low, because tropical food production is low' (ibid.). Thus, with the rate of profit being equalized internationally, the benefits of productivity improvements in the export sector were transferred to the purchasers of sugar. In 1956 Myrdal argued along the same lines that 'as long as there is no scarcity of labour . . . rises in labour productivity would tend to be transferred to the importing industrial countries' (Myrdal, 1956a, 232–3); and Linder argued in 1961 that for the same reason of an unlimited supply of labour, per capita incomes in less developed countries would not rise with increases in productivity in the export sector (Linder, 1961, 41–2). Thus the same wage bargaining argument runs through the writings of a number of cost-of-production economists.

But, for Prebisch, the wage bargaining factor was reinforced by the low income elasticity of demand for primary, as opposed to manufactured products. On average the income elasticity for primary products is probably less than unity (see Helleiner, 1972, table 7), resulting in a decreasing proportion of additional income being spent on primary products. And so, Prebisch argued, as world income expanded, a declining proportion of it would be spent on primary products. In a world of centre/periphery countries, in which the periphery exports primary products in exchange for manufactures and in which there is a relatively low income elasticity of demand for primary products, the commodity or 'barter' terms of trade in the periphery must then have to deteriorate for a given growth in world income. Put another way, the periphery would have a trading deficit *vis-à-vis* the centre, and for a balance of payments to be restored, the exchange rate (or barter terms of trade if we exclude service and capital items) must decline.

The likelihood of this deterioration is increased, Prebisch claims, by the high protection of the agricultural sector in the centre, which would aggravate the slow growth of demand for primary products from the periphery (see Prebisch, in Theberge, 1968, 293). As other writers were later to argue, under certain extreme conditions, the decline in the terms of trade might be so severe, with the growth in the volume of primary product exports, that the periphery could actually end up being worse off than before growth. This is what is referred to, for obvious reasons, as 'immiserizing growth'.

Thus, for Prebisch, there are two factors which generate the tendency for the barter terms of trade of primary producers – the less developed countries – to deteriorate. One is the wage bargaining process; the other is the relatively low income elasticity of demand for primary products. What, if anything, can be done to reverse this tendency? First, Prebisch argued, we have to recognize that 'market forces do not provide an equitable solution for the problem in question' (ibid., 294). In his 1950 article Prebisch had emphasized the priority of industrialization, but in his later articles in the 1960s he stressed that 'the process of remedying the deterioration of the terms of trade in the peripheral countries becomes one vast problem of international redistribution of income' (ibid.). The income to be redistributed could be calculated by indexing primary product prices to those of manufactures and transferring the compensatory amounts back to the primary exporting countries.

Prebisch's earlier emphasis on industrialization had argued that the periphery should reduce the *volume* of its primary product exports by switching resources into an import-substituting programme of industrialization. Such a programme should be pursued until the extra industrial production was worth the same as the marginal primary production (see Prebisch, 1959, 255). Thus by a structure of export duties on primary products or of import duties on manufactures, a switch in production from primary products to manufactures would be encouraged. The production of manufactures, which was socially profitable but privately unprofitable *without* such protective duties, would then become privately profitable *after* the imposition of the duties.

'Optimum tariff theory'

Such an argument for the imposition of duties is one that even the free-marketeers have recognized under the heading of 'optimum tariff theory'. They admit that where the individual country is not a 'price-taker' but a 'price-maker', there is a case for moving away from free trade. Thus in the price-making case, where the price at which a product is sold on the world market is affected by an individual country's own exports, the country's position is analogous to that of a monopolist in a domestic market. That is the country faces a downward-sloping demand curve for its exported product. In such a case the country's exports should be dragged back by export duties to the point at which the *country's* (as opposed to the individual's) profits are maximized, that is to the point at which the country's marginal export revenue is equal to the marginal cost of production.

Thus in Figure 4.1 the price facing the exporting country is shown to

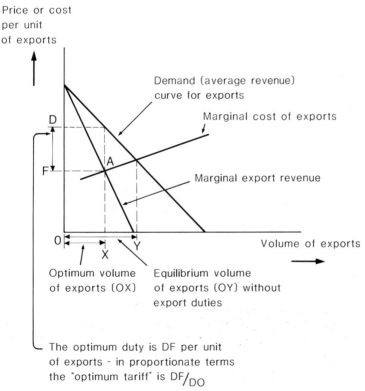

Figure 4.1 The monopolist case for export duties (or optimum tariff theory).

be dependent on its exports; the average revenue curve – the demand curve facing the country – is downward-sloping. Under such conditions the curve showing the *marginal* revenue per unit of exports will drop more steeply. The volume of exports at which the country's 'profits' or net export revenues are maximized will be where the marginal cost is equal to marginal revenue – point A in Figure 4.1, where the country's optimum export volume is *OX*. But because, in the free market, the *individual* producers within the country 'take' a given world price – that is contrary to the country's producers as a whole, they face a horizontal demand curve – they will jointly export quantity *OY*. The country should then impose an export duty sufficient to force production back to the 'optimum' volume *OX*, that is to the point A, where one additional unit of exports brings in the same revenue as it costs to produce. Any exports beyond volume *OX* will cost the *country* more to produce than the revenue earned. At the optimum volume *OX* the duty (per unit of exports) will then be equivalent to *DF*, and in a two-good model and making certain other assumptions, the effect of an export duty will be the same as that of an import duty (see Corden, 1974, 158).

Even the free-marketeers concede that this is a case for interfering with the free market. But they also argue that countries will only rarely be price-makers. In general, their argument goes, an individual country exporting primary products will face close competition either from other countries exporting the *same* primary products or from producers of close substitutes. The first case is anticipated by Prebisch when he argues: 'If the state were to tax exports commensurately with the increase in productivity in export activities, the benefits could be retained just as if wages had been raised; *but all the producer countries would have to adopt the same measure*' (Prebisch, in Theberge, 1968, 290, emphasis added). But at the same time, the problem of close substitutes is ruled out by Prebisch's implied Ricardian assumption that production conditions vary considerably between countries, so that production is specific to particular countries, or groups of countries.

Declining terms of trade?

Since the arguments of Prebisch were put forward there has been extensive discussion about whether the terms of trade of less developed countries have in fact deteriorated – as Prebisch argued they would tend to. But the answer to such a question is not easy; there are a large number of problems involved in measuring the terms of trade. First, we have to decide which definition of the terms of trade is the most appropriate. The usual contenders are the *barter* terms of trade (an export price index simply divided by an import price index) and the *income* terms of trade (the *value* of exports, that is, quantity times price, divided by the import price index). But even if we concentrate on the barter terms of trade on the ground that this is the definition on which Prebisch himself focused, we still have to deal with the following problems:

(1) Over what period do we look at the figures?

(2) Do we look at world primary exports, or all exports of less developed countries, or the less developed countries' exports of primary products?

(3) In constructing price indices are the prices measured at import or at export points, and how are variations in the quality of the product accounted for?

Given these problems, it is not surprising that 'evidence' can be produced for and against a deterioration in the terms of trade, even if attention is restricted to one definition, namely the barter terms of trade. Table 4.2 gives grounds for a number of conflicting conclusions.

But even if, over a long period, the terms of trade were shown unequivocally to improve for the less developed countries, would this necessarily disprove the Prebisch argument? The answer must be no. Prebisch's answer could easily be: admittedly the terms of trade have not deteriorated as predicted, but that is precisely because many less developed countries have taken action in accordance with my advice. That is there *is* a tendency to deterioration, and this tendency would have been revealed but for the countervailing action which the less developed countries have taken in anticipation of this tendency. In which case, as David Evans has argued, 'the empirical evidence of the decline in the developing country and primary commodity terms of trade since the early 1950s [until the early 1970s: see Table 4.2] therefore will be seen as strengthening the proposition that the thesis holds' (Evans, 1979, 267).

In recent years Prebisch's ideas have taken second place to those of another economist, the Greek Arghiri Emmanuel, whose writings are within a similar neo-Ricardian framework, but with a liberal coating of Marxist rhetoric. His book *Unequal Exchange* was first published in France in 1969, and in English in 1972. Most students find the book difficult; it is long, somewhat repetitive and confusing, because of its mixture of neo-Ricardian essence and Marxist flavouring. Section 4.2 attempts to present Emmanuel's influential *Unequal Exchange* clearly and concisely, first, within the Marxist format used by Emmanuel, and then within a more formal Sraffian framework. The latter is more

Table 4.2 A hundred years of the barter terms of trade

	LDCs against DCs		Primaries against manufactures	
	all products	*all products (excluding fuels)*	*LDCs' primaries and DCs' mfrs*	*World primaries and world mfrs*
1880	126	n.a.	130	114
1900	114	n.a.	103	91
1913	177	n.a.	185	106
1928	172	n.a.	178	98
1937	150	n.a.	152	78
1952	115	122	109	118
1962	100	101 (1960)	100	100
1968	101	102 (1965)	97	93
1970	101	105	96	97
1975	143	78	198	156
1980	177	76	309	211

(a) LDCs against DCs – all products:
       1880–1962: Brown, 1974, table 27.
       1962–80: World Bank, 1981a, table 4.
       LDCs against DCs – all products, excluding fuels:
       1952–75: Evans, 1979, appendix table 3.
       1975–80: *UN Monthly Bulletin of Statistics*, October 1978, xxii; IMF, *Financial Statistics Yearbook*, 1982, 76–7.
(b) LDCs' primaries against DCs' manufactures:
       1880–1962: Brown, 1974, table 28.
       1968–80: *UN Monthly Bulletin of Statistics*, December 1973, xix, December 1976, xxiv, July 1982, xxiv, 182; World Bank, 1981a, 30.
       World primaries against world manufactures:
       1880–1962: Brown, 1974, table 26.
       1968–80: *UN Monthly Bulletin of Statistics*, series M, no. 29, rev. 2, 31; *UN Monthly Bulletin of Statistics*, July 1982, XXXVI (7), 182; World Bank, 1981a, 30.

Note: All indices are for the *barter* terms of trade and, therefore, show a relationship between prices only, ignoring the volume of trade. Thus the *income* (or *purchasing power*) terms of trade are not shown. The table is shown in the form of a graph in Figure 8.2, p. 210.

difficult to follow, but shows more clearly both the scope and limitations of Emmanuel's unequal exchange.

4.2 EMMANUEL'S UNEQUAL EXCHANGE

Emmanuel, like Prebisch, rejects the marginal productivity theory of income distribution underpinning the HOS theory. He rejects the neo-classical argument that wages are the effect of prices (see Emmanuel, 1972, 67), instead arguing that 'under capitalist production relations one earns as much as one spends, and . . . prices depend on wages' (ibid., 172). Thus the emphasis is very much a cost-of-production one. He points to the hypocrisy of the apologists of the status quo who, he argues, want to have the argument both ways:

> When it is a question of importing coffee or bananas, which the rich countries do not themselves produce . . . then . . . no allusion to the low wages of the producers is allowed, since . . . these wages are not the cause of prices but their effect. When, however, by chance the poor countries decide to export products such as Indian cotton goods or Japanese transistors, which are already . . . in . . . production . . . in rich countries, then . . . it is discovered that it is only proper that the rich country should make up by means of artificial tariff barriers for the equally artificial difference in wages; thus brusquely and brazenly admitting that wages are not the effect of prices but their cause.
>
> (ibid., 69–70)

Emmanuel's theory is, then, solidly based in a cost-of-production framework. Supply (the cost-of-production) determines prices; demand merely determines the quantity supplied. Wages are given institutionally, through bargaining, and not only may they rise above the Ricardian subsistence level, but in the rich countries, Emmanuel argues, they do. They rise well above subsistence level, because there the trade unions are strong. But in the poor, less developed countries workers are badly organized, unions are weak, and wages in both money and real terms rise slowly, if at all. When this inequality of bargaining power is added to a pattern of international specialization given by technology, and to a tendency towards the international equalization of the rate of profit given by capital mobility, the stage is set for 'unequal exchange'.

The exchange is unequal because the poor countries exchange goods in which more labour-time is embodied for goods in which less labour-time is embodied. The actual situation is compared with a *hypothetical* one in which wages are equal in the rich and poor countries: 'the inequality of wages as such, all other things being equal, is alone the cause of the inequality of exchange' (ibid., 61). Thus whereas in Prebisch the emphasis is on peripheral countries as *primary* producers, for Emmanuel they suffer as low-wage countries regardless of whether they are producing manufactures or primary products (see ibid., xxx). In Emmanuel's world workers in the periphery are more exploited, their labour-time costing less, even allowing for their lower productivity: 'consequently . . . we can be sure that we are on this side of reality if we conclude that . . . the average wage in the developed countries is about 30 times the average in the backward countries, or, allowing for the difference in the intensity of labour, about 15 times that figure' (ibid., 48).

It might be thought that this 'superexploitation' would be temporary and that the workers in the periphery would indirectly benefit from the expenditure of the relatively pampered workers in the rich countries. In other words, some 'trickle-down' effect might be expected with peripheral workers benefiting in terms of employment or an improvement in the terms of trade. But in Emmanuel's model the inequality is cumulative. The higher wages in the centre generate the market for further technical progress and industrialization in the centre: 'once a country has got ahead, through some historical accident . . . this country starts to make other countries pay for its high wage through unequal exchange' (ibid., 130).

Emmanuel's Marxist format

In chapter 2, section 2, of *Unequal Exchange* Emmanuel presents his theory within a 'Marxist transformation' context; here that presentation is followed but slightly modified in the interests of simplification. But in order to understand Emmanuel's own presentation of his theory it is necessary to introduce some elements of the Marxist analysis which he uses.

For Marx, under capitalism the capitalist class has a monopoly of the means of existence. To survive the worker must sell his labour power (essentially, the right to the product of his labour) to a capitalist. And since the worker has no choice but to enter into this arrangement, the capitalist may compel the worker to work for longer than he need do so to 'reproduce' himself, that is support himself and his family. Thus the working-day may be separated into two parts: necessary labour (during which the labourer produces the means of his own reproduction, that is the equivalent value of the necessary commodities) and surplus labour, the fruit of which accrues to the capitalist. Taking a simplistic example, if a worker makes bread and lives by bread alone, he may be able to produce sufficient loaves (say, three in two hours) to feed himself and his family for a day, but he is made to work for eight hours. In this time he can make twelve loaves, but the income resulting from the additional nine loaves goes to the capitalist. In other words, the capitalist appropriates the difference between the value produced by the worker's labour power and its exchange value, namely the worker's wage. Hence a profit is made by selling all commodities at their value.

From this it may be seen that a commodity's value, if said to be determined by the labour embodied in it, has three components. Two of these have been mentioned already: variable capital (v), which is the wage bill, and so called because it creates the second component, surplus value (s). The final component is constant capital (c) (that is raw materials and machinery), which contribute their own value but do not produce additional value. Thus we have the total exchange value of a commodity:

$$EV = c + v + s.$$

From this, Marx defined three ratios:

rate of surplus value or 'exploitation' = s/v;
organic composition of capital $q = c/v$;
rate of profit $p = s/(c + v)$.

Although the basis of a Marxist analysis is laid in these equations, it is important not to fall for the apparently tempting static picture of capitalism implied by them. Marx used the equations as part of a dynamic analysis of capitalist accumulation: capitalism implies a social relationship arising in a particular historical context. Thus the elements of exchange value should not be seen simply as independent of each other, but as arising from the basic struggle between capital and labour. By contrast, the neo-Ricardians tend to view each component (for example, wages) as externally given.

In the first two volumes of *Capital* Marx assumed that goods exchange at their values; it is not until the third volume that the problem of the possible divergence of price from value is discussed. It is in the context of this so-called, still controversial, 'transformation problem' that Emmanuel presents his analysis.

In presenting his theory Emmanuel first gives an example where there is *no* unequal exchange. For this, assume that two goods, namely cloth and corn, are produced in the UK. Further assume that, for each good, the labour-hours embodied in machines and raw materials (what Emmanuel, following Marx, calls 'constant capital') are equal to the labour-hours embodied in the wage goods consumed by direct or 'live' workers (what Emmanuel, again following Marx, calls 'variable capital'). And further assume that the 'unpaid' labour-hours (surplus value) are the same for the two goods. Then, as shown in Table 4.3(i), the labour-times will give the same rate of profit in the production of the

Table 4.3 Emmanuel's format for showing unequal exchange

Country/good	Values (or labour-times) embodied in:						
	Constant capital (c)	Variable capital (v)	Surplus value (s)	Total 'exchange' value (EV)	Profit in money or price terms (P)	Total 'cost-of-production' or price (C + V + P)	
(i) No unequal exchange							
UK – cloth	180	60	60	300	60	300	Prices = exchange values; value is *not* redistributed between product sectors
UK – corn	180	60	60	300	60	300	
– Total	360	120	120	600	120	600	

Rate of profit $= \dfrac{S}{C+V} = \dfrac{120}{360+120} = 25\%$

Where C/V in sector 1 = C/V in sector 2 *and* where S/V in sector 1 = S/V in sector 2

Country/good	c	v	s	EV	P	C + V + P	
(ii) Unequal exchange 'in the broad sense'							
UK – cloth	240	60	60	360	75	375	Prices *not* equal to exchange values; value is redistributed between product sectors
UK – corn	120	60	60	240	45	225	
– Total	360	120	120	600	120	600	→ But this is *not* Emmanuel's unequal exchange

Where C/V in sector 1 is *not* equal to C/V in sector 2

Rate of profit $= \dfrac{S}{C+V} = \dfrac{120}{360+120} = 25\%$
Therefore profit in sector 1 = 25% of $C + V = 75$

Country/good	c	v	s	EV	P	C + V + P	
(iii) Unequal exchange 'in the narrow sense'							
UK – cloth	180	60	30	270	60	300	Prices *not* equal to exchange values; value is redistributed between product sectors
India – corn	180	60	90	330	60	300	
– Total	360	120	120	600	120	600	→ This *is* Emmanuel's

Where S/V in sector 1 is *not* equal to S/V in sector 2

Rate of profit = 25%
Therefore profit in sector

two goods. Thus the prices do not need to deviate from values (or labour-times) in order to equalize the rate of profit. 'Value' or labour-time will not, then, be redistributed between the producers of the goods and there can be no 'unequal exchange' or redistribution of labour-time.

But now suppose that the ratio of constant to variable capital is higher in the production of cloth than in corn, as shown in Table 4.3(ii). In this case, Emmanuel suggests, the equalization of the rate of profit leads to the price of cloth being above its value. Conversely, the price of corn is below its value. There has been a transfer of 'value' (or labour-times) from corn to cloth production as a result of the equalization of the rate of profit. This transfer of value is referred to by Emmanuel as unequal exchange, but it is not the type of unequal exchange on which he wishes to focus attention. Emmanuel emphasizes that this, unequal exchange 'in a broad sense', can occur *within* a country; he wants to emphasize the unequal exchange which arises as a result of the immobility of labour and which is therefore, he claims, specific to the international economy.

For Emmanuel's unequal exchange (unequal exchange 'in a narrow sense') arises as a result of international differences in rates of exploitation. An example is shown in Table 4.3(iii), where the ratio of surplus value (s) to variable capital (v) – the 'rate of exploitation' – is higher in India than in the UK; as a result, other things being equal, there is a transfer of value from India to the UK. Through free exchange, value (labour-*time*) flows from India to the UK; and India suffers from the *international* unequal exchange on which Emmanuel wants to focus attention. It is this unequal exchange which is due to the international immobility of labour because, if labour were as free to move as capital, rates of exploitation would tend to be equalized.

The obvious question that arises from the allegedly higher rates of exploitation in India is: why does capital not flow to India to produce both corn *and* cloth there, since surely with higher rates of exploitation in India, the worldwide rate of profit could be raised by producing *both* goods in that low-wage country? Either the production conditions must be different in the two countries or transport costs must drive a wedge between the prices, so that the costs of transporting the cloth back to the main markets in the rich countries are such that the production of cloth in India is less profitable than in the UK, despite the lower wage costs per unit. The latter is asserted by Emmanuel, as has been pointed out earlier in this section. The markets are concentrated in the rich countries precisely, Emmanuel argues, because of the higher wages of the centre's labour aristocracy. But, in addition, production techniques also vary, so that 'one country is *more* productive in some branches and yet *less* productive in others' (Emmanuel, 1972, 422; emphasis in original).

The next question that arises is: if India suffers from unequal exchange, does this mean that it gains nothing from international trade? The answer is no.

As the formal Sraffian analysis presented later in this section shows, India is still likely to gain from international exchange (at least in a static sense), so that Emmanuel's theory is, like Prebisch's, a complaint about the *distribution* of gains from international trade. But whereas the Prebisch–Singer theory focused on *trends* in the terms of trade, Emmanuel's focuses on a *hypothetical* comparison of prices with and without equal rates of exploitation. That is unequal exchange, as earlier stressed, is defined by comparing a set of prices *without* the equalization of labour exploitation with a set of prices *with* such an equalization.

This basic characteristic of *Unequal Exchange*, as well as the links between Emmanuel's theory and those of Prebisch, Singer and Lewis, are clearly brought out in a formal presentation of Emmanuel along Sraffian lines. Such a presentation is not dishonest to Emmanuel, since it captures the logic of his theory. In any case Emmanuel himself admits that his Marxian 'transformation model' is incomplete inasmuch as the prices of the outputs cannot be calculated from their values without a similar transformation being effected 'simultaneously in the inputs, that is, in constant and variable capital' (ibid., 391). And he argues in the same appendix V of his book that there are similarities between his model and that of Sraffa (see ibid., 407). Furthermore, the Sraffian presentation is useful in showing how Emmanuel's unequal exchange lies clearly within a neo-Ricardian tradition. Technology is given from outside the model, as are wages. The focus is on the resulting redistribution between countries, and not between individuals as for Friedman, or between classes as for Marx (see Chapter 5).

Emmanuel as a neo-Ricardian (or Sraffian)

The Sraffian presentation of Emmanuel's unequal exchange has been pioneered by David Evans, and the presentation followed here owes much to his analysis (see especially the appendix to Evans, 1976). Here, however, I have attempted to simplify further Evans's presentation. (If you find *any* graphical presentation difficult and/or tedious, I sympathize, but try to follow the general flow of the argument, even if you don't grasp the finer details, since the next section helps you to understand both the scope and limitations of Emmanuel's analysis.)

We start with *one* country, say, India. With technology and the real wage both given from outside the model, the relative prices of the two goods can be determined from the Sraffian equations:

$$P_1 = (a_{11}p_1 + a_{21}p_2)(1 + r) + wa_1$$

and

$$P_2 = (a_{12}p_1 + a_{22}p_2)(1 + r) + wa_2$$

where, as in Section 2.3, a_{11}, a_{21}, and so on, are the inputs of one good into itself or into the production of the other good; r is the rate of profit assumed to be equalized in the production of the two goods; w is the wage rate given from outside the model (through a bargaining process); and a_1 and a_2 are the given inputs of labour-time per unit of each good.

With the physical input requirements and the wage rate given by assumption, the relationship between the rate of profit and the *relative* prices (p_1/p_2) can be plotted. This is shown in Figure 4.2(i).

The figure shows that as the price of cloth (good 1) rises relative to that of corn (good 2), the rate of profit in cloth production rises and, conversely, the rate of profit in corn production falls. This is what we would expect. But in a closed or autarkic economy we cannot produce *only* one good, because the other is required as an input. Thus since in autarky both goods have to be produced (on the model's assumptions), there must be a unique equilibrium point (A), that is a unique rate of profit and price of good 1 (cloth) relative to good 2 (corn).

Similarly, if we now take the example of another country (say, the UK) in which the production conditions are the same as in India, but in which the real wage is higher, then again we will have a unique equilibrium point (B), that is a unique price of good 1 relative to good 2, and a unique rate of interest or profit. But this time the rate of profit will be lower than in India (see Figure 4.2(ii)). Again if you think of it, this is obvious. With production conditions the same, but with higher wages in the UK, the rate of profit in the UK *must* be lower.

Now, if the possibility of free trade between the two countries exists as set out in Figure 4.2(iii), the highest rate of profit can be obtained by concentrating *all* production in India, so that with the operation of free markets, the equilibrium point of production will be A. In such a situation trade between India and the UK is *not* profitable. The higher real wages in the UK make the production of *both* cloth and corn less profitable in the UK than in India. On the assumptions of a free market, of identical techniques in the two countries, of given wage levels and of international mobility of capital, all capital will tend to flow to India to produce both goods there, and international trade in goods will tend to be eliminated.

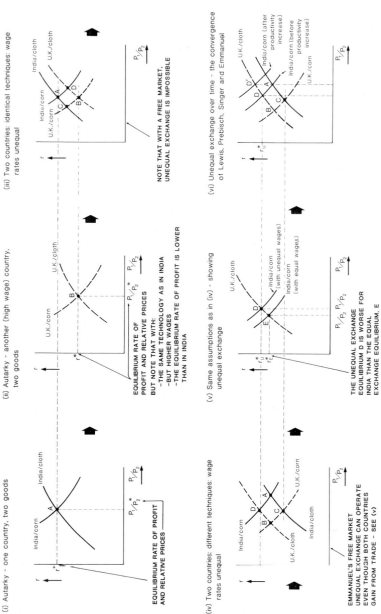

Figure 4.2 Emmanuel's unequal exchange in Sraffian terms.

Clearly, from the situation set out in Figure 4.2(iii) there is no scope for Emmanuel's unequal exchange through trade, unless the assumption of a free market is relaxed, and the use of taxes, tariffs, or even force is admitted. That is discriminatory fiscal or administrative measures will be required to prevent all production from being profitably located in India. This, many claim, is precisely what happened to bring about the de-industrialization of India in the nineteenth century – see, for example, Bagchi, 1976; Clairmonte, 1960, chapter 2. But Emmanuel makes it clear that this is not what he assumes, in general; his unequal exchange is a study in the imperialism of free trade. Thus Figure 4.2(iii) cannot represent the case by Emmanuel.

Indeed, as was argued earlier in this section, Emmanuel does relax the assumption of identical production techniques in the two countries. Once this is done, it is possible that the productivity in one of the industries (say, cloth) in the UK may be so superior to that in India that the rate of profit at a given cloth price will be higher despite the higher real wages paid in the UK. Under these assumptions the situation will be as set out in Figure 4.2(iv). Now the rate of profit can be raised by trade and the resulting specialization of production in the two countries. The autarkic positions of A and B both give a lower rate of profit than the specialization (trading) position of D. At the after-trade equilibrium point D India specializes in corn production, and the UK in cloth. The after-trade rates of profit in both the UK and India are higher than their autarkic rates of profit. And as each country switches to specialization point D so the barter terms of trade are better for *both* countries as compared with autarky.

This may seem a surprising point, but it is clear from Figure 4.2(iv) that as production in India moves from A to D so the price ratio (p_1/p_2) falls, that is p_2 (the price of corn) rises relative to cloth. And since India is specializing in the production of corn, this means that the barter terms of trade must be improving for India. Conversely, as UK production moves from B to D the price ratio (p_1/p_2) rises, meaning that the price of cloth (the good in which the UK is tending to specialize) rises relative to corn. Thus the UK's terms of trade also improve, again compared with autarky.

But if the terms of trade and the rate of profit improve for both countries, with real wages remaining as they were in autarky, then in what sense, it may be asked, can this be said to constitute 'unequal exchange'? For Emmanuel it does, since as stated earlier he defines unequal exchange in terms of a comparison of the unequal situation with a hypothetical one in which the rates of exploitation are equal in the rich and poor countries, that is where wage rates are equal *after* allowing for differences in productivity. This comparison is shown in Figure 4.2(v). The unequal wage equilibrium position of D gives a higher global rate of profit than the equilibrium position of E at which wages, allowing for productivity, are assumed to be equal in the two countries. And this time, in the move from unequal to equal exchange, the terms of trade have improved for India but *deteriorated* for the UK.

This example clearly illustrates Emmanuel's concern with the *distribution* of the gains from trade between countries. The problem is not that, with unequal exchange, India loses absolutely from trade, but that it gains less than it would if unequal exchange were eliminated. The same 'Sraffian' presentation is useful in showing that when Emmanuel puts unequal exchange into a dynamic context, his theory is very close to that of Lewis, Prebisch and Singer. As pointed out in Section 4.1, one strand of Prebisch's argument was that productivity improvements in the rich countries are recovered in the form of higher wages, whereas productivity improvements in the poor countries are not recovered by the workers in the form of higher wages because of their poor bargaining power. Their bargaining power is slight because, as Lewis emphasized, there is a long queue of people ready to work at the existing wage. Thus there is a tendency for the barter terms of trade to deteriorate for the poorer, peripheral country. Emmanuel argues along similar lines, as does Singer. For Emmanuel, the higher wages in the centre generate the market for further technical progress and industrialization in the centre.

Thus the process is cumulative, as shown in Figure 4.2(vi). First, an initial unequal exchange equilibrium of D is assumed. If productivity in cloth production in the UK rises at the same rate as wages, then the UK/cloth curve does not shift. The wage rise cancels out the productivity rise, leaving the rate of profit for a given price ratio the same as before. But if productivity in the production of corn in India improves without a corresponding rise in wages, then the India/corn curve will shift upwards and the trading equilibrium moves from D to D'. The rate of profit has risen globally, but the terms of trade of India have deteriorated, the price of corn having fallen relative to the price of cloth. Thus the poor peripheral country (India in this example) is driven further and further into unequal exchange. Or is it? Many economists have pointed out that there are likely to be tight limits to this process.

Alternative theories of unequal exchange

Two such economists who have themselves put forward a theory of unequal exchange, but have at the same time been critical of Emmanuel's theory, are the Argentinian economist Oscar Braun (see Braun 1974,

1977) and the Finnish economist Otto Andersson (see Andersson, 1971). The latter modified his theories in works published in 1974 and 1976, but here I consider what Andersson himself calls the Andersson–Braun modification to Emmanuel's unequal exchange (Andersson, 1976, 87). The major worry of Andersson and Braun with Emmanuel's theory is described as follows (Andersson 1976, 73): 'Since Emmanuel assumes capital to be internationally mobile, the logic of his theory demands that there should be a constant pressure for capital to be transferred to the less developed countries, speeding up their development and raising their wage levels, thereby causing the unequal exchange to fade away.' Thus the international mobility of capital – a factor in the emergence of unequal exchange – itself sets limits to unequal exchange.

As pointed out in Section 4.1, Emmanuel attempts to counter this objection by: first, arguing that markets are concentrated in the north, so that transport costs are a barrier to relocation; and secondly, resorting to the Ricardian assumption that production techniques are not equally available in all countries, these differing availabilities being explained by the historical accumulation of capital in the centre. By contrast, Andersson and Braun do not resort to the assumption of different technologies to explain why the world's capital fails to flow to the LDCs to take advantage of the lower wages there. Instead they relax Emmanuel's assumption of free trade and argue that unequal exchange results from commercial policies (tariff and non-tariff barriers) which systematically discriminate in favour of the centre. Thus Braun argues that 'The imperialist countries can oblige the dependent countries to sell at low prices by applying a discriminatory commercial policy; by imposing tariffs and other trade barriers for the exports of the dependent countries' (Braun, 1974).

Thus whereas Emmanuel's analysis and policy conclusions tend to be based on the assumption that certain commodities are technologically specific to the Third World, the analysis of Andersson and Braun assumes that the same commodities can be produced in both the centre and the periphery. Similarly, Yeats, an economist within the Geneva-based UNCTAD, has argued that the less developed countries suffer from 'unequal exchange' due to institutional factors and commercial structures which are biased against the LDCs (see Yeats, 1981, chapter 2). Thus for Andersson, Braun and Yeats, unequal exchange results not from the imperialism of free trade, but precisely from the fact that free trade does *not* exist. The developed countries' commercial policies are responsible, and thus the policy solution must be one of breaking down the protectionism in the developed countries and of equalizing the bargaining power of the rich and poor countries. This may require state trading corporations in the LDCs or south–south co-operation in trading. This policy emphasis is somewhat different from that of Prebisch and Emmanuel as Section 4.3 makes clear.

4.3 NEO-RICARDIAN POLICIES ON DISTRIBUTION AND DEVELOPMENT – AN OVERVIEW

In Chapters 2 and 3 it was emphasized that the main effect of the Sraffian 'wing' of neo-Ricardianism in the realm of international trade theory was to attack the neo-classical argument that not only would free trade lead to gains, but that it would also lead to 'factor price equalization'. Thus the writings in Steedman's books (1979a, 1979b) have (among other things) exposed the logical inconsistencies in the argument that free trade will necessarily compensate for restrictions on the international movement of labour. As a result of this 'capital theory' attack, the free-marketeers were forced to retreat into a general equilibrium framework where the world economy is a summation of the billions of individuals and their exchanges, and where restrictions on labour migration must logically be deplored as an unwarranted interference in the free market.

But the Sraffian attack by Steedman and others went further than merely casting doubt on whether free international trade would lead to greater equality. It suggested that individual countries might actually *lose* as a result of changes in the choice of technique induced by trading 'opportunities'. However, Steedman and the others did not identify *particular* countries or groups of countries as being systematically on the losing side from trade. By contrast, what I have referred to as the 'unequal exchange' wing of neo-Ricardianism does identify a particular part of the world – the Third World – as systematically losing out from the world trading system.

Unequal exchange – context and critique

However, these losses are not absolute but *relative*, according to Prebisch, Emmanuel and the other writers whose theories were discussed in Section 4.2. This group of economists argues that although the periphery *may* gain from trade, its gains are likely to be tiny relative to those accruing to the centre, and are certainly small compared to what they would be under a different wage structure in the Third World. Thus, in this relative sense, the periphery loses from trade precisely because capital is internationally mobile, whereas labour mobility is restricted.

The objection to this might be to point to the extensive migration of labour from the south to the north – at least 20 million in the fifteen years from the late 1950s through to the early 1970s. Doubtless Prebisch and Emmanuel's counter to this would be to say that this migration does little to reduce the vast labour surplus in the 'exporting' countries even though it is large relative to the labourforce in the 'receiving' countries – with, by the early 1970s, migrants from Mexico and Turkey constituting 5–20 per cent of the labourforces in the USA and Germany respectively (see Power, 1979). Thus, for Emmanuel, the labour migration, though extensive, has been insufficient to bring the bargaining power of labour in the Third World up to that of the rich countries' labour so as to equalize the rate of exploitation.

But there is another objection that can be levied against Emmanuel's theory. Many economists might agree with Emmanuel that there are large international differences in rates of pay, which more than outweigh differences in productivity. But they would point out also that there are considerable differences *within* countries in the rates of pay for what are, apparently, the same jobs. Various studies in Britain have found considerable differences in pay within nations not only between sexes, races and ages, but also within categories (see Routh, 1980; and other studies quoted in Cairncross and Keeley, 1983, section 2). Presumably Emmanuel's response to this would be to say that the international differences are the most substantial and significant, precisely because of the greater restrictions on job mobility internationally. With such restrictions, labour in the periphery is organizationally weak, and as a result the barter terms of trade of the periphery are worse than they would be if the Third World's labour were better organized and if the same wage rates were paid for the same international job.

Thus whereas the free-marketeers attempted to show that wages would adjust and even be equalized between countries to 'fit' the terms of trade, the argument of Emmanuel and the others was that the terms of trade would adjust to reflect predetermined differences in wage rates. And with wage rates being determined independently of the barter terms of trade (or relative prices), we have Emmanuel's 'imperialism of trade' – the subtitle of his book.

There are some economists who have classified the writers discussed in Section 4.2, and especially Emmanuel, as neo-Marxist (see, for example, Smith and Toye, 1979). Thus my categorization of them as neo-Ricardian is bound to be controversial. My justification for treating them as neo-Ricardians is the ease with which they can be presented within the Sraffian framework. Thus their concern is with the distribution of a technologically fixed surplus between countries with, as a result, attention being focused not on production, but rather on distribution. The emphasis is one of nationalism; thus *countries* lose, not *classes* of people. The argument is less with capitalism than with the fundamental basis on which capitalism is conducted.

This is the drift of the criticism levied at Emmanuel (in an appendix to *Unequal Exchange*) by Charles Bettelheim, a French Marxist. Bettelheim argued that Emmanuel's implicit notion that the surplus is fixed, and that the wage is the independent variable, gave rise to the mistaken argument that workers in the Third World are more exploited than workers in the rich countries, whereas Bettelheim argued: 'the more productive forces are developed, the more the proletarians are exploited, that is the higher is the proportion of surplus labour to necessary labour' (Bettelheim, in Emmanuel, 1972, 302). Thus Bettelheim points out that the relatively precise definition of exploitation in Marx's capital (as the ratio of surplus value to the value of labour power) becomes, in Emmanuel's writing, a much looser term to be applied to any group which is struggling to make ends meet on a very low wage. And it is then not surprising that Emmanuel sees Lenin's bribery of a small section of the labourforce in the north becoming the bribery of the whole of the rich countries' proleteriat. As Emmanuel put it: 'To have a standard of living higher than "the average for the world proletariat", it is today not necessary to belong to the "labour aristocracy" of the rich countries. It is enough to be the humblest of their street sweepers' (Emmanuel, 1972, 197).

Bettelheim did not deny the possibility that one nation might grow rich at the expense of another, but he argued that this is of quite a different order from employing 'the concept of exploitation to describe the effects of international exchange conditions upon the countries with underdeveloped productive forces' (Bettelheim, in ibid., 305). For Bettelheim, 'relations of exploitation cannot be constituted at the "level of exchange"; they necessarily have to be rooted at the level of *production*, or otherwise exchange could not be renewed' (ibid., 300).

No doubt, Emmanuel's response to this would be to say that his theory of unequal exchange *is* based upon the level of production, inasmuch as the wage rate is taken as the determining factor – or 'independent variable'. For Marxists, including Bettelheim, this is the fundamental point at issue. For while they agree with Emmanuel that the wage rate is not determined by the value of the marginal productivity of labour (as the crude, aggregated, neo-classical theory would have us believe), at the same time they deny that the wage rate is the independent variable. The Marxists, while arguing that the wage is determined through class struggle at the level of production, point to the accumulation of capital as the determining factor or independent variable. And it is precisely because the accumulation of capital is such an impersonal force that exploitation at the level of production is by no means obvious and may *appear* to arise in exchange.

While making this point, it is important to emphasize that Bettelheim, in criticizing Emmanuel, does not deny that surplus value may be transferred internationally (as well as nationally) through exchange, as well as more obviously through profit remittances or interest payments. Thus Marxists recognize that Britain maintained its world leadership through the second half of the nineteenth century, and into the twentieth, not so much by renovating its industrial economy but more by the formal construction of a large empire (in which India was much the most important) which served as a source of considerable surplus (see Ross, 1983). But recognizing this, as well as sexist and racist divisions within capitalism, is not the same as saying that these are the *primary*, determining forces in capitalist society.

Further discussion of the Marxist methodology and its approach to international trade theory will have to wait until Chapter 5. Here it is sufficient to point out that the most fundamental criticism of *Unequal Exchange* from the Marxist direction relates to Emmanuel's treatment of the wage as the independent variable. From this, surplus appears as a physical, static concept, and not in a *value* form, originating in the *process* of production.

In so far as Prebisch and Emmanuel focus their attention on a physically defined surplus and its distribution, there are similarities not only between their analysis and that of Brandt, but also between their approach and that of Paul Baran, Samir Amin, Gunder Frank and Immanuel Wallerstein. But I discuss the latter group of 'dependency' writers in Section 5.2, because I think that it will be easier to understand them after my presentation of the Marxist methodology in Section 5.1.

Here, however, it is worth noting two important respects in which the Amin–Frank theories are distinct from that of Emmanuel. First, the Amin–Frank group argue that the periphery not only loses from its integration into the world trading system, but that it loses in *absolute* terms. Thus whereas Emmanuel argues that the Third World is worse off than it would be if the same wage were paid for the same job, the Amin–Frank group argues that the periphery is worse off in absolute terms, as a result of its integration into the world capitalist system, than it would be in an autarkic or isolated situation. Thus the periphery is not only less developed, but *under*developed.

This analytical distinction leads on to the second policy difference. Thus, whereas Prebisch and Emmanuel argue for a modification of the terms on which international trade is conducted, the conclusion of the

Amin–Frank group is that a breakaway from the capitalist system is a precondition for the development of the periphery. This breakaway is necessary to escape from the extraeconomic forces which bind the periphery to the centre and enable its exploitation to be effected.

There is more about the Amin–Frank theories of underdevelopment in Sections 5.2 and 5.3, but in this section I want to consider the policy themes which run through what I have identified as the 'mainstream' cost-of-production (COP) analysis of international economics. For even after excluding Amin and Frank, readers may find it odd that writers as seemingly diverse as Sraffa and Singer, Galbraith and Emmanuel, or Prebisch and Brandt are bracketed together. My argument in defence is that their common link is their 'theory of value'.

Their common emphasis is on a given technology and a struggle over a more or less fixed surplus at the 'political' level of distribution. This approach is vividly illustrated in the algebraic Sraffian formulations, where a fixed surplus is implied by the use of fixed input–output coefficients and where the wage is independent of the production process. Thus labour is treated as an autonomous factor of production, and not as a commodity and item of capital as it is in the Marxist abstract labour theory (see Chapter 5).

With a 'physical', Sraffian definition of surplus, it is not surprising that the primary focus of the COP theory is on a 'political' distribution between competing 'interest' groups. Thus the surplus is not itself the result of class struggle, as it clearly is in the Marxist approaches. And for the COP theorists at the international level, these competing groups logically become nation-states. This focus again contrasts with that of the Marxist abstract labour theory which, as will be seen in Chapter 5, focuses on the class relationships derived from the *control* of the means of production.

Thus I am arguing that there is a common theoretical basis running through a number of economists' writings such that they can be categorized as cost-of-production theorists. The policies of these economists vary in detail, but a common theme is that while they are all critical of the free market, they all look for a restructuring of that market as a solution to the development problem. All conceive of the capitalist system in somewhat static 'political' terms, in which the problem is seen as one of surplus redistribution and use.

Furthermore, there is a tendency for cost-of-production theorists to identify industrialization with development. The analytical emphasis is on an *industrial* society rather than on *capitalism*. In the writings of sociologists in this school as well as those of economists, 'technology appears as its own prime-mover' (Giddens, 1981, 122). Thus the essential problem is seen as one of modifying the institutional structure so as to promote the development of industry and technology.

The exception to this general rule is that branch of the school which hopes, by contrast, to reduce the scale of technology and industrialization to fit the human and physical resources which already exist. This 'minority' section of the cost-of-production school is represented in the 'small is beautiful' writings of Schumacher (1973) and Ivan Illich (1971). Thus, whereas the mainstream of the cost-of-production school argues that institutions need to be expanded to fit advancing technology, writers such as Schumacher tend to emphasize the scaling down of technology to fit smaller-scale political institutions.

The Brandt Report

This theme of holding back technology was echoed in the first Brandt Report, but in highly muted form, when it argued that the 'mounting destruction of the earth's capacity to support life is not, we believe, an inescapable destiny' (Brandt, 1980, 79). Otherwise, in general, the Brandt Report is solidly within the mainstream of the cost-of-production theory. It is very similar to the Pearson Report (1969), which had been commissioned by the United Nations, published a decade earlier and prepared under the leadership of Lester Pearson who, like Brandt, was another ex-Prime Minister, this time of Canada. Even though the first Brandt Report carried a more desperate message in its title (*A Programme for Survival*) than that of the Pearson Report (*Partners in Development*), the theme was similar. Both reports argued that the world ultimately has a common interest in industrialization and development which is obscured by sectional distributional struggles. The only programme for survival is for the countries of the world to become partners in development; in the words of the Brandt Report:

> The North must share its resources, its control of institutions; it must be willing to work for some changes in the way markets operate, which is presently to its advantage. But we do suggest that the North as well as the South gets much in return, both in straightforward economic benefits and in a reduction of uncertainties and instability.
>
> (Brandt Report, 1980, 76)

The general theme of the first Brandt Report was to welcome industrialization and its associated technology, and to ensure that its introduction and use are not impeded by distributional struggles. To avoid such struggles will require 'meeting essential human needs', the most basic of which may even be 'the right to participate in change and to share in the outcome' (ibid., 63), but the Brandt Report is, like the writings of Galbraith and other 'social democrats' ultimately élitist.

It is not difficult to find references in either Brandt or Galbraith attesting to the importance of an impartial, educated élite that stands above, and adjudicates on distributional struggles (see, for example, ibid., 191; Galbraith 1977, 373).

Thus, in these views, what is needed is interference in, and regulation of, the market by a disinterested élite which can arbitrate between the conflicting demands of the various groups, including those of nation-states. It is precisely because the élite does not represent a particular interest group, that it can be representative of society as a whole. What is needed particularly is a strengthening of the institutional structure at the supranational level; such a theme is inherent in the twelve recommendations of Brandt summarized in annex 1 at the end of the 1980 report as follows:

1 more aid and technical assistance to the poorest countries;

2 food aid linked to agricultural research and development including agrarian and trade reform;

3 national population programmes and common action to protect the atmosphere, the environment and ocean resources;

4 intensification of negotiations to end the arms race, strengthening of the United Nations peace keeping role, and an international tax on arms exports;

5 structural reforms inside developing countries combined with encouragement of regional and sub-regional integration or co-operation for economic development;

6 stabilisation of commodity prices at remunerative levels through international commodity agreements to include compensatory financing, combined with the reduction of tariffs and non-tariff barriers on developing countries' processed products;

7 an emergency energy programme to agree on the production, conservation and pricing of oil and on major investment in oil and natural gas exploitation and development in developing countries;

8 expanded free trade in place of protection to support industrialisation in developing countries within an international trade organisation to incorporate both GATT and UNCTAD;

9 effective national laws and international codes of conduct to govern the activities of transnational companies and especially their transfer of technology, investment and pricing policy;

10 reform of the international monetary system to include creation of a new international currency of the IMF with increased liquidity;

11 an increase in aid and loans to developing countries through a world development fund managed jointly by borrowers and lenders with special emphasis on finance to support mineral and energy exploration and development in developing countries;

12 strengthening of the UN system by streamlining public education and summit meetings.   (Brandt Report, 1980, 282–92)

Concluding comments

There is the same suspicion of the free market among all economists within the cost-of-production school, but the suspicion runs deeper than in Brandt in the writings of those like Gerry Helleiner (1972, 1976), Albert Hirschman (1958), Keith Griffin (1971) and Gunnar Myrdal (1956a), who see a strong case for programmes of import substitution and regional integration in the Third World deriving from the structural characteristics of industrialization. Their argument is that the manufacturing sector is characterized not only by economies of scale (both external and internal to the firm), but also by economies over time through learning-by-doing. These economies combine to present a strong case for market interference by national governments so as to promote industrialization through import substitution on either the national scale or through regional co-operation with other Third World states. The switch to manufactures which is necessary to break out of the vicious circle of primary product pauperization will not occur in the free market *because* of the economies of scale and time, and regional co-operation may be advantageous in enlarging the international market and in strengthening the bargaining power of Third World nation-states over the terms of technology transfer (see Helleiner, 1976).

I return to these issues in Chapter 8, but the case for collective action by the periphery to restructure their economies is strengthened when the arguments of Lewis, Prebisch and Singer about the relative wage bargaining in primary products and manufacturing is brought into the picture. In the absence of a substantial redistribution of income from the north to compensate the south for being 'stuck' with primary products Prebisch argues that not only does the case for industrialization through import substitution become stronger, but so does the case for cartel action in the primary products field (see Prebisch, in Theberge, 1968, 290).

As we have seen, Emmanuel's argument is slightly different, though he ends up with similar policy conclusions. His argument is that wage bargaining is weaker in the Third World as a whole, that is in both the manufacturing and primary products sectors. The obvious policy conclusion from such an argument would seem to be for the governments, in the Third World, to collectively raise the wages of the workers in the Third World so 'knocking the centre country workers off their labour-aristocratic pedestal in the process' (Evans, 1979, 271). But Emmanuel dismisses this without further explanation when he says in *Unequal Exchange*: 'A sudden levelling up of their wage levels to those of the advanced countries being, of course, out of the question a priori' (Emmanuel, 1972, 267).

Thus he is left with two solutions to prevent 'from leaking abroad the excess surplus value' that the less developed countries extract from their own workers. The two solutions are either a 'diversification of production through transfer of factors from the traditional exporting branches that can replace imports, which will enable the national consumer to benefit from the low national wage level' or 'a tax on exports that will transfer this excess surplus value to the state' (ibid., 267). The taxes on exports 'presuppose agreement between several producing countries' (ibid., 268), and are likely to be opposed by the developed countries and by 'their' agencies such as the International Monetary Fund (IMF) and the World Bank, as is any extensive programme of diversification through protectionism. Part of the reason for this opposition may lie, Emmanuel suggests, in the size of the stakes involved. For he argues that although the value of exports from the Third World is only $25 billion, this 'in no way prevents the plundering that arises from unequal exchange from assuming the dimensions of 200 or 300 billion' (ibid., 368). The size of this alleged transfer can be gauged by comparing it with the annual official aid figure in the early 1970s of about $20 billion, about one-tenth of Emmanuel's lower figure.

But a discussion as to whether or not OPEC-style producer cartels are feasible for primary commodities other than oil will have to wait until later (Chapter 8), for in Chapter 5 we discuss the basic elements in a Marxist analysis of production and trade in the world of capitalism; by doing this, the essential characteristics of the cost-of-production approach to international trade will be placed in sharper relief.

NOTES ON FURTHER READING

This chapter owes much to the writings of David Evans, and the reader is recommended to look at some of his recent articles in this field. The relative beginner is likely to find Evans, 1979, useful as a starting-point. Then for the early parts of this chapter, you should go on to read some of the articles by Prebisch, 1962, 1964, and in Theberge, 1968; Singer, 1950, 1975; Lewis, 1954, 1958; Myrdal, 1956b. For summaries and discussions of Prebisch's views, look at Meier, 1968; Bacha, 1978; Evans, 1976, 1979; Johnson, 1967, chapter 1.

For more specialized debates on immiserizing growth and trends in the terms of trade, see Bhagwati, in Connolly and Swoboda, 1973; Brown, 1974, chapter 10; Commonwealth Secretariat, 1975, 65–9; Evans and Jairath, 1977; Evans, 1979, 264, 265; Meier, 1968, chapter 3; Ray, 1977; Spraos, 1980. See also further references in Evans, 1979; Spraos, 1980. For a discussion of optimum tariff theory geared to the second-year undergraduate, refer to Corden, 1974, chapter 7.

Generally, of course, it is advisable to read the original texts rather than trust other people's interpretations (including mine); but Emmanuel's *Unequal Exchange*, 1972, is probably an exception to this. The debates between Emmanuel and Bettelheim in Emmanuel, 1972, appendices, are recommended; but, first, read Evans, 1976, 1979; then Ross, 1976; Brewer, 1980, chapter 9; Open University, 1983, section 13, block 4. After reading the recommended Bettelheim in Emmanuel, see the introduction to John Roemer's *A General Theory of Exploitation and Class*, 1982. (If you agree with Bettelheim's criticism of Emmanuel, you will probably also be critical of Roemer's theory for siting exploitation at the level of exchange.) For an interesting discussion of Emmanuel and an attempt at measuring the extent of unequal exchange between Peru and the USA, see Gibson, 1980. The comparison of Emmanuel with Prebisch–Singer in this chapter relies heavily on Evans, 1976.

Oscar Braun's work on imperialism had not been published in English before his untimely death in 1981. The most accessible version for readers of this book may be Braun, 1974, but readers may prefer to look at David Evans's article, 1981a, Andersson, 1976, chapter 5, or the less accessible Evans, 1981b; and Brown and Wright, 1978. The advantage in referring to Evans, 1981b, is that he refers to Andersson's as well as Braun's work (see 16–25) and he distinguishes between Andersson's earlier and later ideas. For Andersson's own later views, look at section 6.8 of Andersson, 1976; appendix 1 also has a summary of the Soviet debate on unequal exchange from the 1950s through the 1970s which the student may find interesting.

For the first Brandt Report, see Brandt, 1980; and for two critiques from the left, see Elson, 1982; Third World First, 1982.

SUMMARY

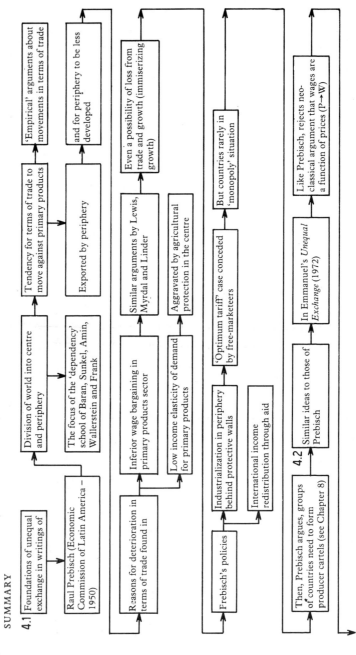

4.1 Foundations of unequal exchange in writings of

Raul Prebisch (Economic Commission of Latin America – 1950)

Division of world into centre and periphery

The focus of the 'dependency' school of Baran, Sunkel, Amin, Wallerstein and Frank

Tendency for terms of trade to move against primary products

Exported by periphery

'Empirical' arguments about movements in terms of trade

and for periphery to be less developed

Reasons for deterioration in terms of trade found in

Inferior wage bargaining in primary products sector

Low income elasticity of demand for primary products

Similar arguments by Lewis, Myrdal and Linder

Aggravated by agricultural protection in the centre

Even a possibility of loss from trade and growth (immiserizing growth)

Frebisch's policies

Industrialization in periphery behind protective walls

International income redistribution through aid

'Optimum tariff' case conceded by free-marketeers

But countries rarely in 'monopoly' situation

4.2 Then, Prebisch argues, groups of countries need to form producer cartels (see Chapter 8)

Similar ideas to those of Prebisch

In Emmanuel's *Unequal Exchange* (1972)

Like Prebisch, rejects neo-classical argument that wages are a function of prices (P→W)

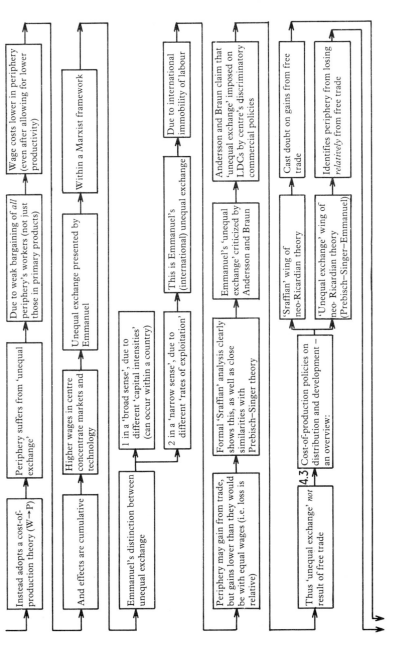

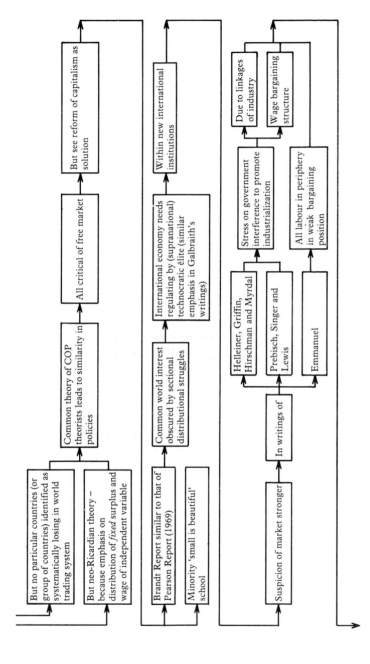

But no particular countries (or group of countries) identified as systematically losing in world trading system

But neo-Ricardian theory – because emphasis on distribution of *fixed* surplus and wage of independent variable

Common theory of COP theorists leads to similarity in policies

All critical of free market

But see reform of capitalism as solution

Brandt Report similar to that of Pearson Report (1969)

Minority 'small is beautiful' school

Common world interest obscured by sectional distributional struggles

International economy needs regulating by (supranational) technocratic élite (similar emphasis in Galbraith's writings)

Within new international institutions

Suspicion of market stronger

In writings of

Helleiner, Griffin, Hirschman and Myrdal

Prebisch, Singer and Lewis

Emmanuel

Stress on government interference to promote industrialization

Due to linkages of industry

Wage bargaining structure

All labour in periphery in weak bargaining position

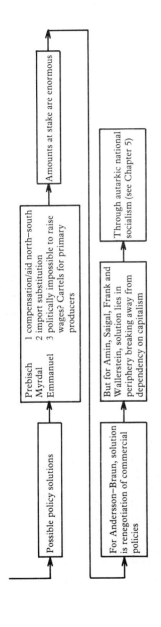

Possible policy solutions

Prebisch
Myrdal
Emmanuel

1 compensation/aid north–south
2 import substitution
3 politically impossible to raise wages? Cartels for primary producers

Amounts at stake are enormous

For Andersson–Braun, solution is renegotiation of commercial policies

But for Amin, Saigal, Frank and Wallerstein, solution lies in periphery breaking away from dependency on capitalism

Through autarkic national socialism (see Chapter 5)

5

Marxist theories – underdevelopment or uneven development?

5.1 MARX'S METHOD AND THE CRITIQUE OF CAPITALISM

Marx, methodology and modes

The purpose of this section is to outline the approach of a third school of economic thought which is quite separate from that of the subjective preference and cost-of-production schools which were introduced in Chapters 2 and 3 respectively. This third approach was pioneered by Karl Marx in the nineteenth century, on the basis of *and* in opposition to the ideas of David Ricardo.

At the time Ricardo's *Principles of Political Economy and Taxation* were published in the early nineteenth century the developing capitalism of north-western Europe was beginning to be subjected to intense criticism on moral grounds. Many of these socialist critics were identified by Marx as 'utopian socialists', because he argued that their criticisms were not founded in a scientific critique of society, but on the basis of a moral opposition. As a result, Marx argued, their policies were bound to lead *nowhere* (the literal translation of the Greek word 'utopia'). Among the leading 'utopian socialists' of the first half of the nineteenth century was a self-educated Frenchman, Pierre Joseph Proudhon. Proudhon, the son of a cooper, was born in 1809, a decade before Marx's birth. Marx always retained a respect for Proudhon's personal devotion to the workers' cause, but by the middle of the century Marx had reached the conclusion that Proudhon's ideas were unscientific, *non-revolutionary* notions, which were unlikely to bring about a political advance for the working class.

In attempting a scientific analysis of capitalism Marx aimed to produce not only a critique of the ideas of the bourgeois utopian and reactionary socialists, but also to provide guidance for the political action that would overthrow capitalism. As Marx and his collaborator, Friedrich Engels, stressed, 'The philosophers have only *interpreted* the world in various ways; the point is to *change* it' (Marx and Engels, 1974, 123; emphasis in original). The effectiveness of the abstract interpretation of capitalism had to be tested by concrete political action in the day-to-day world. Otherwise it would be idle philosophical speculation which would bear the same inadequate relationship to the actual world as masturbation bears to sexual love (see Marx and Engels, 1974, 103). This, then, was Marx's objective in developing an analysis of capitalism based on an abstract labour theory of value. This was the impetus for his painstaking research in the British Museum, as well as his being politically active in European working-class movements.

The completed sections of *Capital* make only occasional references to international trade, but at the same time the foundation was clearly laid for an analysis of trade as an aspect of the social relation of capital, as Marx himself argued (see foreword to Marx, 1973a, 59).

Marx's treatment of the world market as an aspect of the social relation of capital contrasts with both the subjective preference and cost-of-production theories. The other theories take different things as given. Subjective preference theory is essentially ahistorical, in that 'politics' is totally separate from economics. The contrast between them and the cost-of-production theorists is sharper than that between the latter and the Marxists. But the COP theorists tend to concentrate on the nation-state as an entity independent from economic forces, ignoring the dynamics of class relations *within* the state that are at the centre of the Marxist analysis.

Marx's approach to the study of society was one of dialectical historical materialism. Marx developed the dialectical approach from the German philosopher Hegel, which led him to see the 'creative' potential as well as the destructive misery of capitalism. For Hegel, the history of the world was a history of ideas, with each idea, as it is developed, bringing with it another idea which is its negation. In other words, the ideas do battle and out of the contest new ideas develop and thus a dialectical process of change takes place. In place of a battle of ideas as the motive force of history Marx substituted a contest between material or economic forces. Thus no class can rule without bringing another, antagonistic, class on to the stage of history. And the basis of the power of a class lies in its 'economic' control of the means of production. Thus economic questions are not just a matter of exchange relationships (as in the free-marketeers' world), nor are they merely a question of groups relating to an externally determined technology (as in the cost-of-production theory).

For Marx, then, production is always social: an ahistorical world of independent individuals is a myth. Furthermore, social relations are rarely the result of conscious choice. Wage labour and factory production are both the result of a long process of historical change. Any analysis of society must, Marx argued, start from the structure of social relations, and not from individual motivations (see Marx, 1975, 425).

Thus the technical and physical development of society (the material forces of production) interacts with, but ultimately determines, the social relations of production. And it is the totality of these relations of production that 'constitutes the economic structure of society, the real foundation on which there arises a legal and political superstructure and to which there correspond definite forms of social consciousness' (ibid., 425). Thus it is social being that determines consciousness, not consciousness that determines social being. But because the everyday world is highly complex, Marx insisted on the need for abstraction to make sense of this complexity. And at a very high level of abstraction different societies, spanning many centuries, were characterized by quite different forces and relations of production. In short, their *mode of production* was distinct.

Thus, for Marx, *capitalism* is a historically specific mode of production. It was the inability of the 'classical' economists of the late eighteenth and early nineteenth centuries, notably Adam Smith and David Ricardo, to recognize this historical specificity for which Marx criticized them. Inasmuch as they recognized the need for abstraction they were scientific in their approach; inasmuch as they failed to identify capitalism as a mode of production they were bourgeois. For Marx, each mode of production contained in general a pair of opposed classes, a class of direct producers and a non-producing class which exploits them. And the various successive modes of production were stages in the history of mankind. It is this mode of production of material life which 'conditions the general process of social, political and intellectual life' (ibid., 425). Thus capitalism is one of a number of modes of production that Marx identified: 'In broad outline, the Asiatic, ancient, feudal and modern bourgeois modes of production may be designated as epochs marking progress in the economic development of society' (Marx, 1975, 426). A simplified summary of the characteristics of these and other modes of production is given in Table 5.1.

A mode of production, Marx argued, 'engenders the *material conditions* and the *social forms* necessary for an economical reconstruction of society' (Marx, 1973b, 78; emphasis in original). Thus both the joint-stock company and the break-up of the nuclear family are examples of social forms in capitalism which anticipate a transition to communism (see Marx, 1970, 489–90, and 1972, 437–8). But the transition itself is

Table 5.1 Six characteristics of six modes of production

Mode of production	Class of producers	Exploiting class/elements of production owned by exploiting class	Method of appropriating surplus by ruling class	Purpose of production	Do producers organize production?	Which mode of production is likely to follow?
Ancient	Slaves	Slave owners/producers	Coercion/direct	Use value	No	Commodity production/capitalism
Feudal	Serfs/peasants	Landlords/land	Coercion/rent	Use value	Yes on own land; no on lord's land	Commodity production/capitalism
Asiatic	Peasants	Despotic state/land	Coercion/tax-rent	Use value	Yes	Capitalism/communism
Simple (petty) commodity production*	Artisans/peasants	No exploiting class	—	Exchange value	Yes	Capitalism
Capitalism	Proletariat	Capitalists/means of production	Market/labour time and taxes	Exchange value	No	Communism
Communism	Workers	No exploiting class	—	Use value	Yes, collectively	None (?)

Source: Based on Harrison, 1978, pp. 24–5.

* Note that this mode of production is unlikely to be dominant. It is likely to be subordinated to another, for example, capitalism.

likely to come about through a social revolution when 'at a certain stage of development, the material productive forces of society come into conflict with the existing relations of production' (Marx, 1975, 425).

Thus at a certain stage, far from allowing the further development of the forces of production, the social relations of production – the way in which production is organized – hinder their further development: 'Then begins an era of social revolution' (ibid., 425–6). But the outcome is not predetermined. Crises in capitalism, as in other modes of production, provide both restructuring and revolutionary opportunities. Neither is the process of change obvious. To discover it necessitates scientific study, for the social structure is hidden behind the appearance of society. Thus 'all science would be superfluous if the outward appearance and essence of things directly coincided' (Marx, 1972, 817).

Marx and the emergence of capitalism

Capitalism is a historically specific mode of production, in the sense that it has not always existed, but emerged, painfully, from the womb of either the feudal or Asiatic modes of production. These changes from one mode of production to another are not inevitable, but even if they do take place, they may take decades to bring about, so that at any one time in a particular geographic area or social formation (such as the modern nation-state) relations characteristic of several modes of production may be combined, with one of them being dominant.

Above the economic relations of 'civil society' there is the legal and political superstructure which in capitalism includes the legislature, executive and judiciary – in brief, 'the state'. It is virtually an axiom of Marxist theory that the state acts to defend the interests of the ruling, dominant, exploiting class. The latter does, however, have its own divisions or 'factions', so that the interests of the ruling class are not always wholly unambiguous. Thus the state is likely to have a certain flexibility or 'relative autonomy' (for more on this, see Section 9.1).

Thus a particular nation-state will not be coterminous with the capitalist mode of production, even though nation-states and the capitalist mode of production develop together (see Polanyi, 1944). Thus whereas the free-marketeers take the nation-state as a pre-existing institution for a modern market economy, the abstract labour theory of the Marxists sees the development of capitalism as going along with the development of nation-states.

In a particularly lively part of volume I of *Capital* (part VIII) Marx argued that capitalism developed (from feudalism in Europe) through a process of prior or primitive accumulation, in which 'the expropriation of the agricultural producer, of the peasant, from the soil, is the basis of the whole process' (Marx, 1970, 716). But commodity production for the market and, therefore, trade predate capitalism. In a pre-capitalist world, where the surplus is extracted by force, the cost of production of a good is not clearly defined and prices can vary considerably between one area and another. Under these conditions the monopoly of trade can bring considerable profits. Thus it is not surprising that the period from 1500 to 1800 in Europe was dominated by merchants. This was the age of mercantilism. The dominant mode of production was feudal, but the individual ownership of land in feudal Europe and the competition for trade routes between the large merchant companies (such as the Levant and East India) paved the way for the accumulation of money as capital. But Marx realized that merchant capital might both undermine the feudal mode of production and at the same time hinder the development of capitalist production (see Marx, 1972, 334). The transition between feudalism and capitalism would thereby be extended.

Nevertheless, production for exchange would be encouraged by the activities of merchants, and the occasional circulation of commodities mediated by money (C–M–C) would become transformed into the regular mercantile circuit of M–C–M, where M is money-capital. The merchants buy in order to sell, but their aim is to yield a profit, so that the circuit becomes M–C–M', where M' denotes a sum of money greater than that advanced. Now 'circulation sweats money from every pore' (Marx, 1970, 113). But merchants will not be able to sell at a profit unless they have a monopoly of a particular trade. And the struggles between the merchants for such monopolies may take violent forms as in the 'trade' wars of the sixteenth and seventeenth centuries.

But gradually with increasing competition between the merchants (whether in the form of wars or not), the trade monopolies disintegrate. Industry then begins to dominate trade, and with the development of capital beyond the prior or 'primitive' forms of merchant and interest-bearing capital, another source of surplus has to be found. Capitalists must buy and sell commodities at their value and yet make a profit. To do this they must find in the market a commodity which itself is a source of value. Such a commodity is labour power. But this commodity does not arise naturally. It has to be forced into existence. Labourers have to be freed from their restrictive but relatively independent feudal forms, so that they become free in two senses; first, they are free to move from one form of employment to another, a form of freedom extolled by the free-marketeers. But they are also free in a second sense, they are freed of their ownership of land – their means of production – a form of freedom emphasized by Marx and the Marxists. The patent coercion of the serf now becomes the latent coercion of the proletariat, as labourers are forced to sell their labour power as a commodity. Thus capitalism emerges as a system of generalized commodity production in which labour power is squeezed out of the disintegrating pre-capitalist mode by a combination of competition, taxes and, above all, force.

This destruction of the 'natural' economy is vividly described in the Polish-born Rosa Luxemburg's *The Accumulation of Capital* (1963, first published in 1913). Even more than Marx, Luxemburg stressed the role of state power and state force in opening up pre-capitalist areas (and her chapters 27–9 stand in particularly stark contrast to the peaceful neo-classical presentation of developing capitalism in, for example, Myint, 1958). In Luxemburg's account force has been invariably necessary to break down the resistance of the pre-capitalist mode, a resistance which has varied in different areas of the world. Even in such a fertile environ-ment for capitalism as Europe, the English Civil War of the seventeenth century and the French Revolution of the late eighteenth century were necessary to clear the way for capitalism.

The greater resistance of pre-capitalist modes outside Europe and its consequences has been emphasized in more recent writings by P. P. Rey and Giovanni Arrighi. In Rey's *Les Alliances de classes* (1973) and *Colonialisme, neo-colonialisme et transition au capitalisme* (1971) it is argued that in Congo-Brazzaville, the area of his research, the capitalist and pre-capitalist modes co-exist because Congo-Brazzaville is one of the non-western areas which 'apart from Japan have shown themselves and still show themselves to be wretched environments for the development of capitalist relations of production' (Rey, 1973, 11). Thus by impli-cation Congo-Brazzaville remains backward because capitalism has failed to transform the society as much as it did in Europe a century or more before. In Rey's story capitalism coexists with pre-capitalism.

Again, from Arrighi's wider research on Africa south of the Sahara (see Arrighi and Saul, 1973), we get a picture of 'growth without develop-ment' because of the limited penetration of the capitalist mode. Thus for Rey and Arrighi capitalism is progressive but its powers of penetration in Africa have been limited. Their view of capitalism as at least having a 'progressive' aspect is consistent with that of Marx, and in sharp contrast with that of the one-dimensional Amin–Frank theory of the 'develop-ment of underdevelopment' (see Section 5.2).

Capitalism, surplus value and the (falling) rate of profit

Thus even though there is likely to be varying resistance from the pre-capitalist mode, capitalism is always, in the classical picture of Marx, attempting to break down this resistance to the creation of 'free' labour. Once it has done this, the capitalist is free to buy the rather special commodity, labour power. It is special in three senses: first, it is the only commodity which is itself productive of value and therefore a source of profit for the capitalist; secondly, it is not 'produced' in the same way as other commodities; and thirdly, its owner, the labourer, resists it being treated like any other commodity. The second and third factors carry both advantages and disadvantages for the capitalist class. For example, the fact that it is not 'produced' in the same way as other commodities may mean that its reproduction cost can be indirectly subsidized by domestic labour away from the immediate place of work (see West, in Nichols, 1980; Wolpe, 1972).

But the first special characteristic is the most important. For Marx, all commodities have both a use value (they satisfy a want) and an exchange value (they contain socially necessary labour-time), but it is only labour power for which its use value can be said to be 'greater' than its exchange value. For its use value to the capitalist is the amount of exchange value that it can produce in the working-day, and this in general will be greater than the exchange value embodied in itself; otherwise there is little point in the capitalist buying it. At the same time, however, the worker gets paid the 'full value' for his commodity (labour power), and the relationship between him and his employer *appears* as an equal one. This is quite unlike the relationship between the serf and the lord of the manor in feudalism where the exploitation is obvious, since the latter forces the serf to work unpaid on the lord's land for part of the year. By contrast, in capitalism the surplus takes a 'value' form and is hidden beneath the apparent equality of prices. The surplus value is created in production, but is realized and appears in a transmuted form only in exchange.

Thus, whereas the circuit of merchant capital was $M-C-M'$, now with the full development of capitalism, the circuit becomes: $M-C \, {}^{-MP}_{-LP} \ldots$ P $\ldots$ C'$-M'$, where MP denotes the means of production (machines and raw materials), LP denotes labour power and P the production process. Thus, in the view of the abstract labour theory of value, the surplus is not due to abstinence from consumption (as claimed by what Marx called the school of 'vulgar economists'), nor is it a physical surplus fixed by technology as implied by the cost-of-production theorists. With the identification of labour power as a commodity, the path is open for a theory of exploitation in production and the production of surplus *value*.

Thus surplus value is created by the worker having to work beyond the time necessary to reproduce him or herself, but it is hidden by being transformed and distributed in the price forms of profit, rent and interest. The labour process is abstracted from the price form, and thus the social relationships have to be unearthed by the use of an abstract labour theory of value which digs beneath the phenomenal form of prices.

But the capitalist class also compete among themselves, and it is this competition that is the source both of capitalism's huge productive potential and of its destruction. For there is within capitalism, as a direct result of competition, a tendency for the rate of profit to fall. This follows from the introduction of new machinery by capitalists as a part of the attempt to reduce costs and preserve, or improve, competitiveness. The effect of this is to increase the organic composition of capital (constant capital relative to variable capital). Since the rate of profit is $s/(c + v)$, which is the same as $(s/v)/(c/v + 1)$ or;

$$\frac{\text{rate of exploitation}}{\text{organic composition of capital} + 1}$$

this rise in the organic composition of capital tends to reduce the rate of profit.

This tendency can be countered primarily by an increase in the rate of exploitation, which in any case is likely to follow the introduction of the more productive technique. It is a matter of considerable controversy whether this will compensate sufficiently to negate the effect of the rising organic composition. Marx clearly thought that generally it would not and thus talked of the Law of the Tendency of the Rate of Profit to Fall. Thus Marx argued that what, for the individual capitalist, gives an edge over enemies in the competitive war leads, for capitalists as a whole, to a generalized fall in the rate of profit. (For a fuller discussion, see Cole *et al.*, 1983, 220–6; Shaikh, 1978.)

But even those who argue that the rate of profit will tend to fall admit, like Marx, that there are counteracting influences which are likely to slow down its fall (see Marx, 1972, 239). Thus the ratio of s/v may rise as wages are depressed or labour productivity increased, particularly at times of high unemployment. The ratio of c/v may be reduced by a cheapening of c, as a result of the higher productivity or by a devaluation of capital during a crisis. A further countereffect may be provided by a higher rate of profit on capital invested in new areas – in, say, colonies.

The expansion of capitalism

Because of the falling rate of profit and the countereffects, and because of the unplanned character of capitalism, its development is likely to be highly uneven over *time*, with boom periods alternating with periods of crisis. I return to crises and their explanation in Chapter 6, but it is important to note that the process of development is also likely to be uneven over *space*. Thus the *global* expansion of capitalism over *time* is likely to be highly uneven.

The spatial unevenness is likely to be accentuated by the differing resistance of pre-capitalist modes and the varying ability of capitalism to penetrate. For example, Arrighi's writing to which I have already referred points to the difference in the penetration of capital between southern Africa and tropical Africa. The penetration in southern Africa was much stronger because of mineral discoveries, followed by the establishment of a substantial settler–colonial bourgeoisie attracted by the early capitalist boom.

Thus, with these differences in capitalism's penetration, the unevenness of global development is hardly surprising. But capitalism's weakness in some areas was more than compensated by its strength in others and, in the 1840s, at the time of writing the *Manifesto of the Communist Party*, Marx and Engels were certainly in little doubt about capitalism's ability to transform and 'develop' the world (see Marx and Engels, 1975, 38). Their view of capitalism stands in dramatic contrast to that of the Amin–Frank view, in which, as we shall see in Section 5.2, capitalism is relatively stagnant and parasitic in its effect on the periphery.

As mentioned earlier, the first expression of the internationalization of capital was through trade. And as trade expanded, with and despite the monopolization of many of the trade routes, sea and other trading ports were annexed by the mercantile companies. This annexation was a result of military supremacy, itself a result of economic supremacy. The mercantilist period was broadly between 1500 and 1800. In its earliest stages, when Spanish and Portuguese interests were dominant, annexation was limited to trading ports. But in the seventeenth century Spain and Portugal lost control of the sea and of the trading ports, first, to the Dutch, and then to the English and French. An Atlantic trade triangle emerged 'with manufactured goods (especially guns) being shipped to Africa, slaves to the Americas, and sugar back to Europe' (Brewer, 1980, 4).

Later, in the eighteenth and nineteenth centuries, industry began to dominate commerce and the English, French and Dutch trading posts were expanded into territorial possessions. Transport costs continued to fall with improvements in shipping technology in the nineteenth century, and world trade expanded rapidly. Between 1800 and 1870, while world industrial production expanded by something like six times, world trade expanded tenfold (Rybczynski, 1978, 25) and, at the end of this period in 1869, the opening of the Suez Canal provided a further stimulus to the growth of trade.

By the nineteenth century industrial capitalism was well established in north-western Europe. Workers were being herded into factories to obtain economies from a greater division of labour and from increased control. This was the process of what Marx called *concentration*. As yet the use of machines was not dominant, and surplus value was extracted in its *absolute* form by extending the working-hours of the labourforce. In the mid-nineteenth century industrial capital finally pushed aside the mercantile interests. This was the period of *laissez-faire* capitalism, when state power was localized, though less so in continental Europe than in England.

But into the second half of the nineteenth century *laissez-faire* capitalism gave way to a stage of 'monopoly capitalism', during which political power became centralized. Credit grew, and with this growth came the *centralization* of capital, the amalgamation of many capitals into one. This was the age of machinofacture, as the amalgamation of capital was facilitated in the 1860s by the institution of the joint-stock company in England. The most advanced economies were dominated by monopoly capital – not monopoly in the sense of controlling a market, but in the sense of there being few producers within each nation-state, a situation which by no means excluded fierce international competition.

This was the age of the growth of large corporations controlled by the Rockefellers and Carnegies, but with banking or financial capital being integrated with industrial capital, especially on the continent of Europe, to form *finance* capital. This monopolizing centralization process was emphasized by a number of Marxists soon after the beginning of this century, most notably by the Russians, Nicolai Bukharin and Vladimir Ilich Lenin, and by the Austrian, Rudolf Hilferding. The latter's *Finance Capital* was first published in 1910, about a decade before Bukharin's *Imperialism and World Economy* and Lenin's *Imperialism, the Highest Stage of Capitalism*. These writers stressed the integration of finance capital, the formation of monopoly capital in the developed nations and the intensification of competition on a world scale between national blocks of capital. They claimed that the national blocks of capital enlisted state support in grabbing territories and protecting markets through tariffs or other means. Thus the end of the nineteenth and the early part of the twentieth century was a period of the inter-nationalization of finance capital, of colonialism and, ultimately, of war.

This was a period marked by a rapid rise in the stock of foreign investment held by Europeans (see Table 5.2). It should be noted that these investments represent not only capital flows, but considerable reinvestment of profits, and that much of it was in countries of recent settlement (such as Canada, the USA, Argentina and Australia) to which most of the

60 million or so nineteenth-century migrants from Europe had gone (see Nurkse, in Cooper, 1969; and Open University, 1976, 31).

Table 5.2 Stock of foreign capital investment held by Europe 1825–1915 ($ billion)

	1825	1855	1885	1915
UK	0.5	2.3	7.8	19.5
France	0.1	1.0	3.3	8.6
Germany	0.1	1.0	1.9	6.7
Others	—	—	—	11.4
Total	0.7	4.3	13.0	46.2

Sources: Warren, 1980, 62; Brown, 1974, 171.

Table 5.3 Colonies of Europe 1830–1914

	1830	1876	1914	
	Population (million)	Population (million)	Area (million km²)	Population (million)
Colonies				
British	126	252	34	393
French	1	6	11	56
Russian	—	16	17	33
Other European	—	24	13	86
Total colonial population and area	127	298	75	568
Home European states			17	445
Semi-colonial countries (Persia, China and Turkey)			15	361
Others			27	283
Total world			134	1,657

Sources: Brown, 1974, table 15; Lenin, 1970, 77.

This expansion of capital was accompanied by colonialism, the formal annexation of whole territories. In particular, in the last quarter of the nineteenth century, there was a scramble by the 'great powers' for territories, so that by the First World War more than two-thirds of the world's land mass was under the control of the colonial powers, mainly Britain, France, Germany and Russia (see Table 5.3). The struggle for colonial control was frequently violent and justified in the name of the state and of a racist ideology.

Nevertheless, there was a slight possibility of this process of expansion being a relatively peaceful one, for the export of capital in the form of loans from Britain and France to German and American enterprises created a certain solidarity in international capitalism. On the other hand, the growth of German capital on a small land base contrasted with a relatively declining British economy based on a relatively large empire to create 'a situation which is bound to intensify greatly . . . and to lead towards a solution by force' (Hilferding, 1981, 331). And as Bukharin put it, the contradiction between the *actual* national centralization of capital and its *potential* internationalization was likely to drive the system into war and breakdown, a war for which, Lenin said, the proletariat should deny any responsibility.

Lenin's pamphlet on *Imperialism* was much more of a direct attack on those leaders of the working class who failed to oppose the war than were the works of Bukharin and Hilferding. Lenin emphasized that this was a war between capitalists and not a war in which the working class should take sides, except to overthrow capitalism. His *Imperialism* was particularly directed against Karl Kautsky, a prominent member of the Social-Democratic Party in Germany who had put forward, immediately before the First World War, a theory of 'ultra-imperialism', in which the major powers would find it preferable to agree to exploit the world jointly, rather than to fight over the division of the world. Kautsky argued that working-class support for the pro-peace elements within the ruling class would weaken the impetus to war. Lenin vehemently rejected this argument, seeing that it would pull the working class in different countries into all sorts of dangerous 'reformist' alliances.

Not surprisingly these divisions resulted in splits in the organization of international socialism. The Second International, an international association of socialist parties formed in 1889, collapsed during the First World War, a collapse which was, Lenin thought, encouraged by the 'views held by Kautsky and his like' (Lenin, 1970, 12). Lenin argued that imperialism was parasitic and that 'the exploitation of other countries besides China, which means high monopoly profits for a handful of very rich countries, makes it economically possible to bribe the upper strata of the proletariat, and thereby fosters . . . opportunism' (ibid., 100). It was, Lenin said, this group of workers-turned-bourgeois, or the 'labour aristocracy', who were the real agents of the bourgeoisie in the working-class movement (see ibid., 14).

It was, perhaps, an easy step from this theory to one, as in Emmanuel's *Unequal Exchange*, which sees the *whole*, and not just a section, of the working class in the developed countries as a labour aristocracy. And it was, perhaps, not surprising that the general thrust of Lenin's argument – in which monopoly capitalism was depicted as parasitic, decaying and stagnant – was developed and taken out of the polemical context in which it was written.

But capitalism can be seen as both destructive and regenerating, as Marx had emphasized when writing about the role of the British expansion into India: 'England has to fulfil a double mission in India; one destructive, and the other regenerating – the annihilation of old Asiatic society, and the laying of the material foundations of Western society in Asia' (Marx, in Marx and Engels, 1976, 82). With the onset of the First World War, and following the writings on imperialism of Hilferding, Bukharin, and more particularly those of Kautsky and Lenin, two quite different 'Marxist' views on the international expansion of capital developed. One is exemplified in a recent book by Bill Warren which stresses capitalism's regenerating capacity; the other, associated with Amin and Frank, emphasizes the destructive aspects of capitalism. It is the latter view, the 'development of underdevelopment' theory, which Section 5.2 briefly discusses.

5.2 NEO-MARXIST THEORIES OF UNDERDEVELOPMENT – ORIGINS AND ANALYSIS

As we noted at the end of Section 5.1, there has been a split in the 'Marxist' literature on the world economy in the period since the First World War. This split has been particularly evident in the period since 1945, but its origins can be found, as was earlier argued, in the writings of Bukharin, Hilferding, Lenin and Kautsky. At the turn of the century many Marxists hoped and expected that socialism in the centre would overthrow capitalism, and thereby greatly improve the prospects for national liberation and socialist movements in the colonial periphery. But by the 1960s a large and influential section of the left, particularly in the Third World, saw the primary revolutionary potential lying in nationalist movements which would squeeze capitalism in the centre. The experience of the First World War had seemed to counter the argument of Marx and Engels that 'working men have no country . . .

National differences and antagonisms between peoples are daily more and more vanishing' (Marx and Engels, 1975, 56–7).

The first 'underdevelopment' theorists – Lenin and the Comintern

Warren argued that the 'about-turn' came in Lenin's *Imperialism*. The infection of the proletariat with aggressive nationalism had to be explained. Lenin's explanation of the bribery of the upper stratum of the proletariat was one attempt. His target was that section of the Second International which was supporting the nationalist carnage of the war.

The other section of the Second International, the revolutionary elements in the social democratic parties, regrouped with the collapse of the Second International to create, in 1919, a revolutionary Third Communist International or Comintern. But by the time of the Second Congress of the Comintern in 1920 the pessimism induced by the First World War had been reinforced by the defeat of attempted revolutions in Germany and Hungary in 1919 and by the halting of the Red Army at the gates of Warsaw. The Bolshevik Party, which had come to power in the 1917 Russian Revolution, was forced to become defensive. This defensive attitude was reinforced in the 1920s, first, by the collapse of the general strike, in 1926, in Britain, and then by the 1927 massacre of the Chinese Communist Party in Shanghai. By 1928 a beleaguered Comintern was ready to proclaim at its Sixth Congress 'that imperialism was economically retrogressive in the colonies' (Warren, 1980, 107). It declared that revolutionary energy should be channelled into nationalist 'revolutions' similar to those that had taken place in Persia in 1906, Turkey in 1908 and China in 1911.

Thus the historical conditions were favourable for a theory of imperialism which stressed those stagnant, parasitic and decaying characteristics of monopoly capital which had been given prominence by Lenin. Such a theory sidestepped the statements in Lenin's *Imperialism* which had focused on the progressive expansionary aspects of capitalism (see Lenin, 1970, 63). Instead the way was open for a view of monopoly capitalism which stressed:

(a) a tendency to overproduction and underconsumption in modern capitalism, a tendency which had been emphasized so strongly by the British writer Hobson in his 1902 work on *Imperialism* (see Hobson, 1961);

(b) the exploitation of the colonial countries by the decaying, parasitic centre;

(c) the bribing of the *whole* of the working class in the centre from the proceeds of this exploitation.

In short, the way was open for the neo-Marxist theory of the 'development of underdevelopment'. And it was this that was provided by the American Paul Baran in 1957, encouraged perhaps by the lack of social revolution in the First and Second Worlds after the Second World War, by the national independence of India in 1947, the establishment of the People's Republic of China in 1949 and the growth of nationalist movements in much of the rest of the Third World. As Warren put it, 'the Leninist theory of imperialism with its emphasis on robbery, exploitation and parasitism, and its denunciation of Western pillage of the Third World, was perfectly suited to the psychological needs and political requirements of Third World nationalists' (Warren, 1980, 114).

Contemporary underdevelopment theory

Baran's theory was put forward in his *Political Economy of Growth* (1957). Like the later Sraffian wing of neo-Ricardianism, Baran questioned the gains-from-free-trade argument. But while Steedman and other 'Sraffians' query the gains-from-free-trade argument, they do not point to particular countries losing. Baran did. But unlike Prebisch and Emmanuel, who pointed to the possibility of the periphery losing from trade only in a relative sense, Baran's work stressed the absolute losses for the periphery. He emphasized the extractive and parasitic aspects of monopoly capital. And whereas Emmanuel focused on the cumulatively unequal distribution of the gains from trade keeping the poor countries *less* developed, Baran laid the basis for a theory of *under*development in which the wealth of the metropolis was a result of the poverty of the Third World.

It was this theory which was developed further through the writings of Amin, Frank, Wallerstein and at least some of the dependency school. In these writings the losses of the periphery are not relative, they are absolute, and the only way to escape from these losses is through isolation from world capitalism. The dilemma, Baran argued, 'that the majority of mankind faces today is either to liberate itself from both monopoly capitalism and imperialism or to be cut down by them' (ibid., 248).

Baran argued that the political *independence* of the colonial world, if achieved, was likely to be in stark contrast to its economic *dependence*. Thus he saw the development of capitalism in underdeveloped countries

104 THE FRAGMENTED WORLD

as a different process from that which the richer countries had experienced in the nineteenth century. Capitalism had reached, he argued, a monopoly stage which 'far from serving as an engine of economic expansion, of technological progress and of social change . . . represented a framework for economic stagnation, for archaic technology, and for social backwardness' (ibid., 163–4). He argued that the monopoly capitalists not only transfer surplus from the underdeveloped countries (UDCs) to the developed countries (DCs), but fail even to invest it productively in the DCs. Instead these surpluses are wasted in the form of advertising or, more important, military expenditure.

It is this military expenditure which provides the background for imperialist struggles between the capitalist nations, at the same time solving the surplus realization problem inherent in capitalism. That is the immense arms expenditure in advanced capitalism provides a level of effective demand in capitalism which would otherwise be absent. Thus advanced capitalism becomes a 'permanent arms' economy, and here Baran is providing a link between the final chapter of Rosa Luxemburg's *The Accumulation of Capital* and an idea central to Mike Kidron's *Western Capitalism since the War* (1970), published a decade after Baran's *Political Economy of Growth*.

Thus, according to Baran, there is a worldwide tendency to stagnation under monopoly capitalism, but in the underdeveloped countries this stagnation is particularly evident. For not only is most of the surplus transferred out of the UDCs, generally exceeding the inflow of capital (see Baran, 1957, chapter 6), but what remains is generally wasted in conspicuous consumption by the landlord class (ibid., 166) or by 'comprador administrations' (see ibid., chapter 7). Capitalism in the UDCs is distorted and crippled to suit the purposes of Western imperialism. Thus policies of internal reform in the UDCs, such as agrarian reform, are unlikely to provide an antidote to underdevelopment because the other accumulation conditions are not present (ibid., 168). What is needed is a complete break from the world capitalist system. Thus according to Baran, the growth of the relatively isolated Japan in the nineteenth century, compared with the stagnation of colonized India, testifies to this (see ibid., chapter 5).

In the 1960s and 1970s a number of writers followed the lines laid by Baran. These included Samir Amin, Jagdish Saigal, Immanuel Wallerstein and Gunder Frank, the last named of whom has explicitly acknowledged his intellectual debt to Paul Baran (see Frank, 1967, xi).

Thus the underdevelopment theories of Amin and Saigal, and of Frank and Wallerstein, all have one aspect in common. They hinge on the use of forces outside the market for the imposition and maintenance of 'imperialism' and of stagnation in the UDCs. Thus from Chapter 2 to here, there has been a transition from the automatic harmony of the free-marketeers to the imposed imperialism of the underdevelopment theorists.

Unfortunately it is not as easy to grasp the underlying themes in the work of Samir Amin as those of Gunder Frank. Many writers have been critical of Amin's writings, complaining of a lack of consistency (see, for example, Andersson, 1976, 93–6; Brewer, 1980, 233; Evans, 1981b, 28; Smith, 1980). The approach adopted by Evans was to take a joint article by Samir Amin and Jagdish Saigal published in 1973 as expressing the central ideas of Amin on unequal exchange. In that paper Amin and Saigal, like the earlier-discussed Andersson and Braun, reject the imperialism of *free* trade. However, whereas the Andersson–Braun unequal exchange stems from interference with the market (that is from a discriminatory commercial policy), the Amin–Saigal version stems from interference from *outside* the market (that is from extraeconomic coercion).

The Amin–Saigal argument is that the underdeveloped countries have the potential of producing all types of goods. In a free market these would be more profitably produced in the periphery. But the periphery is blocked from producing freely, and 'autocentric', self-accumulating development in the periphery is prevented from taking place. The periphery is complementary to, and dominated by, the centre. It is forced into 'extraverted' development, or production for export of goods which are merely complementary to those of the centre. For in most fields the centre has superior productivity. But this superior productivity of the centre results from, and is maintained by, extraeconomic forces.

In terms of the earlier Figure 4.2 (p. 70), which attempted to summarize Emmanuel's theory in Sraffian terms, the Amin–Saigal position is represented by segment (iii). The periphery could produce, in a free market, both corn and cloth at a higher rate of profit (point A), but because of the constraints imposed by the centre, it is prevented from producing cloth and confined to producing corn for export in exchange for imported cloth. The resulting point of production is represented by point D in Figure 4.2(iii).

Thus unequal exchange is *imposed* by the centre and accumulation in the dependent periphery is 'extraverted', whereas the 'autocentric' development in the centre continues. In Amin's view, 'for the periphery the choice is in fact this; either dependent development, or autocentric development, necessarily original in form as opposed to that of present-day developed countries . . . the periphery cannot just overtake the capitalist model; it is obliged to surpass it' (Amin, 1976, 382–3). The solution, then, is a radical and complete break with the world capitalist system. The problem is how to bring this about. Isn't it simply a matter of the peripheral mass rising up and overthrowing the core? After all, there are more than 3400 million people in the Third World (including China) compared to a mere 1000 million or so in the First and Second Worlds. The answer from the underdevelopment theorists is no, it is not as simple as that.

Frank and Wallerstein, as well as Amin, argue that there is a 'chain' of dependence in the world capitalist system, both between and within nation-states. They, like Amin, argue that capitalism can only be analysed on a world scale. For Frank, as for Wallerstein, 'economic development and underdevelopment are the opposite faces of the same coin. Both are the necessary result and contemporary manifestation of internal contradictions in the world capitalist system', and 'thus at each point, the international, national and local capitalist system generates economic development for the few and underdevelopment for the many' (Frank, 1967, 7–9). Thus this zero-sum game (development for the one meaning underdevelopment for another) does not operate only between nations, but also within them.

In his *The Modern World System* (1974), Immanuel Wallerstein divides the capitalist world system into a hierarchy of three types of state: those of the core, the semi-periphery and the periphery. For him, as for Frank, capitalism is an all-embracing system of monopolistic exchange, which acts to transfer surplus from the periphery through the semi-periphery and back to the core or centre. No place or person is outside the embrace of this system. The strength of the state machine determines the transfer of surplus from the periphery to the core, and it is this surplus which further strengthens the core states. Here as for the other dependency writers, the accumulation in the core is cumulative. But the semi-periphery is a sort of 'labour aristocracy' of states. This inter-mediate tier of middle-income states diffuses the acute conflict that might otherwise lead to revolt.

The semi-periphery is not, however, the only pacifying element in the system. Within each of the semi-peripheral nations, as well as in those of the periphery, there are the ruling classes who owe their position to their place in the chain that runs from the peripheral countryside to the central cities. These ruling classes are not a highly developed capitalist bourgeoisie, but rather a dependent bourgeoisie without an independent momentum of their own. They are, Frank says, a 'lumpenbourgeoisie', and thus in Latin America: 'the "European" lumpenbourgeoisie built "national" lumpenstates which never achieved real independence but were, and are, simply effective instruments of the lumpenbourgeoisie's policy of lumpendevelopment' (Frank, 1972, 58). Thus, as a result, the satellite nations are reduced to a dependence – in the maintenance of which the peripheral ruling class has a vested interest.

Most of Frank's writings focus on Latin America, and it was from Latin America that many of the other dependency writings emerged in the early 1970s (see, for example, Dos Santos, 1970; Sunkel, 1972). Thus the following quotation, from Dos Santos, has a flavour similar to that which can be found in the writings of Frank and Amin:

> By dependence we mean a situation in which the economy of certain countries is conditioned by the development and expansion of another economy to which the former is subjected. The relation of interdependence . . . assumes the form of dependence when some countries (the dominant ones) can expand and be self-sustaining, while other countries (the dependent ones) can do this only as a reflection of that expansion.   (Dos Santos, 1970, 231)

This type of dependency analysis was not confined to Latin America, but was extended in the 1970s to Africa by Samir Amin (1972) and Walter Rodney (1972).

Breaking with the centre: the policy conclusions of underdevelopment theory

Because of the similarity in theory, it is not surprising that the policy solution for Frank and the other writers on Latin America is similar to those of Amin and Baran. If the masses in the underdeveloped countries are to escape from their 'marginalized' position, and if the national market is to be broadened, the chain of dependence has to be broken. For 'short of liberation from this capitalist structure or the dissolution of the world capitalist system as a whole, the capitalist satellite countries, regions, localities and sectors are condemned to underdevelopment' (Frank, 1967, 11). Support for this assertion, Frank argues, comes from the 'fact' that 'no country which has been firmly tied to the metropolis as a satellite through incorporation into the world capitalist system has achieved the rank of an economically developed country, except by finally abandoning the capitalist system' (ibid.), and the temporary spurts of development that have taken place in the satellites have been 'during wars or depressions in the metropolis, which momentarily weakened or lessened its domination over the life of the satellites' (ibid., 12). Economic growth, Frank suggests, has been slowest in precisely those regions (such as north-east Brazil and the sugar exporting areas of the

West Indies) that have had the earliest and most extensive contact with external interests (see ibid., 13).

Thus for the underdevelopment theorists, the solution to under-development lies in escape from the capitalist framework. But, for them, the escape route is not through the 'small is beautiful' lobby, through what Amin calls, the 'hippy' technology (Amin, 1976, 384). Instead, 'under the present conditions of inequality between the nations, a development that is not merely development of underdevelopment will therefore be both national, popular-democratic, and socialist' (ibid., 383).

This breakaway is necessary because for Amin, Frank and many others within the dependency school, capitalism is defined through market exchange, and thus their liberation from capitalism is not the same as the liberation from, and transition to, communism that Marx and Engels had in mind. Instead, 'Much writing on dependency tradition seems to leave one with the vision of an anti-imperialist populist leader uniting his people under a technocratic state' (O'Brien, in Oxaal *et al.*, 1975, 25). This emphasis on a technocratic state is similar to that of the Brandt Report (1980). But the policy conclusion is quite different. For whereas the Brandt Report sees the solution for the Third World in terms of modifications within the capitalist system, Baran and others see the solution as lying outside the capitalist system.

In so far as Baran, Amin and Frank do talk in terms of classes and uneven development, they are closer to the analysis of the Marxist abstract labour theorists. And many of their proposals smack of social revolution which is why no doubt some reviewers, such as Brookfield (1975, 125), refer to these writers as 'neo-Marxist'. Nevertheless, there is a common thread between Baran and Brandt inasmuch as the analysis of the world market is in terms of exchange and distribution; the primary emphasis is on countries, not classes. Thus Baran and others are in a grey area between the cost-of-production and abstract labour theories. Perhaps this is why the strategies that emerge are criticized by so many economists for being vague or even inconsistent. For example, after a review of dependency theory, Gabriel Palma concluded by saying: 'I have elected to stress that the contribution of dependency had been up to now more of a critique of development strategies in general than an attempt to make practical contributions to them' (Palma, 1978, 882).

From the left the challenge to the 'development of underdevelopment' group of writers has come in broadly two forms. One attack has come from writers (such as Laclau, Brenner and Elson) who have argued that the *methodology* is incorrect and that, as a result, as guidance for revolutionary action, the theory may not be reliable. The second form of

attack has been based on the record of development in the Third World.
There are some (notably Warren and Schiffer) who argue that development in the Third World has in fact taken place. These two types of
challenge are discussed in Section 5.3.

5.3 THEORIES OF UNDERDEVELOPMENT – THE CRITICISMS

A number of methodological criticisms have been directed against the
theories of Frank, Wallerstein, Amin and Emmanuel from writers on the
left. Notable criticisms have come from Laclau, Brenner, Schiffer,
Brewer, Warren and Bettelheim. The most important of the attacks on
the theories of the Amin–Frank group can be summarized as:

(a) the conflicting groups on which primary attention is focused are
    countries not classes;
(b) the major conflict is a distributional one over a technologically
    fixed physical surplus, and is fought at the 'political' level;
(c) capitalism is defined as a system of production for the market, and
    not by reference to the control of the means of production and
    employment of wage labour.

As a result of these defects, the theory is an unreliable guide for socialist
political action. Thus it is important to look now at the criticisms in
more detail.

The first and second of the above criticisms are that the Amin–Frank
group identifies the major conflict in the capitalist world as a distributional one between countries, as opposed to a struggle between classes
for control. The picture painted by them is of a somewhat static struggle
over the distribution of a more or less fixed surplus. The source of
surplus and, therefore, of exploitation lies in exchange and not at the
level of production. For example, in Baran's *Political Economy of
Growth*, the term 'surplus' is used in very much a physical Ricardian
sense; and in Amin's writings the term is defined in much the same way
as 'an excess of production over the consumption needed to ensure the
reconstitution of the labour force' (Amin, 1976, 18). Thus the tendency
is to see gains for the centre as *necessarily* being losses for the periphery.
The world constitutes a zero-sum game.

Thus similar criticisms to those levied by the abstract labour theorists
against the Sraffian and unequal exchange 'wings' of the neo-Ricardian
school (see Chapter 4) can also be levied against the so-called neo-Marxist
'underdevelopment' group. For the latter, despite their different

language, make very similar assumptions to those made by the neo-Ricardians, namely that the surplus is a fixed physical one and that the primary conflict arises over the 'political distribution' of this surplus.

This logically leads on to the third criticism of the Amin–Frank group. This is one which was made by Ernest Laclau in 1971 (in Laclau, 1977) with reference to Gunder Frank's *Capitalism and Underdevelopment in Latin America* (1967), but it is a criticism which equally well applies to Amin and Baran. What was wholly unacceptable to Laclau was Gunder Frank's definition of capitalism as a system of production for the market. For Laclau, as for abstract labour theorists in general, a major characteristic of capitalism as a mode of production is the employment of wage labour by capital and the use of labour power as a commodity from which surplus value is extracted. Laclau argued that what is missing in Frank's *Capitalism and Underdevelopment in Latin America* is this conception of capitalism, in which 'the fundamental economic relationship is . . . the free labourer's sale of his labour power, whose necessary precondition is the loss by the direct producer of the ownership of the means of production' (Laclau, 1977, 23). Thus in Frank class relations are displaced from the centre of analysis (see Brenner, 1977, 27), the class hierarchy is buried beneath a spatial hierarchy and the obvious escape route from capitalism is then a spatial one of autarky.

The criticisms which Laclau levies at Frank can also be directed to Samir Amin and Paul Baran, as well as Emmanuel and the other unequal exchange theorists. For all of them confine their attention to the process of circulation within capitalism, whereas for Marx 'The real science of modern economy only begins when the theoretical analysis passes from the process of circulation to the process of production' (Marx, 1972, 337). As a result of confining their attention to circulation, the development-of-underdevelopment theorists pay little or no attention to the concept of class defined by reference to the control of the means of production. This is a defect which Frank has acknowledged in his *Lumpenbourgeoisie and Lumpendevelopment* as follows: 'I am aware that in so limiting the objectives of the present study, I shall have failed to fill in the more serious gaps in my previous work, that is, an analysis of the conditions of the nonbourgeois classes and a proposed strategy of class struggle' (Frank, 1972, 10).

Thus there are a number of criticisms which have been levied from the left at the underdevelopment theorists. But the response may be: so what? Does it matter if they regard the surplus as more or less fixed, that they identify the source of exploitation in circulation and that, therefore, the major conflict is at the level of distribution between, say, countries and not classes? The answer must be, in all seriousness, yes. For one

thing on which Laclau and Frank agree is that theory is a guide to political action; thus Frank argues that 'there can be no successful revolution
without adequate revolutionary theory. Herein lies my purpose' (Frank,
1967, 13).

Of course, it is possible that two different theories may *coincidentally*
lead to the same action. Thus incorrect theory may give rise to correct
action, but clearly it is a risky affair. For example, it is obviously possible
for an alliance between a small, working-class, socialist party and
nationally based capitalists within a Third World country to be regressive or 'progressive', when judged by reference to the interests of the mass
of the people in that country. If the major characteristic of capitalism is
seen as the employment and exploitation of *wage labour*, and conversely,
a major characteristic of socialism is seen as the control of production by
the direct producers, the 'alliance' will be judged by the extent to which
it is thought likely to lead to more control of production by the direct
producers in that country and, perhaps, elsewhere.

But such a criterion is unlikely to be used by the underdevelopment
theorists. For if, instead, capitalism is defined (as it is by Frank, Wallerstein and the others) at the level of circulation and distribution, the
alliance is likely to be judged as 'progressive' if it is thought likely to
reduce the country's foreign trade and other such links with world capitalism. Unfortunately such a move towards autarky may well coincide
with a strengthening of the powers of money-lenders and landlords.
These sections or 'fractions' of capital may well be less 'progressive' (in
terms of developing the production base and of strengthening the
position of workers and peasants within the country) than merchant and
industrial capital. Thus it has been said that much of the Third World
suffers not from *too much* capitalism, but from *too little*.

I return to this issue again in Chapter 10. Here it is sufficient to point
out that the abstract labour theorists are concerned that the (incorrect)
analysis of the underdevelopment school is quite likely to lead to
incorrect action. A similar charge has been levied by Bettelheim against
Emmanuel in the appendix to *Unequal Exchange* (1972). In that discussion Bettelheim argues that Emmanuel's conceptualization of capitalism at the level of exchange is likely to give rise to incorrect policy. Bettelheim argues:

> On the political plane this problematic directs us towards illusory
> reformist solutions. For example, the inequalities of development
> seem to be capable of 'correction' through manipulations of prices and
> wages, whereas only a revolutionary transformation of production
> relations, with the subsequent development of the productive forces,

can make it possible to end the poverty of the dominated countries, who are exploited *at one and the same time* by imperialism and by their own dominant classes.

(Bettelheim, in Emmanuel, 1972, 316; emphasis in original)

Thus the criticisms of the theory of the underdevelopment school are likely to be important in terms of political action. Certainly some critics have argued that the statistical evidence simply does not support the theories of the Baran–Amin–Frank group. Two notable critics arguing along these lines have been Warren (1980) and Schiffer (1981).

Beyond underdevelopment theory: Warren and Schiffer

Warren's book was compiled from notes and articles written before his death in 1978 and, in particular, it makes similar points to those made in an article published in the *New Left Review* in 1973 (see Warren, 1973). His central point is that if we accept the development-of-underdevelopment theory, we would expect economic growth in the periphery to be slow or even negative (Warren, 1980, 186). But, Warren argues, this has not been the case. The growth has certainly been uneven, but not notably inferior in the periphery compared to that in the centre. The same point is made in Schiffer's 1981 article, the targets of which are Baran and Amin, especially the latter. Schiffer deliberately uses data for the 1960s so as to span the same period as that covered by Amin's writings (Schiffer, 1981, 158), and he uses the same spatial distinctions, so that the data are presented in terms of a centre and periphery.

Both Warren and Schiffer argue that in the period since 1950 the Third World's economic growth has been about as fast as the growth in the developed market economies (DMEs), even after allowance is made for population growth. They also point out that manufacturing output has risen more rapidly in the LDCs than in the DMEs (see Table 5.4).

Furthermore, Schiffer argues, the *character* of manufacturing growth, predicted by Amin's analysis, has not materialized. Schiffer claims that 'according to Amin, whatever manufacturing activity occurs in LDCs is directed to the export market and [to] luxury goods consumption by a domestic market limited to a small percentage of the local population, composed mainly of "comprador" elements' (Schiffer, 1981, 521). But according to Schiffer, this is not what has happened. There *has* been a rapid increase in manufactured exports, but this 'has complemented, not replaced, production for domestic markets, and, in many LDCs, has . . . fuelled domestic output by increasing income and thus domestic demand for consumer goods' (ibid.). Thus, Schiffer argues, Amin's case

Table 5.4 Development in the LDCs: the Schiffer–Warren view

Third World has developed rapidly in terms of:

(a) *Output*	*Growth: % per annum*	
	1950–60	*1960–76*
(a) GDP DMEs[1]	4.0	4.4
LDCs	4.6	5.7
(b) GDP per capita DMEs	2.7	3.4
LDCs	2.3	3.3
(c) Manufacturing DMEs	4.5	4.9
LDCs	6.8	7.5

(b) Health[2]	*Life expectancy at birth (years)*	
	1950	*1979*
DMEs	67	74
CPEs (centrally planned economies)	60	72
LDCs middle income	48	61
low income	37	51

(c) Education[2]	*Adult literacy rate (%)*	
	1950	*1976*
DMEs	95	99
LDCs middle income	48	72
low income	22	39

Sources: Schiffer, 1981, 519; World Bank, 1981b, 6.

Notes:
1 DME stands for developed market economy.
2 The countries in the tables on Health and Education exclude China.

that growth in the LDCs is inevitably 'extraverted' is not supported by the evidence.

But the arguments of Warren and Schiffer do not stop at measures of aggregate output. They also claim that, even on broader measures of welfare, the LDCs have done quite well. Life expectancy at birth increased rapidly between 1950 and 1979 in the LDCs as did literacy (Table 5.4). Both Schiffer and Warren challenge the dependency theorists' claim that the mass of the population in the periphery are doomed to 'marginalization'; that is, that the growth of the 'industrial reserve army' in the Third World will be such as to keep wages in check (ibid., 527; Warren, 1980, 211–24).

Thus, Schiffer says, 'the evidence presented suggests that Amin is wrong in just about every aspect of his approach to the development of capitalism in LDCs' (Schiffer, 1981, 532). But Schiffer cautions, 'this does not mean that everything is marvellous in LDCs – far from it!' (ibid., 533), and a sifting of the evidence does not necessarily lead us to the political conclusion that 'open-ended capitalist development [is] not only feasible, but highly desirable (a perspective the World Bank would have)' (ibid.).

Earlier in this section I pointed out that the arguments in Warren's 1980 book were similar to those of his 1973 *New Left Review* article. The latter immediately generated two replies in the *New Left Review*, which were highly critical of Warren's arguments: one was written by Emmanuel (1974), the other by McMichael *et al.* (1974). But to a great extent the argument between Warren on the one hand, and Emmanuel and others on the other, was a 'dialogue of the deaf', since the major source of disagreement was about the *definition* of 'development'. Emmanuel criticized Warren for 'jumping to the unwarranted conclusion that industrialisation (eventually just "manufacturing") and development are one and the same thing' (Emmanuel, 1974, 63). Emmanuel argued that the uneven growth within countries in the Third World, with large backward sections in agriculture and industry, was not equivalent to development (see ibid., 66): 'it is not by transferring its factors from agriculture to industry that a country develops, but by mechanising and modernising *both* of these sectors' (ibid., 67; emphasis in original). Similarly, McMichael and others argued that 'industrial growth in the Third World is clearly not at issue – rather the problem is the *character* of this industrial growth, and what it expresses about international capitalist development' (McMichael *et al.*, 1974, 84; emphasis in original).

Thus the debate between Warren and Schiffer, and Emmanuel, McMichael and others, revolves to a considerable extent on the definition of 'development'. In his book Warren implies that the dependency school makes the mistake of judging the capitalist development in the Third World on the basis of the most *advanced* achievements of capitalism in the First World (see Warren, 1980, 20, 166, 167). Thus the measure of development for Emmanuel, McMichael and others is the standard of living in the Third World *relative* to that of the advanced countries. In his 1974 article Emmanuel's conclusion is consistent with

Table 5.5 Underdevelopment in the Third World – the view of Emmanuel, McMichael and others

The Third World lags behind the DCs in terms of: . . .

(a) National income	*($ per person)*	
	1950	*1980*
DMEs	4,130	10,660
LDCs middle income	640	1,580
low income	170	250
Ratio of DME average to low-income LDCs	24	43

. . . even if 'more valid' comparisons are made in terms of: . . .

(b) Purchasing power	*($ per person) 1980*	
	Exchange rate conversion (as above)	*Purchasing power conversion (see note below)*
DMEs	10,660	8,960
LDCs (middle *and* low income)	850	1,790
Ratio of DMEs to LDCs	13	5

Source: World Bank, 1981b, 6, 17.

Note: 'Converting the GDPs (gross domestic products) of different countries to a common currency at prevailing exchange rates is a misleading way of comparing real incomes. Exchange rates do not necessarily reflect the purchasing power of currencies because they exclude that (often large) portion of GDP which does not enter into international trade' (World Bank, 1981b, 17). Thus the purchasing power conversion is based on a price comparison for *all* commodities and services, traded and non-traded.

the theme of his earlier *Unequal Exchange*, inasmuch as he argues that the struggle is one between nations over a more or less fixed surplus:

We have today reached a point at which, equalisation being impossible either downwards, for socio-political reasons, or upwards, for natural-technical reasons, the only solution lies in a global change in the very pattern of living and consumption . . . the contradictions between classes within the advanced countries, which still undoubtedly subsist, have nevertheless become historically secondary. The principal contradiction, and driving force for change, are henceforth located in the realm of international economic relations.   (Emmanuel, 1974, 79)

Thus the basis of comparison for Emmanuel and the others is a cross-sectional, international one, rather than a historical one looking at development over time. The emphasis is on the international *distribution* of income. Thus the concern is with the growing *gap* in national income per head between the centre and the periphery (see Table 5.5); and if comparisons in national income are rejected on the ground that they are not valid measures of average standards of living, Emmanuel and others would point to the continuing gaps in purchasing power (Table 5.5) and in life expectancy and literacy (see Table 5.4).

As Schiffer and Warren admit: 'everything in the Third World is far from marvellous', but it will never be marvellous, according to Emmanuel, until the Third World is brought up to the standard of living of the presently rich countries. Thus it is hardly surprising that there are acute differences of policy between the development-of-underdevelopment theorists and their critics.

NOTES ON FURTHER READING

For Marx's methods and an introduction to dialectical historical materialism the beginner is likely to find the following most useful: *Manifesto of the Communist Party* by Marx and Engels, 1975; the 'Preface' by Marx, in Marx, 1975; Harrison's *Marxist Economics for Socialists*, 1978; Howard and King's *The Political Economy of Marx*, 1975, but only chapter 1, avoid the others; Cole *et al.*, 1983, chapter 8; Brewer, 1980, chapters 1 and 2.

For Marx's treatment of the capitalist mode of production the new-comer to Marx is likely to find the three volumes of *Capital*: Marx, 1970, 1967, 1972, forbidding, to say the least. Even Marx himself admitted that the manner of presentation was non-popular (introduction to Marx, 1973a, 57) so that his address to the General Council of the First International, later published as *Wages, Price and Profit*, Marx, 1973b, is likely to be more useful. For other Marxist analyses of capitalism, see Harrison, 1978; Cole *et al.*, 1983; Brewer, 1980; as well as Geoff Kay's *The Economic Theory of the Working Class*, 1979, and the earlier book by Paul Sweezy on *The Theory of Capitalist Development*, 1968. Also look at Ben Fine's slim volume on *Marx's Capital*, 1975. On Marx and international trade there is virtually nothing; I return to this issue in Chapter 10 of this book. In general on Marx and his writings, the books by David McLellan are clearly written – in this context the most relevant are McLellan, 1976, 1980.

Many volumes have been written on dependency, colonialism and imperialism. I return to the latter in Section 9.2, but in the context of this chapter Michael Barratt Brown's *Economics of Imperialism*, 1974, will be of interest to students even though it is somewhat lacking in cohesion. Brewer, 1980, chapter 8, has a good coverage of Rey, and is also useful for a brief discussion of the transition to capitalism (chapter 2), as are the first two chapters of Roxborough, 1979; most students find Luxemburg, 1963, reasonably interesting to read, but again Brewer's chapter 3 is a good introduction, as is Bradby, 1975. For Lenin, read Lenin, 1970, but also look at Kitching, 1978, and once again Brewer (this time chapter 5). The latter also provides an introduction to Bukharin, but the student is likely to find Bukharin's *Imperialism and World Economy*, 1972, easy to understand and interesting. By contrast, Hilferding's *Finance Capital* is likely to be less appealing, because of its length; an English translation has recently been published (see Hilferding, 1981). Brewer, 1980, chapter 4, provides a clear introduction to Hilferding.

A brief view of some aspects of imperialism and dependency is provided in Roxborough, 1979, chapter 5, and his chapter 4 also discusses some of the 'development-of-underdevelopment' theory. Within the latter group it is probably logical to start with Baran's *Political Economy of Growth*, 1957. The flavour of this can be obtained from Baran's foreword to the 1962 printing, or from his essay reprinted in *Imperialism and Underdevelopment*, edited by Robert Rhodes, 1970; the reader may find the essence in Brewer, 1980, chapter 6. As argued earlier, chapter 5 of Baran, 1957, makes an interesting contrast with chapter 2 of Friedman and Friedman, 1980.

For Amin's views on unequal exchange, refer to Amin, 1976, chapter 3, section 2; or to Amin, 1977, section IV; or to Amin, 1973. Brewer, 1980, chapter 10, discusses Amin. Stronger criticisms of Amin's writings can be found in Schiffer, 1981; Smith, 1980. Gunder Frank is a prolific writer, but the reader can capture much of his theory from *Capitalism and Underdevelopment in Latin America*, 1967, 1–28; Rhodes, 1970, readings 1 and 6; or Brewer, 1980, chapter 7. Frank's *Dependent Accumulation and Underdevelopment*, 1978, provides a very readable history of the world economy.

For a critique of Frank's methodology, see Laclau, 1977; Brenner, 1977; Bernstein and Nicholas, 1983; and for studies which cast empirical doubt on Frank's claim that Latin American development was greatest when it was least 'connected' with the world capitalist system, see Miller, 1981; Ingham and Simmons, 1981. For Wallerstein's views, see Wallerstein, 1974; or Brewer, 1980, chapter 7; or Brenner, 1977. Brewer's chapter 7 is, however, less useful for an overview of dependency than O'Brien, in Oxaal *et al.*, 1975, or Palma's article, in Seers,

1981. Refer also to Open University 1983, part C, block 4. For a treatment of the theory of development and underdevelopment in historical perspective, see the book of the same name by Kitching, 1982.

In this chapter attention has been focused on the English-language writings on 'dependency', associated with Baran, Frank and Wallerstein. But some economists argue that there is a second school of 'dependent development' which is quite different in emphasis from the 'development-of-underdevelopment' section discussed here. For a text which makes this distinction between two sections of dependency, see Cardoso, 1977. Cardoso claims that the 'dependent development' approach places much more emphasis on factors internal to the LDCs than does the 'development-of-underdevelopment' approach.

Chapters 3 and 4 of Warren, 1980, contain a provocative historical account of 'the theory of imperialism in the international communist movement', but for arguments and 'evidence' about the illusion of the underdevelopment of the Third World, both his chapter 8 and 1973 article are less systematic than Schiffer, 1981. For the counterarguments to Warren's 1973 article, the student is likely to find Emmanuel, 1974, more direct than McMichael *et al.*, 1974.

SUMMARY

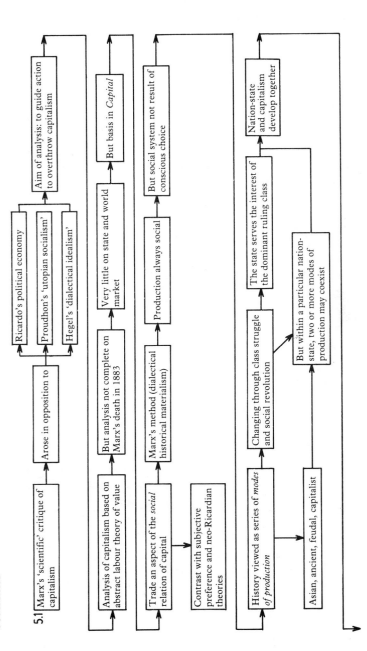

5.1 Marx's 'scientific' critique of capitalism

Arose in opposition to
- Ricardo's political economy
- Proudhon's 'utopian socialism'
- Hegel's 'dialectical idealism'

Aim of analysis: to guide action to overthrow capitalism

Analysis of capitalism based on abstract labour theory of value

But analysis not complete on Marx's death in 1883

Very little on state and world market

But basis in *Capital*

Trade an aspect of the *social* relation of capital

Marx's method (dialectical historical materialism)

Production always social

But social system not result of conscious choice

Contrast with subjective preference and neo-Ricardian theories

History viewed as series of *modes of production*

Changing through class struggle and social revolution

The state serves the interest of the dominant ruling class

Nation-state and capitalism develop together

Asian, ancient, feudal, capitalist

But within a particular nation-state, two or more modes of production may coexist

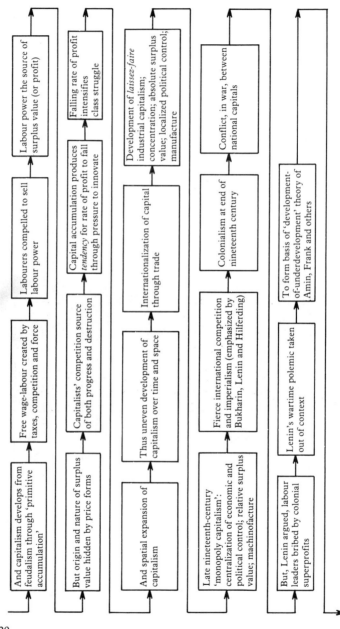

And capitalism develops from feudalism through 'primitive accumulation' → Free wage-labour created by taxes, competition and force → Labourers compelled to sell labour power → Labour power the source of surplus value (or profit)

But origin and nature of surplus value hidden by price forms → Capitalists' competition source of both progress and destruction → Capital accumulation produces *tendency* for rate of profit to fall through pressure to innovate → Falling rate of profit intensifies class struggle

And spatial expansion of capitalism → Thus uneven development of capitalism over time and space → Internationalization of capital through trade → Development of *laissez-faire* industrial capitalism; concentration; absolute surplus value; localized political control; manufacture

Late nineteenth-century 'monopoly capitalism': centralization of economic and political control; relative surplus value; machinofacture → Fierce international competition and imperialism (emphasized by Bukharin, Lenin and Hilferding) → Colonialism at end of nineteenth century → Conflict, in war, between national capitals

But, Lenin argued, labour leaders bribed by colonial superprofits → Lenin's wartime polemic taken out of context → To form basis of 'development-of-underdevelopment' theory of Amin, Frank and others

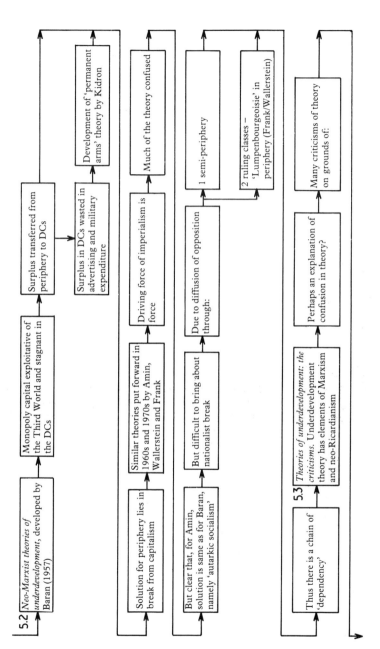

5.2 *Neo-Marxist theories of underdevelopment*, developed by Baran (1957)

Monopoly capital exploitative of the Third World and stagnant in the DCs

Surplus transferred from periphery to DCs

Surplus in DCs wasted in advertising and military expenditure

Development of 'permanent arms' theory by Kidron

Solution for periphery lies in break from capitalism

Similar theories put forward in 1960s and 1970s by Amin, Wallerstein and Frank

Driving force of imperialism is force

Much of the theory confused

But clear that, for Amin, solution is same as for Baran, namely 'autarkic socialism'

But difficult to bring about nationalist break

Due to diffusion of opposition through:

1 semi-periphery

2 ruling classes – 'Lumpenbourgeoisie' in periphery (Frank/Wallerstein)

Thus there is a chain of 'dependency'

5.3 *Theories of underdevelopment: the criticisms.* Underdevelopment theory has elements of Marxism and neo-Ricardianism

Perhaps an explanation of confusion in theory?

Many criticisms of theory on grounds of:

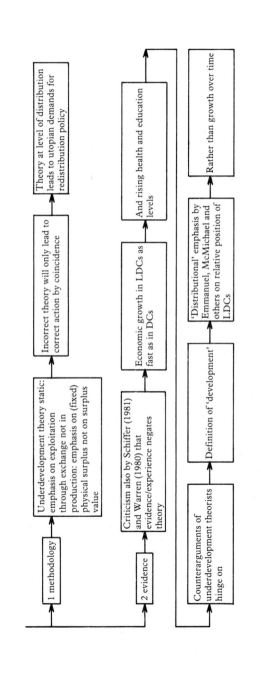

Theory at level of distribution leads to utopian demands for redistribution policy

Incorrect theory will only lead to correct action by coincidence

And rising health and education levels

Underdevelopment theory static: emphasis on exploitation through exchange not in production: emphasis on (fixed) physical surplus not on surplus value

Economic growth in LDCs as fast as in DCs

Rather than growth over time

Criticism also by Schiffer (1981) and Warren (1980) that evidence/experience negates theory

'Distributional' emphasis by Emmanuel, McMichael and others on relative position of LDCs

1 methodology

2 evidence

Definition of 'development'

Counterarguments of underdevelopment theorists hinge on

6

Trade, money and crisis

In this book Chapters 2–5 have discussed the international trade theories of each of the three schools of economic thought. The theories were shown to derive from 'theories of value', that is from sets of fundamental assumptions about the nature of economic causality. But in discussing these trade theories there has been no *explicit* consideration of the roles that money is assumed to play. This separation of 'monetary' from 'real' factors was adopted to clarify the presentation of the theories, but I recognize the dangers in such an approach because the different theories treat money quite differently. The purpose of this chapter is to show these differences and their significance.

The chapter starts by showing how each stream of economic thought attends to money in analysing trading patterns. Thus Section 6.1 looks at the role of money in affecting or determining international trading advantages and balance-of-payments adjustments. Then Section 6.2 looks at each school's descriptions of, and prescriptions for, world economic crises, and the roles that money is seen to play in these crises.

6.1 TRADE, MONEY AND BALANCE-OF-PAYMENTS ADJUSTMENTS

A recap on trade theories

In Chapter 2 the basis of the subjective preference approach to inter-national trade was set out. Theorists within this school argue that countries will gain from free trade because it will allow them to produce according to their *comparative advantage*. And in such a free trade regime total world output will be maximized. Thus the ideological importance of comparative advantage is considerable. But as soon as comparative advantage is mentioned, two questions need to be asked: first, what determines comparative advantage?; and secondly, how, if at all, do the prices which indicate the comparative advantage change, so that a two-way trade becomes worthwhile for profit-seeking traders?

The first question has already been considered in previous chapters. For the Heckscher–Ohlin–Samuelson (HOS) theory of the neo-classicists, the question (what determines comparative advantage) is answered by pointing to differences in factor endowments. They argue that countries have trading advantages derived from their differing endowments of factors, such as land, labour and 'capital'. Indeed, as Chapter 2 pointed out, the HOS theory originally suggested that not only would there be trading advantages from free trade, but the specialization in production resulting from the changing pattern of trade would tend to even out differences in factor prices (wages, rents and the rate of profit) between the trading countries. Free trade could compensate for the immobility of factors such as labour and capital, and if, as in recent decades, some factors such as money-capital became increasingly mobile, then the probability of factor price equalization would be even greater. In other words, investment and trade flows would even out labour scarcities between countries.

And so, the neo-classicists argue, with free trade, individuals in different countries would be paid what they are worth. Plumbers resident in different countries but with the same skills would be paid the same. Entrepreneurs in, say, the UK would be paid differently from plumbers and people operating machines, but would be paid the same as American entrepreneurs, provided they have the same talents. With free trade, worldwide equality of opportunity would exist. Or so it seemed, until the HOS was weakened by neo-Ricardian objections. As was pointed out in Chapter 3, one ('Sraffian') section of the neo-Ricardians argued that, even in a regime of free trade, losses for one or more countries could result from changing trade patterns, once a distinction is made between 'capital' as machines and 'capital' in the form of money.

A slightly different, but politically more powerful, form of attack came from another section of the neo-Ricardians. This 'unequal exchange' section argued that not only *can* some countries lose from free trade, but a particular group of countries (the less developed countries, or LDCs) do lose. The LDCs *systematically* lose out, because their workers are paid less *for the same work* than workers in the rich countries. As a result of the lack of strength of the LDCs' workers and their correspondingly low wages, foreign capitalists tend to move in to LDCs and produce there for the world market. But instead of the low wages being reflected in a high rate of profit which might be retained in the poor countries for reinvestment, the low wages are competed away in the form of low prices for the LDCs' exports. Thus the role played by the international mobility of capital is seen quite differently by the subjective preference and unequal exchange theorists. For the subjective preference theorists, the capital mobility increases the probability of an equalization of wages, rents and other 'factor rewards'. By contrast, for the unequal exchange theorists, capitalist competition perpetuates pre-existing inequalities.

The inequalities are perpetuated because, the unequal exchange theorists say, technology is not equally available throughout the world. This – the equal availability of technology – is another assumption of the Heckscher–Ohlin theory which is rejected by the unequal exchange theorists. Thus the inequalities which are established by the unequal bargaining strengths of workers are perpetuated by inequalities in the distribution of technology. It is argued that production possibilities are not the same throughout the world, because differences in market concentrations have generated, and continue to generate, a concentration of technology in the rich countries. Thus the LDCs are doomed to be less developed than they would be if their workers received the same pay for the same work as workers in the DCs. Thus free trade does not lead to equal pay for equal work; rather, unequal pay generates unequal exchange.

As writers such as Prebisch and Emmanuel have emphasized, trading advantages are determined by 'negotiated' differences in wage rates and by patterns of technology imposed by past colonialism and unequal exchange. They are not determined by the so-called 'natural' pattern of factor endowments. And since wage rates are determined by bargaining, the gains from trade are likely to be 'distorted' and distributed highly unequally between nations, even if all impediments to free trade are removed.

Furthermore, and more generally, neo-Ricardian theorists have not only raised fundamental doubts about the harmonious world of the HOS by emphasizing the role of bargaining in the international distribution of income. Writers in this school have also argued that the costs of *adjusting* production to changing patterns of trade may more than cancel out any gains from exchange. In short, the Sraffian and the unequal exchange wings of the neo-Ricardian school unequivocally challenge the assumption of the neo-classicists that free trade is best for all.

This assumption is also challenged by the Marxists who use the abstract labour theory to analyse and combat capitalism. For the Marxists, the concept of the country – the 'nation-state' – is far from the most important. Indeed, countries are not seen as geographic entities *independent* of the development of capitalism, and the Marxists argue that because the nation consists of antagonistic classes which have their own irreconcilable interests, there can be no such thing as 'the national interest' (see, for example, Harris, in Green and Nore, 1977). Given this, it follows that the abstract labour theorists do not necessarily support either free trade or protection. In their view each situation must be looked at in detail to see what effect it has on the interests of the various *classes* in society and, more broadly, whether it is likely to advance the cause of socialism and communism.

Thus the abstract labour theorist analyses trade in the context of the *capitalist mode of production*. 'Policies' are judged primarily in terms of the interests of world labour and, only secondarily, in the narrower terms of income distribution between nation-states. They are not judged at all in terms of neo-classical concepts such as 'social welfare'. In other words, the abstract labour theorists reject the notion that 'what is good for General Motors is good for the USA'. Or, as the USA-based economist Anwar Shaikh has put it:

> It is not possible to reduce the fundamentally antagonistic relations of classes to the bland homogeneity of a nation-as-a-whole. Christians are not in a position to cheer for lions so long as they both booked to play in the Coliseum. (Shaikh, in Nell, 1980, 216)

It is clear, then, that there are considerable differences between economists in their answers to the first question we have posed, what determines comparative advantage? The neo-Ricardians stress institutionally based differences in technology and wage bargaining, while the Marxists see trading patterns as being moulded by the class-based historical accumulation of capital.

The natural, ahistorical and harmonious picture of the subjective preference theorists is rejected by both the neo-Ricardians and the Marxists. For the latter, comparative advantage has not arisen naturally from the free play of market forces, and market forces are themselves viewed as having operated alongside the use of force. To a considerable extent comparative advantage has been 'created', and for the Marxists, trading advantages have arisen as a result of the capitalists' relentless hunt for profits.

Comparative and competitive advantages – the neo-classical view

These differences between groups of economists about the origins of so-called comparative advantage are accentuated once we look at the second question that was posed earlier, namely how does comparative advantage get converted into a profitable advantage – that is, where a two-way trade is commercially profitable? To answer this question we have to look at the way in which the 'schools' of economists view money and credit and at how they integrate these with trade. I start by looking at how the free-marketeers see the comparative advantage being converted into a profitable one.

The example of so-called comparative advantage used in Section 2.2 was as follows:

	price per unit in terms of international money (say, ounces of gold)	
	UK	*India*
cloth	40	60
corn	45	50

Here both cloth and corn are cheaper (in terms of international money, say, gold) in the UK. Therefore, both will (initially) be produced in the UK and shipped to India in exchange for India's reserves of gold. Thus the UK will run a surplus on its balance of trade, and India a deficit.

This cannot continue indefinitely. There are two possibilities. The first is that the exchange rate between Indian rupees and British sterling changes, with the prices (in terms of gold) in each country changing, so that imports into India become more expensive and exports become cheaper. In other words, the Indian rupee becomes worth less in terms of the pound sterling. It is devalued. The free-marketeers argue that, in this case, the flexible exchange rate will settle at a level at which India's lack of competitiveness is eliminated. India will emerge with a lower price in the commodity in which it has a comparative advantage – the one which previously was, relatively, the cheapest. In the example above this is corn.

The second possibility is that there exists a gold standard (where the domestic currencies are convertible into, or 'backed by' gold), under which the exchange rate cannot be flexible outside the range determined by the cost of transporting gold (the 'gold points'). In such a situation the exchange rate is fixed and gold is effectively the domestic currency in both India and the UK. But according to the free-marketeers, even in this case, there will not be a major adjustment problem. The gold flowing from India to the UK to meet India's balance-of-trade deficit, the argument goes, provides the basis for an expansion in the UK money supply and forces a contraction in the Indian money supply. Then, the free-marketeers argue, the general level of prices in the UK will rise, while that in India will fall.

The simplest way of understanding this process is in terms of the *quantity theory of money*. It is a truism that the stock of money (call this M) multiplied by the speed with which this stock circulates in the economy (call this V for the velocity of circulation) must equal the quantity of goods (Q) bought and sold multiplied by their prices (P). Thus MV must be equal to PQ. But for the monetarists, this is more than just a truism or 'identity'. For them, it is a *causal relationship*, so that changes in M or V lead to changes in P or Q. Furthermore, the monetarists argue, there is generally a stable demand for money, so that V is more or less constant. If this is so, then any changes in money supply M must lead to changes in P or Q. If, in addition, it is assumed that Q cannot easily be increased because the economy is operating at or near its 'natural' level – that is at full employment – then any changes in M must be reflected in changes in P, the general level of prices.

Thus, on the quantity theory assumptions, the flow of gold from India to the UK will cause M to increase in the UK, which increases the level of prices in the UK. At the same time, M declines in India and prices fall there. If, for example, we assume that prices rise by 10 per cent in the UK and fall by 10 per cent in India, then India's earlier *comparative* advantage in corn will be revealed as a *competitive* advantage, as follows:

prices per unit (in terms of gold)

	UK	India
cloth	44	54
corn	49.5	45

Now, after the 10 per cent change in price levels, India has a price advantage in the production of corn, while the UK still has a competitive (or absolute) advantage in the production of cloth – but no longer one in corn. And no longer will merchants find it profitable to sell *both* British-made cloth and corn to India. Instead they will find that they can make a profit only by selling British cloth and buying Indian corn. In this way there will be a tendency for the earlier imbalance of trade to be corrected, and gold will no longer need to flow from one country to another to settle a substantial balance-of-trade deficit. The impetus for changes in the money supplies in the two countries will have slowed, and an international monetary equilibrium will have been reached. Comparative advantage now coexists with a two-way profitable trading advantage.

It is clear from even this brief discussion that the whole story of the free-marketeers is not told by the apparently confident assertion of the American economist Haberler that; 'Even in the land of Adam Smith, Ricardo, J. S. Mill and Marshall, it is . . . necessary . . . to remind certain economists that trade is governed by comparative *not* by absolute advantage and cost' (Haberler, in Ellis and Metzler, 1950, 539–40; emphasis added). For even in the neo-classical world two-way trade is *ultimately* governed by competitive not comparative price advantages. The comparative advantage that is derived from differing factor endowments is converted into a competitive advantage by costless price changes represented by exchange rate changes or induced by international flows of money. The latter mechanism which was suggested two centuries ago by the Scottish economist David Hume is essentially the same as that assumed today by the so-called international monetarists. In the modern version the decrease in money supply, in India, would imply a decrease in the money balances of individuals and firms in India; and in order to restore their money balances consumption and investment spending in India would be cut back. It is this drop in aggregate expenditure which is assumed to lead to lower prices.

Thus the free-marketeers not only assume that *relative* prices in the domestic economy vary according to the marginal productivities of factors – so creating comparative advantage – but in addition assume that the *general* price levels in different countries adjust costlessly and more or less automatically to trade deficits and surpluses, so transforming a comparative into a competitive advantage, profitable for two-way trade. In general, then, in the world of the subjective preference theorists, it is prices that adjust significantly and not 'quantities' such as the level of output and employment. As Harry Johnson put it, in a much-quoted 1972 article: 'the monetary models assume that output and employment tend to full-employment levels with reactions to changes taking the form of price and wage adjustments' (Frenkel and Johnson, 1976, 155). In this monetarists' world the economy is like a barter economy with the only significant role for money being one of means of exchange. In this sense, and somewhat paradoxically, money makes no difference for the free-marketeer monetarists. For them, the earlier neglect of money in the story was of little consequence. As a standard textbook states: 'the requirements for normal balance of payments adjustments are not very stringent and are almost certain to be satisfied in reality' (Yeager, 1976, 69).

But, for the cost-of-production theorists, the neglect of money does matter. For them, money transforms the sad story of unregulated free trade into a potentially tragic one. Admittedly in the nineteenth century Ricardo, in his *Principles of Political Economy and Taxation*, seemed to accept Hume's adjustment mechanism (see Ricardo, 1971, 158). But there are many economists who, while developing in the nineteenth and twentieth centuries a 'cost-of-production' theory of value from Ricardo, have also developed a different view of money and have been sceptical of the ease with which free market adjustments in the balance of trade are made. The disagreement between these followers of Ricardo and the subjective preference theorists is about the speed with which labour and machines can be switched between one line of production and another, and about whether money facilitates or obstructs the adjustment process in an advanced industrial economy.

Comparative and competitive advantage – the cost-of-production view

To pursue these points it is convenient to return to the example at the beginning of this chapter, in which the UK had a price advantage in both corn and cloth, but in which India had a so-called comparative advantage in corn. For the subjective preference theorists, India's comparative advantage is transformed into a competitive advantage by price changes which may be induced by flows of international money which themselves result from the trade imbalance. But for the cost-of-production theorists, the price changes necessary to correct the trading imbalance are by no means automatic.

First, take the example where the currencies are not freely convertible into gold and in which there are floating exchange rates. That is assume that the central banks in the UK and India allow the exchange rate between India's currency (rupees) and that of the UK (pounds sterling) to change without their intervention. If this happens, it may be that the trading imbalance is *increased* rather than corrected. For resources in the UK may be slow to move out of corn production into the production of the more profitable cloth as the exchange rate changes. And, in India, labour and other factors may be slow to move into the production of corn. Initially, at least, following the devaluation of the rupee against sterling, India's balance of trade may continue to deteriorate. If it later moves into balance, the balance of trade will have traced a J-curve, with an initial deterioration – the kink in the 'J' – followed by a much later improvement – the upstroke of the 'J'.

Whether, with devaluation, the balance of trade is ultimately corrected depends on how the total values of imports and exports vary with the changes in prices, and with those changes in national incomes in the UK and India induced by the changes in exchange rates. There will be, in other words, and to use the jargon in the trade literature, both an *elasticities* (price) and an *absorption* (income) effect. For a more detailed discussion of these effects, refer to Sodersten, 1980, chapter 25; or to Hardwick *et al.*, 1982, chapter 28. Here I merely want to point out that the cost-of-production theorists are, in their emphasis on the specialized nature of capital goods and the rigidity of prices, especially wage rates, generally pessimistic about the speed with which trading imbalances are likely to be corrected by changes in exchange rates. More specifically, the price of corn from India may be slow to fall in terms of 'world' or, in this case, sterling prices because Indian agricultural workers may want a rise in wages to compensate for the higher import prices, or Indian landlords and capitalists may want to take the rise in rupee prices in higher rent and profits. Thus the volume of corn exports from India may only increase slowly and India's trading deficit may be corrected slowly, if at all.

Because of this pessimism about the ease of adjustment to changes in exchange rates, the Indian central bank may be reluctant to allow the exchange rate to change freely and may attempt to support it. What happens then will, in the view of the cost-of-production theorists, depend on how it is protected. To clarify this point, first, assume that the Indian government buys rupees and runs down its sterling reserves in order to maintain the exchange rate. In this case the 'money supply' in India may be reduced. Much depends on whether the rupee reserves which commercial banks hold at the central bank are allowed to fall relative to their other assets (mainly loans to bank customers). Even if this reserve ratio is not allowed to fall, the central bank might offset the drop in rupee reserves by pumping rupees into the economy. This it might do through open market operations (OMO) – that is by buying financial securities or 'IOUs' from the public. But even if the central bank refrains from OMO and allows the domestic 'money supply' to fall, the most likely effect (the cost-of-production theorists argue) will be a rise in the rate of interest. Certainly the cost-of-production theorists deny that the prices of corn and cloth in India will fall automatically with a fall in the money supply.

It is useful to look further at the basis of this view. It can be found in the arguments of the 'banking' school of the first half of the nineteenth century, but was further developed about fifty years ago by the British economist John Maynard Keynes. He argued that money is both a medium of circulation and a store of value, but that it is the store-of-value function which means that changes in money demand and supply have their primary effect on interest rates and only an indirect effect on the level of prices. For Keynes, *the rate of interest is a reward for sacrificing liquidity*, that is a reward for *not* holding savings in the form of immediately disposable cash. Thus individuals and companies shift money between current expenditure ('transactions') and financial investment ('speculation') according to expected movements in the rate of interest. With the amount held for speculation varying, the total demand for money is unlikely to be stable relative to income. Thus, the Keynesians claim, the demand for money (relative to income) is not stable. The monetarists (subjective preference theorists) say that it is.

While the monetarists (or subjective preference theorists) accept that money has a store-of-value function, they also argue that money is only one of many possible stores of value in an individual's asset holdings. Furthermore, it is claimed that not only is money highly substitutable with other assets, but that it *will* be substituted by individuals to maintain a certain mix or 'portfolio'. According to these same economists, individuals may find themselves with excess, undesired holdings of money, but they will soon spend these to restore a particular ratio of money balances to other assets. Thus, it is argued, the money-to-income ratio is stable, except for extremely short and temporary periods.

By contrast, Keynes and the Keynesians argue that money holdings will vary according to today's interest rates and expectations of future interest rates. Thus the demand for money with respect to income is not stable, and interest rate changes will result from, as well as cause, changes in the demand for money. It may well be that the instability of interest rates engendered by this 'speculation' will inhibit the decisions of 'entrepreneurs' to invest in new production facilities. This is what Keynes meant when he spoke of 'speculation' dominating 'enterprise' (see Keynes, 1976, 158). It is not necessary for the purposes of this chapter to pursue this point (for a more detailed discussion, see Cole *et al.*, 1983, chapter 6).

Here I want to look at how these views of money and of the rate of interest affect the balance-of-payments adjustments and trading advantages discussed earlier. The assumed situation is one in which the Indian central bank supports the rupee–sterling exchange rate by buying rupees and selling sterling. In the view of subjective preference theorists the government's purchase of rupees will reduce the money supply in India, which will then lead to a cut in expenditure in India and a fall in the Indian price level. But in the view of cost-of-production theorists the primary effect of the support of the rupee – even if reflected in a fall in the Indian money supply – will be to increase Indian interest rates. This rise may attract short-term deposits of money from the UK into India, which may offset India's trade deficit. There may be an overall balance on the total balance of payments, taking these trading and short-term capital accounts together. The Indian foreign exchange reserves and its exchange rate may be protected by the rise in interest rates. But at the same time, the higher interest rate in India may also deter productive investment in the corn industry and may, as a result, reduce the likelihood of the trade deficit ever being corrected. Entrepreneurs are unlikely to be happy about investing in corn production in India, if the interest rates at which they have to borrow are going through the roof. The price adjustments necessary to transform a comparative into a competitive advantage do not occur. If anything, they are deterred.

The situations set out above do not exhaust the possibilities, but they provide enough examples to show the general approach of the cost-of-production theorists, namely that the price adjustments necessary to correct trading imbalances are unlikely to be as smooth or automatic as implied by the subjective preference theorists. The correction of trade deficits may lag behind exchange rate changes because of the J-curve effect. Furthermore, the exchange rate changes, which might lead ultimately to the correction of trade imbalances, may themselves be deterred by short-term 'speculative' movements of money induced by changes in interest rates. And with wage rates being slow to change and capital equipment being highly specialized, adjustments in *output* may precede, if not pre-empt, changes in *prices*.

Thus, in this view, it is quite possible for a country to run a balance-of-*trade* deficit alongside an overall balance on *total* payments for some time. The initial pattern of trading advantages will rule the roost, with trade not shifting according to comparative advantage. In terms of the earlier example continuing 'backwardness' in India is possible, with the country effectively borrowing on a short-term basis from abroad at high rates of interest to finance its trade deficit. However, this may not be just a short-term problem if the high interest rates in India deter companies or tenant farmers from investing in the production of corn, the commodity in which the country has the so-called comparative advantage. And if it is assumed, as the cost-of-production theorists tend to, that technology is highly specialized, investment in such technology may be deterred by a framework of unstable exchange and interest rates. Thus 'speculation' may choke off 'enterprise', and far from international trade providing an 'equality of opportunity', it may merely perpetuate inequality. Indeed, the more internationalized the flow of money becomes, the more probable it is that uneven development will continue, with short-term deposits continually moving in search of quite narrow differentials in interest rates.

This, then, is the cost-of-production view. Comparative advantage does not arise naturally from relative factor endowments, but evolves through differences in technology and in distribution. Furthermore, whereas in the world of the monetarists comparative advantage is transformed into a competitive trading advantage by smooth changes in price levels, for the cost-of-production theorists, this transformation is much less certain. The so-called comparative advantage may lie hidden for a very long time.

Comparative and competitive advantage – the Marxist view

The Marxists – the abstract labour theorists – also reject the picture painted by the subjective preference theorists of smooth price adjustments occurring to reveal comparative advantage. For the Marxists, the process of capital accumulation is an uneven one. Capitalist development is both cumulative and sporadic. It feeds on its own growth; it decays on its own decline. Its tendencies towards concentration (growth in factory size) and centralization (growth in the size of companies) produce agglomerations of control over productive resources. And this tendency for industry to concentrate in established regions results in geographical disparity – in uneven development.

This means that a country or area with a well-established history of accumulation will build up the means for its own growth. It will amass advanced technology and produce a skilled workforce. Other countries will lag behind in productivity and advanced industry, and the first country – say, the UK – will acquire a competitive advantage in the production of many commodities. This pattern of development is likely to establish an international division of labour in which a country with low productivity, in general, can participate in trade only to the extent that it has special advantages due to, say, natural resource availability, transport cost structures, or perhaps a particularly repressive government, which drive down real wages to more than offset the lower productivity.

Thus, for the Marxist, it is not so much a question of an initial temporary pattern of trading advantages being transformed to reveal the so-called comparative advantage, but more a question of a historically derived set of trading advantages being dominant and self-perpetuating, or at least hard to shift. For the Marxist or abstract labour theorist, capitalist development is inevitably uneven through both time and space.

To some extent, then, there are similarities between the views of the cost-of-production theorists and those of the Marxists. For Marx, as for Keynes, international gold flows were likely to be reflected directly in changes in interest rates and only indirectly, if at all, in price levels; in volume 3 of *Capital*, Marx referred to the early-nineteenth-century debate between the banking and currency (the 'monetarist') schools in saying:

It is indeed an old humbug that changes in the existing quantity of gold in a particular country must raise or lower commodity prices within this country by increasing or decreasing the quantity of the medium of circulation. If gold is exported, then according to the Currency Theory, commodity-prices must rise in the country exporting it. . . . But, in fact, a *decrease in the quantity of gold lowers the interest rate* and if not for the fact that the fluctuations in the interest rate enter into the determination of demand and supply, commodity-prices would be wholly unaffected by them.

(Marx, 1972, 551; emphasis added)

And for Marx, as for Keynes, money has significant roles apart from being a means of exchange or medium of circulation. Whereas in the monetarists' view the economy is just like a barter economy, for Marx 'the circulation of commodities differs from the direct exchange of products (barter) not only in form, but in substance' (Marx, 1970, 112), for 'now . . . no one is forthwith bound to purchase, because he has just sold' (ibid., 113). Because for Marx value consists of socially necessary labour time, or *abstract* labour, in opposition to which money stands as a *phenomenal* form, 'the circulation of commodities seems to be the result of the movement of money' (ibid., 116). In fact this is only the superficial appearance, which is why Marx referred to the subjective preference approach as 'vulgar' economics.

Marxists then, like the Keynesians, emphasize the different functions that money plays in a capitalist economy. But whereas Keynes identified the roles of money (as medium of circulation and store of value) within a monetized industrial economy, Marx identified the functions of money within capitalism. For Marx, money, *as capital*, expresses a social relationship – the subordination of labour power. Arising from this, money's prime role in capitalism is as a *measure of value*. And then, arising from this role, with the separation in space of sale from purchase, money functions as a *medium of circulation*. For Marx, as we shall see in Section 6.2, it is this separation of exchange – commodities into money, money into commodities – which provides the potential for crises (see Marx, 1973a, 198).

With the further development of exchange, and arising from the development of money as *capital* in the circuit $M–C–M'$, money appears as an end-in-itself. As capital it is a 'precondition of circulation as well as its result' (ibid., 217); and it becomes related to itself in the form of interest and capital: 'From its servile role in which it appears as mere medium of circulation, it suddenly changes into the lord and god of the world of commodities' (ibid., 221). With the further development of capitalism comes the development of credit, and money then functions as a *means of payment* to settle debts. To perform this function reserves or 'hoards' of money are needed, and may become centralized in the form of banking capital. In its measure of value function money represents social labour-time, but this does not mean that money has to take the form of a commodity which itself embodies values. Rather it must be socially accepted as representing social labour-time. Thus money can and does take the form of paper, backed not by gold, but by the confidence generated by habit and the authority of the state.

So Marx, like Keynes, distinguished between different functions that money performs, whether the money be in the form of a commodity such as gold or a mere token. But whereas for Keynes and the Keynesians the relative importance of these money roles varies with expectations about the rate of interest, for Marx and the Marxists the importance of the medium of circulation role relative to that of money *as capital* or as means of payment varies in the course of capital accumulation, the business cycle and crisis. In a period of prosperity, when the rate of profit is high and when trade credit is being readily extended, the demand for money as a means of payment is low. But in the downswing, in a period of crisis and when confidence is falling along with the rate of profit, the demand for money as capital and as a means of payment is high.

Thus the significance of the different money functions varies, in the view of the Marxists, with the structural conditions of capitalism, whereas in the view of the Keynesians, they are determined by 'psychological propensities'. For Marxists, the substitutability of money for commodities is conditional upon the *structural* conditions. For Marx, in the upswing, commodities are as good as money in providing a store of value. Also according to Marx, in the upswing, money is generally substitutable with, or equivalent to, commercial credit. But in the crisis, Marx argued, money alone is value. Thus:

> On the eve of the crisis, the bourgeois, with the self-sufficiency that springs from intoxicating prosperity, declares money to be a vain imagination. Commodities alone are money. But now [in a crisis] the cry is everywhere; money alone is a commodity.   (Marx, 1970, 138)

Thus, for the Marxists, balance-of-trade deficits may be covered by credit advances when the world capitalist economy is in a period of upswing, but in a period of crisis devaluations will be forced and are even likely to become competitive, either directly in the form of exchange rate changes or indirectly in the form of trade controls.

While at a superficial level there are strong similarities between the Marxist (abstract labour) and the Keynesian (cost-of-production) theories, there are also some marked differences. They agree that changes in prices (including that of the rate of interest) and flows of money may well play a 'perverse' role, in the sense that far from leading to an elimination of trade deficits, surpluses and economic crises, they may defer or exacerbate them. And they both emphasize that money functions other than as a medium of circulation. But for the abstract labour theorists, the roles of money within capitalism have to be seen as integral to *capital* accumulation, and thus the different aspects of money vary in importance according to stages in the capitalist crisis.

Thus not only does each school of economic thought have different views of the determinants of trade arising from their different theories of value. They also have different views of money, again rising from their 'differing views of the world'. I return to these differences in Chapter 10 of this book; but in Section 6.2 we look in more detail at how each school of economic thought views the role that money plays in economic crises and, more broadly, at their descriptions of and prescriptions for economic crises.

6.2 WORLD CRISIS – EXCESS MONEY SUPPLY, DISTRIBUTIONAL CONFLICT, OR CAPITALIST CONTRADICTION?

Almost all economists agree that the world economy has been in a state of crisis for much of the 1970s and in the early 1980s. But among these economists, there is considerable disagreement on the major aspect; on the cause; and on the cure for the crisis.

World crisis: the monetarist view

For the subjective preference theorists, the school that unequivocally advocates free trade, the major characteristic of the crisis is inflation. In the 1970s and the 1980s prices rose rapidly in the advanced capitalist countries (see Figure 6.1). And prices rising in general is *the* problem. Unemployment is of secondary importance, because it is the result of rising prices. It is the deflationary 'hangover' after an inflationary 'binge'.

Rising prices are the main enemy, and their cause is excessive public expenditure reflected, in general, in an excessive money supply. As explained in Section 6.1, with the demand for money assumed to be stable, the velocity of circulation (V in the formulation of the quantity theory of money) is constant. This being so, any changes in the stock of money and of its supply (M) must then be reflected in changes in either P

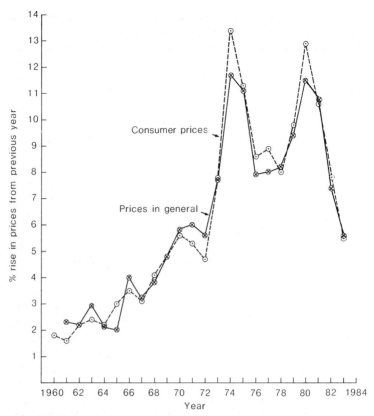

Figure 6.1 Prices in the advanced capitalist countries since 1960.

Notes and sources:
1. Consumer prices, for all OECD countries:
     1960–64: OECD, 1978, 127
     1965–81: OECD, 1982b, 151
     1982: OECD, 1983b, 167
     1983: IMF, 1983, 175
2. Prices in general: these are the percentage rises in the price indices for the gross domestic products (or national outputs) of all OECD countries (except Greece, Portugal, Spain, Turkey and Yugoslavia):
     1961–66: World Bank, 1981a, 30
     1967–81: OECD, 1978, 1983a
     1982: OECD, 1983b, 56
     1983: IMF, 1983, 170

(the general level of prices) or Q (the volume of transactions). The monetarists argue that, in general, Q will be constant unless and until labour productivity rises. This is because, in the absence of government intervention, the economy will tend to operate at a 'natural' level of unemployment – a level consistent with 'equilibrium' in the labour market. Thus with Q constant, any increase in M (the money supply) must be reflected in a rise in the price level P.

According to American economists Milton Friedman and Anna Schwartz, this is exactly what happened in the USA between 1867 and 1960. Friedman and Schwartz claimed to have found a close relationship, over these years, between changes in the money supply and changes in the money national income (see Friedman and Schwartz, 1963). They claimed this was a causal relationship with the changes in M causing the changes in money income, which with the volume of output Q fixed must mean changes in P.

And so inflation (an increase in the general level of prices) is caused by an increase in the money supply. But so what? Even if we accept this monetarist argument of a causal relationship between money and price increases, why do we need to worry? What is so damaging about inflation anyway? The answer of the subjective preference theorists is that inflation is pernicious because it interferes with the delicate workings of the free market. As Milton Friedman put it in his Nobel prize acceptance speech: 'The more volatile the rate of general inflation, the harder it becomes to extract the signal about relative prices from the absolute prices: the broadcast about relative prices is, as it were, being jammed by the noise coming from the inflation broadcast' (Friedman, 1977, 27).

Thus inflation is a problem because it throws a spanner in the works of the delicate free market machine. Given this argument, it is hardly surprising that Friedman went on to argue in his Nobel speech that 'the average level of unemployment would be raised by the increased amount of noise in market signals' (ibid.). Thus although unemployment is a secondary problem, it is likely to be higher on average, the more unstable is the general level of prices. And given this, we might expect to welcome a low level of unemployment as the sign of an efficient economy. But this is not the case according to Friedman, for 'a low level of unemployment may be a signal of a forced-draft economy that is using its resources inefficiently' (ibid., 16).

Unemployment can only be reduced below the 'natural' rate when inflation is unexpected – that is not fully anticipated. It is temporarily reduced below the natural rate by the confusion of the market signals caused by the government unexpectedly pumping extra money into the economy. Initially employers and employees perceive this as an increase

Table 6.1 Rising government expenditure in advanced capitalism 1960–80

	Total government expenditure[1] as a percentage of GNP	
	1960	1980–1
USA	28	38
Canada	28	34
Japan	29	40
EEC countries	32	48

Source: Morgan Guaranty Trust, May 1982, table 3.

Note:
1 Total government expenditure includes purchases of goods and services and transfer payments by central, state and local government.

in demand and, accordingly, increase output and employment rises. But then it is realized that it was only a 'monetary illusion' – the increase becomes expected, the inflation is built-in and unemployment returns to the natural level. It may even overshoot the 'natural' rate as workers and employers find themselves locked (again temporarily) into inappropriate contracts. But once inflation becomes correctly anticipated, unemployment will settle at its natural rate.

This natural level will not necessarily be the same for all countries. There will be a variation in natural rates because of variations between countries in the inducements given to leisure (through social welfare payments) or in labour market rigidities. But whatever the natural rate is in a particular country, unemployment will tend to approach it. All this might seem fine, except that it seems difficult to define the 'natural' rate except tautologically as that rate at which inflationary pressures are small. And yet we are told that the complete adjustment of expectations 'may well extend over decades' (ibid., 24).

Nevertheless, the lesson from the monetarists is clear. The crisis is monetary in nature, and has been reflected, in the 1970s, in inflation. The inflation has been caused by an excessive supply of money, generated by irresponsible governments interested in short-run political gains at the expense of the long-run efficiency of the economy. Similarly, in the view of the monetarists, the 1930s depression was caused by too little liquidity – that is by governments *not* printing enough money (see Leijonhufvud, 1971, especially 45; Friedman and Friedman, 1980, chapter 3).

In general, say the subjective preference theorists, any attempt to regulate the economy by changing government expenditure is not just unneccessary; in general, it is undesirable. Certainly the expansion of government expenditure in the advanced capitalists countries since 1960 (see Table 6.1) fills the hearts of the monetarists with dismay. They argue that economies are bound to suffer regardless of the way in which the public expenditure is financed. If it is financed through borrowing, savings for the private sector will be squeezed or 'crowded out' by rising interest rates; if it is financed by increased taxes, incentives to innovate and increase productivity will be choked off; and if the expenditure is financed by printing money, then individuals and companies will offload the increase in their money balances, and prices will rise. But the last alternative is the political soft option, and inflation is all too likely to be generated by governments attempting to buy temporary political support in this way.

This has been a problem not only at the level of the nation-state. The monetarists argue that an excessive money supply has also been the cause of inflation at the international level. They argue that the accelerating inflation in the advanced capitalist countries in the 1960s and early 1970s (see Figure 6.1) was caused by an increase in the world money supply. The principal agent of this increase and therefore the guilty party was the US government which, it is argued, financed the war in Vietnam not by higher taxes or increased borrowing, but by the printing of money. As the economist Harry Johnson argued in 1978: 'The proximate cause of the world inflation was excessive monetary expansion in the USA' (Johnson, in Brunner, 1978, 224).

But how can this be so? How, if the US government expands the supply of dollars, can this be translated into an excessive supply of French francs or German marks? Surely with separate currencies in existence, the American dollar will simply be devalued? How does this inflationary expansion in the American money supply get transmitted internationally, when each country has its own separate money? The answer from the monetarists is to point to the more or less fixed exchange rates of the 1960s, and with fixed exchange rates, it is argued, there is effectively one world money. Furthermore, the US share of the world money supply was so weighty that a large American increase was bound to be reflected in a significant increase at the world level. For at the end of the 1960s at least one-half of the world's reserves of foreign exchange was held in the form of dollars (see Caves and Jones, 1977, 387–8).

The argument, then, is that to finance the rising expenditures of the Vietnam War the US government resorted to printing money. This

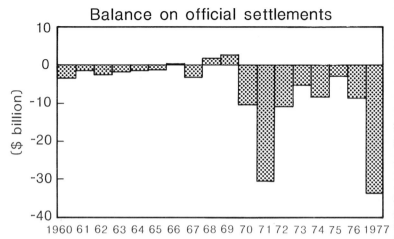

Figure 6.2 The USA's balance of payments, 1960–77 ($ billion).

Source: OECD, 1979a, pp. 10–13.

expansion in the money supply was inevitably reflected in deficits on the US Balance on Official Settlements as individuals and companies tried to spend their excess money balances, and the excess expenditure 'spilt over' into an external deficit (see Figure 6.2 for the balances during 1960–77).

The dollars could be exported without being devalued, because individuals and companies in other countries were willing to accept them; and they were willing to accept them partly because 'other advanced countries also became generally more willing to resort to inflationary monetary policies' (Johnson, in Brunner, 1978, 224). Thus at the level of the world economy, during the period of fixed exchange rates (that is until the early 1970s), there was a correlation between the stock of world money and the world price level. The figures used by Johnson are shown in Figure 6.3. This was, the monetarists argue, a *causal* correlation, with the increase in money supplies causing the increase in prices.

There are some economists who see this expansion of dollar liabilities overseas as part of a deliberate policy by the USA to gain 'seigniorage' (see, for example, Parboni, 1981, 40–9). Seigniorage is usually defined as the profit obtained from the issue of paper or token money. The profit may be obtained by a lord ('seigneur') or by a country. Since the cost of issuing the money, in terms of real resources, is less than the resources which it 'measures', a profit is obtained from issuing it. But the view that the USA's objective was to acquire 'seigniorage' is not shared by other economists (see, for example, Williamson, 1977, 153).

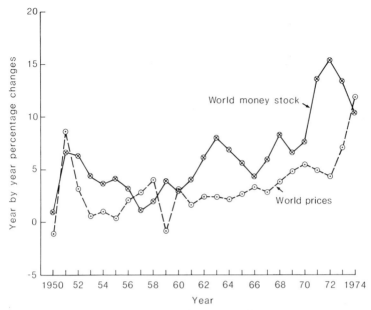

Figure 6.3 World money and world prices, 1960–74.

Source: Johnson, in Brunner, 1978, table 1.

Whatever the motive, the monetarist view is that the excessive expansion in American money supply in the 1960s and early 1970s generated the expansion in world prices. But when in the early 1970s the fixed exchange rate system collapsed, first partially in 1971 and then more comprehensively in 1973, there was no longer one world money. Nationally independent money supplies were possible, and with independent money supplies, one would expect to find as a monetarist more variation in the rates of inflation between one country and another. This has been the case (see Table 6.2). But this variation only appeared with some delay. Although the fixed exchange rate system collapsed in early 1973, rates of inflation did not vary significantly between countries until 1974. This delay is explained by 'the time dimension of adjustment to changing circumstances' (Johnson, in Brunner, 1978, 226).

But in all the major economies inflation continued, despite floating exchange rates. Why was this? Johnson's explanation for the widespread inflation is that policy-makers found it convenient (by continuing to print money) to allow increases in import prices (particularly oil) to be reflected not in changes in *relative* prices, but in changes in the *general* level of prices.

Table 6.2 Variations in national inflation rates (1960–75)[1]

Year	Percentage deviation[2]
1960	9.2
1961	9.0
1962	17.7
1963	19.4
1964	14.2
1965	12.1
1966	10.5
1967	6.4
1968	11.2
1969	14.5
1970	13.8
1971	14.1
1972	14.5
1973	12.4
1974	37.0
1975	34.1[3]

Source: Johnson, in Brunner, 1978, 227.

Notes:
1 For ten industrial countries: Belgium, Canada, France, West Germany, Italy, Japan, Netherlands, Switzerland, UK and USA.
2 Sum of percentage deviations from average rate of inflation.
3 Preliminary estimate.

From this analysis the policy solution is clear. Governments must control the supply of money. Furthermore, to prevent enterprise from being swamped by tax increases and to prevent private investment from being 'crowded out' by government borrowing, public expenditure needs to be tightly controlled. In order for the government to control the money supply an independent monetary policy is needed, in which case the exchange rate needs to be allowed to float.

Thus floating exchange rates are generally advocated by the subjective preference theorists. I say generally, because there are those like the German-born economist Friedrich von Hayek who argue that fixed exchange rates are attractive for the simple reason that they do *not* allow independent monetary policies to be followed by governments who are prone to irresponsibility. In this view fixed exchange rates are a necessary condition for international stability, since they impose 'upon the national central banks the restraint essential if they are successfully to resist the pressure of the inflation-minded forces of their countries' (Hayek, 1975, 21).

Thus there are some differences among subjective preference theorists about the desirability or otherwise of fixed exchange rates. But they are in unanimous agreement about the desirability of controlling the money supply, for it is this that causes inflation, which is their major concern. For them, inflation is the crisis.

World crisis: the cost-of-production view

By contrast, the cost-of-production theorists differ both about the description of the crisis, and particularly about its diagnosis. Unemployment, the associated loss of output and regressive distribution of income are, for them, the major problems. It is on these that attention needs to be focused. The growing rates of unemployment in the advanced capitalist countries in the 1970s are far from 'natural'. They are caused, the cost-of-production theorists argue, by the incorrect regulation of the economy. For them, struggles over distribution – the share of the cake – are reflected in rising costs. Rising costs are reflected in rising prices, and rising prices are reflected in rising money supplies. Thus, in general, the money supply merely accommodates the rising prices. For writers like the Cambridge economist Nicholas Kaldor the causal direction between money supply and the level of prices is reversed with the velocity of circulation (V) and the level of output being more variable in the medium-term than the monetarists assume (see Kaldor, 1980, 294).

But Kaldor and others admit that the inverse relationship between increases in wage costs and the rate of unemployment which seemed to hold until the 1960s now no longer holds (see Figure 6.4). This inverse relationship is usually referred to as the Phillips curve after the name of the economist who identified the relationship (see Phillips, 1958). The monetarists explain the situation shown in Figure 6.4 by saying that in the long run there is a vertical Phillips curve at the natural rate of unemployment, but that this is superimposed on a number of sloping short-run Phillips curves – the latter representing temporary adjustments to unstable prices.

By contrast, the cost-of-production theorists stick essentially to a cost-push explanation, with the Phillips curve being shifted outwards from the origin by expectations of inflation combined with labour militancy. Thus to a limited extent they agree with the monetarists inasmuch as inflationary *expectations* are seen to play a role in continuing or even increasing the rate of inflation. But the initial impetus is not provided by

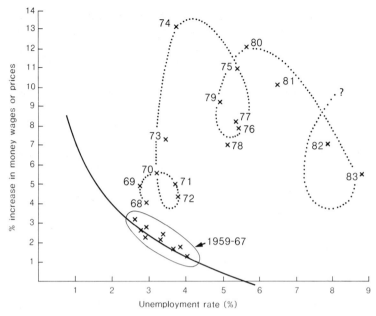

Figure 6.4 The breakdown of the Phillips curve and spiralling stagflation since the late 1960s.

Notes and sources:
The Phillips curve (full line), showing the inverse relationship between increases in money wages and the rate of employment, based on British experience from 1861 to 1957: Phillips, 1958.
Points (crosses) showing the percentage increase in *consumer prices* and the rates of unemployment for every year from 1959 to 1981 for the major seven OECD member countries: OECD, 1982a; OECD 1983b, 167 and 169; IMF 1983, 174–5.

excessive money supplies, nor is the momentum of inflation continued by rising money supplies. Indeed, for Kaldor, 'Control over the "money supply", which has in any case been ineffective on the government's own criteria, is no more than a convenient smokescreen providing an ideological justification for such anti-social measures [as shrinking effective demand and reducing the bargaining power of labour]' (Kaldor, 1980, 294). Or as the American economist James Tobin put it as bluntly in a similarly anti-monetarist paper: 'it is gratuitously optimistic to think that fundamental distributional conflict can be resolved by shrinking the pie over which the parties are contesting' (Tobin, 1981, 39).

The fundamental distributional conflict, to which Tobin refers, may change over time. In Ricardo's view the fundamental conflict was between the landlords and the tenant–capitalist farmers; Keynes shifted the focus to a conflict between rentiers and entrepreneurs; while the emphasis of cost-of-production theorists since 1945 has been on the distributional conflict between wages and profits, with a subsidiary emphasis being placed on the rising prices for 'monopolized' primary products, particularly oil.

Such distributional conflicts are seen to be the cause of inflation at the level of the world economy as well as that of national economies. In general, prices are 'sticky'. Contrary to the belief of monetarists, they do not adjust quickly. The cost-of-production theorists argue that prices are 'administered' in the industrial sector 'where the greater part of production is concentrated in the hands of large corporations' (Kaldor, 1976, 217). Thus in this sector it is not prices but quantities that adjust to changes in demand. In the primary commodity sector prices are more responsive to changes in demand, but when they do rise, they are passed on in the industrial sector on a cost-plus basis. And 'added to this is the price-induced rise in wages caused by "real wage resistance" – the reluctance of workers to accept a cut in their standard of living' (ibid., 219). Thus prices rise through what Kaldor, Prebisch and others have called a 'ratchet' effect. Prices only rise in the industrial sector; they rarely, if ever, fall. On this view, then, inflation crept up in the 1950s and 1960s because there were at work 'powerful social forces which make for constancy in relative earnings in different trades and occupations' (ibid., 221).

Moving on to the rapid inflation of the 1970s Kaldor rejects the monetarist explanation of Johnson set out earlier in this section, and instead sees the 'basic cause as increased trade-union militancy mainly attributable to the sharply rising deductions from the pay packet for payment of income-tax and insurance contributions' (ibid., 224–5). This was aggravated by the sharp, speculative rise in commodity prices in 1972, and then by the further rises in the price of oil in the later part of 1973 and again in 1979 (see Figure 6.5).

Thus the cost-of-production argument is that inflation is not caused by an excess supply of money, but rather by distributional conflicts. The rising prices may be accommodated by an increased money supply, but if the money supply and the level of effective demand are cut back sharply, then it will be the level of output and not prices that will take the brunt of the attack: 'If prices are "sticky", therefore, one can see how efforts to control money will tend to work; via high interest rates, an overvalued exchange rate, with some effect on prices but a major effect on real incomes and output' (M. Miller, 1981, 77).

Thus if attempts are made to control prices by indirect measures such as controlling money supply and cutting government expenditure, then

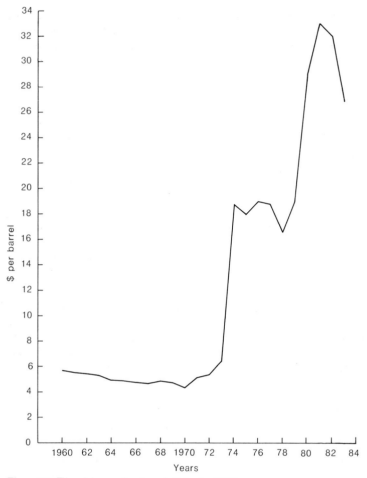

Figure 6.5 The rising real price of oil in the 1970s.

Sources: World Bank, 1981a, 92; IMF, 1983, 177.

Notes: The price is for Saudi Arabian light crude oil. It is the average realized price f.o.b. at Ras Tanura for 1980 with prices for earlier years revalued using the prices of manufactured exports from DCs to LDCs.

unemployment will be the *primary* result with the *secondary* effect being only a slight abatement in price increases. Thus to get inflation down by these indirect methods is a wasteful business. 'In the United States', Tobin argues, 'up to 90 per cent of reductions in monetary spending for a year goes into output rather than prices' (Tobin, 1981, 38), and even the conservative International Monetary Fund admitted in its 1982 *World Economic Outlook* that 'During the past two years, a disappointingly large proportion of the reduction in growth of aggregate nominal demand engendered by the tightening of monetary policy has taken the form of shrinkage in the growth of real economic activity, rather than lower inflation' (IMF, 1982, 10–11).

Thus in the cost-of-production view the cost of controlling inflation through monetary policy alone is enormous. In 1981 the average level of unemployment in the major industrialized market economies (the member countries of the Organization for Economic Co-operation and Development – the OECD) exceeded 7 per cent of the labourforce, with the cost of this being (conservatively) estimated at more than $340 billion, equivalent to about one-half the annual income of France (see OECD, 1982a, 11). This is the cost of the 'lost output', calculated as the value of the difference between output at a hypothetical 'full employment' level and the output at its actual 1981 level.

The cost, then, in terms of lost output is considerable. In terms of human degradation it is immense and, the cost-of-production theorists argue, the cosy picture painted by many monetarists of a large proportion of the unemployed preferring leisure to work is false. The 30 million or more who are currently (early 1985) unemployed in the OECD countries do not choose to be in the unemployment and social welfare queues. For the vast majority, the situation is both painful and degrading. This is, the cost-of-production theorists argue, the high personal cost of the impersonal market.

The cost-of-production policy implications are clear. Governments must mediate in the distributional conflicts. The cause of inflation must be tackled head on, using if necessary incomes policies and price controls. The solution is not as simple as that given by the monetarists, but then nor, say the cost-of-production theorists, is the world. Government intervention in the market is essential both at the level of the nation-state and of the world economy.

It is essential at the level of the world economy, because the increasing internationalization and interdependence of the world economy requires international regulation of financial and commodity markets. The need for this regulation is acute, because of the output-cutting impetus given to the world economy by the asymmetry in balance-of-payments measurements and adjustments. The apparent deficit on current account balances (trade and invisibles) at the world level has grown (see Table 6.3), so that an increasngly deflationary bias is imposed on the world economy as governments of countries with apparent surpluses are reluctant to allow their currencies to float upwards, and the brunt of the

Table 6.3 World payments imbalances on current account 1973–83 ($ billion)

	1973	1978	1983
Industrial countries	20	33	16
Developing countries:			
oil exporting countries	7	2	−27
non-oil developing countries	−11	−41	−68
Total*	16	−6	−79

Source: IMF, 1983, p. 185. Note that other sources give different figures – see, for example, table 2, p. 48 of Veil, 1982.

* Reflects errors, omissions, and asymmetries in reported balance-of-payments statistics on current account, plus balance of listed groups with other countries (mainly the USSR and other non-member countries of Eastern Europe and, for years prior to 1977, the People's Republic of China).

adjustment is taken by those countries in deficit. The latter countries, to prevent devaluations being reflected in a cost–price spiral, are all too ready to accompany devaluations with demand-reducing policies.

Thus restrictive demand management policies are used to cure inflation which has not been caused, it is argued, by excess demand in the first place. The restrictive demand policies cause output to fall, while the devaluations provide an additional impetus for prices to rise; thus we experience 'stagflation', a combination of stagnation and inflation.

What is needed, say the cost-of-production theorists, is a set of policies appropriate to the particular set of problems at any one time. Once a policy objective is identified, the most appropriate policy instrument must be selected to achieve that objective. This process is sometimes referred to as the principle of 'efficient market classification', a term coined by an American economist, Robert Mundell (see Mundell, 1962). The principle is simple; the application not so simple. Succcessful implementation is dependent on a correct diagnosis of the problems and of their appropriate cures, and on the aims (and means) being compatible with one another. A detailed discussion of 'efficient market classification' can be found in Sodersten, 1980, chapter 28. Here it is sufficient to take a brief look at some of the difficulties in applying it.

If, for example, there is thought to be a Phillips-style tradeoff between inflation and unemployment, then near-full employment can be obtained together with reasonable price stability by varying net government expenditure, that is by fiscal policy. But if full employment does not coincide with an external balance, a change in the exchange rate may be needed to avoid a deficit on the balance of payments. Thus two policy instruments (fiscal and commercial policy) are necessary to achieve two ends (full employment and external balance).

However, as argued earlier, the Phillips curve broke down in the late 1960s. Another policy (perhaps prices and incomes restraint) may then be needed to control inflation, while fiscal policy is used to regulate the level of output (and employment). Thus we now have three means to achieve three ends.

But then if exchange rate changes are thought to work only slowly because of a J-curve effect, import controls may be thought necessary to achieve an external balance. Alternatively, monetary policy may be used to regulate the external balance, if short-term money flows from one country to another are highly sensitive to changes in interest rates. Indeed, if it is thought that with the internationalization of capital markets, stable interest rates are incompatible with stable exchange rates, monetary policy may be dictated by changes in the balance of payments arising from movements of short-term capital. Thus governments may be forced to raise interest rates to stop sudden outflows of money. It has been argued in an article in the August 1981 issue of *Barclays Review* that 'Germany . . . and other members of the European Monetary System (EMS) block . . . have been forced to acquiesce in the high interest rate regime essentially as a result of exchange rate considerations even though domestic activity has been depressed' (Davies and Wright, 1981, 52). Thus Germany and other countries have had to get their interest rates in line with those in the USA. Otherwise short-term capital would flow out of the country, the exchange rate would be pushed down and a further impetus would be given to cost-push inflationary forces in the economy.

Under free market conditions, and in the present stage of development of the international monetary system (examined in Chapter 7), policy-makers have to treat the rate of interest as being linked with the exchange rate. To de-link these, and to enable independent commercial and monetary policies to be followed, exchange controls on the international flow of money may need to be reintroduced. Otherwise, as Kaldor puts it, 'with the vast amount of liquid funds now floating around the world, the possibilities of de-stabilising capital flows are so large as to make it too risky to pursue a policy of manipulating the exchange rate itself with a view to restoring . . . competitiveness on trading acount' (Kaldor, 1980, 318). And if national governments are to regain control of capital flows, they have, according to another cost-of-production theorist, Paul Davidson, only two choices: 'they can attempt to prevent or restrict all movements of funds into and out of each country . . . or they can join together into a supranational organisation to control international liquidity' (Davidson, 1982, 240).

Thus, for cost-of-production theorists, the continuous modification of policies is likely to be necessary to regulate a changing industrial economy. In view of their pragmatic approach it is, perhaps, not surprising that the choice between fixed and floating exchange rates is problematic. The advantage of fixed rates is that they may discourage speculation and give entrepreneurs a more secure environment in which to make investment decisions; the disadvantage is that the country's interest rate may be even more closely tied to that of other countries, and a policy instrument (interest rate changes) is taken away. Thus floating exchange rates provide an additional policy instrument, but one which may carry the associated risk of great speculation.

But to get back to the main topic of this section – the crisis. There is clearly a marked contrast between the views of the cost-of-production and subjective preference theorists about the crisis and about the form of government intervention that is required. For the cost-of-production theorists, state intervention is essential for regulating an increasingly complex capitalist economy. Prices for them are 'sticky' because technology is increasingly rigid and inflexible, wage bargains are institutionally struck and industrial companies are large and powerful. Production decisions have to extend over ever longer periods, and with the conflicts over distribution ever present, state regulation is essential if permanent stagflation is to be avoided.

World crisis: the Marxist view – capitalism, crisis and the rate of profit

It might seem from a superficial reading of the manifestos of political parties that the views on crisis of the cost-of-production theorists are the same as those of the Marxists, the abstract labour theorists. But the manifestos of centre and left political parties (at least in Europe) do not reflect accurately the theories of these schools of economists. In the same way as these groups of economists differ in their views on the roles that money plays in a capitalist economy (see Section 6.1), so there are differences in their views of the causes and consequences of the economic crisis.

Whereas for the cost-of-production theorist the crisis is a disequilibrium based in conflicts over distribution and the inflexibility of modern technology, for the abstract labour theorist the crisis is rooted in the production conditions of capitalist accumulation. Far from being a temporary disequilibrium, the crisis is fundamental to capitalism as a *mode* of production. Far from being accidental, unemployment, falling output and the restructuring of capital are all integral parts of capitalism's existence. The crisis is an expression of the basic contradiction in capitalism between the *social* division of labour and the *private* appropriation of surplus value. In other words, 'The real barrier of capitalist production is capital itself' (Marx, 1972, 245).

The way in which this barrier reveals itself is through a falling rate of profit. This tendency for the rate of profit to fall was analysed in Section 5.1, but since for Marx it was 'the most important law of modern political economy, and the most essential one for understanding the most difficult relations' (Marx, 1973a, 748), it is worth recapping.

The falling rate of profit stems from the accumulation process itself. The rate of profit (r) is equal to the total surplus value in money terms (s) divided by total capital. The latter consists of constant capital (c) – machines and raw materials – and variable capital (v) – the value of labour power. Thus:

$$r = s/(c + v)$$

which is the same as:

$$r = (s/v)/\{(c/v) + 1\}.$$

From this it can be seen that, if with the accumulation of capital and with the competitive quest for greater productivity, more machinery per worker is introduced and c/v rises, then s/v (the rate of exploitation) will have to rise to maintain the rate of profit r. But if productivity is stagnant or rising only slowly, s/v may not increase even if real wages are not rising. It is, then, possible for the rate of profit to fall even *without* a rise in real wages.

Certainly Marx thought the ratio of machines to labour, which he called the *technical composition of capital*, was bound to rise with the accumulation of capital. That is under the pressure of competition and the urge to accumulate companies are bound to increase the number of machines per worker. Measured in terms of 'original', 'old', or 'base' prices, the price equivalent of this, which Marx labelled the *organic composition of capital*, would also rise. About this there is little controversy. (Though it is worth stressing that Marx used the term organic composition of capital to refer to the c/v ratio expressed in 'old' prices, since many economists fail to make this distinction.)

But when we refer to the c/v ratio in terms of 'new' prices, there has been considerable controversy as to whether this is likely to rise. For when companies introduce new machines, their purpose is to get a step

ahead of their competitors. Ultimately their competitors must also introduce new machinery or die. The effect of this competitive process will be
to reduce the labour-time or value embodied in the commodities and,
therefore, their prices. If the prices of wage goods are reduced, then we
would expect v to fall and c/v (in terms of 'new' prices) to rise. But it is
likely that with increasing productivity, constant capital, as well as
variable capital, will become 'cheaper' and embody less and less labour-
time, so that c/v in terms of the new values and prices – the *value
composition of capital* – may well remain the same, rise, or fall. In
general, Marx thought, it would rise, due to the warlike nature of competition (for references which go into more detail on this, see the 'Notes on
further reading' at the end of this chapter.)

All of this is quite difficult to grasp at the theoretical level, but it is
extremely important. For what Marx is saying is that capitalism, being a
system of production for profit through the employment of wage-labour,
contains the nucleus of its own destruction, and that this is revealed
through the tendency for the rate of profit to fall. However, the theoretical complexity is reflected in further problems when we come to look at
the rate of profit and the composition of capital at the empirical level.
For its measurement is difficult. First, because in each crisis capital will
be devalued as companies go bankrupt and as the crisis is partially
resolved. Secondly, because we are concerned with the ratio of c to v in
the private sector and data may not be produced separately for the public
and private sectors. And thirdly, because data are often produced in
terms of capital–output ratios and not in terms of c/v ratios. In so far as
the capital–output ratio is taken to be a reasonable proxy for the c/v ratio
there seems to be conflicting evidence as to whether it has fallen or risen.
The British economist Bob Rowthorn, looking at data for the USA over
a period of almost seventy years which included the 'public utilities'
sector, has argued that the capital–output ratio has not risen, but has in
fact fallen (see Rowthorn, 1980, 103); whereas another British economist, Sean Hargreaves-Heap, looking at data for a number of countries
over a shorter period and covering only the 'industrial' sectors, argues
that (with the exception of Italy) capital–output ratios have risen, and
that this may provide 'important evidence in favour of the operation
during this period of Marx's famous "Law of the tendency of the rate of
profit to decline"' (Hargreaves-Heap, 1980–1, 81).

As stated above, if the c/v ratio is rising, then the rate of exploitation s/v
has to rise at least as fast to maintain the rate of profit. This it has
patently failed to do, and the rate of profit has fallen. There has been a
profits squeeze, which has been particularly evident in the 1970s in most
of the advanced capitalist world. Not only did the price of oil and other

primary commodities rise in the early 1970s, but real wages in the manufacturing sectors of most of the major capitalist countries also rose faster
than productivity, whereas in the 1960s productivity growth had been
rising faster than real wages, at least in the UK, USA and Japan (see
ibid., 71).

Thus with the ratio of fixed capital to output rising since the 1950s,
there has been a decline in the rate of profit – and a particularly rapid one
since the early 1970s. Figure 6.6 shows the trend in the rate of profit for
the major OECD countries since 1955. Thus the factors which might
counteract the tendency of the rate of profit to fall (increasing intensity of
exploitation, depression of wages, cheapening of constant capital and the
overseas expansion of the capitalist mode were the major ones identified
by Marx – see Marx, 1972, chapter XIV) have not been strong enough to
prevent the rate of profit from falling and with a falling rate of profit the
crisis has occurred.

Thus for the abstract labour theorists, crisis is endemic to capitalism;
it is rooted in the accumulation process. It is not, as for the cost-of-
production theorists, the result of a conflict simply at the level of distribution. As Marx stated in volume 3 of *Capital*, 'Both the rise in the rate
of surplus value and the fall in the rate of profit are but specific forms
through which growing productivity is expressed under capitalism'
(ibid., 240). Marx further argued that

the highest development of productive power together with the
greatest expansion of existing wealth will coincide with depreciation

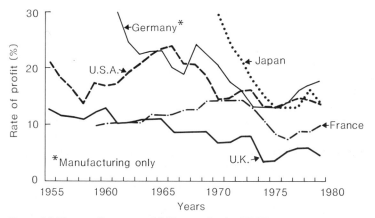

Figure 6.6 Twenty-five years of falling profits in OECD countries, 1955–80.
Source: DTI, 1981, p. 17; non-financial corporations; net rates of return to fixed capital.

of capital, degradation of the labourer, and a most straitened exhaustion of his vital powers. These contradictions . . . lead to explosions, cataclysms, crises in which by momentary suspension of all labour and annihilation of a great part of capital, the latter is violently reduced to the point where it can go on . . . fully employing its productive powers without committing suicide.

(Marx, 1973a, 750)

Thus by this reasoning, the present (early-1980s) crisis is unlikely to be the last, that is if capitalism survives it at all; it certainly isn't the first. There were slumps in the second and last quarters of the nineteenth century and in the second quarter of this century. In between there have been upswings, and a recent report by the United Nations Conference for Trade and Development (UNCTAD) argued, 'The most striking common feature is that the periods of upswing are invariably associated with the introduction and diffusion of new technologies (UNCTAD, 1981, 26). But what surely needs to be explained is why these technologies were introduced when they were? That is, why was accumulation renewed at particular times? The approach of the abstract labour theorists is to look at capitalism's characteristics as a *mode of production* to answer these questions. And the same approach is used to explain inflation.

I argued in Section 6.2 that for abstract labour theorists money acts not just as a measure of value and as a medium of circulation, but also as the material representative of wealth and as a means of payment. For money to act as a means of payment hoards or reserves are essential; in advanced capitalism these reserves become centralized in certain institutions such as the commercial banks, with the use of paper or 'token' money being possible because of the backing of state credit. Now whether the crisis is reflected in sharply rising prices depends not only on the bargaining power of labour and capital, but also on the reaction of the state and of the banks to the crisis.

As argued above, the *essence* of the crisis is revealed in the falling rate of profit. But the crisis may be revealed most obviously in a *financial* form. For, Marx argued, the demand for and supply of money-capital is likely to change quite dramatically over the economic cycle. In the upswing of the cycle, when the rate of profit is cyclically high and so is confidence, commercial or trade credit will be freely given and bank credit will not be much in demand. At the international level exchange rates are likely to be fairly stable as credit is readily extended through the international economy. Then at the peak of the cycle, with labour reserves used up and the capital–output ratio rising, the rate of profit is likely to fall as is confidence. Both the rate of profit and confidence may continue to decline, for 'as soon as it is no longer a question of sharing profits but of sharing losses . . . competition . . . becomes a fight among hostile brothers' (Marx, 1972, 253).

As the crisis deepens trade credit is likely to be restricted, and as credit restrictions tighten the demand for money as a *means of payment* will rise. This may become desperate if bank credit is restricted soon after commercial credit is squeezed. Interest rates are likely to rise, at precisely the same time as the rate of profit-in-general is falling, so putting even greater pressure on profit-as-enterprise. If anything, this will accentuate the demand for money as a means of payment. This tendency for the rate of interest to rise above the rate of inflation – that is to rise in real terms – as the crisis deepens was dramatically illustrated in 1981–2. With the rate of return on capital falling and the real rate of interest rising in these years, the 'pure profit' rate fell sharply in the manufacturing sector in the USA, West Germany and the UK (see OECD, 1983b, 57).

Thus the crisis may well *appear* as a financial one, the lack of real returns being hidden in this paper world. But the severity of the financial crisis may be modified by governments – the 'state' – expanding the money supply and providing handouts to failing companies – the 'lame ducks'. This extension of state credit allows the expansion of production on the expectations, possibly false, of future profits and accelerates the process of capital centralization, as the larger companies are likely to receive preferential treatment from the state. Otherwise, if they collapse, a general crisis of confidence or political instability is the more likely. Thus an extension of credit may accompany the further centralization of capital and 'postpone' the crisis without tackling the fundamental problem, namely the falling rate of profit. In other words, the extension of credit by postponing the restructuring of capital and the associated 'depreciation' of capital does nothing to prevent the crisis from ultimately occurring. Credit suspends the 'barriers to the realisation of capital only by raising them to their most general form' (Marx, 1973a, 623).

It is, then, the extension of credit backed by the state that enables production to be maintained by commodities being sold at higher prices. But the underlying *cause* of the rise in prices is not, as the monetarists claim, the extension of state expenditure and the expansion of the money supply. Instead it is the falling rate of profit which necessitates an increase in the money supply and state credit in order to allow production to be sold at higher prices. Thus the rise in prices may appear to

be based in an expansion of money supply, and to the 'vulgar' economists, as Marx called them, this appearance *is* the basic cause. But as Marx
pointed out, the 'sudden transformation of the credit system into a
monetary system adds *theoretical* dismay to the actually existing panic,
and the agents of the circulation process are overawed by the impen-
etrable mystery surrounding their own relations' (Marx, 1977, 146).
The expansion of the money supply may allow production to be realized
at higher prices, and it *is* the result of deliberate state action. This is
because the state, in the Marxist view, attempts to regulate or moderate
an existing crisis on behalf of capital; but the expansion does not bring it
about.

Similarly, the rise in prices may *appear* to be due to rising wages or the
result of the actions of 'monopoly' companies in raising their prices.
Again, in abstract labour theory, these play a role, but they are not the
fundamental cause of the crisis. To restore the rate of profit real wages
must rise more slowly than productivity, and if they do not the rate of
profit will fall even more rapidly. But this is not the same as saying that
without wages rising, the rate of profit would not fall and the crisis
would not occur. And again when the largest companies in the private
sector receive preferential credit to preserve confidence and prevent
deep pockets of unemployment, while in the public sector, prices are
raised to finance growing public expenditure, it may appear that
'monopolies' cause inflation by raising prices. But once again these are
reflections of the crisis, not its cause.

Indeed, initially at least, the state may allow prices to rise in an attempt
to reduce the real wages of labour. But if this fails, then the state will be
forced to attempt to restore the rate of profit by other means. Ultimately
credit may be blocked to force companies to increase productivity on
pain of bankruptcy. Unemployment will grow and with it the disciplin-
ing of the labourforce. The surpluses of those sections of the public
sector supplying wage goods will be raised by raising prices. Then
profitable sections of the public sector will be returned to the private
sector. Public expenditure, particularly on social welfare, is cut. The
booms become shorter. The slumps longer. This is the world of Reagan-
omics and Thatcherism. But it is not a world of irrational Ronnies or
mad Maggies. It is the result of the deepening crisis of capitalism.

This is the view of the abstract labour theorists. The cause of the crisis
has to be found in the basis of capitalism. Capitalism is a system of
production for profit. And when profit shrinks, so does the basis of
capitalism. Accumulation slows: fixed investment drops (see Figure
6.7). The foundations have to be restored, or the edifice tumbles.
Expanding the money supply is not the cause of the crisis but merely a

Net business fixed investment as percent of GNP

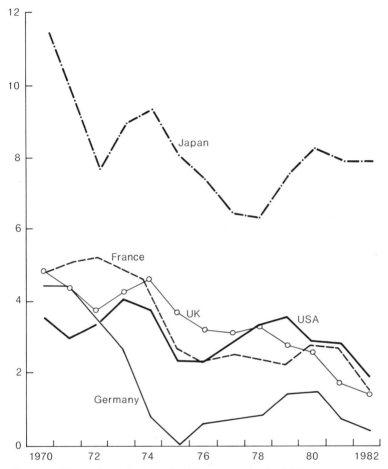

Figure 6.7 The decline of private fixed investment in the 1970s.

Source: Morgan Guaranty Trust, May 1982, 3.

way of papering over the cracks, so that the structural defects are less obvious. Rising real wages may or may not make the crisis worse, depending on the pace of productivity increases; but again they are not the *fundamental* cause.

These arguments of the abstract labour theorists stand apart from those of the cost-of-production theorists and are in stark contrast to the

Table 6.4 Economists' views of the crisis

Whose view?	What is the crisis?	What causes it?	Spin-off?	Cure?
(School of economists)	(Major characteristic or definition or focus of the crisis)		(Secondary effects)	(Policy solutions advocated)
Subjective preference theorists (monetarists, neo-classicists)	Rising prices ('inflation')	Excess money supply (public expenditure)	Inefficient economy (long-term rise in unemployment)	Less state intervention (control of money supply/public expenditure)
Cost-of-production theorists (neo-Ricardians)	Unemployment, falling output	Distributional conflict	Accommodating rise in money supply	More state intervention (incomes policy, import and exchange controls)
Abstract labour theorists (Marxists)	Falling rate of profit	Capitalist contradiction (social production/ private appropriation)	Political attempts to postpone crisis generate inflation	Recession and repression or revolution (abolition of capitalist mode)

views of the subjective preference theorists. The contrasts are summarized in Table 6.4. As hinted above, each of the schools of economics has a different view of the roles that the capitalist state can and does play in resolving or managing the crisis. But the role of each nation-state is increasingly constrained by the growing internationalization of capital, or to put it differently, by the increasing integration and interdependence of the world economy. In Chapter 7 I look in more detail at the integration of the world monetary system and at the growth and nature of the transnational corporations. Then in Chapter 8 I examine the growth of nations and the birth of the so-called Third World in the postwar period, and the twists and turns that policies have taken in those countries. In Chapter 9 I shall look at the different views of economists on the nature of capitalist and so-called 'socialist' states and on the consequences of the crisis for conflicts between these states.

NOTES ON FURTHER READING

On trade, money and balance-of-payments adjustments, see Sodersten, 1980, chapters 1 and 3, for a straightforward explanation of comparative advantage. For references critical of free trade, refer to 'Notes on further reading' at the end of the previous chapters. In the context of comparative advantage some readers may find chapter 6 of Emmanuel's *Unequal Exchange*, 1972, useful. A good reference for the ideas in the first section of this chapter is Anwar Shaikh's article on 'Foreign trade and the law of value'. This first appeared in two parts in *Science and Society* in late 1979 and early 1980: see Shaikh, 1979, 1979–80; but it can be found in one piece in a book edited by Ed Nell: see Shaikh, in Nell, 1980. The main focus of the first part of this chapter was on the transformation of comparative into competitive advantage. You will find many similarities (but a few differences, as well) between Shaikh's discussion and mine. Thus his writings should be read alongside the first section of this chapter.

On the components of the balance of payments and on adjustment mechanisms (mostly from a cost-of-production viewpoint), see Sodersten, 1980, part IV; Crockett, 1980, chapters 3–6; Hardwick *et al.*, 1982, chapters 18 and 28. For more specific writing on targets and policy instruments, see Sodersten, 1980, chapter 28; Hardwick *et al.*, 1982, chapter 26. For more on Hume's specie-flow mechanism, the quantity theory of money, and on the monetarist and Keynesian views of money in general, see Hardwick *et al.*, 1982, chapter 22; and specifically on Keynes and money, see Cole *et al.*, 1983, chapter 6; or, perhaps, better still go to Keynes (1976) himself. His *General Theory* is not the easiest book to read, but you may find a reading of chapters 13–16 rewarding in the context of this chapter. For a Keynesian view of money, look at the article by Davidson and Kregel, in Nell, 1980, and in the international context see Davidson, 1982.

Marx wrote very little on foreign trade, but much of his work on the nature and roles of money in capitalism can be found in his *Contribution*: Marx 1977, 64–187, and in *Grundrisse*: Marx, 1973a, 115–238. Rosdolsky, 1980, chapters 5–8, provides a good summary of Marx on money. But to repeat, the best source for the first part of this chapter is unquestionably Shaikh, in Nell, 1980.

On world crisis, the articles used in this chapter to show the approaches to the world economic crisis of the three major 'schools' of economists are Johnson, in Brunner, 1978; Kaldor, 1976, Bullock and Yaffe, 1975. The last is long and difficult in parts, but is worth persevering with.

For monetarist views similar to those of Johnson, refer to Parkin, 1974; Zis, 1975. For an interesting and more fundamental theoretical debate between monetarists and anti-monetarists, see the papers by Laidler, Tobin, Matthews and Meade presented at a conference on monetarism, held in July 1980: see the *Economic Journal*, March 1981. For an excellent attack on monetarism with particular reference to the UK, see Kaldor, 1980 and 1982.

For a view of stagflation on a similar cost-of-production basis to that of Kaldor, 1976, and which puts the case for incomes policies, see Meade, 1982. For a clear and succinct presentation of the Phillips curve, see Trevithick, 1980, chapter 4. The latter summarizes Friedman's interpretation of the Phillips curve; and for Friedman's own words, see Friedman, 1977. For American Phillips-style data covering the past ninety years, see Sachs, 1980.

I consider Bullock and Yaffe, 1975, to be still the best starting-point for an orthodox Marxist view of the crisis. Despite its length, Bullock and Yaffe's piece is more concise and clearer than Mandel's much-publicized *Late Capitalism*, 1978. Before ploughing through the latter, the reader is advised to read the review of it in Rowthorn, 1980, chapter 4; chapter 5 of the same book entitled 'Inflation and crisis' is also worth reading.

For an interesting comparison of Marxist and non-Marxist theories of crisis, see Shaikh's article, in URPE, 1978. The reader may also find Pillay's article, 'International economic crisis' useful: see Pillay, 1981. Less coherent, but written in his usual racy and readable style is André Gunder Frank's 'Reflections on the world economic crisis': see Frank,

1981a. For more articles on the crisis written in the same neo-Marxist, underdevelopment framework, see the book by Samir Amin *et al.*, 1982.

Writings on the crisis which I have found more satisfying than those of Frank, Amin and the other underdevelopment theorists are Sutcliffe, 1983; Harris, 1983; Glyn and Harrison, 1980, chapter 1. The latter chapter, entitled 'World capitalism in crisis' is readable and informative, as is their appendix on the profits squeeze. The latter denies that Marx's Law of the Tendency of the Rate of Profit to Fall (LTRPF) can explain the fall in the rate of profit since the mid-1960s. For a counterview, see Hargreaves-Heap, 1980–1. And for a fuller theoretical discussion of Marx's LTRPF than has been possible in this chapter, see the debate in the *Cambridge Journal of Economics*: for references to this debate, see Salvadori, 1981; Weeks, 1981, 1982; Fine, 1982, chapter 8.

6.1 Trade, money and balance-of-payments adjustments

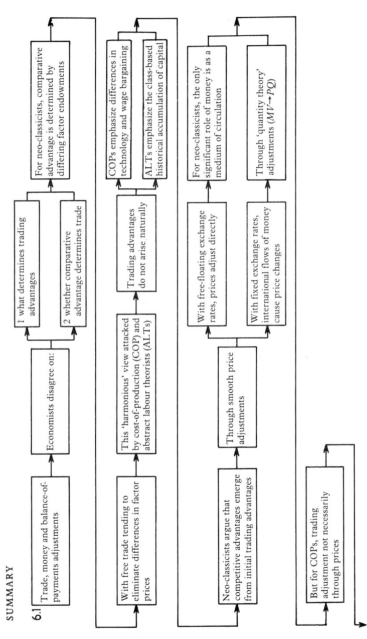

Economists disagree on:

1. what determines trading advantages
2. whether comparative advantage determines trade

For neo-classicists, comparative advantage is determined by differing factor endowments

With free trade tending to eliminate differences in factor prices

This 'harmonious' view attacked by cost-of-production (COP) and abstract labour theorists (ALTs)

Trading advantages do not arise naturally

COPs emphasize differences in technology and wage bargaining

ALTs emphasize the class-based historical accumulation of capital

Neo-classicists argue that competitive advantages emerge from initial trading advantages

Through smooth price adjustments

With free-floating exchange rates, prices adjust directly

With fixed exchange rates, international flows of money cause price changes

For neo-classicists, the only significant role of money is as a medium of circulation

Through 'quantity theory' adjustments ($MV \rightarrow PQ$)

But for COPs, trading adjustment not necessarily through prices

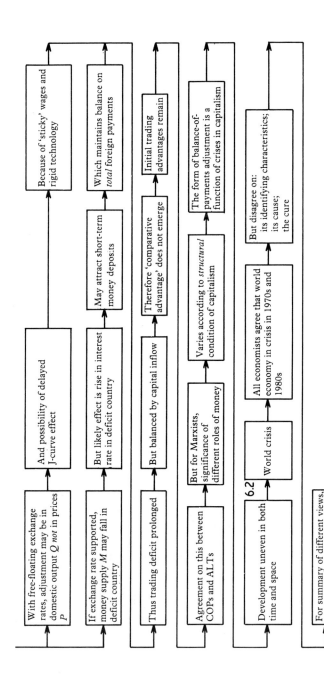

6.2

165

7

Capitalism, international money and transnational corporations

7.1 THE EXPANSION OF CAPITALISM

The second section of Chapter 6, which discussed the growing economic crisis of the 1970s, presupposed the growing integration of the world economy without discussing it in detail. And in the first section of Chapter 5, which introduced the views of the abstract labour theorists on the development of capitalism, we focused our attention on the relentless global expansion of capitalism. In this view the *intensive* development of capitalism and the rise of machinofacture has been accompanied by the global expansion of capitalism. With the growing *concentration* of capital into more intensive factory production in the early nineteenth century, there was an increasing exchange of commodities through world trade. And then in the second half of the nineteenth century as capital became increasingly *centralized* in bigger and bigger companies, so there were increasing flows of money-capital between nation-states.

In the last half of the nineteenth century the international expansion of money-capital was dominant, while since the beginning of this century industrial investment has been rapidly internationalized. But whereas in the nineteenth century the outward expansion of capital was accompanied by an outward flow of labour, in this century the growing centralization of capital in the transnational corporations (TNCs) based in the rich northern countries has been accompanied by a flow of labour which has been from south to north, rather than from north to south.

Thus in the nineteenth century trade or the flow of *commodity*-capital gave rise to a flow of *money*-capital, which in turn gave rise to a flow of industrial or productive capital, as transnational (or as they are sometimes called, multinational) corporations expanded their control of productive investments in a number of different nation-states. The total circuit of capital ($M–C–M'$) expanded and bridged national boundaries as the process of internationalization gathered steam and capitalism expanded. New nation-states were both formed and transformed by the expansion of capital.

More broadly, in the past century the global expansion of capitalism has been expressed in both the expansion of the international capital market (and the development of an integrated, but unplanned, world monetary system) as well as in the growth of the TNCs. The internationalization of financial capital has been particularly marked since the 1960s with the rapid growth of the Eurocurrency market. The latter followed the uneven de-regulation of the financial markets – a process which is still going on. Thus in the late 1970s US pension funds were allowed to invest overseas, and the final vestiges of British exchange controls were swept away, and then in the past few years Japanese exchange controls have been relaxed and a new offshore banking centre established in New York. In this period – indeed in the whole of the period since 1945 – the expansion of the international money market and the growth of TNCs have been parallel, symbiotic developments, and the purpose of this chapter is to discuss them and their effects in more detail.

There has been a considerable controversy over the effects of TNCs and the direction and magnitude of capital flows, and transfers of 'surplus'. Some of this controversy is due to the different definitions of capital used – definitions which result from the different theoretical frameworks within which the analyses are conducted. Some economists have argued that there has been a drain of surplus from the Third World into the rich north with the TNCs being the main agents of this drain; others have argued that there has been a net income gain for the countries hosting foreign investors with the TNCs being the cause of much of this gain. To enlarge on these issues is the main purpose of Section 7.3 in this chapter, where we look at the roles and effects of TNCs in a comparative framework.

But before that, in Section 7.2, I trace the development of the international monetary system, largely within a Marxist framework; unlike the previous chapters, the treatment is less rigorously comparative in order to keep the section reasonably brief.

7.2 THE INTERNATIONAL MONETARY SYSTEM

The subject of this section is the global expansion of international money-capital, and the development of an integrated international monetary system (IMS). What is it? How has it developed? How does it relate to, affect, or perhaps even cause a world economic crisis?

For the abstract labour theorists, the development of the IMS is seen as integral to the capitalist mode of production; it is linked with the international accumulation of capital, and reflects the relations between national economies. This view is somewhat at odds with that of the monetarists who see the IMS as being consciously developed to facilitate the growth of an international barter system. The cost-of-production theorists see the IMS as being less functional. In this respect they agree with the Marxists. But in so far as they see the evolution of monetary institutions as being inherently subject to national and international control *within* capitalism, they differ from the Marxists.

At a less abstract level the IMS is concerned with flows of funds on both the current and capital accounts of the balance of payments, these flows ebbing and flowing with changes in interest rates and pro- ductivities in nation-states, and thus both affecting and being affected by changing currency exchange rates. Thus the IMS simultaneously causes and clears international balances; adjusts and clears imbalances in the balance of payments; and gives rise to and supersedes international institutions.

To understand the present IMS it is useful to consider its historical development. But to be brief, the treatment will be less comparative than it has been in previous chapters. It may be helpful to see the develop- ment of the 'world' monetary system in four phases, as follows:

(a) the domestic gold standard;

(b) the sterling–gold standard;

(c) the dollar–gold exchange standard;

(d) the international credit system.

Most of this section will be devoted to a discussion of the last of these phases and of the financial crises of the 1970s and 1980s; the other phases are discussed briefly to throw into historical perspective some of the problems associated with the present structure.

The domestic gold standard

In the eighteenth and nineteenth centuries gold was money (as measure of value, medium of circulation and material embodiment of wealth) both within and between legislative areas. In this sense there was no such thing as a 'national' balance of payments. As capitalism and the exchange of commodities had developed in north-western Europe from the fifteenth through to the nineteenth century, so gold (due to its specific characteristics of uniformity, divisibility, durability and concen- trated value – see Marx 1973a, 166) had become money.

As capitalism developed, so did credit, and currencies began to emerge as moneys within specific legislative areas or nation-states. National tokens based on gold developed as confidence in exchange developed with habit and repetition. Thus these national currencies were partly 'fiduciary' (based on trust or faith) and partly gold-backed (that is convertible into gold). The fiduciary issue was backed by the authority of the legislative area (the city-state or national government), so that domestic became separated from international money, for national tokens had to be exchanged for gold through central authorities to settle international debts.

The sterling–gold standard

Thus by the nineteenth century national currencies were linked through gold. Some economists have suggested that the international monetary system operated, before the First World War, on the basis of a 'fairly automatic' gold standard with trade surpluses and deficits being quite quickly 'cleared' through shipments of gold. But even before the First World War, there is considerable evidence to suggest that the gold standard was far from automatic in the way that, for example, Hume's gold-specie theory suggested.

According to the detailed two-volume study of the gold standard between 1914 and 1934 by the American William Brown, the system was very much linked with credit centred on the City of London, and when a crisis did occur in 1914, it

> showed the difficulties that arise when an attempt is made to force gold to serve as a balancing item in international payments when credit is disorganised. The crisis caused moratoria, suspensions of specie payments and legal and de facto gold export embargoes in many countries.   (Brown, 1940, 27)

Brown went on to point out that 'it is a paradox that during the war, countries went off gold in order to preserve to the maximum possible degree the psychological and economic advantages of . . . the gold standard' (ibid., 39). Even before the First World War, trade and financial imbalances were not cleared through the free 'automaticity' of the gold market, but were instead regulated through the control of imports and foreign borrowing (see ibid., 87; Lindert, 1969; Triffin, 1947); in essence even before the war, the international monetary system was on a sterling-gold exchange standard (see Brown, 1940, 133; Kindleberger, 1981, 68, 190).

The demand for gold was irregular. In the upswing of an industrial and trade cycle when exchange was regular and international credit abundant, there was little demand for gold as money, but in a down-swing when credit was withdrawn, there would be a mad scramble for gold. Thus the international gold standard, often presented as working smoothly and automatically before the First World War, is said, by some economists, to have operated in a quite different way. Its functioning was linked to the ebb and flow of international capitalism, so that the apparent adequacy of reserves was never static, but varied according to the state of the trade cycle. In an upswing credit would be overextended; in the downswing the chickens would come home to roost and the demand for gold would seem to be infinite.

This ebbing and flowing of the international monetary system is described in detail in Brown's study. According to him, the period between 1914 and 1928 was dominated by 'an effort to preserve as far as possible the illusion of merely temporary deviations from normal gold standard conditions, to be followed by an early return to normal after the war' (Brown, 1940, xxi). For while the worldwide dominance of sterling was in decay by the time of the First World War, the dollar was not immediately substituted for the pound. That is the international credit system was not quickly reconstructed on the basis of the dollar. There was instead a period of highly unstable exchange rates between 1918 and 1922 (see *Barclays Bank Review*, November 1982, 79, fig. 1), as the world adjusted to a new set of productivity levels in the capitalist econ-omies, and to a new dollar centre of gravity in the world financial system.

The dollar–gold exchange standard

From 1922 for a period of approximately fifty years until the late 1960s and early 1970s the IMS was based almost exclusively on the dollar. During this period as capitalism and exchange became yet more exten-sive, gold became less important as a medium of circulation and inter-national credit more important. The basis of this expansion was the dollar – and the dollar was strong because the American economy was strong.

Although during this period gold was not *generally* in great demand, at *particular* periods of crisis it was. This was especially so during the 1931 financial crisis – so much so that the convertibility of the pound into gold was suspended. Thus in the interwar period the proportion of reserves held by central banks in the form of foreign exchange fluctuated con-siderably. In 1913 the major European central banks held only about 12 per cent of their reserves in the form of foreign exchange; by 1927 this had risen to more than 40 per cent; but by 1932 the proportion had again fallen back, this time to less than 10 per cent (see Grubel, 1978, 131).

The crisis of the 1930s was marked by fluctuating exchange rates and trade restrictions as each national government rushed to defend its capital against foreign competition. It was, ostensibly, to prevent a recurrence of this instability that an agreement was signed in 1944 by the governments of the major capitalist countries at Bretton Woods in New Hampshire, USA. This Bretton Woods agreement established the International Monetary Fund (IMF) and the International Bank for Reconstruction and Development (IBRD) or World Bank. Some characteristics of these organizations are summarized in Table 7.1, but briefly the IMF

Table 7.1 The IMF and World Bank: some institutional facts

Brief details	Location of head office	When set up	Members	What it is	Voting basis
International Monetary Fund (IMF)	Washington, DC	1944	147	'International central bank'	Financial contributions
International Bank for Reconstruction and Development (or World Bank)	Washington, DC	1944	134 (1979)	International development bank	Financial contributions

More on the IMF – the IMF is a 147-member club of governments. They pay subscriptions or quotas, determined by the size of their economies. Quotas determine: a member's voting power (250 votes, plus one for every $100,000); and the amount of foreign exchange which it may draw when in balance-of-payments need. The more it borrows, the more stringent the borrowing conditions.

But in addition to getting subscriptions from member governments, the IMF also borrows from surplus countries and 'creates' its own money – the latter being the so-called special drawing rights' (SDRs), the value of which, since 1981, has been set in terms of a bundle of five currencies – namely the US dollar, Deutschmark, sterling, French franc and the yen. These borrowed and created funds are also lent to member countries.

The USA has about one-fifth of all the votes and the IMF is run by a board of twenty-two executive directors – a 'Committee of 20'. Six countries appoint directors – the world's five biggest economies (USA, UK, Germany, France and Japan) plus Saudi Arabia (one of the biggest creditors) – China is a permanent member and the remaining fifteen directors are elected by the remaining members grouped into 'constituencies'.

The *World Bank's* head office, in Washington, DC, is next door to the IMF's. The World Bank is governed in the same way, and it is therefore dominated by the most powerful economies and, particularly, the USA. Most of its loans are at commercial interest rates, but some loans are 'soft' – that is the interest rates and repayment terms are 'concessional'. In 1983 the USA had 21 per cent of all votes.

Sources: The Economist, 1979; van Meerhaeghe, 1971; Sodersten, 1980; Latin America Bureau, 1983, glossary and chapter 2.

is an international central bank collecting deposits and providing short-to medium-term loans to member countries, the conditions attached to these loans varying with their size, with the country's outstanding overdraft with the IMF and with the recipient government's political leanings. The major purpose of the World Bank was to provide longer-term multilateral 'aid' for particular projects.

Thus the IMF was to provide programme loans independently of the World Bank's provision of project aid, but in recent years as the crisis has deepened the loans of the twin organizations have been increasingly co-ordinated. This co-ordination is made easier by the American dominance of both organizations. Now (1985) the USA holds about 20 per cent of all IMF votes. Although this is lower than the 36 per cent share held by the USA at the formation of the IMF, it is sufficient to give the American government a dominant position in the Fund.

The announced purpose of establishing the IMF was to regulate exchange rates by supervising the expansion of international money. Against the chaotic and crisis-ridden background of the 1930s the regulation of international liquidity was seen as necessary to prevent uncontrolled fluctuations in exchange rates. But a different emphasis sees the establishment of the IMF as an assertion by the USA of its international power – of its hegemony. In this view it was the relative economic importance of the USA that 'enabled [it] virtually to dictate terms at the negotiations leading to the Bretton Woods Agreement' (*Barclays Bank Review*, November 1982, 80). The US Treasury opposed the creation of an international money – such as the 'bancor' proposed at Bretton Woods

Table 7.2 The USA's balance of payments 1947–80

Years	Balance on current account (trade and services) ($ billion, p.a.)	Basic balance (including long-term capital) ($ billion, p.a.)	Balance on official settlements (including short-term capital) ($ billion, p.a.)
1947–9	3.8	1.1	1.1
1951–6	−0.2	−1.2	−1.1
1958–62	1.0	−1.8	−2.5
1963–6	4.0	−1.2	−1.2
1967–71	−0.8	−4.6	−8.1
1972–6	5.0	−4.5	−8.9
1977–80	−5.8	−18.4	−16.7

Sources: Sodersten, 1980, 451; OECD, 1979a, 10–11; IMF, 1981, 580.

by Keynes – and instead promoted the use of the dollar as the international currency or medium of circulation (see Brett *et al.*, 1982, 134).

In fact, in the postwar period, the dollar has played the major role in
the international monetary system. The role of the IMF has been a subsidiary one. In the postwar period world liquidity expanded considerably, but it was not an international currency issued by the IMF which
provided this increase in liquidity, but the growth of foreign holdings of
US dollars. Initially the US dollars were provided through the Marshall
Plan, the programme of military and civil aid and reconstruction in
western Europe financed by the US government, and 'sold' to the US
Congress against the spectre of the communist threat in Europe. Then
through the 1950s and 1960s, and into the 1970s, the supply of world
liquidity was provided by the USA running 'basic' balance-of-payments
deficits which were funded by dollars accumulating outside the USA
(see Table 7.2). Such a structure ensured that 'seigniorage' accrued to
the USA, since the only way that the rest of the world could acquire US
dollars was by running an autonomous or 'basic' balance-of-payments
surplus, thus transferring real resources (or claims to real resources) to
the USA (see Grubel, 1978, 143; Parboni, 1981, 40).

By the end of the 1960s the deficit on the basic balance of payments
(current account plus long-term capital) of the USA had grown substantially (see Table 7.2), as direct foreign investment by US companies
grew in the 1950s and as in the 1960s US military expenditure in Vietnam escalated. Gold flowed out of the USA, and by the end of the 1960s
American gold reserves were less than one-half the level of the early
1950s. By 1970 the gold holdings of the USA were only about 30 per
cent of world official stocks compared to 69 per cent in 1950 (see Figure
7.1). And in 1970, when the Nixon administration tried to combat a
recession in the USA by lowering interest rates, there was a large outflow
of short-term funds from America into Europe and Japan. This outflow
totalled $7 billion which was on top of a basic deficit in the same year
(1970) of $3 billion. The pressure on the dollar was overwhelming, and
in May 1971 the Deutschmark was revalued against the dollar. But still
the pressure against the dollar continued. The basic US deficit increased
to more than $10 billion in 1971, and with the world economy more
closely integrated than ever – with transnational corporations able to
switch huge amounts of money between currencies – it was not surprising that the postwar system of relatively fixed exchange rates collapsed.

The weakening of US competitiveness, which was reflected in a deficit
on the American current account in the late 1960s (see Table 7.2) had to
be reflected in a devaluation of the dollar. In August 1971 dollar
convertibility was officially suspended, and for the next few months the

Top three gold holders

Percentage of total official stocks (IMF members only)

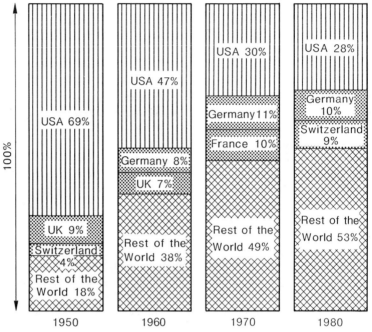

Figure 7.1 Official holdings of gold 1950–80.

Source: Barclays Bank Review, February 1982.

major currencies were forced to float. In December 1971 a meeting of the Group of 10 capitalist countries (see Table 7.3) was convened at the Smithsonian Institution in Washington, DC. The Group of 10 agreed to devalue the dollar and to revalue the mark (again) and the Japanese yen, as well as to widen the band within which the IMF would allow the currencies to fluctuate. President Nixon hailed the Smithsonian realignment as the 'greatest monetary agreement in history' (quoted in Sodersten, 1980, 460). It lasted fourteen months.

The dollar continued to be under pressure, and by March 1973 after spectacular, speculative worldwide movements of money, the pegged dollar–gold exchange rate system of Bretton Woods was finished with. American hegemony was being challenged by German and Japanese economic power, the rate of profit was falling rapidly and the world had moved into the present, highly unstable phase of the IMS.

Table 7.3 The Groups of 5, 10 and 24

The Group of 5 consists of:

> USA
> UK
> West Germany
> France
> Japan

These countries constitute the five western permanent members of the IMF's Executive Board (see Table 7.1). Since the early 1970s this has been the group of countries most commonly involved in international monetary negotiations. Sometimes this is 'stretched' to include Italy, and the discussion group is sometimes further expanded to . . .

The Group of 10, which consists of ten industrialized countries belonging to the IMF, namely the Group of 5, plus:

> Italy
> Belgium
> Canada
> Netherlands
> Sweden

The central bankers of the Group of 10 meet monthly under the umbrella of the Bank of International Settlements (BIS), based in Basle, Switzerland. The BIS is the bank through which currency swaps are arranged and the central banks clear their accounts with each other.

The Group of 24

This is the LDC counterpart to the Group of 10, though nowhere near it in terms of strength and effectiveness. It was established in the early 1970s to review the IMS from an LDC position. It is the monetary equivalent to the Group of 77, the LDC's pressure group within UNCTAD and other United Nations organizations.

Sources: Latin America Bureau, 1983, glossary; Tew, 1982.

The international credit system

The present IMS is characterized by considerable instability. The postwar period, and especially the period since 1960, has been characterized by:

(a) a decline in the importance of the dollar as an international currency. Even over the relatively short 1973–80 period the proportion of official foreign exchange reserves (that is excluding gold) held in the form of dollar deposits in the USA fell from 61 to 43 per cent (Figure 7.2);

(b) a relative decline in the early 1970s – and then a rise in the late 1970s – in the importance of gold (valued at market prices) in international reserves (Figure 7.3);

(c) a rapid growth in private international liquidity mostly in the form of Eurocurrencies (Figure 7.3).

This last-mentioned characteristic, the growth of Eurocurrencies, is only partly a reflection of the decline of the dollar, for the latter remains the major trading currency. It is more a result of the continuing integration of the world economy – with the growing internationalization of productive and financial capital – and of increasing competition between financial institutions, especially the commercial banks. This growth in banking competition has been both due to *and* despite a reduction in exchange controls and restrictions on banking.

Official holdings of foreign exchange reserves

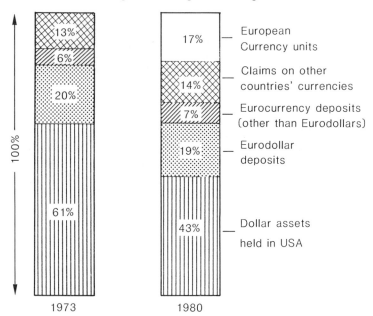

Figure 7.2 The decline of the dollar in the 1970s.

Source: As Figure 7.1.

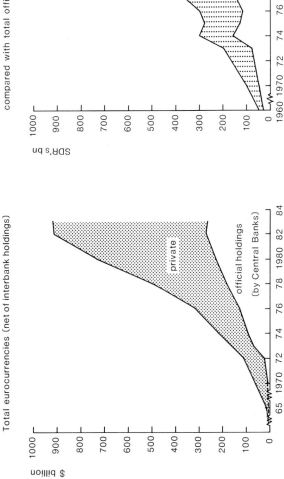

Figure 7.3 The growth of Eurocurrencies 1960–80.

Sources: Morgan Guaranty Trust, September 1983, 15; Argy, 1981, 69, 83; *The Economist*, 1982, 9.

But what is a Eurocurrency? Eurocurrency deposits are quite simply bank deposits that are not subject to domestic banking legislation. They are generally, but not in all cases, held in countries outside or 'offshore' from the country in which they serve as legal tender. The rapid growth in Eurocurrencies shown in Figure 7.3 has accommodated a large part of the growth in world trade over the past twenty years. This growth has been in Eurocurrencies rather than other monetary forms because the Eurocurrency market has provided funds to borrowers with few conditions, while at the same time offering depositors higher interest rates than would otherwise have been available. These higher interest rates were made possible by the fewer regulations imposed on 'offshore' banking as compared with those imposed on the banks' domestic operations.

Eurodollars first became significant with the growth in the Eurodollar deposits of the USSR. In the immediate postwar years the USSR and some east European countries had had little option but to hold their dollar balances in banks in the USA. For at that time the dollar was only exchangeable or 'convertible' for sterling and other European currencies through the central banks. But in the 1950s Cold War climate, and with the return to dollar convertibility of European currencies, the USSR preferred to hold its balances in those banks in Europe which were willing to accept deposits denominated in dollars. The incentive for depositors to keep their dollar balances outside the USA had increased in 1956 with the freezing (albeit for a brief period) of some dollar deposits by the US government at the time of the Suez War. Further incentives for the growth of Eurodollars were given by restrictions imposed on interest rates in the USA, and by restrictions imposed on capital outflows by the US government after 1964 (for more details, see Tew, 1982, 105, 141). In general, these restrictions neither reduced the amount of overseas investment by US companies nor reduced the growth of US banks. Instead their main effects were on the way in which the investment was financed and on the location of the banks' expansion (see Lomax and Gutmann, 1981, 24).

The Eurodollar market grew even more rapidly in the 1970s. This was also true of the Eurocurrency market in general, for banks dealing in any 'offshore' banking centre (whether or not in Europe) enjoy the advantage of some, or even complete, exemption from *reserve* requirements. In general, central banks act as ultimate lenders, or 'lenders of last resort' to the commercial banks. That is the central banks are prepared to bail out the commercial banks in the event of difficulty. But, not surprisingly, this guarantee is not given for nothing. In return the commercial banks are subjected to controls of one sort and another. In particular, they are required to hold a mix of assets – that is lend to a variety of sources – with some bearing higher interest rates than others. Their most liquid assets, and ones which carry the lowest or even zero interest rates are those held with the central banks. These liquid assets or 'reserves' help to ensure the long-term existence of the commercial banks, but at the same time reduce their short-term profits. An exemption from, or avoidance of, such reserve requirements can make a very large difference to short-term profits (for an example, see Grubel, 1982, 41–3). And in the context of the high interest rates of the 1970s, when the cost of holding idle reserves with central banks was particularly costly, even a partial exemption from reserve requirements was valuable.

The same principles apply to all Eurocurrencies. In the same way as the fewer restrictions on overseas banking led to the growth of the Euro-dollar business in US overseas banks, so banks controlled in the UK, Germany, France, Italy and Japan developed their 'offshore' banking activities. Thus the joint effect of exchange controls and looser banking regulation overseas was to encourage the growth of the offshore banking market dealing not just in American dollars, but also in British pounds, Japanese yen, Deutschmarks, and so on. Quite simply, the 'necessary condition for the development of an offshore market for deposits and loans is that a particular financial transaction is less extensively regulated there than a similar transaction is in a domestic market' (Aliber, 1980, 512).

And so there developed a Eurosterling market in Paris, a Euromark market in Luxemburg, and a variety of Eurocurrency markets in London and in Switzerland. Offshore banking also developed in the Bahamas, the Cayman Islands and Panama. All this development was the result of competition in 'fiscal laxity' with the commercial banks based in the UK, Germany, Japan, and so on, successfully pressurizing their central banks to allow them to compete internationally by *not* being obliged to carry the reserves on overseas operations which applied to their 'home' operations. The significance of this 'fiscal laxity' was highlighted in a recent book by the American economist Paul Davidson, who writes: 'Even in the current, fashionable, anti-regulation milieu, no one could seriously argue for the *complete* absence of all government regulation in domestic credit markets; yet such a phenomenon appears to exist in so-called Euromarkets' (Davidson, 1982, 218–19; emphasis in original).

The scale of the Eurocurrency market is difficult to precisely determine because of the size of the *interbank market*. This is an approximately $1000-billion-dollar wholesale market in short-term deposits between banks so as to raise money or to offload surplus liquidity. The deposits taken by offshore banking in London have generally exceeded

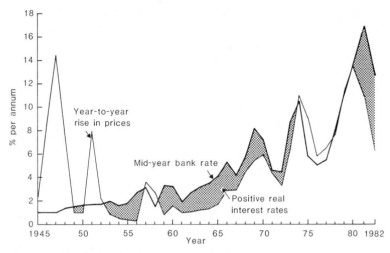

Figure 7.4 Nominal and real interest rates in the USA, 1945–82.

Sources: USA bank rate, from 1945 to 1954, the discount rate of the Federal Reserve Bank of New York; from 1955 to 1981, the Federal Funds rate: US Government, 1982, 1983, tables B67. Prices; year-to-year percentage change in consumer prices: US Government, 1982, 1983, tables B54–B55.

Note: The real interest rates would, in general, be higher if deflated by price indices for national output; they would be lower if allowance is made for tax, since interest costs are tax-deductible for many borrowers in both the corporate and household sectors.

loans to non-bank customers, so that London has supplied funds to off-shore banking elsewhere, as well as to banks doing 'home' business in the UK (see Aliber, 1980, 516). As a result, the cost of funds in the vast interbank market has been set by the London Inter-Bank Offered Rate (LIBOR). This has become the base interest rate for the Eurocurrency market in general. Thus one dollar 'could show up on the books of three or four banks as it sped round the inter-bank circuit' (Mayer, 1980, 134), and as a result, the gross liabilities of the Eurocurrency market are about double the net liabilities to the non-banking world.

But another development which is of greater concern to some economists because they allege that it generates a net increase in worldwide liquidity is the expansion of official (central bank) holdings of Euro-currencies since the early 1960s (see Tew, 1982, chapter 13; McKenzie, 1981, 126) (Figure 7.3). The incentive for this was provided by the high interest rates in the 1960s and 1970s. When the Bretton Woods system was created, nominal interest rates were relatively low compared to those offered in the 1960s – for nominal and real interest rates in the USA since the war, see Figure 7.4 (see also Morgan Guaranty Trust, March 1983, 3; OECD, 1983a, tables 10.7 and 10.9). Thus the opportunity cost to central banks of holding idle reserves rose; and as the cost rose, so central banks increased their deposits with commercial banks both inside and outside the USA. But when the reserves were redeposited in Euro-dollars, the velocity of circulation of dollars was likely to increase, since these newly deposited Eurodollars were likely to be lent to a customer (possibly an LDC in deficit) which in turn would spend the loan.

Thus, it is argued that the central banks, by recycling the dollars acquired from a US balance-of-payments deficit, effectively created loanable funds over and above those that would have been created had the dollars not been redeposited in the Eurodollar market. It is hard to believe the view of the British economist Brian Tew that the effect of the redepositing by the central banks in increasing total liquidity was only gradually realized in the 1960s but, in any case, it was not until 1971 that the Group of 10 reached an agreement to limit the amount of their reserves which they pushed back into the Eurodollar market. Unfortunately this agreement did not commit the central banks of the oil exporting countries, and as their surpluses grew with the massive oil price rise in the first half of the 1970s, so the official holdings of Eurocurrencies continued to grow (see Figure 7.3).

There is some agreement that the Euromarket credit coefficient is greater than one, with an initial deposit creating further deposits (see Parboni, 1981, 44; Argy, 1981, chapter 7). Given the multiplication of credit resulting from the lower reserve ratios of the Eurocurrency market and the reinjection of money into the system by central bank holdings of Eurocurrencies, it is not surprising that the 'euro-currency market grew on average (between 1965 and 1978) at something like three times the growth in the world money supply' (Argy, 1981, 69).

Thus through the 1960s and 1970s the monetary system has become less and less subject to the control of central banks, either individually or collectively. The system has been privatized. The IMF's direct role has shrunk despite its issue of 'new money'. For the first time, in 1969, the IMF issued 'special drawing rights' (SDRs) in proportion to members' quotas or deposits in the Fund, and since the borrowings of member countries are proportional to their quotas, the issue of SDRs effectively enlarged their 'overdraft' rights. Until 1971 the value of the SDR was fixed in terms of the dollar, but since then it has been set in terms of a weighted average or 'basket' of national currencies. But despite interest being payable on holdings of SDR, the rate was too low to provide an effective counterweight to the attractions of the Eurodollar market. As a result, the SDRs are far from being the 'principal reserve asset' that they were hailed when first issued.

Thus in terms of creating a multilateral credit system in the 1960s and 1970s the IMF was by-passed, and by the end of the 1970s SDRs were still less than 10 per cent of world reserves even with gold valued at the 'official' price. Some economists (such as the Italian, Riccardo Parboni – see 1981, 62) have claimed that this slow growth of IMF 'money' was due to American opposition. He claims that the US government has consistently opposed an extensive expansion in SDRs, either through new issues or through allowing them to be substituted for dollar holdings. Thus although the IMF has retained a prominent role as 'lender of last resort' to the poorest of the LDCs, its importance in relation to world liquidity in general has declined.

But its influence has not been replaced by that of a particular national government. American power has also declined, and in the highly integrated world economy of the 1980s with its high capital mobility, 'the autonomy of any single national monetary authority is considerably circumscribed' (McKenzie, 1981, 110; see also Davidson, 1982, 223). The Eurocurrency system increases the sensitivity of capital flows to variations in interest rates, so that any attempt by any one central bank to enforce a particular monetary policy is likely to be negated by offsetting international capital flows. And the dilemma is that the more the national governments allow their financial sectors to be internationally competitive, the less control will they have over monetary and exchange rate policies.

With the growing integration of the world economy, speculative movements of money become ever greater. Thus whereas in the massive run on the pound in August 1947 the maximum amount of daily speculation was under $100 million, in May 1971 more than $1 billion moved into the Deutschmark in less than an hour (see Cooper, 1972, 167). It is not, then, surprising that; 'exchange rate movements have been (during the 1970s) larger than justified by any kind of inflation or productivity criteria' (Lomax and Gutmann, 1981, 3). Thus the average monthly variation in effective (import-weighted) exchange rates increased in the 1960s and 1970s as follows (see UNCTAD, 1981, 76):

	for DCs	for LDCs
1967–73	1.1%	1.7%
1973–8	1.7%	2.4%

These fluctuations in exchange rates may not matter if domestic prices are also fluid, but if the latter are 'sticky' the first casualty in a country's attempt to fight inflation through monetarism is likely to be competitiveness (see Buiter and Miller, in Eltis and Sinclair, 1981, 172). The argument is that as credit is made tighter and interest rates rise in the domestic market (in say, the UK), deposits of money flow into the UK forcing up the exchange rate and making UK producers less, not more, competitive. Thus any benefits, in terms of competitiveness, from reduced domestic inflation are offset by the rising exchange rate. Furthermore, if prices are sticky domestically and continue rising, so that money balances are slow to fall in real terms, then even the monetarists will have to concede that the demand for money will fall slowly. This will mean that interest rates have to rise very sharply to 'ration' the money supply.

This rise in interest rates will have to be very sharp indeed, if banking reserve ratios are falling as they have done with the growth in the Eurocurrency market. (Indeed, as emphasized earlier, the Eurocurrency market has grown precisely because of the lower reserve requirements in the less regulated offshore markets.) For the lower the reserve ratio, the greater the rise in the interest rate which the central bank has to impose in order to force the commercial banks to cut back on their lending (see M. Miller, 1981, 75–7). And so we have the following sequence:

A crisis occurs and exchange or interest rate controls are imposed by one or more countries;

with high capital mobility and banking competition, attempts to maximize banking profits by escaping from the controls result in a rapid growth of the Eurocurrency market;

this means that average banking reserve ratios fall;

national monetary policies must then be *highly* restrictive to cut back on domestic money demand;

the resulting sharp rise in interest rates attracts short-term funds into the economy which raises the exchange rate;

this rise in the exchange rate chokes off production both for exports and import substitutes and reduces output;

and the more sticky are domestic prices and wages, the greater the drop in output.

Thus we have a situation in which 'authorities who try to control money without penalising the banking industry will tend, in a world of floating rates and mobile financial capital, to control money by damaging non-banking – largely manufacturing – industry' (ibid., 77).

From a cost-of-production viewpoint, it is easy to see that a Keynes-type conflict between speculation and enterprise will be sharpened, not reduced by international capital mobility. With greater fluctuations in interest and exchange rates, there is likely to be an ever increasing emphasis given by companies to liquidity and short-term investments. In this view the long-term effects of greater capital mobility are likely to be harmful.

The viewpoint of an abstract labour theorist differs in emphasizing the *capitalist* context of international money. In this view the relationship between the rate of interest (determined by the demand and supply for money-*capital*) and the overall rate of profit is emphasized. Thus the lower the rate of profit-in-general, the more serious will be the effect of fluctuations in interest rates. Thus in a crisis, when the rate of profit-in-general has fallen to a low level and capital accumulation has been over-extended relative to the rate of exploitation, the effects of 'speculation' are likely to be particularly severe, making the prospects for profit-in-enterprise even less certain than before. Thus the falling rate of profit is likely to be associated with an acute crisis of confidence in the international financial system. There was such a crisis in the mid-1970s, and a further, deeper crisis is occurring in the 1980s.

The financial crisis of the 1970s and 1980s

In 1982 concern was expressed by a number of top-level bankers about the stability of the international monetary system. For example, the ex-managing director of the IMF, Johannes Witteveen, was reported as saying that 'the chances of an early international banking crisis are undoubtedly higher than for many years past' (*The Economist*, 16 October 1982, 21), and in the following month the chairman of the Basle Committee of Central Bank Supervisors, Peter Cooke, urged commercial banks to increase their provisions for international bad debts, since: 'we find ourselves in a situation where there has been a deterioration of assets generally' (*Financial Times*, 5 November 1982). The cause of this instability was the overexpansion of credit (particularly through the Eurocurrency market) in the 1960s and 1970s, leading to a crisis which has its roots in the overaccumulation of capital and declining profitability.

This general crisis of a declining rate of profit has been exacerbated by the imbalances caused by the sharp rise in the price of oil in 1973–4 (see Figure 6.5, p. 148). This caused severe adjustment problems, similar to those analysed by Marx in the context of a poor grain harvest. Marx had argued in the *Grundrisse* that such a 'grain crisis' could cause imbalances in the economy which were likely to be reflected in a financial crisis (see Marx, 1973a, 129–30). Similarly, the fourfold increase in oil prices at the end of 1973 and the beginning of 1974 had its reflections in a financial crisis. In 1973 the West German Hessische Landesbank suffered heavy losses, the US National Bank of San Diego collapsed and the Israel–British Bank ran into problems. But in June of the following year there was an even greater crash, when the prominent West German Bankhaus I. D. Herstatt collapsed. Herstatt's collapse gave rise to panic in the international monetary system, particularly in the Eurodollar market: 'For months afterwards, the euro-dollar market remained sub-dued [and] interest rates in it jumped sharply' (Reid, 1982, 116).

It was in the wake of the Herstatt collapse, in the second half of 1974, that the governors of the central banks of the Group of 10 (see Table 7.3) attempted to tighten the regulation of the commercial banks and to clarify the central banks' lender-of-last-resort responsibilities to overseas banks. Specifically the principle was adopted that 'host' central banks would be primarily responsible for the losses of the *subsidiaries* of banks, while the 'source' central banks would have to bail out the *branches* of commercial banks (see Artis and Lewis, 1981, 105). Thus if the British-based Barclays Bank had a subsidiary company in the USA which was in trouble, the primary responsibility for the solvency of that subsidiary company seemed to rest with the American Central Bank (the Federal Reserve). Whereas, if Barclays was in trouble, the losses of its American branches would have to be met by the British central bank (the Bank of England). The agreement was hazy since not only were these responsi-bilities labelled as 'primary' ones, but also an attempt was made to dis-tinguish between the related issues of solvency and liquidity.

Although in the early 1980s this lack of clarity in the agreement was revealed, the central banks' new principle of parental responsibility stimulated improvements in supervision. In 1975 the Basle-based Com-mittee on Banking Regulations and Supervisory Practices (later to be renamed the Standing Committee of Banking Supervisory Authorities) was established to tighten and co-ordinate banking supervision among the Group of 10, plus Switzerland and Luxemburg. (The Committee is also sometimes referred to as the Cooke Committee after the present chairman, Peter Cooke.)

According to an account of these developments by the *Financial Times* journalist, Margaret Reid, much of the initiative for this Basle Concor-dat was taken by the then Governor of the Bank of England, Gordon Richardson. But then, as Reid points out, '[Richardson] had had recent experience through the Lifeboat of just such a problem of crumbling confidence' (Reid, 1982, 116). The 'Lifeboat' referred to was the rescue operation launched by the Bank of England in early 1974 to bail out major British commercial banks as a number of secondary or fringe banks went bust (see ibid., chapter 7). There were similar rescue schemes in the USA, so that credit expanded in both the USA and UK, and as it did so, real interest rates fell (see Figure 7.4). But profitability also continued to decline, as did fixed investment, and so the financial crisis was deferred by the expansion of bank credit only to reappear in the early 1980s. In July 1979 the Governor of the Bank of England had told a conference; 'it would . . . be prudent for those who work in the supervisory area to be alert to the possibility that the international banking system may be tested again in the next few years' (ibid., 118). The Governor was right – the banking system did come under strain in the next few years.

Again the financial crisis was triggered by a sharp rise in the price of oil (see Figure 6.5), this time resulting from the Iran–Iraq war. As the crisis deepened, so the demand for money as a means of payment rose, but restrictive monetary policies were followed by the Thatcher and Reagan governments elected in 1979 and 1980 respectively, and interest rates rose in real as well as in nominal terms.

In 1982 the financial crisis broke; there was a sharp rise in bankruptcies among industrial capital, and this put pressure on a number of banks and other financial institutions. In May 1982 the American broking firm Drysdale went bust and, as a result, Chase Manhattan Bank suffered heavy losses and the Federal Reserve Bank was forced to pump some $3 billion into the banking system (*The Economist*, 16 October 1982, 21). In mid-1982 the chairman of Banco Ambrosiano, Italy's largest private bank, was found dead under a London bridge as that bank ran into trouble. And as it was revealed that BAH, Ambrosiano's financial affiliate in Luxemburg had failed, the Basle Concordat was put to the test, as BAH's creditors looked to the Italian central bank for payment. The response was not as generous as BAH's creditors hoped, and the Ambrosiano case revealed that 'not all host authorities accept the same degree of responsibility' (see *ibid.*). (For this and other limitations of the present system of international regulation of banking, see the 1982 semi-official report by Richard Dale of the USA-based Brookings Institution on *Bank Supervision Around the World*.)

But worse was to follow. In August 1982 Mexico suspended its foreign exchange dealings as it ran into difficulties in meeting interest and capital payments on its debts. About three-quarters of its $80 billion official external debt was due to be repaid to commercial banks, with more than $20 billion being owed to American banks. But Mexico was not the only LDC claiming that it had to reschedule its debts and defer

Table 7.4 The debts of LDCs and eastern Europe to
the commercial banks 1981

	Total at end-1981 ($ billion)	*US banks' % share of debt*
Non-OPEC LDCs[1]		
Mexico	57	38
Brazil	53	32
Argentina	25	34
Korea	20	45
Chile	11	55
Philippines	10	53
Others	83	22–75
	259	36
OPEC LDCs		
Venezuela	26	40
Others	47	16–47
	73	32
Total LDCs	332	35
Eastern Europe		
USSR	16	3
Poland	15	13
East Germany	11	9
Yugoslavia	11	25
Others	19	7–15
	72	11

Source: Morgan Guaranty Trust, October 1982, table 2.

Note:
1 Excludes countries that are offshore banking centres.

repayments. Brazil and Argentina were also revealed as being likely to default, and their debts, like Mexico's, were very much higher than those of Poland which previously had run into problems (see Table 7.4).

An immediate rescue operation to save Mexico (and the commercial banks which were owed money by Mexico) was launched by the IMF, the Bank of International Settlements (BIS) and their member central banks, but at the time of writing (1984–5), the financial crisis persists. There is a real danger that lending to countries as well as companies will be restricted sharply as individual commercial banks try to protect themselves against bankruptcy. Such evasive action by individual banks is likely to result in collective bankruptcy, for the scale of the crisis is considerable. Between 1975 and the end of 1983 the debts of more than twenty countries were rescheduled, as the terms of trade of the LDCs (particularly for those not exporting oil) deteriorated (see Table 4.3) and real interest rates rose.

As the terms of trade deteriorated, and as interest rates rose, so did the debt repayment burden. As pointed out previously, much of the lending to the LDCs in the 1970s had come from the commercial banks, and much of this had been on a short-term basis. This meant that by the late 1970s a growing proportion of the debt was having to be rolled-over very frequently. In general, the capital was rolled-over and interest paid because, the banks claimed, if interest payments were not met, they would be forced to classify the loans as 'non-performing assets'. In other words, for the banks, 'rolling loans gather no loss'. But as the loans were rolled-over, so the terms became more stringent, with repayment periods shortened and interest rates raised.

Thus by the end of 1981, of the total debt of $271 billion owed to commercial banks by twenty-one major LDCs, almost one-half – about $127 billion – was due to be repaid in a year or less (see Morgan Guaranty Trust, May 1982, 8). For the non-oil exporting LDCs, the ratio of debt payments (on medium- and long-term debt) to exports of goods and services rose from 21 per cent in 1973 to 37 per cent in 1982. If short-term debt is included, the debt service ratio for twenty-one major LDC borrowers rises from something like 30 per cent to more than 70 per cent (see ibid., February 1983, 5). And for some countries, particularly the 'middle-income' countries in Latin America, the debt service ratio (including short-term debt) in the late 1970s was very high indeed (see Table 7.5).

As debts were rescheduled, so interest rates were raised. In 1979 and 1980 the interest rate on new loans contracted by Third World countries was rarely above LIBOR (London Inter-Bank Offered Rate) plus 1 per cent. But in 1982–3 the rates on recontracted loans were being set at 2 per cent or more above LIBOR with, in addition, refinancing commissions of 1–1.5 per cent being charged (see *South*, July 1983, 63; Bogdanowicz-Bindert, 1983, 830). Given the scale of Third World debt, the burden of a 1 per cent rise in interest rates can be enormous. The total outstanding external debt of non-oil developing countries rose from

$130 billion in 1973 to $336 billion in 1978 to $664 billion in 1983 (see
IMF, 1983, table 32). Clearly a rise in the interest rate of 1 per cent
increases the servicing burden by almost $7 billion a year, or almost $20
million a day.

It is clear that the present financial balance is delicate; the crisis acute;
the basis for confidence fragile. This is particularly evident when the

Table 7.5 LDCs and debt: the growing burden in the 1970s and 1980s

All non-oil exporting LDCs	1973	1977	1982
Debt service payments		*($ billion)*	
interest	4.6	10.1	40.8
repayments	10.7	20.6	67.0
total	15.3	30.7	107.8
Debt service as % of exports of goods and services		*(%)*	
interest payments ratio	5	8	12
repayment ratio	16	17	25
total debt service ratio	21	25	37

The top ten debtor LDCs, 1982	*Debt service payments as % of exports of goods and services*		
	Total	*Interest*	*Capital repayments*
Argentina	179	44	135
Mexico[1]	129	37	92
Ecuador	122	30	92
Brazil	122	45	77
Chile	116	40	76
Venezuela[1]	95	14	81
Colombia	94	25	69
Philippines	91	18	73
Peru	90	21	69
Turkey	68	13	55

Sources: IMF, 1982, 33; Morgan Guaranty Trust, October 1982; Cline, 1983, 130–1.

Note:
1 These countries are net oil exporters.

Table 7.6 Banks and capital-asset ratios: the world's twenty biggest banks, 1981

Bank (and head office)	Total assets ($ billion)	Capital and reserves ($ billion)	Capital-asset ratio (%)
Bank of America Corporation (San Francisco)	116	4.1	3.5
Citicorp (New York)	113	4.3	3.8
Banque Nationale de Paris (Paris)	106	1.4	1.3
Credit Agricole (Paris)	98	4.9	5.0
Credit Lyonnais (Paris)	94	0.9	1.0
Barclays Group (London)	93	4.3	4.7
Société Générale (Paris)	87	n.a.	1.6 (1980)
Dai-Ichi Kangyo Bank (Tokyo)	85	2.8	3.3
Deutsche Bank (Frankfurt)	85	2.6	3.1
National Westminster Bank (London)	83	4.2	5.1
Sumitomo Bank (Osaka)	79	2.5	3.1
Midland Bank (London)	78	2.8	3.5
Fuji Bank (Tokyo)	76	2.7	3.5
Mitsubishi Bank (Tokyo)	76	2.5	3.3
Chase Manhattan Corp (New York)	74	3.5	4.8
Royal Bank of Canada (Montreal)	70	2.1	3.0
Sanwa Bank (Osaka)	68	2.3	3.4
Banco do Brasil (Brasilia)	65	4.3	6.6
Dresdner Bank (Frankfurt)	58	1.7	2.9
Norinchukin Bank (Tokyo)	57	0.3	0.6

Source: The Banker, June 1982, p. 185.

capital base of the commercial banks is examined. As Marx pointed out: 'The more advanced is bourgeois production, the more these [reserve] funds are restricted to the indispensable minimum' (Marx, 1977, 147); and so we find that in 1981 the ratio of the banks' own capital to total assets was around 4 per cent (see Table 7.6); whereas in the early nineteenth century the ratio had been about 40 per cent (see Revell, 1980). Thus, for example, the loans to Mexico from the world's largest private bank (Bank of America) amount to more than 70 per cent of the bank's capital (*The Economist*, 16 October 1982, 23), and the nine largest US banks have nearly 300 per cent of their capital exposed in loans to developing and east European countries (see Cline, 1983, 121).

Thus the banks have a collective interest in the debts of countries such as Mexico being rolled-over. If they are not rolled-over, the pressure (both direct and indirect) on the banks' capital resources increases. Indirect pressure comes from the recessionary effects of an enforced cut-back in imports by the defaulting countries. It has been estimated that if net bank lending to the LDCs expands at 'only' 10 per cent a year compared with the recent annual growth rate of 20 per cent, income in the OECD countries will be at least 0.5 per cent lower (see Morgan Guaranty Trust, October 1982, 7). This puts increased pressure on the already hard-pressed industrial capital of the OECD countries, and defaults on their debts to the banks become even more likely. Very large companies such as AEG in Germany, Massey-Ferguson in Canada, or International Harvester in the USA, which have been on the brink of bankruptcy, might be tipped over the edge.

Thus the thirst for money which typifies the present financial crisis continues. If that thirst is not quenched, the financial crisis will become even sharper and the depression even more severe. In the second half of 1982 there was a sharp drop in new international bank lending from the private banks, but since then agreement has been reached for an increase (an effective doubling) in the IMF's resources. First, quotas have been increased by about one-half, and in 1983 the amounts available under the IMF's general arrangements to borrow (GAB) were increased. Nevertheless, many economists think that these resources are likely to be less than adequate to resolve the financial crisis; they point out that these increases will contribute only about $22 billion in new lending, whereas the reserves of the LDCs have declined by more than $80 billion in two years (1981 and 1982). And even if the IMF's quotas were doubled – a move which has been resisted by the US government – the Fund's resources would still be no more than about 5 per cent of world imports in 1983–4 compared with 12 per cent in the mid-1960s (see ODI, 1983, 5).

Although it is likely that these increases in the IMF's resources – supplemented by loans from Saudi Arabia – will give some renewed impetus to commercial bank lending (see Morgan Guaranty Trust, February 1983, 12), such an extension of credit will do little to resolve the longer-term basis of the crisis, namely the declining rate of profit. Once again, as in the mid-1970s, the crisis may be deferred but its root cause not eradicated. This is the view from the left. It is one which is pessimistic about radical reforms being achieved within the framework of capitalism. Thus the Latin America Bureau's recent booklet on the IMF and Latin America argues: 'It is difficult to see . . . how proposals for increased lending will resolve LDC problems in anything but the immediate future' (LAB, 1983, 118).

In general, the left sees the burden of the crisis as most likely to fall on the poor, if capitalism is to continue. The international monetary system, as presently structured, is seen as highly unstable. In particular, the Eurodollar credit system is seen as greatly reducing the power of democratically elected governments as well as multiplying the risk of a banking crash (see Coakley and Harris, 1983, 49).

By contrast, those on the right of the political spectrum see less cause for alarm in the present 'debt crisis'. The latter is seen as arising from the mismanagement of economies in the DCs as well as, but particularly, in the debtor countries. The solution is seen as a continuation of stringent financial control and of 'getting the prices right' – in particular, getting exchange rates right. If such policies lead to defaults, then this 'would impose losses on the parties that should bear them – bank stockholders and management personnel whose jobs would be at stake' (Schwartz, 1984, 130).

The prospect of widespread defaults is not viewed so optimistically by cost-of-production theorists. In their view widespread defaults, whether caused by a squeeze or initiated by a 'debtors' cartel', would set off a chain reaction and lead to a worldwide banking collapse. If the bank debt is to be restructured, it is argued that it needs to be done systematically. There have, for example, been proposals for international institutions to take over the debts of the commercial banks, perhaps at a discount (see Bogdanowicz-Bindert, 1983, 835). In any case, among these economists, there is agreement that internatioinal institutions, such as the IMF, need to provide more, not less, money for the Third World. And this money needs to be lent over long periods. For the problems of the Third World are seen as arising not so much from internal mismanagement, but rather from external forces. Writers such as William Cline, Sidney Dell and Tony Killick all point to a similar source (see Cline, 1983; Dell, 1981; Killick, 1984a, chapter 8). In Cline's words, 'the analysis . . . shows the overwhelming rate of exogenous shocks in the world economy in creating the current situation (oil price shocks, sharply higher interest rates, and declining export prices and volumes caused by global recession)' (Cline, 1983, 123). Cline's estimates are shown in Table 7.7.

Given such a structural problem, devaluation is no panacea. Dell points to not only social and political, but also economic, objections to devaluation (see Dell, 1981, 20–1). He argues that 'for countries whose exports consist mainly of primary products . . . it cannot be assumed that an increased share of the market can invariably be obtained by cutting export prices in terms of foreign currency, with or without devaluation' (ibid., 21). To deal with the exogenous shocks imposed on them the LDCs need more time and 'exogenous money' (ibid., 24). But new loans

Table 7.7 Impact of exogenous shocks on external debt of non-oil developing countries

Effect	Amount ($ billion)
Oil price increase in excess of US inflation, 1974–82 cumulative[1]	260
Real interest rate in excess of 1961–80 average: 1981 and 1982	41
Terms of trade loss, 1981–2	79
Export volume loss caused by world recession: 1981–2	21
Total	401
Memorandum items	
Total debt: 1973	130
1982	612
Increase: 1973–82	482

Source: Cline, 1983, table 4.

Note:
1 Net oil importers only.

are not being provided on the scale or on the terms called for. In 1983 the borrowings of developing countries were 24 per cent down on the 1982 level of borrowings, and the lowest total for this group of countries since 1977 (see Morgan Guaranty Trust, January 1984, 2). As a result, Cline argues, there is some cause for concern about the growing incentive to default (Cline, 1983, 88), for in 1983 the developing countries made net *payments* of $12 billion to the commercial banks compared to net *receipts* two years earlier of $16 billion (*Financial Times*, 19 March 1984).

If there are widespread defaults, the fear of a chain reaction of banking collapses remains. For despite some attempt in 1983 to clarify the earlier Basle Concordat on supervisory responsibilities and jurisdiction, there is still considerable vagueness about the 'lender-of-last-resort' responsibilities (see Dale, 1983; Cline, 1983, 103–4).

The *fundamental* basis of the instability remains, namely capitalist competition in both the industrial and financial spheres. The increasing integration of world capitalism continues, along with the threat of its disintegration. At the end of 1980 exchange controls were relaxed in Japan, so opening up 'a further alternative source of funds to the corporate sector' (*Barclays Bank Review*, August 1981, 56), and at the end of 1981 new offshore banking centres (International Banking Facilities) were created in the USA (notably in New York) in response to pressure from

US banks to counteract the alleged loss of Eurobanking business for them. Thus the competition in 'fiscal laxity' continues, as does the considerable uncertainty about the lender-of-last-resort responsibilities. At the same time, the links between banks are strong. At present UK banks have a higher volume of loans to banks in offshore centres than directly to non-oil LDCs and OPEC countries combined (ODI, 1983, 3). Thus if one large bank goes under, it is likely to drag the others down with it.

A basic contradiction remains. If the national banking regulations and controls are loose, the demand for bank credit is met from 'traditional' channels; while if they are tight, then financial innovations (such as the Eurocurrency market) may arise to meet the demand (see McKenzie, 1981).

McKenzie argues that 'Ultimately, any regulations governing activities undertaken within the system will require the careful coordination of all international monetary policies' (ibid., 110). But can such a co-ordination be achieved without nationalizing the banking industry? This is a question raised by Davidson, when he writes: 'As long as we leave banking functions to the private sector and profit-making proclivities, bankers will, given sufficient time and the absence of vigilant control, invent devices to circumvent government and constitutional rules concerning the money supply if such restraints hamper the process of endogenous finance' (Davidson, 1982, 228–9). Thus there seems to be a need for vigilant control of the banks at an international level, or the nationalization at the level of individual countries of the banking industry. But then these alternatives may lead to further controls. For as is emphasized in Section 7.3, the internationalization of financial capital has been accompanied by the internationalization of industrial capital. The growth of the international money market and the internationalization of industrial capital have been parallel, symbiotic developments. They must be considered together.

7.3 TRANSNATIONAL CORPORATIONS

The internationalization of industrial capital

Transnational corporations (TNCs) – otherwise known as multinational corporations (MNCs) or multinational enterprises (MNEs) – are broadly defined as those corporations which have direct and majority control over investment outside the 'home' countries in which they are based. Therefore, such investments are usually referred to as direct foreign investments. Considering their importance in the world economy, the information on TNCs is sparse, although in recent years the quality and amount of information has improved. The main focus of the UN's Centre on Transnational Corporations, since its start in 1975, has been on improving the collection of information on TNCs.

Data collected by the Centre show that there are more than 10,000 TNCs, and that these TNCs control the activities of more than 80,000 affiliates and subsidiaries in the world. Of these, about three-quarters are located in the richer developed countries. The stock of direct foreign investment in the world in 1978 was $369 billion (Stopford *et al.*, 1980, xiv), and today is considerably more than $400 billion. Ten years ago it was less than one-third of that, revealing an annual growth rate of more than 11 per cent, far faster than the growth in income of the rich countries over the same period.

The growth of the TNC is largely a post Second World War phenomenon and has paralleled the growing concentration and centralization of capital in the DCs. This growth in centralization has been accompanied by the increasing internationalization of production within the large corporations. For most of the last century international trade has grown faster than world production and the international flow of capital has been significant. But whereas in the period before the Second World War, and particularly in the half-century before the First World War, most of the capital investment was in 'portfolio' or fixed interest form without direct control, the past three decades have been characterized by a massive flow of direct investment and by the growth of the TNC; and by 1979 about two-fifths of the $500 billion US assets held abroad consisted of direct investment. It is the period since the Second World War which has seen the development of the international car, cassette recorder, television, or home computer with different components being produced in different countries under the same corporate control.

This integration of production presents formidable problems of control for individual states. These problems confront the governments of the rich DCs as well as those of the poorer LDCs, since most of the flow of direct foreign investment has taken place between the rich countries. By the mid-1970s the greatest proportion had been invested in Canada (about 17 per cent of the world total), followed by the USA (12 per cent), the UK (9 per cent), and West Germany (8 per cent), with Japan relatively untouched with a mere 1 per cent, the latter being much less than the direct investments in some of the LDCs, such as Brazil (4 per cent) Indonesia (3 per cent) and Mexico (2 per cent). About one-half of the investment in the rich north is in the manufacturing sector with the rest shared equally between extractive industries and services. In the LDCs the pattern of investment varies considerably with the majority of the direct foreign investment in the OPEC countries being in

Table 7.8 The world's twenty biggest industrial TNCs

Name of corporation	Country	Industry	Total sales (1978) ($ billion)	Sales of overseas subsidiaries as a % of total corporation sales (1978)
Exxon	USA	Petroleum	64	74
General Motors	USA	Motor vehicles	63	22
Royal Dutch/Shell Group of Companies	Netherlands/UK	Petroleum	46	58
Ford Motor Co.	USA	Motor vehicles	43	35
Mobil	USA	Petroleum	37	60
Texaco	USA	Petroleum	29	66
British Petroleum	UK	Petroleum	28	78
Standard Oil of California	USA	Petroleum	24	59
International Business Machines	USA	Office equipment	21	52
Gulf Oil	USA	Petroleum	20	51
General Electric Co.	USA	Electrical	20	20
Unilever Ltd/Unilever NV	UK/Netherlands	Food, drink and tobacco	19	33
Standard Oil (Indiana)	USA	Petroleum	16	26
Ente Nazionale Idrocarburi	Italy	Petroleum	16	25
VEBA AG	Germany	Petroleum	16	8
Fiat SpA	Italy	Motor vehicles	16	N/A
International Telephone & Telegraph	USA	Electrical	15	52
NV Philips Gloeilampenfabrieken	Netherlands	Electrical	15	91
Siemens AG	Germany	Electrical	14	12
Chrysler	USA	Motor vehicles	14	19

the extractive industries (notably oil), whereas in India, Brazil and Mexico the major target was manufacturing.

The centralization of capital

Since size and activity overseas are, as one might expect, closely associated, TNCs have grown with the increasing *centralization* of economic power in the hands of fewer and fewer corporations. Information on centralization is generally more widely available for the extractive and manufacturing sectors than for the banking and other 'service' sectors, and Table 7.8 lists the twenty biggest of the world's industrial TNCs. As the table shows, the sales of each of the top ten TNCs in 1978 exceeded $20 billion, with the net output of each of them probably exceeding $7 billion, the latter equivalent to the total income of Bangladesh in the same year. Thus the biggest of the TNCs are very big indeed.

The sales of the largest TNC of all – the oil company, Exxon Corporation – average about $7 million per hour, and its net output in 1978 was larger than the net output (or gross domestic product) or more than seventy of the 100 or so LDCs. The combined net output of the fifty largest industrial TNCs was more than double India's net output, and the largest 500 companies in the world probably 'account' for more than 15 per cent of the world's income. In general, the larger the corporation, the larger the ratio of overseas to total sales.

But not only is industrial capital highly centralized, the centralization process continues. The largest corporations have growth rates higher than the economies in which they are based, as shown in Table 7.9. The

Table 7.9 The industrial TNCs grow faster

	Average growth rate (in sales) of the largest industrial TNCs (% p.a.) (1957–77)	Average growth rate of national industrial production (% p.a.) (1960–77)
Japan	15	9
France	15	5
West Germany	13	4
USA	8	4
UK	8	2
Canada	8	5

Sources: Average growth rate of the largest industrial TNCs: Droucopoulos, 1981, 39, table 2; average growth rate of national industrial production: US Government, 1981, table B-108.

centralization process is encouraged by economies of scale in production, research and development, finance and marketing, and is facilitated by the periodic crises of capitalism. For example, in the USA each crisis and drop in the level of output is accompanied by a rise in bankruptcies. In 1970 the index of industrial production in the USA fell by about 3 per cent, and in the same year there was an increase in bankruptcies (as measured by the value of company liabilities involved) of more than 65 per cent; similarly, in 1975 the index of industrial production fell by about 9 per cent, and business failures again rose – this time by more than 43 per cent (see US Government, 1981, table B-91). These business failures devalue capital and give the big fish an opportunity to swallow up the small, for not only do the larger corporations have greater financial resources to withstand the crises, but it is rare for governments to allow the largest corporations – for example, Chrysler – to collapse.

The (relative) decline of British and American TNCs

Table 7.9 shows that Japanese, French and German TNCs grew faster than those based in the UK and the USA in the 1960s and 1970s. As a result of the slower growth of American and British companies, the share of the USA in the total stock of direct foreign investment fell from 50 per cent in 1967 to 45 per cent in 1977, while the British share fell from 15 to 11 per cent over the same period. Nevertheless, the American and British shares are still the largest, with West Germany (9 per cent in 1978) and Japan (7 per cent in 1978) running third and fourth respectively. It is, then, hardly surprising to find that twenty-seven out of the top fifty industrial TNCs are based in the USA.

A similar American dominance is found in the *banking* sector. Information on transnational banks (TNBs) is even less detailed than the data on industrial transnationals, but a 1981 report by the UN Centre on Transnational Corporations revealed that of eighty-four TNBs having subsidiaries or branches in five or more countries in 1975, twenty-two were based in the USA, and ten each in Japan and the UK (UNCTC, 1981). However, the largest of the Japanese banks are bigger than those in other countries, and they accounted for 22 per cent of the total assets of the world's biggest 500 TNBs (outside the USSR and the other so-called 'socialist' countries). This is considerably more than the 15 per cent share of the biggest US banks. The same pattern of growth is evident in the banking as in the industrial sector, with TNBs in general growing rapidly (accompanying the rapid growth of the Eurocurrency

Table 7.10 The growth of the biggest TNBs – especially rapid for Japanese, French and German banks

	Share of deposits of top 500 banks %			Name	World's ten biggest TNBs	
	1960	*1970*	*1979*		*1978 assets ($ billion)*	*Annual % growth in assets (1973–8)*
USA	47	33	15	Bank America	92	14
				Citicorp	84	14
				Chase Manhattan	60	10
Japan	9	17	22	Dai-Ichi Kangyo	66	18
France	4	5	9	Banque Nationale de Paris	78	21
				Credit Lyonnais	74	21
West Germany	5	9	14	Deutsche Bank	80	27
				Dresdner Bank	61	24
UK	11	7	6	Barclays	49	12
				National Westminster	45	10

Source: Rhoades, 1983, 435; UNCTC, 1981, tables 1 and 15.

markets), but with Japanese, German and French TNBs all growing faster than their British and American competitors (see Table 7.10).

Some views on TNCs

So far in this brief discussion of TNCs we have a picture as follows:

(1) a massive growth in direct foreign investment and of TNCs since the Second World War, and particularly since 1960;
(2) American TNCs being dominant and controlling almost half of the world's transnational capital;
(3) American dominance, however, being challenged in the 1970s by Japanese, French and West German TNCs in both the industrial and financial sectors.

But what are the effects of this growth in the TNCs? Should the TNCs' operations be controlled, and if so how? There is no agreed answer to these questions; indeed, there are considerable disagreements between economists and politicians on such issues.

Those on the right of the political spectrum, the subjective preference theorists, argue that the effects of TNCs cannot and should not be judged simply in terms of capital flows to and from the countries in which they operate, since, they claim, the TNCs produce an increase in value added in those countries. That is the profits remitted by the TNCs from the LDCs are not a full measure of the value created by their activities. In this view the TNCs provide organizational skills which *supplement* rather than substitute for local resources. Thus the profits are a reward for exceptional services rendered. Therefore, controls on TNCs' activities are unnecessary and nationalization is likely to be counterproductive, for as the British economist Peter Bauer has put it: 'Capital is much more likely to be productive when deployed by those groups and persons who accumulated it because accumulation and effective deployment require much the same abilities, motivations and institutions' (Bauer, 1976, 103).

This view is in marked contrast to that of the 'dependency' or 'underdevelopment' group of economists, who have argued that the gains to the TNCs are generally at the expense of the 'host' countries, and particularly the LDCs. Here the argument is that advanced monopoly capitalism is senile and stagnant in the richer developed countries, and that any increases in income accruing to the DCs are generally at the expense of the LDCs, so that the latter suffer from the 'development-of-underdevelopment'. The TNCs are an important agent of this underdevelopment inasmuch as the profits which they drain from the poor peripheral countries are greater than the amounts invested. In the view of this 'dependency' group the TNCs do not supplement local resources; indeed, they are a poor substitute for them, since with more than 90 per cent of research and development concentrated in the rich countries, the TNCs adopt inappropriate, capital-intensive technologies in the poor periphery, so creating little employment. The TNCs are also said to generate inappropriate patterns of consumption, forcing processed foods on semi-literate and helpless populations with the aid of advertising which is misleading but persuasive. For the advertising agencies are concentrated in the DCs; of the biggest fifty advertising agencies in the world, thirty-six are based in the USA, and ten in Japan (see UNCTC, 1979).

Furthermore, it is argued, the drain of surplus from the LDCs revealed through the official balance-of-payments figures probably *understates* the losses to the Third World arising from TNC activities. An increasing proportion of world trade – probably, by the late 1970s as much as one-third of the total trade outside the 'socialist' or centrally planned economies – consists of trade *within* the TNCs. This intrafirm trade provides, it is argued, a golden opportunity for the practice of 'transfer pricing', whereby the TNCs fix their prices between subsidiaries so as to reduce taxes on profits or to avoid controls on profit remittances, or even to swindle local minority shareholders in joint ventures. Local directors in joint ventures are likely to find it difficult – even if they want to – to enforce independent, 'arm's length' prices, since for many components or services such free market prices may be difficult to determine (for a fuller discussion of transfer pricing, see Murray, 1981).

But this is not all. In addition to the extra drain arising from transfer pricing, further losses may arise from other characteristics of TNC operations. It has been alleged that TNCs restrict the exports of their subsidiaries back to their 'home' country to prevent intrafirm competition, so that the exporting potential of the LDCs is not realized (see UNCTAD, 1978). Yet another argument is that for certain products, particularly those such as clothing that are exported back by the TNCs from free trade zones (FTZs) in the newly industrializing countries, the TNCs absorb the export quotas which would otherwise be available to local firms. The dependency theorists argue that the operations of the TNCs in these FTZs illustrate, perhaps in a somewhat exaggerated form, the costs of TNC activities in general. The TNC activities in FTZs are isolated, enclave activities with few linkages with the rest of the economy; the profits are not taxed and the labourforce is so low paid that its costs of reproduction are borne by other sectors of the economy. This 'superexploitation' is possible because of the enclave nature of the workforce. Rapidly turning over, consisting disproportionately of women and isolated in the free trade zones, the prospects for trade union organization among the workforce are bleak.

But if there are so many losses arising from the operations of the TNCs, why are they allowed in to the LDCs? Briefly, two reasons are given by the dependency theorists; first, the TNCs are alleged to have monopoly control over 'packages' of technology and markets; and secondly, they effectively bribe the local politicians to gain access. Thus whereas the view of the Brandt Commission (see Brandt, 1980, 200) is that the TNCs need to be subjected to codes of conduct (such as those devised by the OECD in 1976 and by the ILO in 1977 – for details, see Labour Party, 1977, appendices) which would provide more systematic information on their activities, the dependency theorists argue that such codes of conduct will not effectively control the TNCs. Indeed, they question whether there is the will to control TNCs given the present political structure in most LDCs.

As argued earlier, the views of the 'dependency' theorists have been attacked by a number of economists from a Marxist direction – see, for example, Brenner 1977. The Marxists question whether the TNCs monopolize markets as depicted by the dependency theorists. In contrast, they emphasize the voracious competition between the TNCs, although they do agree that the TNCs have immense economic and political power as a *group*. Thus they agree with the dependency theorists that the TNCs tend to dominate governments as well as aspects of 'cultural' life, including the press (see Labour Research Department, 1981).

But from the viewpoint of the orthodox abstract labour theorists, *all* capital is suspect, not just the TNCs. Thus an expansion of those TNCs based in LDCs such as Brazil, India, or South Korea is unlikely to provide a solution to mass poverty in the world. For the Marxists, the control of TNCs then becomes a means to an end, not an end in itself. The crucial question is: who does the controlling, and on whose behalf?

For the abstract labour theorists, the view presented by the Brandt Commission of national governments in the north and south representing more or less equally the various groups in society is grossly misleading. This is not to say that codes of conduct or the slightly tighter planning agreements proposed (but not implemented) by the 1974–9 Labour government in the UK (see Labour Party, 1977, 52) should not be supported. They should. Support may also be warranted for attempts by regional groupings of countries such as the Andean Pact or the European Economic Commission (EEC) to impose conditions on the operations of TNCs in the member countries. Indeed, this is one argument from the left in Britain for continuing British membership of the EEC, namely that the TNCs are so transnational, so big and so powerful that effective countervailing power has to be at the international level (see Rowthorn and Grahl, 1982).

Nevertheless, there are considerable doubts on the left about the willingness and ability of social democratic governments to control TNC activities. There are those on the left who have argued that the internationalization of productive capital has tended to weaken the nation-state and heavily circumscribed the power of national governments. For example, Robin Murray has argued that 'there is a growing territorial non-coincidence between extending capital and its domestic state' (Murray, in Radice, 1975, 129), and that 'from British experience at least, it is the corporate rather than the national division of labour that dominates and determines the features of the international economy' (Murray, 1973, 35). Views of this sort have been challenged by Bill Warren, who has argued that 'the idea of national states cowering before the Paul Chambers [ex-head of the British chemical TNC, Imperial Chemical Industries] of this world is wholly fanciful; the reality is national states deliberately encouraging the creation of gigantic competitive units' (Warren, in Radice, 1975, 137).

Thus Warren's argument is that capital has not become stateless. A further discussion of this will have to await Chapter 9, in which I discuss various views of the state. Here it is sufficient to point out that the dominant view of Marxists is not only that the state in capitalism generally acts in the interests of capitalism, but also that the nation-state itself arises with, is transformed by and itself affects the accumulation of capital. All this suggests that relying on guidelines and codes of conduct to control the TNCs is unlikely to be particularly effective. Almost any countervailing power is to be welcomed, but this is likely to be stronger the more directly this comes from the class interest of labour.

Unfortunately labour organization is often weak, particularly in the LDCs where the industrial labourforce is small and more fragmented than in the DCs. At the international level the organization of labour is, if anything, weaker. The International Metal Workers and the International Chemical Workers have established close links over a range of companies (see Labour Party, 1977, appendix K), but the International Federation of Trades Union has been roundly criticized in a recent report (see Thomson and Larson, 1978) for being a 'labour aristocracy' susceptible to being bought off – a view echoing that of Lenin in his pamphlet on *Imperialism* more than sixty years previously.

NOTES ON FURTHER READING

On the internationalization of capital, in general see the extract by Palloix and the article by Hymer (both in Radice, 1975) for a discussion of the different forms taken by the internationalization of capital. Also for a general discussion of the expansion of capitalism, see Brown, 1974, chapters 6, 8, 9 and 11; Open University, 1976, chapter 6.

On the international monetary system I have come across no texts, among the hordes of books and articles on the IMS, which give a useful long-term history of its development from a Marxist viewpoint. For the sterling–gold period, it is probably easiest to start with Grubel, 1978, part 2, then to go to Brown, 1940, starting with the guide on pages xx–xxi and the overview in chapter 21, and then to Bloomfield, 1959; Lindert, 1969; Triffin, 1947. Moving to the dollar–gold exchange standard, you may find Nurkse, 1944, useful. For a very clear description of the sterling area, I recommend the second chapter of the clear and stimulating book by Coakley and Harris, 1983.

For the immediate post Second War period, look at Gardner, 1969; Horsefield, 1969. The latter is a history of the IMF to 1965. But there are good, briefer treatments of the IMF's history and development in Dell, 1981; Open University, 1983, case study 9. For good discussions of the IMF's role in the debt crisis and particularly on its relations with Third World countries, look at Dell, 1981; Open University, 1983, case study 9; Killick, 1984a; LAB, 1983. Also look at Cline, 1983, chapter 6. For particular-country case studies of the IMF's involvement, see Open University, 1983, case study 9 (for Jamaica); Killick, 1984b (for Latin America, Indonesia, Jamaica and Kenya); LAB, 1983 (for Jamaica, Chile and Peru).

For more general treatments of the postwar IMS, I recommend Parboni, 1981; Scammell, 1980; Tew, 1982; Crockett, 1980, more or less in that order, though there is little to choose between them. For a briefer introduction, look at Sodersten, 1980, part V.

The history of the World Bank and a critical appraisal of some of its operations can be found in Bello *et al.*, 1982; Payer, 1982.

For the specific topic of Eurocurrencies, Sodersten, 1980, is unsatisfactory, and it is best to go to the relevant chapters of Tew, 1982, and Crockett, 1980. Try also Mayer, 1974, chapter 17; Argy, 1981; Lomax and Guttmann, 1981; as well as the briefer and readable pieces in *The Economist*, 1979 and 1982. Other brief, useful sources are Cairncross and Keeley, 1983, chapter 5; Coakley and Harris, 1983, chapter 3. An article which I have found informative (if you feel inclined, skip the algebra) was McKenzie, 1981.

For the financial crisis of the 1970s and early 1980s, Reid, 1982, chapter 9, is useful, but on this topic it is generally best to go to the bank reviews and periodicals, since things are moving fast. In the UK the *Midland Bank Review* and *Barclays Bank Review* are easy to read, as is the weekly *Economist*, but more useful than these is the Morgan Guaranty Trust's *World Financial Markets*, produced monthly from New York. In addition, look at the articles in the monthly *Banker* and in the Bank of England's *Quarterly Bulletin*. For financial crises more generally, see Kindleberger, 1981; Minsky, in Altman and Sametz, 1977. Chapter 4 of Coakley and Harris, 1983, is excellent. Finally, one highly readable but not very analytical source is Anthony Sampson's *The Money Lenders* 1982, while two stimulating novels on banking and finance are Paul Erdman's *The Billion Dollar Killing*, 1973, and Christina Stead's *House of All Nations*, 1938.

More specifically, on Third World debt useful sources are ODI, 1983; Cline, 1983; Cairncross and Keeley, 1983. Similar diagnoses of the problem can be found in Dell, 1981; Killick, 1984a. For up-to-date statistics, look at the Annual Reports of the IMF, the World Bank and UNCTAD.

On transnational corporations useful general statistics are in UN, 1978, the encyclopaedic Stopford *et al.*, 1980, and the UNCTC publications, in particular, UNCTC, 1983. On trading and pricing within the TNCs, look at Helleiner, 1981; Murray, 1981; Vaitsos, 1974. For an introduction to some of the important issues more generally, refer to Bodington, 1982, chapter 1.

For more detailed coverage of TNC issues, look at the readings in Radice, 1975, and at Hymer, in Nell, 1980, and then at Hood and Young, 1979. Readers may well find Dunning, 1981, as boring as I have, but Sanjaya Lall's collection of essays is more readable: see Lall, 1980a.

For news items on individual companies, see the monthly *Multinational Monitor*, produced by the Corporate Accountability Research Group based in Washington, DC; for fuller reports on individual companies, see the periodic issues of the Counter-Information Services (CIS) based in London. For a broader discussion of TNCs and imperialism, see 'Notes on further reading' at the end of Chapter 9, but the readings in Radice, 1975, by Warren, Murray, Mandel and Rowthorn are a good start.

SUMMARY

7.1 Expansion of capitalism →

Nineteenth and twentieth centuries: internationalization of
commodity-capital (through trade)
money-capital (through banks)
industrial-capital (through TNCs)
→

Growing integration of international monetary system (IMS)
→

7.2 The IMS

Development of the IMS with growth of capitalism →

Through:
1 domestic gold standard
2 sterling–gold standard
3 dollar–gold exchange standard
4 international credit system
→

Since 1960s, marked by:
1 a slow decline in the dollar
2 a rapid growth in private international liquidity

With the growth of the Eurocurrency market in 1960s and 1970s →

Sharp fluctuations in exchange rates →

A series of financial crises in 1970s and 1980s →

Root cause in falling rate of profit

Lender-of-last-resort paradox faces central banks →

Dilemma as to whether to →

extend credit (and defer crisis)

or attempt to control restructuring of capital →

At the risk of total financial collapse

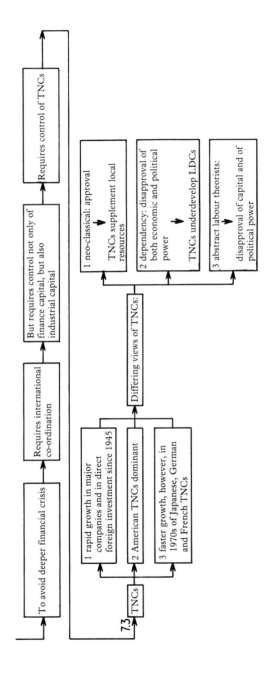

7.3 TNCs

TNCs
1 rapid growth in major companies and in direct foreign investment since 1945
2 American TNCs dominant
3 faster growth, however, in 1970s of Japanese, German and French TNCs

Differing views of TNCs:

1 neo-classical: approval
↓
TNCs supplement local resources

2 dependency: disapproval of both economic and political power
↓
TNCs underdevelop LDCs

3 abstract labour theorists: disapproval of capital and of political power

To avoid deeper financial crisis → Requires international co-ordination → But requires control not only of finance capital, but also industrial capital → Requires control of TNCs

8

The Third World, nationalism and a NIEO

8.1 THE GROWTH OF THE THIRD WORLD AND IMPORT SUBSTITUTION

One characteristic of the postwar period has been the growth of new nations, particularly in the southern hemisphere. In the 1950s and 1960s the so-called Third World was born. As colony after colony obtained its political independence the number of member countries of the United Nations rose from 51 in 1945, to 59 in 1955, to 141 in 1975 and to 157 in 1982. In 1960 in a speech to the South African Parliament, Harold Macmillan, then British Prime Minister, referred to this process of de-colonialism as 'this wind of change'. Some indication of the speed of this wind in the postwar period is given in Figure 8.1.

As new nation-states arose to form the so-called Third World, so the demand for industrial development grew in these countries. During the Second World War, when competition from the DCs had been blunted by shipping blockades and the like, a small industrial bourgeoisie had arisen in some of the LDCs. Some of these manufacturers as well as traders and merchants in the richer of the Third World countries looked

Figure 8.1 This wind of change: the new states of the world 1945–80.

Notes and sources: The map shows the proliferation of new (politically) independent states since 1945. Generally, only countries with a population (at the end of the 1970s) of more than 1 million are included. The main sources used were Kidron and Segal, 1981, map 2; Kurian, 1978; Mitchell, 1982; Spuler, 1977. States are defined as in Kidron and Segal, 1981: 'Sovereign states are those that are generally accepted as such by other sovereign states and by international agencies', and 'all states and boundaries conform to those given in the *Times Atlas of the World.*'

Note that East and West Germany are shown as new states because neither existed in its present form before 1945; Nepal, until 1947, had extensive treaty obligations to Britain and, therefore, is shown as becoming politically independent between 1945 and 1959; Oman joined the UN in 1971 and is shown as a new state since 1970; and Greenland is constitutionally part of Denmark.

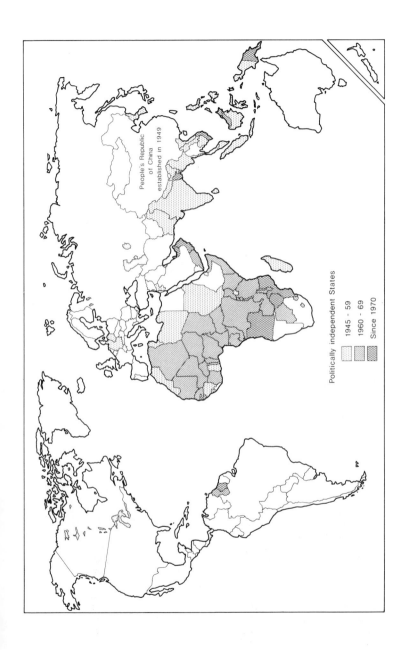

People's Republic
of China
established in 1949

Politically independent States

1945 - 59

1960 - 69

Since 1970

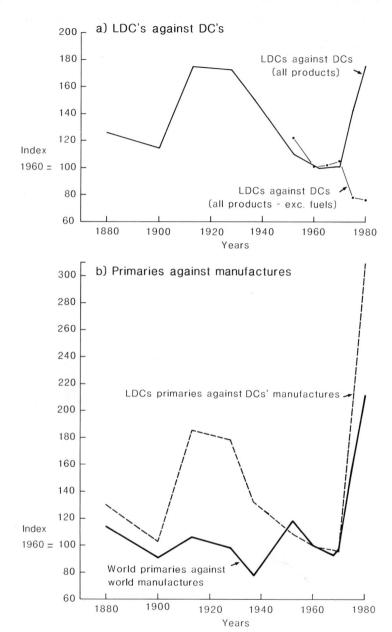

Figure 8.2 The barter terms of trade for primary commodities and for LDCs: a tendency to decline?

Notes and sources: see Table 4.2 above, p. 62.

to the manufacturing sector for continued capital accumulation. And politicians in the newly independent countries were looking at industrialization as a path to development not only for the countries, but also for themselves. Some at least of the politically powerful saw a potential for their own material gain in the development of locally based industrial companies in which directorships might become available.

Furthermore, since this political and material appeal could be buttressed by theoretical argument, the motivation for industrialization was strong. For, as pointed out in Section 4.1, by the 1960s there was a general pessimism about the growth potential of primary production being expressed by economists such as Prebisch, Lewis and Myrdal. From the 1920s through to the 1960s the barter terms of trade of LDCs had deteriorated in general (see Figure 8.2(a)) as had the terms of trade for LDCs' primary products in particular (see Figure 8.2(b)). LDCs' primary products seemed to be particularly hard hit compared to primary products in general, for the barter terms of trade between *world* primaries and world manufactures was as high in the 1960s as it had been in the 1920s – again, refer to Figure 8.2(b). The deterioration of LDCs' primaries was thought by many, following Prebisch's lead, to be inevitable, given the low-income elasticity of demand for LDCs' primary products, the low wages in the primary sector in the LDCs and the high protective barriers for competing primary production in the DCs.

Not only was the protection given to agriculture in the DCs considerable, but also there was little prospect that the institution set up soon after the war to promote free trade, namely the General Agreement on Tariffs and Trade (or the GATT), would be able to reduce this protection. For although the Geneva-based GATT had been set up in 1947 to promote non-discriminatory trade, it has not been active in pursuing free trade in agriculture because of opposition from, first, the USA and, more recently, the EEC. And even though – despite some EEC opposition – a GATT committee on agriculture was established at the ministerial summit held in November 1982, there seems to be little optimism that the committee will be very effective.

Thus by the 1960s there was considerable pessimism about the revenue-generating potential of primary products. But this was not all. Economists, such as the American Albert Hirschman or the Swedish Gunnar Myrdal, also argued that the primary sector was inherently backward compared to the manufacturing sector, because of the latter's *linkages* (both within the sector and between the manufacturing industries and other parts of the economy), and because of the allegedly greater *economies of scale* in manufacturing (see Hirschman, 1958;

Myrdal, 1957). Thus once a manufacturing industry was established, it was much more likely to attract other activities around it, because of its demands both on supplies from other industries and on a supporting infrastructure, as well as through its turnover of a skilled and disciplined labourforce. As a result of these linkages and 'external economies', manufacturing industries were less likely to develop in an 'enclave'. And the development of manufacturing industries was thought more likely to release the LDCs from the balance-of-payments constraints which would otherwise bedevil them with a pattern of growth based on agriculture.

Thus the promotion of industrialization by government intervention found both 'material' support in the LDCs and theoretical justification. It was argued that this promotion would have to come from *protection* – from reserving domestic markets for newly founded industries. For these were *infant industries*, which needed a period of nurturing away from the cold winds of world competition. It was argued that as the market grew the industries would benefit from economies of scale, and with time and experience, they would become more efficient. Then having grown up, they would be able to compete in the world market. And so the infant industry argument was used to justify the protection which developed in the Third World in the 1960s.

The protagonists of infant industries pointed out that all countries that had industrialized, had done so behind protectionist walls (see Brown, 1974, 148). And not surprisingly, their arguments find echoes from infant industry supporters in the LDCs of the past, for the same argument was used by Alexander Hamilton and by Frederick List to justify protectionist policies in eighteenth-century America and nineteenth-century Germany respectively (see ibid., 147–8). But the opponents of protectionism have counterattacked by alleging that the levels of protection in the present LDCs are high even by the protectionist standards of the past (see Table 8.1).

Unfortunately the measurement of protection is not as simple as at first it may appear. For the forms of protection vary considerably, ranging from a series of non-tariff barriers (quotas, multiple exchange rates, government subsidies, import deposit schemes, discriminatory regulations, government procurement preferences and even slow customs clearance) to the relatively easy-to-measure import duties. But even in the case of import duties the most obvious measure – the percentage import duty on the finished product – is not necessarily the one which accurately reflects the protection given to the *producer*. It may be that the producer has to pay (because of protection on inputs) higher than world prices for the raw materials and intermediate goods used in

Table 8.1 Growing free trade in the north and protectionism in the south 1902 to the 1970s

| | *Average tariff (nominal) rates for manufactures (%)* | | | |
The north – DCs	1902	1925	1962	1970s
USA	72	37	12	—
France	34	21		
Germany	25	20		
Italy	27	22		—
Common Market			11	
Japan	9	—	16	—
The south –LDCs				
Argentina	28	29	141 (1958)	74
Pakistan	—	—	93 (1963–4)	85
India	3	16	—	—
Philippines	—	—	46 (1961)	25
Mexico	—	—	22 (1960)	24

Sources: Little *et al.*, 1970, 162–3; Magee, 1980, 88.

the finished product, so that to measure the effective protection from foreign competition given to domestic manufacture we need to take account of the protection on the inputs. To do this we need to calculate what is usually called the effective rate of protection (ERP). This is the level of protection given to the domestic production activity. In general, this will not be obvious from the published tariff lists. As shown in Figure 8.3, it is likely to differ considerably from the nominal rate of protection on the finished product.

Theories for and against protectionism

For the free-marketeers, government intervention to promote industry is bad enough. The hidden nature of protection, if anything, compounds the misery. In their view protection is not justified, except in the limited case where the country is a price-maker for a particular product, that is where the import price of a product falls when the country restricts its imports by imposing a tariff on the product. This is the *optimum tariff* case, which was discussed earlier in Section 4.1. In this case the country's policy-makers are justified, even in the eyes of the free-marketeers, in imposing a duty to maximize the net export earnings from (or to minimize the import costs of) the product, for the country is in an

SUMMARY

a) BEFORE TARIFF

ASSUME THAT:-

1. The commodity being produced is cloth:

2. It is produced using cotton, labour and machines:

3. The price of cloth imported into India is 1,000 rupees per square metre:

4. The costs of cotton and labour to produce a square metre of cloth are:-

RUPEES

COTTON 500
LABOUR 200

5. Then we have:-

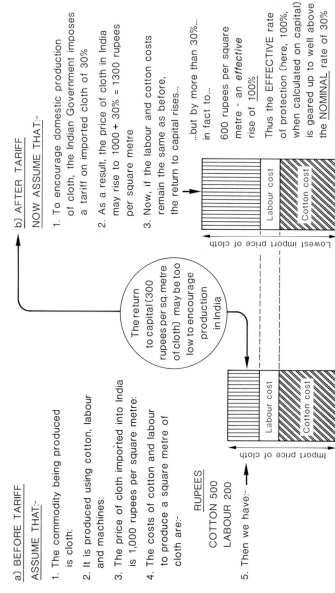

Import price of cloth

Labour cost

Cotton cost

The return to capital (300 rupees per sq. metre of cloth) may be too low to encourage production in India

b) AFTER TARIFF

NOW ASSUME THAT:-

1. To encourage domestic production of cloth, the Indian Government imposes a tariff on imported cloth of 30%

2. As a result, the price of cloth in India may rise to 1000 + 30% = 1300 rupees per square metre

3. Now, if the labour and cotton costs remain the same as before, the return to capital rises...

...but by more than 30%... in fact to...

600 rupees per square metre - an *effective* rise of 100%

Thus the EFFECTIVE rate of protection (here, 100%, when calculated on capital) is geared up to well above the NOMINAL rate of 30%

Lowest import price of cloth

Labour cost

Cotton cost

Figure 8.3 The effective rate of protection (ERP): an example.

analogous position to that of a monopolist (or monopsonist) in an industry (see Figure 4.1, p. 59). But this case, the free-marketeers argue, is rare. Rarely will countries be in a monopoly (or monopsony) situation. But where they are, the correction to the otherwise free market prices should be made by imposing an export or import duty on the 'monopolized' commodities.

The free-marketeers admit that an export duty may give indirect protection to producers of products other than the 'monopolized' one, but they argue that this in no way justifies giving these producers *direct* tariff protection. The free-marketeers argue that commercial policies should be aimed as directly as possible at their stated objective, for then the effects of the policy will be easier to perceive.

Thus the first acknowledged exception to a policy of completely free trade is that of the *optimum tariff*. The other exception acceptable to the free-marketeers is to preserve *national security*. But again, they argue, this is a limited exception in theory, though it is a widely claimed one in practice. Here again the general principle is to apply the policy as directly as possible. Thus the most direct way of protecting national security is best, and this is likely to be through preferential procurement by the government, rather than through the less direct method of import duties protecting the activity that is thought to be in the 'overriding national interest'.

For the free-marketeer, then, there are only two cases which constitute valid exceptions to the free trade principle: the first is the optimum tariff case where the country's own exports of a particular product are thought to directly affect the world price; and the second is where it is thought desirable to promote domestic production on the ground of national security. But, the free-marketeers argue, both these cases are limited in extent, do not justify the indirect support given by import tariffs and non-tariff barriers, and in no way justify the levels of protection commonly found in today's LDCs. In this view the infant industry argument is not a valid one. If there are *internal* economies of scale, then the profit-seeking industrialist will find them so long as the capital market is efficient and allows the entrepreneur to finance production on a sufficient scale to exploit the economies; and if the capital market is not efficient, then the answer is to improve it, *not* to provide protection. If the industry is an infant one because of *external* economies, then the answer is, once again, to tackle the external economies at source and to internalize them (by, for example, subsidizing education or training facilities, or by promoting integrated industries through capital market improvements), rather than to impose tariffs which provide arbitrary protection from world competition. The latter will obscure the basis of the policy-making at the national level and may promote competitive protectionism at the international level.

In general, the free-marketeers' argument goes, protectionism will lead to a loss of welfare, as shown in Figure 8.4. The losses from protection are shown by the shaded areas, and consist of a loss resulting from the higher domestic production costs (area ABC) as well as the loss (area DEF) resulting from the domestic consumers being forced to buy less of the product at higher prices than they would otherwise have done.

Furthermore, the free-marketeers argue, home supply costs may rise *as a result* of the introduction of protective tariffs. That is, the supply curve may shift upwards after protection is imposed. Domestic companies, protected from the bracing breezes of foreign competition may become less efficient, or they may spend resources on 'public relations' to persuade ministers and other policy-makers of their case for protection. The latter costs have been referred to as *rent-seeking* costs (see Krueger, 1974a; Nelson, 1981).

The free-marketeers are adamant that if, on the ground of misplaced nationalism, import substitution *is* to be encouraged, it is better that direct cash subsidies rather than tariff protection be given to the promoted industries. For with subsidies, the domestic market will not be reduced to the same extent, and the cost of the policy will be more explicit. Whereas with tariff protection, the costs of the policy will be hidden, particularly if there are tariffs on the raw material inputs as well

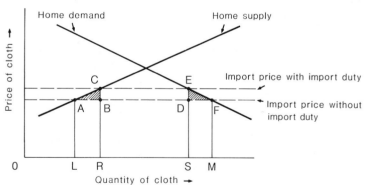

Figure 8.4 The losses from protectionism.

Source: Greenaway and Milner, 1979, 40–41.

Notes:
Imports of cloth BEFORE import duty = LM
Imports of cloth AFTER import duty = RS
Losses from protectionism = ABC (higher cost of supplying quantity, LR) + DEF (consumers' loss)

as on the outputs of finished goods. With tariff protection, considerable domestic resources may be used to generate small foreign exchange savings, and yet this domestic resource cost (DRC) may not be at all obvious.

The cost-of-production theorists counterattack by arguing that there are difficulties in applying subsidies. First, subsidies are subject to close scrutiny from the GATT; and secondly, government expenditure is usually heavily constrained, so that the opportunity cost of subsidies is high. Neither of these arguments is convincing to the free-marketeers nor, for that matter, do they win over the abstract labour theorists.

The latter, the Marxists, are sceptical about protectionist policies. They argue that within a capitalist state protectionism is likely to benefit capital at the expense of labour, for it is generally capital which makes and breaks the rules within such a state. I look at the nature of the state in more detail in Chapter 9, but here it is sufficient to point out that once again the abstract labour theorists look very carefully at which class is likely to benefit from the policy.

In general, they argue, protectionist policies are acceptable if they lead to greater workers' control of production, but this is unlikely in a state dominated by the interests of capital. Nevertheless, since the effects of protectionism are rarely obvious (especially in the longer term), the debate about protectionism on the left is a lively one. Witness the present debate about the British left's Alternative Economic Strategy, a major part of which concerns the extent to which, and conditions under which, import controls are acceptable. To go into this in more detail is beyond the scope of this chapter; here it is sufficient to emphasize that, once again, the abstract labour theorists emphasize the heterogeneous, class structure within nation-states in contrast to both the subjective preference and cost-of-production schools of thought.

It is the case, then, that both subjective preference and abstract labour theorists are sceptical about protectionist policies, though for very different reasons. They point out that the experience of import-substituting policies has not been a successful one, and even cost-of-production theorists admit to some disappointment. There is acknowledgement from the latter that the protection on consumer goods may have been excessive and become entrenched. That is, the protection on consumer goods has bred resistance to any further protection designed to promote the production of intermediate and capital goods. As can be seen from the example in Figure 8.3, p. 214, any tariff on cotton imports is likely to reduce the effective rate of protection on cloth production, and therefore is likely to be met with resistance by cloth-making capitalists as well, perhaps, as by workers in the cloth industry.

The cost-of-production theorists also acknowledge that the protection-ist policies followed in the LDCs have not led to much of a drop in imports (see Sodersten, 1980, 217), and that the industries protected have only very slowly, if at all, emerged from infancy to become competitive in the world market. They acknowledge that, in many LDCs, the domestic markets for some consumer goods have been so small that economies of scale have not been reaped in those protected industries. But their response to this disappointment has differed from that of the free-marketeers. The latter have argued that the correct policy solution is to turn to free trade, on the ground that such a policy will encourage export growth from those activities which have a 'compara-tive advantage'. They point to the success of Singapore, Taiwan, Hong Kong and South Korea in growing on this basis, and argue that other countries can and should follow their example (see Little *et al.*, 1970; Balassa, 1980a, 27). By contrast, the cost-of-production theorists are sceptical about the possibilities of a wide range of LDCs increasing their manufactured exports in a world of free trade, and instead look to regional co-operation among groups of LDCs in providing the assured, larger market base for industrial expansion.

The arguments for and against regional integration are examined briefly in Section 8.3, but before that we look briefly, in Section 8.2, at the experiences of the LDCs which have followed so-called 'outward-looking policies' to facilitate the exports of manufactured goods.

8.2 THE NEW INDUSTRIAL COUNTRIES – A NEW INTERNATIONAL DIVISION OF LABOUR?

In the 1960s exports of manufactures from the LDCs grew rapidly from about $3 billion in 1960 to more than $9 billion in 1970 (UNIDO, 1981); even expressed as a percentage of total world trade in manu-factures, there was a slight rise from a little under 4 per cent in 1960 to 5 per cent in 1970. But in the 1970s this growth was particularly rapid, and by 1980 manufactured exports from the LDCs totalled more than $80 billion or a little over 9 per cent of the world total. For the free-marketeers, this growth in manufactured exports, particularly from the 'open' economies of Singapore, Hong Kong, Taiwan and South Korea, provided a vindication of comparative advantage. Their claim is that these countries have relatively abundant endowments of labour, and that they can, they should and do export goods which are relatively labour-intensive.

It is this growth in exports from the new industrial countries (NICs) which has prompted some economists (not all of them free-marketeers) to talk of a new international division of labour (NIDL) (see, for example, Frobel *et al.*, 1980). The free-marketeers argue that the emergence of the NICs not only signifies a NIDL, but also provides proof that a free market provides opportunities for exchange and specialization that can benefit everyone. It provides a continuing justification for the 'open-economy' policies of the World Bank and of the IMF. Thus, at present, the World Bank's policy is to 'encourage' tariff reform by tying credit to the implementation of 'structural adjustment programmes'.

By contrast, cost-of-production and 'dependency' theorists are sceptical both about the benefits from the past expansion in manufactured exports and about the possibilities for continued expansion in the future. They argue that the past growth has been from a very small base, and that there is little hope of meeting the target of the United Nations Industrial Development Organization (UNIDO), set in 1975 at Lima, Peru, namely that manufacturing in the LDCs should be one-quarter of the world's total by the end of the century (see Frank, 1981b, 98). They point out that the bulk of the LDCs' manufactured exports come from only a small number of countries. More than 80 per cent of the total comes from ten LDCs (Argentina, Brazil, Hong Kong, India, Malaysia, Mexico, Pakistan, Singapore, South Korea and Taiwan). And they raise questions about whether the experience of this small group of LDCs can or should be imitated by LDCs in general.

The sceptics admit that, at present, the major market for LDCs' manufactured exports is in the north. Thus at the end of the 1970s more than 60 per cent of all LDCs' manufactured exports were sold to the DCs. But they also emphasize that this market is limited by both the high levels of protection in the DCs and the high risk of further protection in the future.

The *level* of protection is high, for not only do tariff barriers in the DCs escalate according to the stage of processing, so that the effective rates of protection on manufactured goods are much higher than the nominal rates (see Figure 8.5), but also there is some evidence that non-tariff barriers in the DCs are higher for exports from the LDCs than they are for exports from the other rich DCs. Thus the Generalized System of Preferences (GSP), which was introduced in the DCs in the 1970s and which offered preferential tariffs for a range of exports from LDCs, has been overridden for many important exports by non-tariff barriers such as quotas (see *South*, October 1980, 20). A prominent example of a range of products which has been hit by import quotas into the DCs is that of textiles and clothing. Cotton textiles have been subject to 'informal' or voluntary restrictions from as early as 1962, but since the early 1970s a wider range of textiles and clothing have been subject to formal quotas

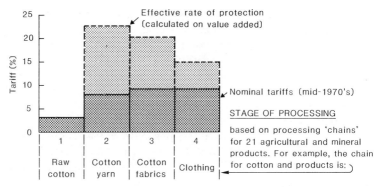

Figure 8.5 Escalating protection in the north.

Source: World Bank, 1981b.

Notes: 'While industrial-country tariffs add only 3 per cent to the cost of imported raw materials, they rise to more than 20 per cent as the degree of processing increases . . . (see above). These higher rates are, of course, intended to encourage firms in industrial countries to import raw materials and process them there . . . [And] in 1974, developing-country commodity exports were heavily concentrated in the lower stages of processing': World Bank, 1981b, 23.

under the Multi-Fibre Arrangements (MFAs) (see World Bank, 1981, 28).

But those who question the wisdom of 'open-economy' policies object not only to the level of protection. They also point to the *uncertainty* of protective barriers and, therefore, of access to DC markets. They argue that the very success of a few LDCs in expanding manufactured exports has generated, and will continue to generate, pressures in the DCs for higher tariff and non-tariff barriers. For example, the MFAs have become more, not less, restrictive each time they have been renegotiated (see ibid.), and it is argued that it is unlikely they will become more liberal in the current recession. This is in spite of the imports of manu-factures from the LDCs being a relatively small threat (in total) to jobs in the north. For not only do they represent less than 5 per cent of the DCs' total consumption of manufactures, but also more jobs are 'lost' in the DCs through new technology or restructuring than because markets are lost to competition from the LDCs. Nevertheless, the competition from the LDCs is highly 'sensitive', because many of the industries (for example, textiles) affected in the north are located in especially depressed areas. For such products the threat of legislated protection – through, for example, 'trade reciprocity' measures – is considerable. This is bad enough, but there is also some evidence that administered protection is growing faster than legislated protection (see Nelson, 1981).

The pessimism about access to DC markets is not confined to manufactured goods. The agricultural sector in the DCs is also highly protected, and this, as argued earlier, encourages a pessimism about the likely terms of trade for non-manufactured exports which in turn discourages policies of export-led growth.

The cost-of-production theorists question whether a policy of relying on exports provides a sufficiently secure basis for a programme of economic development, especially in the depressed conditions of the 1970s and 1980s. It is argued that the LDCs have little bargaining power in negotiations over protection, since the DC markets are generally more important to the LDCs than vice versa.

Where there is bargaining power, and where exports from the LDCs do have genuinely preferential access, it is often because the LDCs' exports are produced by TNCs which provide a powerful lobby for access to the markets of the north. Thus some products (such as electronic components imported into the USA) carry import duties on their value added only, and not on the full import price (see Helleiner, 1973). But, the dependency theorists argue, even if the TNCs do provide a firmer foothold in the DC markets, TNC dominance is too high a price to pay for this acquisition and retention of overseas markets. It is too high a price to pay because the control and regulation of TNCs is difficult, particularly in the vertically integrated industrial sectors such as electronic components, where the threat of nationalization is a weak one, given the specialized nature of the product.

Not only are questions raised about the prospects for a continued expansion of exports; questions are also raised about the development benefits alleged to accrue from a policy of export-led growth. The dependency theorists argue that benefits are negligible or even negative, in general. This is particularly so for the manufactured exports produced, or rather assembled, in the free trade zones (FTZs) of the LDCs. Detailed figures on the exports from FTZs are not available, but I estimate that in 1978 something like one-third of LDCs' manufactured exports came from FTZs (see Table 8.2). And of the estimated 6 million workers directly employed in the LDCs to produce manufactured exports, about 2 million were employed in the FTZs. These are crude estimates, but one thing is certain: the ratio of exports from the FTZs to total manufactured exports from the LDCs grew throughout the 1970s. Thus in so far as the dependency theorists are particularly critical of the FTZ activities, the benefits from manufactured exports in general must have been growing slowly, if at all.

Table 8.2 Manufactured exports from LDCs 1978

(a) Total and destination	1978 ($ billion)	$ billion	%
World exports of manufactures:	778		
of which, from LDCs	63		
of which, to DCs		40	63
to other LDCs		22	35
to CPEs		1	2
		—	—
		63	100
		—	—

Source: UNIDO, 1981.

(b) Product composition and origin	% of LDCs' manufactured exports	
	Total	From FTZs
Textiles, clothing	33	10
Office, telecommunications and other electrical equipment	18	15
Others	49	8
	—	—
	100	33
	—	—

Sources: My estimates based on Frobel *et al.*, 1980; Lall, 1980b.

The dependency theorists give many reasons for doubting the worth of FTZ activities. They point to the enclave effect of the export processing zones and to the lack of linkages with the rest of the economy; to the rapid turnover of labour in these industries and the lack of skills embodied in the work; and to the tax-free nature of the operations so that, given the extensive foreign ownership in the FTZs and the flow of tax-free profits overseas, and given the large import component and low wages, the domestic value added and balance-of-payments benefits are negligible. They also argue, by pointing to the predominance of unmarried women in FTZ employment, that the industries do not employ those who are actively looking for work, but generate instead a net increase in the labourforce.

Some writers, such as Gunder Frank, even argue that workers in the FTZs are 'superexploited', with their wages not even covering their full costs of reproduction (see Frank, 1981b, chapter 5). This superexploitation is made possible, it is argued, by repression both of trade unions and, more generally, of political opposition to the ruling regimes. In most of the countries in which FTZs are significant, human rights are (or have been in recent history) violated. Thus martial law has been in force in Taiwan for thirty years. In the Philippines martial law was declared in 1972, strikes were prohibited and controls imposed on labour organizations. In Singapore political opposition was crushed in 1963 under the aptly named 'Operation Cold Store' and trade unions were placed under firm governmental control. And in South Korea strikes are banned and the trade unions tightly controlled by the government (see Frank, 1981b, chapter 6).

Thus the dependency theorists are profoundly pessimistic about the benefits from open-economy policies; their general conclusion is that access to the DC markets will only be on terms such that any growth in manufactured exports from the LDCs 'will not lead to the creation of an indigenous, self-expanding capitalist development in the Third World, but to dependent industrialisation as part of a new form of imperialist domination' (Landsberg, 1979, 50).

Other economists, while not seeing the growth of manufactured exports as a beneficial vindication of free trade theory, are not as pessimistic as the dependency theorists. Some, such as the American James Cypher, argue that this growth in Third World industrialization is a slow and uneven process, but one which nevertheless represents a further internationalization of capital. The argument is that the growth of industrialization in the Third World can best be understood in terms of an analysis of *capitalism*, and that it is hardly surprising if the development of industry in the south is uneven, since *capitalist* development has never been a smooth process (see Cypher, 1979).

Thus, for abstract labour theorists, Third World industrial development heralds neither a wholly new international division of labour (NIDL) nor a new international economic order (NIEO). The expansion of manufacturing in the LDCs is creating an industrial proletariat, but it is a small one, hemmed in by anti-union laws and, in the FTZs especially, segmented from the rest of the economy both spatially and psychologically. Thus labour organized in trade unions tends to be even rarer within than outside the FTZs. Neither unfortunately does the widespread employment of women in the FTZs signify their liberation from male oppression – for further discussion on this, see the excellent article by Elson and Pearson, in Young *et al.*, 1981. Thus at present the labourforce in the FTZs is far from likely to lead an anti-capitalist struggle.

But for the abstract labour theorists, the growth of manufactured exports from the LDCs is not necessarily more limiting than industrial-ization based on import substitution. The way ahead within capitalism is bound to be uneven. And if capitalism is seen as the major problem, then it is hardly surprising if the same Marxists hold out little hope for the salvation of the poor majority in the Third World within a framework of national capitalism; and this doubt is not removed even if the LDCs combine together – either in the form of regional associations or of commodity cartels. But cost-of-production theorists, with their greater emphasis on distribution between nation-states, attach greater hopes to these south–south combinations, as I attempt to show in Sections 8.3 and 8.4.

8.3   SOUTH–SOUTH CO-OPERATION AND REGIONAL INTEGRATION

In the 1960s cost-of-production theorists increasingly turned to south–south co-operation in the form of regional integration schemes as the way forward to development. For by the late 1960s even cost-of-production theorists were forced to acknowledge the problems associ-ated with import-substituting industrialization when intermediate and capital goods industries failed to develop in the wake of the establish-ment, behind tariffs, of consumer goods industries. Thus the prolifer-ation of regional groupings in the 1960s and early 1970s (see Figure 8.6) met with the approval of these economists. In terms of degree of economic integration the regional groupings varied from loosely integrated free trade areas like the Latin American Free Trade Associ-ation (LAFTA) to customs unions with a common external tariff such as the Caribbean Community (CARICOM). The types of regional schemes are summarized in Table 8.3.

Generally, cost-of-production theorists view these attempts at regional integration with sympathy. The broad argument is that such regional groupings provide LDCs with access to larger markets than are possible within the national boundaries under a programme of import substi-tution. At the same time, not only are these regional markets more secure than the world markets, but also the regional grouping provides the member countries with more bargaining power *vis-à-vis* the developed countries than they would have if they adopted a 'go-it-alone', open-economy policy (see Stewart, in Helleiner, 1976; Vaitsos, 1978).

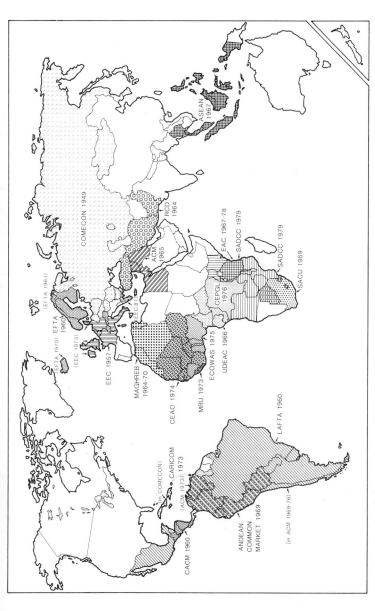

Figure 8.6 Regional integration in the world.

Notes and sources: see Table 8.3, p. 227.

Table 8.3 Regional integration in the world – where, what and when

(a) Types (or stages of) regional integration

Type	Characteristics	Examples
Free trade area	Common internal tariffs, but differing external tariffs	EFTA, LAFTA
Customs union	Common internal and external tariffs	UDEAC, CEAO
Common market	Common tariffs and few restrictions on factor mobility	EEC, Comecon
Economic union	Common monetary policies	—

(b) The where and when of regional integration (since 1945)

Year	Grouping	Main provisions
1949	Council for Mutual Economic Assistance (Comecon): USSR, Bulgaria, Czechoslovakia, GDR, Hungary, Poland, Romania, Mongolia and Cuba	Trade and development agreements and contracts
1957	European Economic Community (EEC): France, West Germany, Italy, Belgium, the Netherlands and Luxemburg	Common Market (common internal and external tariffs and common agricultural and industrial policies)
(1973: plus UK, Ireland, Denmark) (1981: plus Greece)		
1960	European Free Trade Association (EFTA): UK, Switzerland, Austria, Denmark, Norway and Sweden	Common internal tariffs but not common external tariffs
(1961: plus Finland as an associate member) (1970: plus Iceland) (1973: minus UK and Denmark)		
1960	Latin American Free Trade Association (LAFTA): includes Mexico and all of South America, except the Guyanas	Free trade area (no common external tariff) and sectoral agreements
1960	Central American Common Market (CACM): Costa Rica, El Salvador, Guatemala, Honduras, Nicaragua	Common market (but note that Honduras has reimposed some tariffs)
1964 (broke up in 1970)	Maghreb Permanent Consultative Committee: Algeria, Morocco and Tunisia	Co-operative agreement
1964	Regional Co-operation for Development (RCD): Iran, Pakistan and Turkey	Sectoral agreements (not a free trade area)
1965	Arab Common Market (ACM): Egypt, Iraq, Jordan and Syria	Trade agreements

(continued)

Table 8.3—continued

Year	Grouping	Main provisions
1966	Union Douanière et Economique de l'Afrique Centrale (UDEAC): Cameroon, Central African Republic, Congo, Gabon	Customs union with common central bank
1967 (broke up in 1978)	East African Community (EAC): Kenya, Tanzania, Uganda	Common market
1967	Association of South-East Asian Nations (ASEAN): Indonesia, Malaysia, Philippines, Singapore and Thailand	Some regional trade preferences and sectoral agreements
1969	Southern African Customs Union (SACU): Botswana, Lesotho, Swaziland and the Republic of South Africa	Customs union
1969	Andean Common Market (ACM): Bolivia, Chile, Colombia, Ecuador and Peru	Common market envisaged, common policy on foreign investment
(1973: plus Venezuela) (1976: minus Chile)		
1973	Caribbean Community (Caricom): Antigua, Barbados, Belize, Dominica, Grenada, Guyana, Jamaica, Montserrat, St Kitts-Nevis-Anguilla, St Lucia, St Vincent, Trinidad and Tobago	Common market (Caricom) succeeded free trade association – Carifta – in 1969 with agricultural and industrial integration
1973	Mano River Union (MRU): Liberia and Sierra Leone	Customs union
1974	Communauté Economique de l'Afrique de l'Ouest (CEAO): Ivory Coast, Mali, Mauritania, Niger, Senegal, Upper Volta (a re-formed West African Customs Union)	Customs union; joint sectoral policies
1975	Economic Community of West African States (ECOWAS): Benin, Gambia, Ghana, Guinea, Guinea-Bissau, Ivory Coast, Liberia, Mali, Mauritania, Niger, Nigeria, Senegal, Sierra Leone, Togo, Upper Volta	Common external tariff envisaged by 1990 – free movement of labour
1976	Economic Community of the countries of the Great Lakes (CEPGL): Zaire, Rwanda and Burundi	Trade agreements
1979	Southern Africa Development Co-ordination Conference (SADCC): Angola, Botswana, Lesotho, Malawi, Mozambique, Swaziland, Tanzania, Zambia, Zimbabwe	Sectoral integration

Sources: Morton and Tullock, 1977, chapter 8); Robson, 1980, introduction.

Note: Many of the above agreements are now (1985) defunct.

The larger markets are an essential precondition, it is argued, for reaping the economies of scale associated with many industries. For in 1980 more than one-half of the 120 or so LDCs had populations of less than 5 million (see World Bank, 1981b, table 1), and most of these had national incomes of less than $1 billion. Even these statistics may give a misleading impression of the effective size of some markets given the constraints associated with lack of transport and communications. Thus larger, regionally based markets may be an essential precondition of industrial development; as the UNCTAD-based economist Sandy Yeats puts it:

> If economic integration results in larger markets and the achievement of scale economies, it can be an important catalyst for increased production, investment and employment. Such economies seem especially important in manufacturing processes like steel, machinery and chemicals. Since these items are often inputs into other production processes, the scale economies may have important linkage effects.   (Yeats, 1981, 35)

In general, the free-traders question the significance of scale economies (see Friedman, 1955), but say that even if they do exist, they can be best exploited by opening the economy to the world market under a regime of free trade. In this view regional integration schemes are seen as 'second best' arrangements, admittedly better than a national-based policy of import substitution, but inferior to a policy of non-discriminatory free trade. This is the approach of the classic work on customs unions by a Canadian economist, Jacob Viner, who saw such regional groupings as desirable in so far as they are a step towards free trade, but decried them in so far as they are a move towards protectionism (Viner, 1950). In his view the correct method of analysing the effects of regional groupings is to balance the 'trade creation' against the 'trade diversion' effects. If the regional grouping is likely to lead to net trade creation by reducing the trade barriers confronting low-cost producers, then it is superior to the previous trade structure even though still a 'second best' arrangement when compared to a system of completely free trade. Thus Viner's test quite simply looks at the extent to which the regional union has contributed towards free trade, and this is still a widespread approach in the theory of regional integration.

Stewart and Yeats, and other cost-of-production theorists, criticize this approach by arguing that it is limited to the *static*, or allocative effects of the regional union, whereas, they claim, the major effects of a customs union are likely to be the less easily quantified, but none the less important, *dynamic* effects. The cost-of-production theorists emphasize the longer-term and, therefore, more secure nature of the regional markets, as well as the improved bargaining which may accrue to the countries belonging to the regional grouping. They ague that the regional union should *change* the economic conditions in the member countries, so that the test should not be one of *trade* creation and diversion, but rather of *development* creation and diversion (see Dosser, in Bird and Head, 1972).

Yeats has argued that the static effects are likely to be tiny relative to the dynamic effects (see Yeats, 1981, 34), and he and Frances Stewart stress that the maximization of benefits from a regional union may require accompanying changes in technology, in institutions and in transport systems (changes both inside the union as well as in the region's shipping and other connections with the outside world). For, according to Stewart, not only have trading patterns had a north–south straitjacket imposed on them by the colonial development of transport routes, but in exporting to the markets of the north the LDCs have a technology imposed on them by having to compete in those markets (Stewart, in Helleiner, 1976, 96, 99).

Thus unless a policy is followed which deliberately counters this, the LDCs (especially the smaller ones) are likely to find themselves in a permanent state of 'less development', if not 'underdevelopment'. For Stewart alleges that the development process follows a path of what Myrdal calls 'cumulative causation', with an economy's current efficiency being a product of its past history. Stewart argues that such a process of cumulative causation benefits the north and may harm the south, and therefore is unlikely to be challenged by the rich countries. Indeed, it may be perpetuated deliberately by the north, in which case, Stewart argues, 'The best counter to the colonial and neo-colonial policy of divide and rule is unite and fight' (ibid., 100).

But Stewart's unity is far from simple to achieve, for 'in recent years the integration schemes of the Third World have almost everywhere been under stress . . . and . . . the outcome has been dissolution in one or two instances (such as the East African Community, which broke up in 1978 after a history of fifty years) and stagnation in others' (Robson, 1980, 9). What are the reasons for this stagnation? The free-traders argue that a major factor is 'that the agreements contained no mechanism for weaning protected infants and gradually exposing them to global competition' (Havrylyshyn, 1982, 36). Not surprisingly, Havrylyshyn goes on to argue that the optimum policy for the member countries of ASEAN to follow is one of 'go it alone' liberalization. Failing that, the next best policy is that of across-the-board preferential liberalization, with global liberalization to follow. He concedes that global liberalization might be used as a bargaining counter to get reductions in trade barriers in the DCs – and, in particular, to a reduction in the textile barriers under the Multi-Fibres Arrangement (MFA) – but the basic point made by Havrylyshyn is that a policy of trade liberalization is preferable to what he calls 'the mercantilist formulas of complementation agreements and selected product lists' (ibid.).

Thus for free-traders like Havrylyshyn, LAFTA failed because of its mercantilism; whereas a quite different picture is given in Constantine Vaitsos's survey of regional integration schemes among the developing countries (see Vaitsos, 1978). Vaitsos argued that LAFTA ran out of steam because no major local industrial group in LAFTA wanted effective trade liberalization (ibid., 723); and that local capitalists saw LAFTA as a 'Trojan horse' through which foreign companies might penetrate national restrictions on imports and investment. Thus Vaitsos's reasoning runs totally counter to Havrylyshyn's, and he argues that

> In interpreting causal relationships it is important to stress that it was not that the selection of policy instruments led to the poor performance of LAFTA. Instead, powerful social groups, which would have been affected by integration, pressured their governments to adopt measures and policies which were consistent with the groups' interests.
> (ibid.)

But, Vaitsos emphasizes, the opposition to economic integration has not always come from local capital, and cites Central America as an area in which strong opposition to a certain type of integration came from the US government (see ibid., 728). In particular, he argues, the US government 'intervened continuously against regional industrial planning in Central America' (ibid., 729).

Similarly, Vaitsos argues that transnational corporations (TNCs) are likely to oppose, and have opposed, forms of integration likely to be accompanied by controls on their activities (ibid., 733). Thus they are likely to oppose schemes in which regional industrial programming is significant, particularly if it is accompanied by the co-ordinated treatment of foreign investment. In this view TNCs are seen as a major obstacle to effective economic integration among the LDCs, which is not surprising since a major purpose of economic integration in the south is to provide a stronger basis for the control of TNCs (ibid., 735, 736).

In general, then, Vaitsos, like the cost-of-production school, sees an increase in links between the countries of the south as a necessary element in Third World development strategy, but argues that links in the form of a reduction in trade barriers are unlikely to be enough. For 'trade liberalisation will accentuate inter-country polarisation effects' (ibid., 746), with some countries suffering significant losses from their membership of the regional union. Examples of such countries are Uganda in East Africa, Bolivia in the Andean Pact, and Honduras in Central America (see ibid., 748).

Thus Vaitsos, in arguing for sectoral programmes and industrial complementation agreements, disagrees radically with the free-traders like Havrylyshyn. And in seeing 'the process of economic integration as a social phenomenon . . . consequently benefiting or damaging specific economic and political interests' (ibid., 721), Vaitsos's approach is clearly similar to that of abstract labour theorists. However, although it goes much further than the asocial approach of the free-traders, it does not perhaps go far enough in analysing the effects of regional integration schemes on the class structure *within* the LDCs. This is the sort of question that was raised by Miguel Wionczek in a comment on Vaitsos's survey, when he wrote, 'if the . . . governments are not autonomous . . . entities but are the products of power relationships within under-developed societies and of their external dependence, how can one expect from them the pursuit of rational, long-term "common interest"?' (Wionczek, 1978, 782).

Hilferding has said: 'The proletariat avoids the bourgeois dilemma – protectionism or free trade – with a solution of its own; neither protectionism nor free trade, but socialism' (Hilferding, 1981, 366). But in terms of political strategy the difficult task for the abstract labour theorist is that of analysing the relationship between a regional integration scheme and world capitalism, and of deciding on the basis of that analysis whether the scheme is likely to further the cause of democratic socialism, both within and outside the regional union.

Such a judgement is far from easy, as can be seen from the debates on the political left about the advisability of continuing British membership of the European Economic Community (see, for example, Currie, 1979; Rowthorn and Grahl, 1982).

8.4 SOUTH–SOUTH CO-OPERATION – THE NEW INTERNATIONAL ECONOMIC ORDER (NIEO) AND COMMODITY CARTELS

The growing demand for a NIEO

In the 1960s there was disillusionment in the Third World with the programmes of import substitution that had been adopted in the late

1950s and the early 1960s. In the 1970s there was similar disappointment with the regional integration schemes that had been adopted in the
wake of import substitution. And so, in the early 1970s, the hopes of
many in the Third World switched to the demand for a new international economic order (NIEO). The main, detailed focus of the NIEO
was on world trading arrangements and specifically on the prices of
commodities exported from the Third World. The more general
concern was and still is with the distribution of power in the world, with
the Third World complaining that the control of the most powerful of
the world's multilateral institutions, such as the World Bank and the
IMF, was vested in the hands of the wealthiest of the OECD countries
(see Table 7.1, p. 171).

Admittedly in the UN's General Assembly, voting is on a one-
member-one-vote basis, but even at the UN (in the Security Council) the
most powerful can veto resolutions. And within the framework of the
General Agreement on Tariffs and Trade (GATT), even though each of
the eighty-eight contracting countries has one vote, few decisions are
voted on. The GATT is a loosely knit organization, albeit with a permanent Geneva-based secretariat; and, as noted earlier, it acts more as a
pressure group than a formal institution with enforceable powers. When
the GATT was signed in 1947, it was intended to be only an interim
arrangement until a formal UN agency was established to deal with trade
and related issues.

The formal agency envisaged – which had been under discussion since
the end of the Second World War – was the International Trade Organization (ITO). But the ITO was stillborn because of fundamental disagreements over its objectives between the north and the, then much
smaller, south. A group of countries from the south, led by India, Brazil
and Chile, wanted the ITO to have economic development as one of its
major aims. In particular, the south wanted specific concessions for the
LDCs built into the ITO Charter, with provisions being made for
controls on international investment, and for trade preferences for the
LDCs. But the US government wanted the ITO's objectives to be
limited to multilateralism in world trade and vehemently opposed the
'wider' objectives of the south. The ITO was never ratified.

Thus the birth of the new nations of the south in the 1950s and 1960s
(see Figure 8.1) occurred within a framework of world economic institutions dominated by the north. In these decades a 'trade union of the
south' developed. A series of meetings of the self-styled 'non-aligned'
nations took place – the first significant meeting was held, in 1955, in
Bandung, Indonesia. But a 'trade union of the Third World' could be
said to date from the first United Nations Conference on Trade and

Development (UNCTAD), held in Geneva in 1964. As Scammell describes it: 'a coalition of the leading Third World countries challenged the United States and the industrial countries as a group and found them in great disarray. Thereafter Third World operations in the GATT, the IMF and the United Nations Assembly were conducted as a group operation' (Scammell, 1980, 106). After the first UNCTAD, seventy-seven LDCs issued a joint declaration, and since then the LDCs within UNCTAD have been known as the 'Group of 77', even though there are now more than 120 of them. After its second session, held in New Delhi in 1968, UNCTAD became a permanent organization, based like the GATT in Geneva.

By this time most of the Third World was politically independent, but further encouragement for this 'trade union of the south' came from other sources. Not only were significant anti-colonial wars being fought in Angola, Mozambique, Zimbabwe and Vietnam, but in the late 1960s and early 1970s a Third World commodity cartel was successfully flexing its muscles. This was the Organization of Petroleum Exporting Countries (OPEC).

OPEC had been founded in 1960 by a number of oil producing LDCs to fight for higher royalties and taxes from oil production for the member countries. The royalties were based on 'posted prices' which had been falling through the 1950s in not only real but also nominal terms. But through the 1950s and into the 1960s the proportion of the world's consumption of oil accounted for by OPEC's exports had increased rapidly (see Table 8.4). And since the importance of crude oil in world primary energy consumption was also growing (from 30 per cent in 1950 to 42 per cent in 1965 – as shown in Table 8.4), OPEC's market power increased significantly.

By the early 1970s most of the oil producing LDCs had negotiated more favourable royalty and participation agreements, and between 1970 and 1973 a number of agreements had been reached between the governments and the oil companies that resulted in an approximate doubling of the oil export price. But in October 1973, and again in January 1974, further price rises were enforced by OPEC members, so that by the end of January 1974 the oil export price was about four times as high as at the beginning of October 1973. The co-ordinated action of the OPEC members, many of them Arab countries (see Figure 8.7), was encouraged by the 1973 Arab-Israeli war in west Asia (or the Middle East to Eurocentrics), and the oil price rise in turn encouraged the Group of 77 LDCs to raise its demands.

The report which Raul Prebisch had produced in time for the 1964 UNCTAD (see Prebisch, 1964) had summarized the arguments current

Table 8.4 OPEC and world oil

	1950		1965		1980	
	(million tonne)[1]	*(%)*	*(million tonne)*[1]	*(%)*	*(million tonne)*[1]	*(%)*
Production of oil[1]						
OPEC	171	32	720	46	1356	44
OECD	292	54	492	32	711	23
USSR, Eastern Europe and China	44	8	270	17	728	24
Rest of the world (ROW)	32	6	78	5	284	9
Total world production	539	100	1560	100	3079	100
Consumption of oil[2]						
OPEC	51	9	147	9	173	6
OECD	364	68	990	63	1836	61
USSR, Eastern Europe and China	44	8	246	16	627	21
ROW	78	15	188	12	366	12
Total world consumption	537	100	1571	100	3002	100
World consumption of primary energy	1776		3725		6893	
% of oil to primary energy	30		42		44	

Surplus (or deficit) of production over consumption of oil		*% of world cons.*		*% of world cons.*		*% of world cons.*
OPEC	120	22	573	37	1183	39
OECD	(72)	(13)	(498)	(32)	(1125)	(37)
USSR, Eastern Europe and China	—		24	2	101	3
ROW	(46)	(9)	(110)	(7)	(82)	(3)
World	2	—	(11)	—	77	2

Sources: 1950 and 1965: UN, 1976, 2, 193–9, 203, 209–213, 216; 1980: BP, 1981, 6, 8, 12; UN, 1981, 301.

Notes:

1 Oil is defined as crude petroleum and natural gas liquids; all tonnages are in oil equivalents; for conversion rates, see UN, 1976, xx, xxi.

2 Consumption figures for 1950 and 1965 are apparent figures derived from production plus or minus deficit and surplus respectively; and the deficits and surpluses for these years are net imports and net exports respectively.

OPEC (Organisation of Petroleum Exporting Countries)

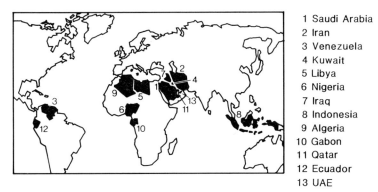

1 Saudi Arabia
2 Iran
3 Venezuela
4 Kuwait
5 Libya
6 Nigeria
7 Iraq
8 Indonesia
9 Algeria
10 Gabon
11 Qatar
12 Ecuador
13 UAE

Aims: to unify oil policies within the member countries
Founded in September, 1960. H.Q. in Vienna

Figure 8.7 The ABC of OPEC.

Source: see Table 8.4.

at the time among many of the south's economists and politicians. And, as pointed out earlier, Emmanuel's *Unequal Exchange* written at the end of the 1960s further encouraged the view that the terms of trade of the less developed primary producers were 'poor' because of the weak bargaining position of the direct producers. Thus the cost-of-production approach of both Prebisch and Emmanuel encouraged the LDCs' leaders to believe that the prices of exports from LDCs were up for grabs – that they could be raised by negotiation. It was not, then, surprising that OPEC's actions were seen as endorsing the arguments of Prebisch and Emmanuel.

In 1973 the non-aligned movement (NAM) adopted an economic declaration at an Algiers summit meeting which called for a NIEO. These demands were submitted to the UN General Assembly in April 1974, and adopted, without a vote, in the form of resolutions by the Assembly in May 1974. The demands for a NIEO have particularly focused on commodity issues, although many other issues were covered by the resolutions (see Table 8.5). The commodity issues were: (1) access to the north's markets; and (2) an integrated approach through a Common Fund to *stabilize* and *support* the prices of commodities exported from the LDCs.

These demands were echoed in the first Brandt Report (see Brandt, 1980), and most economists were quick to endorse the demand for better

Table 8.5 The NIEO proposals and resolutions: a summary

(a) *Technology:*	easier transfer of technology through
	    (i) new patent laws and commercial practice;
	    (ii) an international code of conduct *appropriate to the LDCs*

(b) *Transnational corporations:*	more regulation in the interests of LDCs through the formulation, adoption and implementation of *an international code of conduct for TNCs*
(c) *Debt, finance, aid:*	*more control by the south* of the international monetary system and of its institutions; more aid and rescheduling of debts; more recycling of surpluses to the LDCs, and linkage of development aid to the creation of SDRs
(d) *Commodities, trade and shipping:*	greater share of the south in world *shipping* improved *access* to the north's markets, especially for processed commodities and manufactures an 'integrated' approach through a Common Fund to *stabilize* and *support* commodity prices: 'to achieve stable conditions in commodity trade, including avoidance of excessive price fluctuations at levels which would be remunerative and just to producers and equitable to consumers'

Sources: Grubel, 1977: Cuddy, 1980; Reubens, 1981.

access to the north's markets. For as pointed out earlier, there is a general recognition by economists that the upgrading of primary products from the LDCs is discouraged by the escalating protection in the north which, *some* economists claim, is made worse by a structure of shipping charges, which escalate according to the value of the commodity (see Yeats, 1981) and which add to the discrimination against the upgrading of primary products in the LDCs.

Table 8.6 The commodity dependence of LDCs

For selected LDCs, percentage of total export value represented by exports of
particular commodities (average 1977–9)

Country	Petroleum	Others	Country	Coffee	Others
Iraq	97	—	Uganda	93	—
Saudi Arabia	94	—	Ethiopia	72	—
Iran	90	—	Colombia	62	—
Nigeria	88	—	Madagascar	42	—
Algeria	84	—	Guatemala	42	—
Venezuela	66	—	Tanzania	35	—
Syria	64	15 (cotton)	Kenya	34	16 (tea)
Indonesia	58	—	Ivory Coast	31	24 (cocoa)
Angola	43	—	Cameroon	29	21 (cocoa)
Tunisia	42	—	Dominican Republic	19	26 (sugar)
Ecuador	42	15 (coffee)	Brazil	16	—
Mexico	39	—	Zaire	15	44 (copper)
Egypt	23	22 (cotton)	Ecuador	15	42 (petroleum)
All LDCs	46		All LDCs	3.2	
World	13		World	0.9	

Country	Cotton	Others	Country	Copper	Others
Sudan	57	—	Zambia	89	—
Mali	44	—	Chile	50	—
Yemen Arab Republic	41	—	Zaire	44	15 (coffee)
Upper Volta	38	—	Peru	21	—
Egypt	22	23 (petroleum)			
Syria	15	64 (petroleum)			
All LDCs	0.9		All LDCs	1.3	
World	0.5		World	0.5	

Country	Others
Ghana	cocoa (69)
Guinea	bauxite (64)
Bolivia	tin (53)
Malawi	tobacco (53), tea (19)

(continued)

Table 8.6—continued

Country	Others
Nepal	rice (44), hides/skins (29)
Burma	rice (39), timber (27)
Morocco	phosphate rock (34)
Senegal	groundnut oil (27)
Bangladesh	jute (22)
Malaysia	rubber (19)
Mozambique	maize (18)
Sri Lanka	tea (16), rubber (15)
Philippines	coconut oil (16)
Zimbabwe	tobacco (16)
Thailand	rice (15)

Source: World Bank, 1981a, table 11.

Note: The table shows only those LDCs with a population of more than 5 million in 1979, and for whom a commodity's exports were more than 15 per cent of the country's total exports between 1977 and 1979; for the trade classifications covered by each commodity, see World Bank, 1981a, table 11; and for similar tables, see Magee, 1980, 14, 15; Morton and Tulloch, 1977, 97; Yeats, 1981, 26; and also Kidron and Segal, 1981, figure 21.

However, there is much less agreement among economists on the need for an institutionalized attempt at stabilizing and supporting commodity prices. Thus the proposals for the establishment of a Common Fund have run into considerable opposition, and there has been little progress in getting a fund off the ground in the ten years since the NIEO resolutions were passed in the General Assembly.

The free-marketeers who oppose the Common Fund are pleased at this lack of progress; indeed, they see it as some indication of the theoretical bankruptcy of the ideas behind it. They argue that the NIEO is promoted by faceless bureaucrats in cumbersome international institutions like UNCTAD – which, it has been suggested, could stand for 'Under No Circumstances Take Any Decision'.

Not surprisingly, the cost-of-production theorists see the lack of progress as the result of *different* vested interests at work which themselves make a Common Fund necessary. Their argument is that both the stabilization and support of commodity prices are desirable, because of the heavy dependence (for export income) of many LDCs on one or two primary commodities (see Table 8.6). A series of buffer-stocks is desirable to provide the necessary support, and this support, it is argued, will be cheaper to provide through a Common Fund. The main purpose of the fund is to be the financing of buffer-stocks for a number of commodities of special interest to the LDCs; but it is envisaged that some

Table 8.7 Petroleum and the 'Common Fund' commodities – their importance to the south

| Commodity | Commodity's importance | | Concentration of exports in the south | | |
| | World export value ($ billion) (average, 1977–9) | % of all world exports | Percentage of exports from: | | |
			3 biggest LDC exporters	5 biggest LDC exporters	All LDC exporters
The '10 core'					
Cocoa	3.1	0.2	57	78	95
Coffee	12.0	0.9	39	48	92
Cotton	1.8	0.1	15	21	48
Copper	7.3	0.5	40	51	63
Jute	0.2	–	88	93	94
Rubber	3.2	0.2	88	94	98
Sisal	0.1	–	80	92	98
Sugar	7.8	0.6	12	18	38
Tea	1.8	0.1	58	66	79
Tin	2.4	0.2	66	80	84
The 'other 7'					
Bananas	1.1	0.1	43	58	93
Bauxite	0.7	0.1	61	74	86
Beef and veal	6.2	0.5	11	13	17
Iron ore	5.7	0.4	29	33	42
Rice	3.6	0.3	29	33	45
Wheat	10.1	0.8	6	7	7
Wool	3.1	0.2	9	10	17
Petroleum	175.8	13.1	45	58	91
Other exports	1097.5	81.7	3	4	13
All world exports	1343.5	100	6	8	26
Sources:	World Bank, 1981a, table 9	World Bank, 1981a, table 11	World Bank, 1981a, table 10	World Bank, 1981a, table 10	World Bank, 1981a, table 10

finance would be made available through a 'second window' to promote the upgrading and further processing of commodities. UNCTAD suggested that about $500 million be allocated to the second window mainly for research and development in jute, hard fibres, tea, bananas and rubber.

But the bulk of the money going into the Common Fund was intended for the financing of buffer-stocks. In successive meetings the original eighteen commodities became seventeen, which represent about three-quarters of the LDCs' total non-petroleum mineral and agricultural exports, but priority was attached to ten 'core' commodities – for a list of the seventeen, with their 1980 export values and export concentration in LDCs, see Table 8.7. The ten core commodities were alleged to have characteristics suitable for price stabilization through buffer-stock schemes. The remaining seven were not included in these arrangements, but were intended to be covered by the second window – that is by measures to improve market access or to stimulate local processing.

According to UNCTAD, a primary attraction of the Common Fund is that commodity agreements would be less costly if financed jointly, partly because of the interlocking financial requirements of individual commodity agreements, and partly because a joint fund would be able to obtain better terms in the world's capital markets. Even so, through a simulation exercise, UNCTAD estimated that the fund's capital requirements for the ten core commodities would be about $6000 million, and some estimates are even higher, since there are considerable disagreements about the required size of the fund. For example, looking at just one of the ten core commodities, namely copper, a simulation exercise has suggested that to have held the market price within 15 per cent of the long-run or 'trend' price between 1955 and 1974 would have required a maximum copper stock valued at well over $3000 million in 1977 prices (see MacBean, in Sengupta, 1980, 62). Thus the estimated requirements for the *total* Common Fund have ranged from $3800 million to almost $12,000 million (see Harris *et al.*, 1978, 48).

The Common Fund was 'agreed' in 1980 after four years of haggling in UNCTAD. The Common Fund's Articles of Association gave the LDCs more votes (47 per cent of the total) than the OECD countries (42 per cent), the rest of the votes (11 per cent) being shared among the Soviet bloc and the People's Republic of China. The majority of the money for the fund (68 per cent of the total) was to come from the OECD grouping, with the Soviet bloc and China contributing 22 per cent and the LDCs 10 per cent. But the Common Fund 'agreement' will only come into effect when countries providing at least two-thirds of the contributions have ratified it. And this had not (in early 1983) happened, even though the total contributions into the fund from member countries have been scaled down to less than $500 million (see *South*, February 1981, 70).

As stated earlier, there has been considerable controversy about the Common Fund proposals; the flavour of much of the debate can be obtained by looking at two recent articles – one by Grubel (1977) and the other by Helleiner (1978), commenting on Grubel's paper. Unfortunately in the theoretical debate, there has been some confusion between price stabilization and price support, partly because in practice the dividing line is difficult to draw. Here I divide them and, first, look briefly at the arguments for and against *stabilization* before going on to discuss the feasibility and desirability of commodity cartels and price *support*.

Price stabilization schemes – the pros and cons

What, then, are the arguments for and against *stabilization*? It is frequently argued that short-term variations in the prices of primary commodities exported from the LDCs cause sharp changes in their total export earnings, which in turn cause domestic income instability, handicap economic planning and damage prospects for growth. Thus in the Brandt Report we find: 'It is generally acknowledged that more stable prices would be beneficial to exporting countries by helping to maintain foreign exchange earnings and to facilitate fiscal planning and economic management' (Brandt, 1980, 148). On this reasoning price stabilization is likely to be beneficial. But there are a number of stages in the argument, each of which needs to be subjected to close scrutiny.

First, do the stabilization schemes need to focus on commodities from LDCs in particular? That is, are the primary products exported from LDCs subject to greater price instability than commodities in general? The short answer seems to be yes. For all LDCs, the average annual percentage variation of export prices from long-run average prices seems to have been greater than for the DCs (see Thoburn, 1977, 21). And fluctuations in commodity prices seem to have been increasing over the period 1950–80 (see Lutz and Bale, 1980, 350).

But even if this is so, the next question that needs to be asked is: is the price instability reflected in an instability in *export earnings*? Again the answer for the LDCs as a whole seems to be yes, but there is considerable variation between LDCs. For the LDCs accounting for a large minority of the world's population (Brazil, China, India and Indonesia), instability in export earnings was no greater than the world average over the twenty-year period 1951–70 (MacBean, in Sengupta, 1980, 60). And for these larger countries, the share of all exports in total national income is generally small – in general, less than 10 per cent – so that even if they experienced export earnings instability, the effect on their national income would be small. But for some of the smaller LDCs which are heavily dependent for their export earnings on one or two primary commodities, and for which export earnings generate a large share of national income, the impact of export instability is likely to be more serious. About twenty-five LDCs are in this position – that is combining a higher-than-average degree of export earnings instability with a dependence of national income on exports of more than 20 per cent. Out of these twenty-five, ten are oil exporters. And 'of the remaining 15, three are major exporters of manufactures, Hong Kong, Singapore and Taiwan, not noticeably handicapped by their highly unstable export earnings' (ibid., 61). Thus MacBean adds, 'only a relatively few countries . . . are particularly liable to suffer from the effects of commodity export instability' (ibid.).

The next question that needs to be asked is: even if some countries' export earnings are unstable, is there any effect on national income? In the less developed countries, it has been argued, export stabilization will lead to faster growth. With greater stability of exports, a country can carry smaller foreign exchange reserves and, therefore, make better use of its export earnings. Thus export stabilization means faster growth. But, in a recent book on commodities, Adams and Behrman have argued that 'there is no evidence that fluctuations in prices, as compared to a smooth path of prices, have a substantial impact on economic perform-ance as measured by capacity utilization and growth' (Adams and Behrman, 1982, 294: see also Coppock, 1962, and MacBean, 1966, who both denied any effect on growth, and Yeats, 1981, 73, who argued that growth has been reduced by instability). This issue is clearly highly contentious.

But even if few, or any, *countries* are likely to suffer a loss of income from price instability, it may be that individual producers *within* the LDCs will suffer. To analyse this issue requires not only an examination of the organization of production to find out who is affected and how seriously by price instability, but also an analysis as to whether price instability is reflected in income instability. Free-marketeers have contended that if the price instability is due to shifts in supply (due, say, to bad harvests), then *price* stabilization through a buffer-stock is likely to de-stabilize rather than stabilize *earnings*, since if output falls but prices remain the same, income will also fall; whereas, without stabilization measures, prices would have risen to compensate, at least in part, for the fall in output. On the other hand, if the shift or 'shock' comes from the demand side, price stabilization will be accompanied by earnings stabilization.

The 'static' demand and supply analysis behind this reasoning is shown in Figure 8.8, but the realism of such an analysis has been challenged by many economists. The analysis is criticized for not accurately depicting the position of 'small' producers, who are price-takers and who, therefore, face horizontal ('perfectly elastic'), and not downward-sloping, demand curves. Furthermore, many economists have argued that, even for large producers, this is not how markets work in practice. In particular, it is argued, the analysis as to who gains and who loses from price stabilization and by how much is very much affected by assumptions about producers' expectations (see references in Figure 8.8).

But even if the free-marketeers are forced to concede that the stabilization of prices is *always* reflected in some stabilization of incomes – that is the picture depicted in the bottom half of Figure 8.8 is the realistic one – they have another line of attack. They say that the resource costs of stabilizing prices (for example, the interest and storage costs of operating a buffer-stock) have to be shown to be less than the gains from price stabilization for the whole cumbersome operation to be worth while. This they claim is not the case. MacBean argues that it is improbable that international civil servants will be able to outspeculate the commodity speculators (MacBean, in Sengupta, 1980, 62). And an analysis by MacAvoy (1976) of the costs and benefits from price stabilization suggests that there would be a net loss (or net costs) of more than $500 million a year from operating a Common Fund (see Table 8.8).

However, in view of the earlier discussion, it is not surprising to learn that there are considerable differences of opinion about both the benefits and costs. For example, the income gains from stabilizing the prices of copper and tin are shown in Table 8.8 to be $82 million plus $19 million, or a little over $100 million in total. By contrast, a study on price stabilization by Cuddy, an UNCTAD economist, suggests that the income gains from the price stabilization of these two commodities would be ten times as much, totalling more than $1000 million (see Cuddy, 1980).

There are differences between the two studies in the estimates of particular effects, but the main difference is in what effects are included. In Cuddy's study major gains are shown to accrue from the long-run effects on the production and consumption of copper and tin, and from the broader effects that fluctuating prices have on the world economy. As another UNCTAD economist, Yeats, states: 'less volatile commodity prices could facilitate stabilisation of the world economy at higher levels

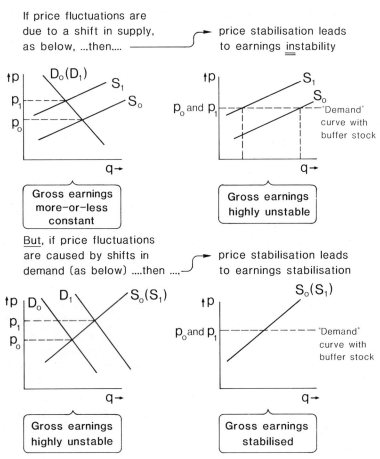

Figure 8.8 Price and income instability – the 'static' demand and supply approach.

Source: Brook et al., 1978; references in Harris et al; Salmon and Smith, 1978; but see Cuddy, 1980, 245, for criticisms of this model.

of activity' (Yeats, 1981, 72). The argument is that price stabilization would raise output in the developed countries, because volatile commodity prices are reflected in general price rises (inflation) in the DCs due to institutional rigidities in the labour and other markets. And, then, in the course of attempts to reduce inflation output is sacrificed. Thus the price instability of LDCs' exports is reflected, through the 'ratchet' effect, in output losses in the DCs.

Table 8.8 Gains and losses from commodity price stabilization: one estimate ($ million at 1974 prices)

Commodity	Income gains (losses):			Cost of price stabilization[1]	Net gains (losses)
	to producers	to consumers	Total		
Coffee	29	(9)	20	25	(5)
Cocoa	21	(7)	14	12	2
Tea	8	(2)	6	12	(6)
Sugar	226	(67)	159	133	26
Cotton	26	(6)	20	81	(61)
Rubber	(2)	4	2	15	(13)
Jute	0	0	0	0	0
Sisal	2	(1)	1	0	1
Copper	(50)	132	82	555	(473)
Tin	(10)	29	19	82	(63)
Total	250	73	323	915	(592)

Source: MacAvoy, 1976.

Note:
1 Cost of storage and of interest at 10 per cent p.a.

These alleged 'macroeffects' of price stabilization have been subjected to considerable criticism. The free-marketeers have challenged the 'ratchet' effect by saying that it is only when governments follow incorrect monetary policies that the *relative* changes in commodity prices will be reflected in *general* price increases. And MacBean argues,

> Given the fact that all eighteen of the UNCTAD commodities are only some ten per cent of Developed Countries' imports and less than 2 per cent of their national incomes . . . and given the very limited amount of commodity price stabilisation likely to emerge from ICAs [international commodity agreements], it [the ratchet effect] does not seem a very powerful argument in support of the UNCTAD proposals.   (MacBean, in Sengupta, 1980, 67)

Given all these differences, it is not surprising that Harris *et al.* (1978, 46–7) say that 'Our analysis of price variability leads us to judge that few firm conclusions are possible from economic analysis regarding the costs and benefits of stabilisation'. In general, the cost-of-production theorists argue for price stabilization, because for them the uncertainties generated through price volatility are invariably reflected in losses in output.

Against this, the free-marketeers argue that buffer-stock operations would generate net costs, and that it is better to facilitate the smoothing out of earnings of individual farmers and LDCs through improvements in capital markets, or to compensate them through national marketing boards or the IMF. And against this, the cost-of-production theorists argue that earnings compensation and price stabilization are not mutually exclusive (see Gulati, in Sengupta, 1980, 180), and Yeats argues that 'The fact that industrial countries have found it necessary to adopt internal price support and stabilisation policies for domestic producers of agricultural raw materials and other commodities works strongly in favour of the common fund and its policy objectives' (Yeats, 1981, 74).

Commodity cartels and price support – feasibility and desirability: the subjective preference view

But this parallel with the price support measures in the industrial countries is precisely what worries the free-marketeers. They are concerned that the Common Fund will end up as a wasteful income support scheme along the lines of the Common Agricultural Policy (CAP) of the European Economic Community (EEC), even if its *initial* objective is to stabilize prices. Thus the free-marketeers are concerned that commodity prices and incomes will be *supported* rather than *stabilized* by a Common Fund, and that the latter will have the same tendency to encourage over-production and to generate wasteful 'commodity mountains' and 'lakes' as has the EEC's CAP. Cost-of-production theorists are much less worried about this possibility, for in their view the waste would be a small price to pay for the resulting redistribution of income between DCs and LDCs. Nevertheless, they would prefer to see prices stabilized by a Common Fund with price support coming from production quotas and controls administered by a commodity cartel along the lines of OPEC.

In any case they argue that the stakes are high. Price support for LDCs' exports would go some way to eliminating the unequal exchange to which Emmanuel refers. He argues that the loss inflicted on the LDCs from unequal exchange, and which could be recovered through a system of collective export taxes, is of the order of $200–$300 billion dollars a year, a figure which, for example, swamps the $10–$15 billion dollars in world 'aid' each year (see Emmanuel, 1972, 368). Thus it is important to examine the feasibility of cartels for commodities other than oil, and the gains likely to accrue to the cartel members.

The subjective preference theorists argue that oil is both a limited and a special case. It is limited for the reason that the gains accruing to OPEC members will be short-lived because of the inherent fragility of cartels. Cartels are fragile both because cartel members invariably have different interests and because the rising price of the cartel-dominated commodity invariably brings forward substitutes. The latter are likely to take the form of increased production of the same physical commodity from outside the cartel (for example, North Sea or Alaskan oil) or of substitution by a commodity which has a different physical form but which provides the same utility (for example, coal or even insulation). Thus even OPEC's success, according to the free-marketeers, will be short-lived. But cartels for other commodities, they argue, will have an even shorter life. For OPEC and oil is a somewhat special case.

Oil is allegedly a special case because of the unusual characteristics of oil supply and demand. First, let us look at the latter – the demand characteristics. A minimum condition for a cartel's success is a low price elasticity of demand for the commodity around which the cartel is organized. Thus a low price elasticity, of, say, minus 0.5, means that a reduction of 10 per cent in the quantity supplied will be reflected in a price increase of 20 per cent and, therefore, an increase in total gross sales or revenue of 8 per cent (90 per cent multiplied by 120 per cent yields 108 per cent).

Thus even if the cartel loses revenue in the longer term through substitution, the short-run gains may be worth while for the cartel as a whole, for the additional short-term revenue can be used to generate further gains in the long term. Whether the cartel's operations are worth while and hold together depends on the size of the gains to the cartel as a whole, and on the distribution of those gains within the cartel.

Thus an important first question in assessing the viability of any cartel is: by how much will the price of the commodity increase following a reduction in its total supply? The answer is not easy to give, since the price elasticity of demand for a commodity is not easy to measure. Other factors (such as the prices of other commodities and the incomes of buyers) have to be isolated, and the time period carefully specified. But looking at the seventeen primary commodities (Table 8.9) identified by UNCTAD for its Common Fund, it is probable that less than one-half are favourably placed in this respect. The beverages (cocoa, coffee and tea) are reasonably well placed in this respect, although to some extent they compete with one another; the minerals (copper, tin, bauxite and iron ore) are also favourably placed; while the price elasticities for the foodstuffs (sugar, bananas, beef, rice and wheat) are generally thought to be higher, because of substitution from other foodstuffs; and the other

Table 8.9 Commodity cartels: prospects for UNCTAD's '17'

In 'core 10'?	Commodity	Cartel profitability		Cartel feasibility		Particularly favourable or unfavourable factors?
		Little immediate increase in production elsewhere? [3]	Large rise in price if supply reduced	Few major exporting countries [1]	Rapidly growing market?	
	Petroleum [2]	F [3]	F	F	F	Major producer (Saudi Arabia) can 'afford' to cut supply; divisions among importing countries
	Beverages					
Yes	Cocoa	F?	F?	F	U?	Some doubts about price elasticities of supply and demand
Yes	Coffee	F?	F	U	U?	Less than one-half world's exports from five biggest exporting countries
Yes	Tea	F?	F	F	U	Considerable differences in production costs between major producers
	Other foodstuffs					
Yes	Sugar	U	F	U	U?	Dispersed production
	Bananas	U?	U	F	U	High price elasticity of demand
	Beef	U	U	U	F	Dispersed production
	Rice	U	F?	U	U	Dispersed production
	Wheat	U	F?	U	F?	Dispersed production
	Minerals					
Yes	Copper	F?	F?	F?	U	Production not highly concentrated; substitution threat from other metals
Yes	Tin	F?	F	F	U	Large US stockpile of tin
	Bauxite	F?	F?	F	U	Substitution threat from other metals
	Iron ore	U	U?	U	U	Dispersed production

Table 8.9—continued

Commodity	Cartel profitability		Cartel feasibility		Particularly favourable or unfavourable factors?
In 'core 10'?	Little immediate increase in production elsewhere?	Large rise in price if supply reduced	Few major exporting countries[1]	Rapidly growing market?	
Other materials					
Cotton Yes	U?	U?	U	U?	Strong competition from synthetics
Jute Yes	F?	U	F	U	Strong competition from synthetics
Rubber Yes	F	U?	F	U	Strong competition from synthetics
Sisal Yes	F?	U	F	U	Strong competition from synthetics
Wool	U	F?	U	U	Dispersed production

Notes:
1 Considered favourable if >50 per cent of exports come from five biggest LDC exporters (see Table 8.7).
2 Petroleum is included for purposes of comparison; it is not one of the UNCTAD 17.
3 F = condition favourable to a commodity cartel; U = an unfavourable factor; '?' expresses some doubts.

industrial raw materials (cotton, jute, natural rubber, sisal and wool) suffer extensive competition from synthetic, petroleum-based sub-stitutes.

Thus in respect of its low price elasticity oil (crude petroleum) is copied by probably less than one-half of the UNCTAD 17. But, in addition, oil has a high *income* elasticity of demand; that is as individuals get richer, so their expenditure (direct and indirect) on oil increases proportionately. This income elasticity of demand is relevant because, if it is high, the cartel is likely to be subjected to less internal strain. For it is clear that the cutback in a cartel's production necessary to bring about a given price increase will have to last for a shorter period of time when the market is growing rapidly than when it grows slowly. This is likely to mean that less strain is imposed on those producers within the cartel who are bearing the brunt of the cutback in production. But again few of the UNCTAD 17 commodities are favourably placed in this respect; that is few have a high income elasticity of demand – see the column in Table 8.9 headed 'Rapidly growing market?'.

The situation, the free-marketeers claim, is no more favourable when we look at some of the supply characteristics of the UNCTAD 17. A cartel is likely to be more cohesive, the more the world's supply of a commodity is concentrated in a few countries. The world production of oil and particularly the world exports of oil are dominated by relatively few producing countries. The same can be said for only a few of the UNCTAD 17, especially when close substitutes are considered.

Thus the free-marketeers claim that oil is a special case. No other commodity has all of the same favourable characteristics for the forma-tion of a successful commodity cartel. This, they add, is why so few have been formed, and why none, apart from OPEC, has held together. The cost-of-production theorists accept that oil is particularly well placed but argue that it is not unique. That is although oil has *particularly* favour-able characteristics for the formation of a cartel, some of the UNCTAD 17 have *sufficiently* favourable characteristics for cartel formation to be worth while.

Commodity cartels: the cost-of-production view

But the cost-of-production economists argue that for many of the com-modities, cartel formation has been blocked by the DCs. Thus, it is alleged, the US stockpile of tin – equivalent at about 200,000 tonne in 1980 to one year's world production – has been used to weaken the market and to fragment the cohesiveness of the main producing countries. Similarly, the free-marketeers' explanation for the absence of a tea cartel differs from that of the COP theorists. In explaining the failure of the main tea producing countries to agree on the allocation of global export quotas the subjective preference theorists emphasize inter-country differences in unit production costs, arguing that Kenya (as a low-cost producer) is likely to favour a collective export tax to bring down production, since this is likely to eliminate the high-cost producers in Sri Lanka and India, while the south Asian producing countries are more likely to favour proportional export quotas. While conceding that there are these differences, the Sri Lankan and Indian negotiators allege that British tea interests in Kenya are responsible for Kenya's uncooper-ative attitude (see *Third World Quarterly*, July 1982). And again, although the price elasticity of demand for bananas is not sufficiently low to hold out the hope of high cartel profits, cost-of-production theorists stress also the *structure* of the market in explaining the absence of an effective producer's organization based on bananas. As Harris *et al.* (1978, 56) say: 'the failure of the 1974 increase in export taxes was possibly due more to the failure of many producing countries to support the action and to the power of the companies involved, who destroyed bananas rather than pay the tax'.

By contrast, in the case of oil, the cost-of-production theorists claim that the undoubtedly favourable market characteristics of the com-modity were reinforced by other factors. Thus Peter Odell, an ex-Shell company economist, has pointed out that in the late 1960s and early 1970s there was support for an oil price rise from some sections of capital (in particular, the oil TNCs and the petrochemical companies in the USA) and, more generally, from the US government (see Odell, in Payer, 1975, 31). Furthermore, when in 1973–4 the oil export price rose sharply, the effect on consumption in the rich countries was muted by government action. For the developed country governments did not increase indirect taxes on petroleum products in the same proportion as the rise in international oil prices; and so whereas 'in real terms, inter-national prices of those products [gasoline, kerosene and fuel oil] were about 350 per cent above their 1972 levels . . . domestic prices . . . in industrial countries [were] only 62 per cent higher' (World Bank, 1981b, 46). Thus OPEC's actions were reinforced rather than countered by government policies in the DCs.

The cost-of-production theorists thus argue that it is partly because of support from at least some of the DCs that OPEC has achieved its success; and that far from the DCs supporting the attempts to form cartels for other commodities, there has in many cases been powerful opposition. Thus the barter terms of trade for most of the UNCTAD 17 continue to deteriorate.

But why, the subjective preference theorists ask, focus on the *barter* terms of trade? If the focus is on the reward for work, then other measures (of the terms on which trade is conducted) are more relevant. One such measure is the *income* terms of trade, defined as the *value* of exports divided by the import price index. The income terms of trade may show a quite different trend from that of the barter terms of trade; indeed, the price of an export commodity may decline precisely *because* the volume of exports has expanded rapidly. But, the SPTs claim, even the income terms of trade may be misleading as a measure of the 'reward' to the factors producing the commodities. If productivity is rising very rapidly, then the income as well as the barter terms of trade may be declining, and yet the wage per labour-hour may be rising.

A more detailed discussion of the 'best' measure is beyond the scope of this book. The COP theorists argue that the barter terms of trade is a reasonably good measure of the relative payments for the labour, raw material and machine inputs into commodities. But they also argue that if the income terms of trade is used as a measure, then it is the income that is *retained* in the country that needs to be calculated. They admit that these, the *retained value terms of trade*, do seem to have improved for the LDCs in general, but they argue that there are some important exceptions (for example, tea) to the general improvement and that, in any case, the improvements are generally from a very low level. Thus the developing countries invariably retain less than one-quarter of the commodity's value added (for examples, see Clairmonte, in Payer, 1975; *South*, November 1981, 54).

Cartels and capitalism: the views of the abstract labour theorist

Abstract labour theorists are neither 'for' nor 'against' commodity cartels in general, but emphasize the need to consider each case individually and answer the question: who will benefit? Thus they place much less emphasis than do cost-of-production theorists on the distribution between *countries* of the revenue from commodities. Instead the emphasis is on the *production process within capitalism*.

Thus abstract labour theorists analyse the potential for commodity cartels by focusing on the activities of capital in the process of reproducing commodities. They follow Marx in arguing that *market* prices are determined by the relationship of supply and demand, and are likely to differ from longer-run prices of production, the latter being determined by (but, note, *not* equal to) the socially necessary labour-time or exchange value of the commodity. The time required for supply to approximate demand, and for market prices to get close to long-run prices, depends on the conditions of production and distribution for particular commodities.

Thus, for Marxists, the margins are likely to differ between producers, even when surpluses are defined in price terms, that is as sources from which interest, rent and profit-as-enterprise are paid. For even when the market price of a commodity is equal to the price of production, some producers are bound to be more efficient than others and, therefore, make an above-average profit. Thus the process of competition between capitals produces *actual* differences in profit rates as well as an equalization *tendency*.

The possible divergence of market prices from prices of production clearly provides a possibility for a successful commodity cartel. For if the reproduction of a commodity (or of its more or less equivalent use value) is 'awkward' or is blocked, then demand is likely to exceed supply, and market price will rise above the long-run price of production. An above-average rate of surplus will accrue to the producers of the commodity. Thus agriculture may be 'awkward', in as much as capital may be slow to flow into it, either for technical reasons or because landlords block its introduction. If landlords are effective, as a group, in slowing the flow of productive capital into agriculture, then above-average rates of surplus will be available, and rent may have to be paid by tenant farmers even on the worst bits of land in use. This is the source of what Marx called 'absolute' rent.

It is easy to see how, on similar reasoning, gains can accrue to a commodity cartel. For if capital has difficulty in reproducing a particular use value (for example, energy), then the market price of a particular commodity possessing that use value (for example, oil) may rise well above its long-run price of production, if a major group of producers such as OPEC collectively cuts back on its supply. Thus absolute rent or superprofit will accrue to the cartel – OPEC in this case.

The Marxists' emphasis on the capitalist framework in their discussion of commodity production immediately raises two further points about commodity cartels. First, the emphasis on the *capitalist* nature of commodity production raises questions about who is likely to gain from a commodity cartel. Specifically doubts are raised as to whether the peasants or wage-workers directly engaged in the production of a commodity which is to be cartelized will gain to any significant extent. In the same way as the price support policies for agriculture within the EEC seem to have benefited the richer farmers rather than the agricultural labourers, so it is likely that commodity cartels will benefit the landlords, rentiers and entrepreneurs dominating the production of the commodities within UNCTAD's list of 17.

The second point concerns the opposition of DC governments to the formation of commodity cartels by the LDCs. Marxists agree that these influences are important, but they doubt whether such a monolithic conspiracy exists to oppose such cartels as was implied by Gunder Frank when he argued that 'The ability of Third World countries to form cartels and exercise monopoly power is further limited by the developed countries' policy of divide and rule' (Frank, 1981b, 125). For in the same way as the theories of value of abstract labour and the dependency theorists (such as Frank) differ, so they also have different theories of the structure of the state in capitalism; these differences are examined in more detail in Chapter 9. Here it is sufficient to point out that blocks of capital (even within the same nation-state) are likely to be in competition, even though they have a common, more general interest towards wage-labour. And this competition may well lead them in different directions in respect of particular commodity cartels.

If anything, this makes the abstract labour theorists more pessimistic than the cost-of-production theorists about the feasibility of commodity cartels. It certainly makes them more pessimistic about the gains accruing to the direct producers (the wage-labourers and the peasants) of these commodities. But their analysis differs from that of the subjective preference theorists, who are similarly pessimistic about the feasibility of commodity cartels. The latter feel vindicated, if not positively pleased by the failure, so far, of attempts to get the Integrated Programme for Commodities and the Common Fund off the ground.

To date, commodity agreements exist only for cocoa, tin, natural rubber and sugar, but these are not financed in common, and only one has been formed since the call was made for a Common Fund. Similarly, progress has been slow on the other components of the NIEO demands and other north–south issues such as the restructuring of international institutions with no progress being made at, or since, the north–south summit meeting at Cancun, Mexico, in 1981. Nor is much progress expected in the near future; there was little progress made at the Sixth Session of UNCTAD, held in 1983.

NOTES ON FURTHER READING

On the growth of the Third World and import substitutions, see Greenaway and Milner's Hobart paper, 1979, for the clearest exposition of the subjective preference theorists' case against protectionism. Little *et al.*,

1970, also put a forceful case against protectionism from a similar view-point – a summary of the arguments can be found in their chapter 1. For a case from the left against import controls, see the Socialist Workers Party's pamphlet by Harris and Hallas, 1981.

For more general discussions of the cases for, as well as against protection, see Sodersten, 1980, part III; Streeten, 1973, section 3; Helleiner, 1972, chapter 7; Cairncross and Keeley, 1983, chapter 4; Hardwick *et al.*, 1982, chapter 29, the last two having the merit of being particularly concise. Also refer to Stewart, in Helleiner, 1976. For dis-cussions within a more historical context, refer to section 8.4 of Colman and Nixson, 1978, and to chapter 7 of Brown, 1974.

Optimum tariff theory is explained clearly in Corden, 1974, 158–76; for a concise introduction to the effective rate of protection (ERP), see Helleiner, 1972, chapter 8. For more detailed discussions on ERP, see Corden, 1971; Edwards, 1975, section 3.3; Grubel and Johnson, 1971 section 1. For examples of the many ERP empirical studies, see Balassa, 1971; Edwards, 1975.

On NICs and a NIDL, for statistical overviews of the expansion of manufacturing exports from LDCs, see Lall, 1980b; World Bank, 1981b, chapter 3; UNCTAD, 1981, part III, chapter 3, and part IV, chapter 4; UNIDO, 1981. For brief general discussions of the subject, look at Edwards, 1980, and the debate in the *Far Eastern Economic Review*, 25 June 1982, 6 August 1982, between on the one side Gunder Frank, and on the other Linda Lim, Huo Bide (both Singaporeans), Simon Osnos and Stephen Haggard (both Americans).

For a generally optimistic, free-marketeer view of the expansion of manufactured exports from the LDCs, see Balassa, 1979. For a pessi-mistic dependency viewpoint, look at chapters 3 and 5 of Frank, 1981a, and at Landsberg, 1979. For a critical look at the dependency picture, see Cypher, 1979. A more particular discussion of the role of TNCs in LDCs' manufactured exports can be obtained from Helleiner, 1973, and Trajtenberg, in Zarembka, 1977.

A detailed study by Frobel *et al.*, 1980, focuses on the establishment of world market factories by German companies, but it also looks at the effect on industries in Germany. More general discussions of the 'adjust-ment problem' in the DCs can be found in FCO, 1979; OECD, 1979b; Riddell, 1979. In a 1983 book Michael Beenstock has argued that stag-nation in the OECD countries was largely caused by the rapid industrial-ization of the developing countries since the mid-1960s: Beenstock, 1983. For a brief counter to this view, look at Cairncross and Keeley, 1983, 82–3. AMPO, 1977, is useful for a discussion of FTZs in particu-lar, and UNCTAD, 1983a contains much useful material, but I strongly recommend Elson and Pearson, in Young *et al.*, 1981, for a thought-provoking look at the role of, and effects on, women workers of employment in export manufacturing zones.

For some details of protectionism in the DCs, look at Balassa, 1980b; IMF, 1982, 135–7; Nowzad, 1978; *South*, October 1980, 18–20, May 1982, 70–1, July 1982, 56–7.

On regional integration, for a summary of the issues, refer to chapter 20 of Sodersten, 1980, and chapter 8 of Morton and Tulloch, 1977. Concise discussions can also be found in Stewart, in Helleiner, 1976; and in the third chapters of Yeats, 1981, and of Hardwick *et al.*, 1982. Most students will find it unnecessary to go beyond these, but for more refer to Vaitsos, 1978; Robson, 1980; Milner and Greenaway, 1979, 87–93; UNCTAD, 1983b.

For the NIEO and commodity cartels, details of the resolutions of the United Nations on the NIEO can be found in the appendix to Yeats, 1981, and in the first chapter of Reubens, 1981. Much has been written on the background or buildup to the NIEO. I have found the following useful: Frank, 1980, chapter 5; Reubens, 1981, chapter 1; Rangarajan, 1978, chapter 1; Sodersten, 1980, chapters 18–19. Chapter 9 of Morton and Tulloch, 1977, is less useful, but chapter 20 of Sampson, 1982, is worth looking at for a discussion of the links between the NIEO and the first Brandt Report.

Blow-by-blow accounts and up-to-date news of the north–south negotiations in UNCTAD and elsewhere can be found in the monthly *South*, and in the *Third World Quarterly*. A good grasp of the different theoretical positions on the NIEO can be got from Abdel-Fadil *et al.*, 1977; Grubel, 1977; Helleiner, 1978.

An introduction to the orthodox position on *price stabilization* can be found in Brook *et al.*, 1978. Good, more general introductions can be found in Harris *et al.*, 1978, 32–49; Yeats, 1981, chapter 4; MacBean, in Sengupta, 1980; Cuddy, 1980; Magee, 1980, sections 4.4 and 6.5. These are all relatively brief; for a much longer treatment, see Hallwood, 1979; Adams and Behrman, 1982.

On price support and cartels the following are likely to be useful: Radetzki, in Helleiner, 1976; Harris *et al.*, 1978, 50–64; Laursen, 1978; Hallwood, 1979, chapter 9.

Finally, for individual commodities and commodity schemes, see Gemmill, 1981; Payer, 1975; Rangarajan, 1978, chapter 2. There is a useful listing of postwar commodity schemes in the first appendix of Morton and Tulloch, 1977.

SUMMARY

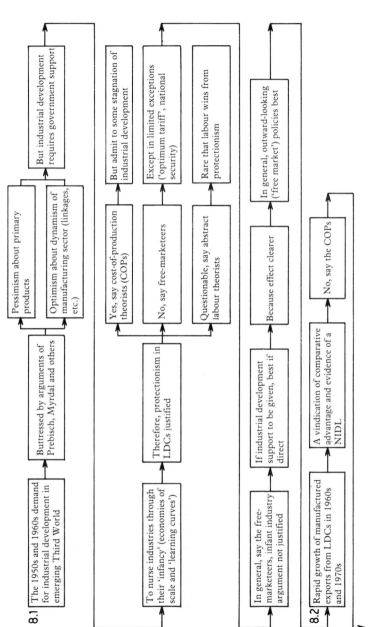

8.1 The 1950s and 1960s demand for industrial development in emerging Third World

Buttressed by arguments of Prebisch, Myrdal and others

Pessimism about primary products

Optimism about dynamism of manufacturing sector (linkages, etc.)

But industrial development requires government support

To nurse industries through their 'infancy' (economies of scale and 'learning curves')

Therefore, protectionism in LDCs justified

Yes, say cost-of-production theorists (COPs)

But admit to some stagnation of industrial development

No, say free-marketeers

Except in limited exceptions ('optimum tariff', national security)

Questionable, say abstract labour theorists

Rare that labour wins from protectionism

In general, say the free-marketeers, infant industry argument not justified

If industrial development support to be given, best if direct

Because effect clearer

In general, outward-looking ('free market') policies best

8.2 Rapid growth of manufactured exports from LDCs in 1960s and 1970s

A vindication of comparative advantage and evidence of a NIDL

No, say the COPs

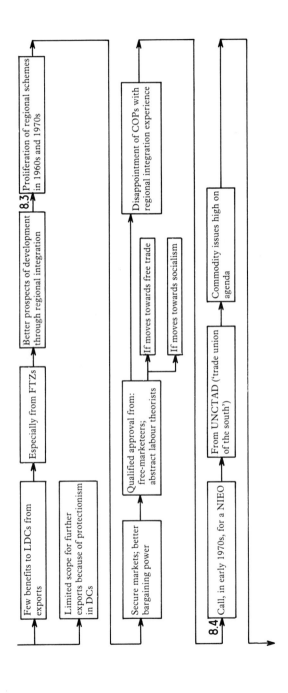

Few benefits to LDCs from exports

Limited scope for further exports because of protectionism in DCs

Especially from FTZs

Better prospects of development through regional integration

8.3 Proliferation of regional schemes in 1960s and 1970s

Secure markets; better bargaining power

Qualified approval from: free-marketeers; abstract labour theorists

If moves towards free trade

If moves towards socialism

Disappointment of COPs with regional integration experience

Call, in early 1970s, for a NIEO

From UNCTAD ('trade union of the south')

Commodity issues high on agenda

8.4

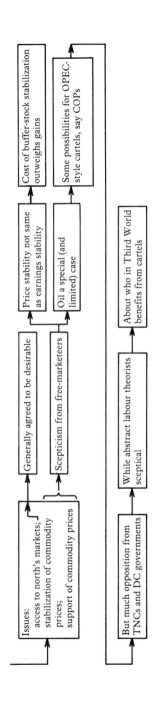

9

The state, imperialism and socialism

9.1 THE CAPITALIST STATE

The subject of this book has been the world economy and ways of looking at it. Throughout I have argued that there is no one view which is
universally acknowledged to be correct by all economists. Furthermore,
it has been argued that it aids understanding to systematically distinguish between different schools of economists on the basis of their
fundamental assumptions or 'theories of value'. By now, no doubt, you
will be in a position to agree or disagree with this.

If you disagree, so be it. But whether or not you agree with my arguments so far, you will realize that if different 'schools' are identified on
the basis of their theories of value, then it is likely that each of these
schools will have different 'theories of the state'. This has been implicit
throughout the previous eight chapters, but the explicit purpose of this
section is to summarize and compare these theories of the state.

At the risk of oversimplifying things I start with a highly schematic
summary. Table 9.1 summarizes the approaches of each of the broad
schools of economic thought identified in this book. The table is a useful
starting-point but needs amplifying. For not only does each school mean
different things by 'economic' and 'political', but they also use the terms
'competitive', 'imperfectly competitive' and 'monopolistic' somewhat
differently. So we need to look at each approach in more detail.

The focus of the *subjective preference* school is on the individual. As
argued in Chapter 2, for this group of economists, the best economic
system is one in which individuals are free to exercise their talents and
express their tastes. The 'economic' is here defined quite precisely as the
'allocation of resources between competing ends', and good government
consists of providing a framework within which voluntary contracts can
be formulated and upheld. The 'market' is the context within which
individuals can and should express their subjective preferences.

From this it follows that the economic system is also in a sense a

Table 9.1 Political economy and the state: competing views

School of economists	The 'economic' sphere	The 'political' sphere
Subjective preference	Competive (generally)	Competitive (ideally, based on ballot box)
Cost-of-production	Imperfectly competitive (generally)	Imperfectly competitive (pluralist consensus, ideally)
Underdevelopment	Monopolistic (generally)	Monopolistic (generally)
Abstract labour	Imperfectly competitive ('capitalistically competitive')	Monopolized (by dominant class, generally)

political one, in which each individual votes with his (or more rarely her) dollar, pound, or whatever, but the ideal system of government is one in which individuals are represented *as* individuals. That is, the ballot box and voting on single issues (through referendums, for example) is generally preferred to the politics of pluralism or the oppression of open meetings. It follows that the role of the state organs (the legislature, judiciary and executive) should be limited to protecting and enforcing the market.

It is not surprising, then, to find that the subjective preference theorists are opposed to non-military aid provided by the state (see Bauer, in Duignan and Rabushka, 1980; Bauer and Yamey, 1981; Friedman, in Bhagwati and Eckaus, 1970). For these economists, aid is acceptable if provided through non-governmental organizations (NGOs), such as Oxfam, because then the money comes from direct voluntary donations. And state-to-state *military* aid meets with their approval so long as it is used to support governments which are upholding the free market. But state-to-state civilian aid is proscribed, because it 'reinforces the disastrous politicization of life in the Third World. It intensifies the hold of government over the rest of society by increasing the money, patronage and power at its disposal', and such a situation 'inevitably diverts attention and energies from the ordinary business life to the political sphere' (Bauer and Yamey, 1981, 5).

The upholding of the free market is, then, the yardstick by which governments are judged; such a yardstick leads to fine distinctions being drawn by politicians on the right. Thus Jeane Kirkpatrick, President Reagan's Ambassador to the UN in 1982, was able to distinguish between 'authoritarian' Latin American military dictatorships which were acceptable allies of the USA since they could be 'reformed', and 'totalitarian' communist regimes which were unacceptable because they could not.

The view of the cost-of-production theorists is quite different. Their view is that because the economic system is imperfectly competitive, the state also needs to be 'imperfectly competitive' in order to provide a balance of power. The primary 'economic' problem is seen as one of preventing struggles over distribution from interfering with the development of technology. But since the main protagonists in the distributional struggle are constantly changing, so the public institutions required to regulate these struggles need to change.

In general, then, a strong state is needed, but one which is based on a pluralist consensus. What is needed in the new industrial system, according to Galbraith, is an 'educational and scientific estate' which is above the narrower sectional interests of the big corporations and organized labour (see Galbraith, 1977, 373). And according to another writer in this school, many of the less developed countries suffer particularly not only because their educational and scientific estate is weak, but also because they are 'soft states', characterized by a 'general lack of social discipline, signified by deficiencies in their legislation' (see Myrdal, in Streeten, 1969, 229). Thus narrow sectional interests have even more scope in the 'soft states' of the Third World than in the north.

According to the cost-of-production theorists, sectional interests arise from distributional roles. And clearly since a group of individuals can have a distributional interest in common, they are quite likely to have common political interests. The role of 'good' government is to minimize these differences by achieving a balance of power. The mould of antagonistic groups has to be broken, and a new 'consensus' found. This is more likely to be achieved within a system of proportional representation.

Unfortunately the primary obstacle to the achievement of this consensus changes over time. It is a moving target. Thus in the early nineteenth century, in Ricardo's view, it was the landlords; in the interwar years, in Keynes's view, it was the rentiers; and more recently, according to Galbraith, it has been the technostructure within the 'two bureaucracies' of the private corporations and the public sector (see Galbraith, 1975). In all these cases countervailing power needs to be encouraged in opposition to these all-too-powerful vested interests. Income distribution between groups needs to be managed.

This applies to income distribution *between* as well as *within* countries. International income distribution needs to be managed, if necessary by establishing new international institutions which will identify and achieve a common interest. This is the basic theme of both Brandt reports (1980, 1983). Not surprisingly, the argument on aid of the cost-of-production theorists runs directly counter to that of Bauer, Yamey and Friedman. State-to-state civilian aid must be supported, both to rectify imbalances in income distribution and to promote the development of technology, whereas military aid is acceptable only if it supports governments based on a consensus, preferably elected through a parliamentary system based on proportional representation.

For the cost-of-production theorists, it is both normal and desirable, in an industrial economy, for the political structures (the 'state') to be separate from the economic (the 'civil society'). Such a separation is necessary if the state is to ensure that liberal values are upheld and a balance of power achieved. Thus the 'best' government is not necessarily the one that has the greatest support in an absolute sense, but one which has the greatest support in the sense that it generates the least opposition. In the UK these aims are most closely pursued by the Liberal–SDP (Social Democratic Party) alliance.

It will come as no surprise when I say that the view of the abstract labour theorists, the Marxists, is radically different from that of the cost-of-production theorists. For the Marxists, civil society in the capitalist mode of production is characterized by a warlike competition particularly during periods of acute economic crisis. This is not the atomistic, perfect competition of the subjective preference school. The relentless concentration and centralization of capital prevents that. And it is markedly different from the cartelized world of Galbraith's techno-structure. For blocs of capital, particularly in crisis periods, 'fight like hostile brothers'. Thus within the civil society 'It is not monopoly or conspiracy upon which uneven development rests, but free competition itself' (Shaikh, in Nell, 1980, 227). And even when at the level of the nation-state the fire of competition is dampened temporarily, it is likely to continue to rage at the international level.

Unfortunately 'ever since the publication of Lenin's *Imperialism*, it has become a commonplace to assert that capitalism has entered its monopoly stage' (ibid., 208). For, in his *Imperialism*, Lenin had written that 'the deepest economic foundation of imperialism is monopoly [which] inevitably engenders a tendency to stagnation and decay' (Lenin, 1970, 95–6). But as was emphasized in Section 5.1, Lenin's *Imperialism* was primarily a polemic. He had emphasized the monopolistic aspect of capitalism for two reasons: first, because of the geographical context in which he wrote *Imperialism*; and secondly, because of its contemporary political context. In writing *Imperialism* Lenin drew many examples from the Germany of his time. And the Germany of the late nineteenth and early twentieth century *was* more monopolistic in structure than capitalism elsewhere, with financial capital being more closely integrated with industrial capital. But Lenin also overemphasized the monopolistic aspect of capitalism because of the contemporary context of *Imperialism*. For he wanted to convince his readers that the First World War was a war between national blocs of capital, and as such should be opposed by workers everywhere. It was this emphasis on monopoly capitalism that was picked up by many on the left, even though, on the same page that Lenin had written about the tendency to stagnation and decay, he had also written: 'monopoly under capitalism can never completely, and for a very long period of time, eliminate competition in the world market' (ibid., 96).

I believe that it is more accurate, within the context of an abstract labour theory of value, to emphasize the competitive nature of capitalism at the level of 'civil' society. To some extent this is not how things appear. With the prevalence of big factories and massive transnational corporations, 'civil society' appears to be dominated by monopolies. But appearances are deceptive. The force of competition is exercised 'behind the backs', so to speak, of individual capitals through the social abstraction of labour.

At the political level appearances are similarly deceptive. For within capitalism power is monopolized, even though it appears to be 'shared'. Not only does access to the state apparatus *appear* to be fluid, but the powers of that apparatus appear to be greater, for groups in opposition to capital, than they are in reality. For, in reality, the capitalists' collective monopoly of the means of production is reflected (though in a somewhat distorted form) in a monopoly of power. In the words of the *Communist Manifesto*, 'The executive of the modern state is but a committee for managing the common affairs of the whole bourgeoisie' (Marx and Engels, 1975, 35).

Thus 'According to Marx . . . the capitalist state is a sham because its claims to universality (as embodied in declarations of the freedom, equality and dignity of all citizens) are shown upon examination to protect the sectional interests of the dominant capitalist class' (Giddens, 1981, 204). But furthermore,

> The capitalist state, for Marx, is a sham in a much more profound sense . . . in so far as the 'universal' political rights accorded the whole community of citizens only embrace one restricted segment of their existence. The right to elect a government at fixed periods leaves

untouched . . . the power of capital over the worker in the production
process.   (ibid., 205)

Capitalism turns pre-capitalist society on its head. In the latter (in
what Giddens characterizes as class-divided societies) direct political
control gave rise to the control of resources. Whereas in capitalism it is
control over resources which confers political power on the capitalist
class as a whole. Thus for Marx and the Marxists, 'The transcendence
of the state, in a socialist society is . . . very much bound up . . . with
the recovery by the worker of control over the production process'
(ibid.).

But, the abstract labour theorists stress, the political power of the
capitalist class as a whole is not at all obvious. For within capitalism, 'the
ruling class does not rule'. That is the personnel of the state are not
drawn exclusively from the ranks of the capitalist class. As Giddens puts
it, 'The capitalist class's business *is* business' (ibid., 211). Thus although
it may be useful to analyse empirically the composition of the personnel
of the state (for a British example, see Miliband, 1969), it is incorrect to
project from such an analysis that with a change of personnel there
would be a radical change in the nature of the state. For the powers of the
state in capitalism tend to be conditional upon the way in which they are
exercised.

At the same time, however, the capitalist state is not simply an undis-
torted reflection of the capitalist class. The state does have *some*
autonomy from the broad interests of capital. Thus to apply the term
'state monopoly capitalism' to late-twentieth-century capitalism in any
one nation-state is, I believe, not very useful. The state cannot *directly*
sanction the exploitation process through violent means, whereas it can
in class-divided societies. And although the state can influence the
accumulation process through its own revenues and expenditures, it
does not control the process directly. For the state in advanced
capitalism rests, in general, upon the *institutional* separation of the
political and economic.

The views of the cost-of-production and abstract labour theorists on
the desirability and permanence of this separation differ considerably.
For the cost-of-production theorists, this separation is both a desirable
and permanent feature of the industrial society, with some writers such
as Dahrendorf going so far as to say that it signals the transcendence of
capitalist society (Dahrendorf, 1959). But for the abstract labour theorists, 'far from marking the disappearance of capitalist society, this has
from the beginning been a distinguishing feature of that society'

(Giddens, 1981, 229). Despite this, the separation is fragile, incorporating as it does a strong ideological element.

And so, in the view of the abstract labour theorists, the state is not the class-neutral agency of social reform, which it is for the cost-of-production theorists. But neither is it a mere functional vehicle for the capitalist class, even though it is class-based and class-dominated. As Giddens emphasizes, 'the state is directly enmeshed in the contradictions of capitalism' (ibid., 219–20). In recent years a number of Marxist writings have provided useful insights into the nature of the capitalist state, both in general and within particular nation-states. A detailed discussion can be found in the 'Notes on further reading' at the end of this chapter, but here it is important to note that there is rough agreement that even though, in general, a ruling class dominates the state, the institutions of the state are autonomous, to some extent at least, of the dominant class. In practice, of course, the divisions within the political left, over the extent of this autonomy at particular points in time, and about the precise nature of particular state structures have been sharp. The bitter debate between Lenin and Kautsky that destroyed the Second International was perhaps the most prominent, but certainly not the only one. For when both dominant and subordinated classes are further analysed into subgroups and put into an international context, the nature of particular states becomes very complicated.

This applies equally to both the developed and the less developed countries, with in the latter case the debates on the nature of the 'post-colonial' and 'neo-colonial' states being quite involved. Here there is only space for a few general remarks. In the LDCs where national private capital is generally weak, it is recognized that the state may be *particularly* autonomous. Indeed, some parallels have been drawn between certain states in the LDCs and the situation in mid-nineteenth-century France which Marx discussed in 'The 18th Brumaire of Louis Bonaparte' (see Marx, 1976). In Marx's view the Bonapartist state was particularly autonomous of any specific class. Bonaparte himself ostensibly represented a class (the smallholding peasants), but the peasants' lack of cohesion made them 'incapable of enforcing their class interest in their own name whether through a parliament or a convention' (ibid., 239).

It is perhaps not surprising that some parallels have been drawn between this Bonapartist regime and the 'post-colonial' state in many newly independent LDCs. For the 'post-colonial state' may combine the following 'class' ingredients which produce a highly unstable concoction:

(a) a weak national industrial capitalist class;

(b) a trained bureaucracy;

(c) a powerful and entrenched financial and industrial foreign capital;

(d) a historically powerful but declining landlord class;

(e) a fragmented but large and newly enfranchized peasantry;

(f) a small but increasingly cohesive and newly enfranchized urban working class.

Such a structure may produce a 'Bonapartist', or what Kalecki called an 'intermediate' regime (Kalecki, 1976), with no one class in obvious control. Some writers (notably Raj, 1973; Jha, 1980) have suggested that India is an example of an intermediate regime, in which the 'ruling class' consists of many disparate elements such as rich peasants, small traders and civil servants. In such a situation, it is argued, the state has to make itself responsible for capital accumulation. Other Indian writers on the left have seen the contemporary Indian state as being much less auton-omous than this. For example, the present Indian state is seen by the Communist Party of India (Marxist) as 'the organ of the class rule of the bourgeoisie and the landlord, led by the big bourgeoisie who are increas-ingly collaborating with foreign finance capital in pursuit of the capital-ist path of development' (quoted in Harriss, 1982, 12).

The debate goes on, and not just in and about India, for as stated earlier, there are a myriad writings on the left about the state. But I think that it is fair to say that the dominant view of the abstract labour theorists is that specific class divisions can be identified both within the LDCs and within 'foreign capital', and that these divisions 'qualify' the role played by foreign capital. Thus Peter Evans, in writing about contem-porary Brazil, sees political power as effectively being in the hands of a 'triple alliance' of the state, local capital and multinational capital (P. Evans, 1979). And in writing more generally about Latin America, but at the same time more restrictively about the role of TNCs, Rhys Jenkins sees the 'relationship between the state and the TNCs . . . [as] consisting of islands of conflict within a sea of cooperation and mutual accommodation' (Jenkins, 1983, chapter 7).

Thus the class–state linkage of the abstract labour theorists provides a vivid contrast to the 'pluralist' view of the social democrats and the 'representative' view of the conservatives. The contrast with the 'depen-dency school' is not so stark. But there is a difference. For, whereas the abstract labour theorists stress the existence of class divisions *within* the

LDCs and the competing interests of 'fractions' of capital, the dependency writers tend to adopt a more monolithic view of class relationships. Their tendency is to work at one level of abstraction only.

The dependency theorists see civil society as monopolistic, and the state as a reflection of this. Thus they tend to see the state as a monolithic mass with control being exercised by capital as a homogeneous entity. 'Aid' is seen as directly and universally reinforcing this control, a view summed up in Theresa Hayter's *Aid as Imperialism* when she says 'aid can be explained only in terms of an attempt to preserve the capitalist system in the Third World' (Hayter, 1971). In this dependency view, then, the state is simply functional to capitalism. And in the LDCs 'local classes' become wholly symbiotic to foreign capital. They are a wholly 'comprador' group – a mere functional link in the drain of surplus to the metropolis from the periphery.

As I have argued earlier (in Section 5.3), I do not think that the dependency approach to the analysis of capitalism is consistent with an abstract labour theory of value. This is particularly true of the writings of the early dependency writers such as Paul Baran and Gunder Frank, for whom surplus in capitalism is not surplus value but a physical product, and for whom classes are defined more by reference to the distribution of income than by control of the means of production. These writers have, I think, overreacted to the atomistically competitive, harmonious picture of the world painted by the free-marketeers, and have overemphasized the monopolistic aspects of 'civil society'. And since, for them, the political sphere is simply a functional reflection of the economic, the state is also presented in more monolithic terms than it is, in general, by the abstract labour theorists.

For the latter, the analysis of capitalism has to be conducted at various levels of abstraction. Thus it is important to move from the high level of abstraction involved in analysing the capitalist mode of production in general (the world of the *Communist Manifesto*), to the more complex world of 'fractions' of capital and of subclasses (the world of the '18th Brumaire').

9.2 IMPERIALISM

It was argued in Chapter 5 that Lenin's pamphlet on *Imperialism* was extremely influential and played a major role in the development of dependency theory. I also argued both in Section 5.1 and in the first section of this chapter that there were specific reasons for Lenin's strong

THE STATE, IMPERIALISM AND SOCIALISM 269

emphasis on the monopolistic cohesiveness of national capitals. At the same time, criticizing this approach is not the same as saying that imperialism never existed or does not now exist. Lenin had argued that imperialism was the highest stage of capitalism, and that it arose as a result of the concentration and centralization of capital. He argued that

> Private property based on the labour of the small proprietor, free com-
> petition, democracy . . . are things of the distant past. Capitalism has
> grown into a world system of colonial oppression and of the financial
> strangulation of the overwhelming majority of the population of the
> world by a handful of 'advanced' countries.   (Lenin, 1970, 11)

Does this mean that imperialism has disappeared with the ending of colonialism – with the 'wind of change', the spread of political independence – in the 1950s and 1960s?

It is impossible to examine this complex question in very much detail here. The interested reader will have to go to some of the books referred to in the 'Notes on further reading' at the end of this chapter. In Brewer's *Marxist Theories of Imperialism* – an excellent review of the theories – the most common use of the term 'imperialism' is said to be 'the domination of one country over another' (Brewer, 1980, 102). This implies that blocs of national capital are more cohesive than other 'fractions'. This was the theme developed by Lenin and another Russian, Nikolai Bukharin, in their books on imperialism written during the First World War. Both Bukharin and Lenin were highly critical of Karl Kautsky, the German political economist, who had argued, in 1915, that a new ultra-imperialist phase of capitalism was thinkable (see Kautsky, 1915 and 1970).

'Ultra-imperialism' was the term applied to the international unification of state-bound capitals which might eliminate wars and political convulsions; ultimately the concentration and centralization of capital on a world basis could be such as to override the conflicts between national blocs of capital. Lenin agreed that 'There is no doubt that the development is going *in the direction* of a single world trust that will swallow up all enterprises and all states without exception'; but in the next sentence he added; 'the development in this direction is proceeding under such stress, with such a tempo, with such contradictions, conflicts and convulsions . . . that before a single world trust will be reached, before the respective national finance capitals will have formed a world union of "ultra-imperialism", imperialism will inevitably explode, capitalism will turn into its opposite' (Lenin's introduction to Bukharin,

1972, 14). Bukharin also argued, after condemning Kautsky's 'opportunist optimism', that

> The process of the internationalisation of economic life can and does sharpen, to a high degree, the conflict of interests among the various 'national' groups of the bourgeoisie. Indeed the growth of international commodity exchange . . . can be accompanied by the growth of the most desperate competition, by a life and death struggle. The same is true of the export of capital. (Bukharin, 1972, 61–2)

Thus, Bukharin argued, in opposition to Kautsky, that not only does capitalism necessarily expand internationally to permit its reproduction and expansion, but

> Significant as this [internationalization] process may be in itself, it is, however, counteracted by a still stronger tendency of capital towards nationalisation, and towards remaining secluded within state boundaries. The benefits accruing to a 'national' group of the bourgeoisie from a continuation of the struggle are much greater than the losses sustained in consequence of that struggle. (ibid., 138)

The international expansion is accompanied not only by international alliances between sectoral blocs of capital, but also by alliances, within nation-states, of blocs of capital. The contradiction between an internationalization of productive forces and the territorial division of appropriation is if anything heightened, rather than reduced, as capitalism expands.

What implications does this have for 'imperialism'? Earlier Brewer was quoted as saying that the most common use of the term was the domination of one country over another. But it is useful to enlarge on this 'definition', by using the following quotation from the 1973 article by Bill Warren, entitled 'Imperialism and capitalist industrialisation': 'Imperialism has been popularly and rightly conceived as both the domination of the non-socialist world by a few major powers and as the attempt of the major capitalist powers to suppress or eliminate socialist states' (Warren, 1973, 43–4). Thus Warren provided a dual definition of imperialism; domination within the non-socialist world and the suppression of socialist states and socialist forces. He then went on to argue that, in the 1970s, the former element – the direct domination of the *non*-socialist Third World – was becoming less important, while the latter – the suppression of *socialist* forces – was becoming stronger. It is worth looking at his arguments more closely.

Warren argued that strong nationalist forces in the Third World were compelling the spread of industrial capitalism into the less developed countries, and that these 'social forces compelling industrialisation have developed . . . in advance of the development of a stabilised bourgeoisie' (ibid., 43). In further arguing that 'this partly explains the importance of the state in most underdeveloped countries where it often assumes the role of a bourgeois ruling class prior to the substantial development of that class' (ibid.) Warren was clearly painting an 'intermediate-regime' picture of the state in the Third World. Warren then went on to argue that although these 'intermediate regimes' are tied to imperialism internationally, there are nevertheless sufficiently autonomous national interests in the Third World to maintain the impetus towards industrial capitalism.

Thus, in Warren's eyes, no single developed nation is sufficiently powerful or has a sufficiently strong motivation to prevent industrial capitalism in the Third World. Thus, he argues, the obstacles placed in the way of industrialization in colonial India were temporary rather than permanent, and have been shown to be the exception – admittedly an important exception – rather than the rule (see ibid., 42). Thus the 'development-of-underdevelopment' thesis is argued to be inaccurate.

But in attacking the development-of-underdevelopment argument Warren does not deny the existence of imperialism in his second sense, namely forces used to hold back the development of socialism. This imperialism must, he says, be opposed, but he argues that it is also extremely important to distinguish between quarrels and bargaining between capitalist less developed and developed capitalist states, and anti-imperialism in this second sense (see ibid., 44). These arguments of Warren are broadly consistent with an abstract labour theory of value and Marxist methodology. If they are accepted, then clearly imperialism is *unlikely* to disappear with the further development of capitalism. And yet this is what has been argued both on the political right as well as on parts of the left.

On the political right writers like Joseph Schumpeter have argued that imperialism is (or rather has been) a relic or 'hangover' from a feudal age. Schumpeter's writing on imperialism was produced at about the same time as Lenin's, that is at the end of the First World War. In it he argued that 'Nationalism and militarism . . . are the forms assumed in the environment of the modern world by habits of emotion and action that originally arose under primitive conditions' (Schumpeter, 1951, 127 n.). Thus as these 'primitive conditions' receded with the development of capitalism, so it was likely that imperialism would be eliminated. Meanwhile on the political left, as pointed out above, Kautsky argued that national antagonisms and imperialism were likely to be submerged by 'ultra-imperialism' as capitalism advances.

From the point of view of an analysis based on abstract labour theory, both Schumpeter and Kautsky are wrong. Schumpeter's argument is not rooted in a materialist analysis, and Kautsky, as we have seen, was attacked from the left for paying far too little attention to the contradictions within capitalism. In attacking Kautsky, Bukharin did not deny the possibility of states being combined peacefully. But he argued that the antagonisms between such federations and the rest of the world were likely to become even greater. Thus in *Imperialism and World Economy* he wrote: 'even were *all* of Europe to unite, it would not signify "disarmament". It would signify an unheard of rise of militarism because the problem to be solved would be a colossal struggle between Europe on the one hand, America and Asia on the other' (Bukharin, 1972, 139–40).

Could this 'colossal' struggle be avoided by other than military means? An English writer, John Hobson, certainly thought so. In his *Imperialism: A Study*, first published in 1902, Hobson argued that the 'economic taproot' of imperialism was deficient demand in the advanced industrial countries. Thus he wrote. 'it is not industrial progress that demands the opening up of new markets and areas of investment, but mal-distribution of consuming power which prevents the absorption of commodities and capital within the country' (Hobson, 1961, 85). Although, in his work on *Imperialism* Lenin paid tribute to Hobson's work, he nevertheless rejected Hobson's conclusion that imperialist wars might be avoided by wage rises in the advanced industrial countries. For Lenin argued: 'if capitalism did these things [raise the standard of living of the masses] it would not be capitalism' (Lenin, 1970, quoted in Brewer, 1980). Clearly Hobson's emphasis was on distribution, and in that sense very much within a cost-of-production mould.

Thus the position of the abstract labour theorists is that both the violence of intercapitalist competition and imperialism (used in Warren's second sense of opposition to socialist movements) are rooted in capitalist production and the nature of the capitalist state. Similarly, it is clear that once the capitalist dominance of the state is established, then arms expenditure may be more than just a defence against 'external' threats. It may also be a necessary expenditure to guard against threats to the ruling class from *within* the nation state. For not only has capitalism developed within a military 'cockpit' in which the expansion of industrial production was seen by ruling groups as the condition of national survival (see Giddens, 1981, 190), but so military expenditure has been, and continues to be, necessary to the survival of national capitalism.

Thus a combination of factors – the need for internal repression as well as external defence/aggression – leads to massive military expenditure on a world scale, as shown in Table 9.2. The total expenditure in 1981

Table 9.2 World arms expenditure and income: the massive burden

1981	Arms expenditure ($ billion)	Population (million)	Arms expenditure per capita ($)	Income (GDP) per capita ($)	Arms expenditure as % of income
USA	158	230	687	12,820	5
Other OECD countries	151	490	308	10,320	3
USSR	140	268	522	4,800[1]	11
Other CPEs (excluding China and Vietnam)	15	113	133	2,500[1]	5
OPEC countries	54	351	154	1,635	9
Other LDCs (including China and Vietnam)	94	3,104	30	644	5
Totals (and averages)	612	4,556	134	2,665	5

Sources: Arms expenditure statistics from SIPRI, 1982, 63, adjusted for inflation during 1979–81, since SIPRI figures are in 1979 prices; population and income figures: World Bank, 1983, table 1.

Note:
1 Estimate.

amounted to more than 5 per cent of world income. More strikingly, world military expenditure amounts to more than $20,000 in every second of every minute of every day. But not only is the expenditure large; it is growing. It is growing in absolute terms and, at least in the early 1980s, it is expected to grow in relative terms. From 1972 to 1981 world military expenditure increased, in real terms, by about one-quarter from $416 billion in 1972 to $519 billion in 1981, and US government budgets in the early 1980s have set aside an increased share of government expenditure and of national income for 'defence expenditure' (see SIPRI, 1982, 27, 63).

On the political left there has been a sharp debate about the role, in capitalism, of arms expenditure. A number of writers have argued that arms expenditure has a directly economic role to play within capitalism (see Baran and Sweezy, 1966; Kidron, 1970). Kidron was one of the main proponents of the 'permanent arms economy' argument, which gave two reasons why arms expenditure could stabilize and prolong the life of capitalism. The main emphasis was on demand. Here the reasoning was similar to that of Hobson, namely that capitalism was always liable to suffer from deficient demand. But, Kidron argued, the *particular* virtue of arms expenditure as opposed to wage rises in curing deficient demand was that state expenditure on arms would prevent the rate of profit from falling. Thus as Kidron argued, 'since arms are a "luxury" in the sense that they are not used . . . in the production of other commodities, their production has no effect on profit rates overall' (Kidron, 1970, 49).

Unfortunately for capitalism, this is not the case. So long as the arms industry is subject to similar accumulation and competitive pressures as other sectors of capitalism, then the tendency will still be there for the rate of profit to fall as a result of a rising value composition of capital. Of course, if for some reason, the state finds it easier to 'subsidize' industry by channelling the subsidies through the arms sector rather than through other sectors, then certainly the arms sector will be especially beneficial to capitalism. But there is little reason to suspect that this is the case.

This is why I think that the role of arms expenditure within capitalism has to be seen in broader political terms. Its crucial role is to create the 'economic and political conditions which are favourable to capital' (Rowthorn, 1980, 261). Arms expenditure essentially creates these conditions by being 'part of a whole system of power in which the ruling bloc . . . maintains its position and intensifies its exploitation of the rest of society' (ibid.). It may also provide some technological 'spin-off' which is valuable to capital, but this is by no means certain. Its major role is that of supporting the *political* power of capital. Thus, in the context of the abstract labour theory of value, the role of arms expenditure is political, and in that sense 'indirect'. It does not play a direct 'economic' role as suggested by those like Kidron, Baran and Sweezy, who emphasize the tendencies towards deficient demand (or 'underconsumption') in capitalism.

Similarly, the role of imperialism defined in Warren's second sense of attacking socialist forces, has to be seen in a broad context. Thus the US government supports repressive forces against the Liberation Front in El Salvador and against the Nicaraguan government not because of the narrow economic interests of US capital in those countries, but rather because of the wider implications of that struggle for the interests of US and to a lesser extent other capital in Central America and elsewhere.

9.3 SOCIALISM AND THE SOVIET STATE

Views on socialism

In Section 9.2 two forms of imperialism were distinguished. One, and according to Warren the increasingly important one, consists of attacks by one or more capitalist states on socialist states or socialist movements within national boundaries. Clearly in deciding on whether state action constitutes imperialism defined in this sense, and in deciding on whether or not to support or oppose such action, we need to be able to identify socialism and socialist movements.

Unfortunately the term 'socialism' has been used in even more diverse ways than the term 'imperialism'. Thus the first part of this section looks at the various approaches to 'socialism' in broad, general terms. The discussion is necessarily brief, but I attempt to illustrate some of the more abstract points by looking at the USSR as a 'case study'.

The position of the subjective preference theorists on socialism is straightforward. For them, it is quite simply equated with a tendency towards totalitarianism. The natural state of society is one of free competition between individuals; thus freedom in the 'market-place' or 'economic freedom' is a necessary (though not sufficient) condition of political freedom. Therefore, anything which reduces economic freedom must be opposed. Thus socialism must be opposed. There is, of course, something of a paradox here, for it is argued that force (political 'un-freedom') is likely to be necessary to enforce economic freedom, which is a necessary condition of political freedom. But as the Friedmans put it (though in a somewhat different context), 'Freedom cannot be absolute . . . some restrictions on our freedom are necessary to avoid other, still worse restrictions' (Friedman and Friedman, 1980, 94).

The cost-of-production emphasis is quite different. Writers within this group are more favourably disposed towards 'socialism', which they define in terms of equality of opportunity and of income. According to economists like Galbraith, 'the central problem of the modern economy is unequal development' (Galbraith, 1975, 294). There is unequal development in the advanced industrial societies, between a monopolistic, privileged sector and an unorganized, deprived sector. To eliminate this unevenness, the industries in the monopolistic sector have to be made more accountable; and 'the only answer for these industries is full organisation under public ownership' (ibid., 297). This is because 'the market system is generally deficient in relation to the planning system', and it is important to 'recognise the logic of planning with its resulting imperative of coordination . . . government machinery must then be established to anticipate disparity and to ensure that growth in different parts of the country is compatible' (ibid., 300, 337).

Thus for Galbraith, as for other cost-of-production theorists, the increasing complexity of a technologically advanced industrial society demands planning. This applies whether that society be the USA or the USSR. These societies tend to 'converge' with the 'convergence between the two ostensibly different industrial systems [occurring] at all fundamental points' (Galbraith, 1977, 384). Thus socialism, defined as state planning and state control of major industries, is desirable and inevitable in advanced industrial societies.

By contrast, in the eyes of the abstract labour theorists, socialism is far from inevitable. Its attainment without a struggle is by no means automatic, but then, for them, socialism has a quite different meaning. It involves much more than state planning and ownership – much more than social reform. Indeed, the very term 'socialism' was by-passed by Marx and Engels in their *Manifesto of the Communist Party*, precisely because it *was* a byword for social reform, and because socialism was in the mid-nineteenth century a middle-class movement. But apart from the *Communist Manifesto*, Marx and Engels wrote little on the probable or possible shape of post-capitalist societies. What they did write was generally in the form of a polemic against others' interpretations of socialism. Thus what I consider to be the best of Marx's few writings on the subject is the 'Critique of the Gotha programme' (see Marx, 1974), and Engels's most notable writing on the problem was a criticism of a piece by Eugen Duhring, a prominent member of the German Social Democratic Workers Party. Extracts from this 'Anti-Duhring' were later published as *Socialism: Utopian and Scientific* (Engels, 1975).

In his 'Critique of the Gotha programme' Marx emphasized that socialism was a transitional stage towards communism. In a more advanced phase of the latter, Marx argued:

> when the enslaving subjugation of individuals to the division of labour, and thereby the antithesis between intellectual and physical labour, have disappeared . . . when the all-round development of individuals has also increased their productive powers and all the springs of cooperative wealth flow more abundantly – only then can society wholly cross the narrow horizon of bourgeois right and inscribe on its banner: from each according to his abilities, to each according to his needs! (Marx, 1974, 347)

But, Marx emphasized, socialism was a transitional stage to communism, and as such will have emerged from a capitalist society; thus:

> In every respect, economically, morally, intellectually, it is . . . still stamped with the birth-marks of the old society from whose womb it has emerged. Accordingly the individual gets back from society – after the deductions [to cover investment, insurance, administrative, and welfare costs] exactly what he has given it. (ibid., 346)

Thus socialism is a system of payment according to work, a transitional stage to communism – a system of payment according to need. But even for payments to be made according to work, and for no surplus (value) to be appropriated by another (capitalist) class, the direct producers must have control of the means of production.

Thus, for Marx, socialism is not just control of production by the state, but also control of production by the direct producers, by the mass of the people. This is unlikely to be a process of mere reform; instead

> between capitalist and communist society lies a period of revolutionary transformation from one to the other. There is a corresponding period of transition in the political sphere and in this period the state can only take the form of a *revolutionary dictatorship of the proletariat.*
> (ibid., 355; emphasis in original)

And so, Marx emphasized, in order to control the means of production, the workers have to control the state.

As many questions are raised as are answered by Marx's 'definition' of socialism. What precisely does the revolutionary dictatorship of the proletariat imply for a range of human rights? Is 'socialism in one country' feasible? If socialism in one country is impossible, what does the 'path' to international socialism look like? How can we tell if a country or group of countries in a particular part of the world is moving in the direction of socialism? Can the 'antitheses' between town and country, between manual and mental labour, between central planning and democracy ever be resolved, and if so how? And more abstractly, can or should the law of value operate within socialism, how can we avoid making labour into a commodity, and can politics be in command without creating excessive bureaucratic control?

Within the last ten years or so, since the late 1960s, these questions have been raised by Marxists, and the debates have been lively and vigorous. Until the 1960s there was an unfortunate tendency for Marxists, following Marx, to avoid such questions. The general argument was that Marx had no wish to produce just another version of utopian socialism, in which detailed blueprints of the future utopia would be drawn up. But there are two counterarguments to this. One is that 'utopia' is the Greek for 'nowhere', and to advocate a revolutionary path without discussing the destination itself smacks of utopia. The second counterargument is the more practical political point that 'socialism' has had such a bad press in the past half-century or so, that at least an outline, if not a blueprint, is needed to reassure, let alone convert, the many sceptics in the public. For as Giddens points out: 'this is the era of the

Gulag, of confrontations of a warlike character between socialist states, of Pol Pot and of something close to genocide in Kampuchea' (Giddens, 1981, 249).

All sorts of 'crimes' have been committed in the name of socialism, and it is incumbent on those who advocate revolutionary socialism either to justify such action and to show that it was not criminal or to show that the governments that initiated such action were not truly 'socialist'. For if capitalism has fashioned a world which is a 'unique conjunction of the banal and the apocalyptic' (ibid., 252), the history of the USSR has failed to furnish, for many, an attractive prototype of a post-capitalist world. In view of this it is not surprising to find a vigorous debate within, as well as between, the 'economic' schools about the nature of the Soviet state.

Views on the Soviet state

For the subjective preference theorists, the USSR is the anti-model for the ideal society. For them,

> there is a fundamental conflict between the *ideal* of 'fair shares' . . . and the *ideal* of personal liberty. This conflict has plagued every attempt to make equality of outcome the overriding principle of social organisation. The end result has invariably been a state of terror; Russia, China, and, more recently, Cambodia offer clear and convincing evidence. (Friedman and Friedman, 1980, 167)

Thus for the subjective preference school of economists, societies with the aims and structure of the USSR are bound to be exploitative, and, they say, it is inevitable that 'Russia is a country of two nations: a small privileged upper class of bureaucrats, Communist party officials, technicians; and a great mass of people living little better than their great-grandparents did' (ibid., 179).

In the cost-of-production theorists' discussion of socialism there is also an air of inevitability. But for them what is inevitable, at least in advanced industrial economies, is socialism itself. Because by this they mean the public planning and control of production. In Galbraith's words, 'organisation – bureaucracy – is inescapable in advanced industrial technology' (Galbraith, 1977, 17). The difficult problem is not one of avoiding 'socialism', but of moulding it so that it has a 'human face'.

The problem, for Galbraith, is how to achieve what he calls 'New Socialism', a state in which the bureaucracy is made responsive to the majority of the public. And this, 'the emancipation of the state begins . . . with the legislature. This, not the executive branch of the government, is the natural voice of the public purpose against the technocratic purpose' (Galbraith, 1975, 239). But, Galbraith argues, there are grounds for optimism, for 'the industrial system . . . brings into existence, to serve its intellectual and scientific needs, the community that, hopefully, will reject its monopoly of social purpose' (Galbraith, 1977, 391). In this view, for the industrial system's monopoly to be rejected, the legislature must *not* be directly connected with 'narrow distributional interests'. Such a separation is assisted by a move to proportional representation (see Owen, 1981, 14–15).

There are, of course, variations in attitudes to the USSR within both the subjective preference and cost-of-production schools. For example, in terms of a theory of value, the position of the Communist Party of the Soviet Union (CPSU) is somewhat similar to that of Galbraith, inasmuch as the essence of socialism is understood as state ownership of the means of production together with economic planning. But undoubtedly the CPSU's interpretation is different from that of Galbraith. The CPSU clearly believes that 'the working class has achieved full equality and has captured real political power' (URPE, 1981, iii), whereas Galbraith argues that 'The technical complexity, planning and associated scale of operations that took power from the capitalist entrepreneur and lodged it with the technostructure, removed it also from the reach of social control' (Galbraith, 1977, 116).

When we come to look at those analyses of the USSR which have been carried out within a Marxist framework (that is using a Marxist methodology), there are two major streams that can be identified.

First, there is the view of the Fourth International and of some other Trotskyist groups that the USSR is a non-exploitative, transitional society. It is said to be transitional because the social relations of production are neither capitalist (because of the planned nature of the economy) nor socialist (since the management of social life is not in the control of the direct producers): 'Consequently the economic order is governed by the conflict of two antagonistic logics – the logic of the plan and the logic of the market' (Mandel, in URPE, 1981, 35).

In this view there is a clear conflict between the planned social character of the economy, and a parasitic bureaucracy primarily concerned with the defence of its own privileged position. Thus the Soviet economy has a 'non-capitalist mode of production' underlying a 'bourgeois mode of distribution' with, as Trotsky put it, 'the bureaucracy [enjoying] its privileges under the form of the abuse of power' (Trotsky, 1972, 249–50). The origins of this abuse of power can be traced to the backward state of Russia at the time of the Bolshevik Revolution in 1917, together with the impact of western imperialism. The small size of the working class in 1917 and the isolation of the USSR after 1917 enabled a bureaucratic stratum to gain control of the country. And so there exists a 'bureaucratically degenerated or deformed workers' state' (Mandel, in IMG, 1973, 19). But because the USSR 'does not display any of the *fundamental* aspects of a capitalist economy' (Mandel, 1968, 560), the Soviet drive for expansion is not as strong as that of the capitalist west, and in general, in international politics, the USSR should be supported when in conflict with capitalist states.

In this view what is required to transform the Soviet state into a social-ist one, is 'only' a political revolution, not a 'wider explosion of the social structure and social institutions' (Lane, 1976, 39). Two influential Marxists, Paul Sweezy and Charles Bettelheim are not as optimistic. Both Sweezy and Bettelheim see the adoption of market forms in eastern Europe as a movement along the road to capitalism. In Sweezy's view three factors (control of enterprises by managers, co-ordination through the market and reliance on market incentives) suggest a 'strong tendency toward an economic order which, whatever one may choose to call it, functions more and more like capitalism' (Sweezy and Bettelheim, 1971, 4). Thus for Sweezy and Bettelheim, Soviet society is unlikely to be transformed into socialism without at least a Chinese-style 'cultural revolution'.

However, despite this stated tendency towards capitalism, Sweezy does not go so far as to refer to the USSR as 'state capitalist', which is the position of the Socialist Workers' Party (SWP) in Britain. This is the second of the 'Marxist' views that I want to discuss.

The best expression of this view can be found in books by Tony Cliff (1964, 1974). He argues that the state bureaucracy is a ruling class because of the dominant role it plays in the production process. The bureaucracy effectively controls the means of production and exploits the working class, extracting *surplus value* from it (see Cliff, 1964, chapter 6). The economic reforms are seen as yet further indications of the growing role of commodity production, of production for profit and of the operation of the law of value in the Soviet economy.

In Cliff's view the October Revolution in 1917 swept away the last remnants of feudalism and gave a tremendous boost to the development of the productive forces. Indeed, 'the fulfilment of the bourgeois tasks [of developing the forces of production] was the *central* problem in post-October Russia with its low level of national income' (ibid., 106). This 'historical mission of the bourgeoisie' had to be carried out by the Soviet bureaucracy, despite the contrary 'wishes and hopes of the actors them-selves' (ibid.). And all this happened because the Russian Revolution did not spread to the more advanced capitalist west (see ibid., chapter 4). With the implementation of the first Five Year Plan in 1928, the bureaucracy became a ruling class; all remnants of workers' control were abolished, coercion was introduced into the labour process and all social-political life was forced into a totalitarian mould (see ibid., 107). Social-ism in one country, at least in one as backward as early-twentieth-century Russia, was impossible. The state capitalist view would seem to require more than just a political revolution; 'the final chapter can be written only by the masses, self-mobilised, conscious of socialist aims and the methods of their achievement and led by a revolutionary Marxist party' (ibid., 349).

Cliff argues that the form of capitalism in the USSR is state capitalism – a form different from that of 'monopoly' or 'competitive' capitalism. Despite this difference in form, it is argued that the USSR acts like any other major capitalist power in the world – especially in relation to the Third World. This has been an argument also advanced, and with par-ticular vehemence, by the Chinese Communist Party – see, for example, *Ugly Features of Soviet Social-Imperialism*, a pamphlet published, in English, in 1976 (CCP, 1976). The term 'social-imperialism' (used by Lenin in his *Imperialism*: 1970, 105), implies that the USSR is socialist in words, but imperialist in deeds. It is admitted that the Soviet imperial-ist drive may come from a different source from that of American imperialism – namely (in the Soviet case) from the state backed by state corporations, rather than (as in the USA) from privately owned com-panies backed by the state. Nevertheless, despite the different structure, Soviet imperialism is said to exist.

Even some of those who categorize Soviet society as something other than state capitalist speak of Soviet imperialism – but it is those like the Chinese Communist Party who argue that the Soviet Union is state capitalist who most consistently identify Soviet foreign policy as imperialist. The USSR, it is argued, has sucked surplus both from its 'satellite countries' in eastern Europe and from the Third World. The surplus was extracted from eastern Europe, first, through excessive reparation payments from 1945 to 1960, and then, more indirectly, through the trade and investment contracts arranged under the umbrella of the Council of Mutual Economic Assistance (Comecon) (see URPE, 1981, 67–75; CCP, 1976, 33; Lavigne, 1974, chapter 7). And Soviet/Third World economic relations are said to share three important characteristics with western/Third World ties; high profits earned from high prices, reinforcement of an unequal international division of labour and export of capital (see URPE, 1981, 76).

Interestingly 'most of the pieces on the internal structure of the Soviet Union argue that the USSR is a socialist society of one sort or another, while the articles on the role of the USSR in the world today reflect the view that the USSR is imperialist' (ibid., viii). Many of the 'internal studies' suggest that the law of value does not operate and that production is not solely for profit, and yet the 'external studies' frequently assume a capitalist drive for surplus extraction. The two sets of studies are rarely linked (ibid.).

I have argued earlier that there is a similar sort of national–international dichotomy in the 'Marxist' studies of capitalism. Those who have studied capitalism and the capitalist crisis at the level of the nation-state have tended to emphasize the competitive aspects of western capitalism; whereas those who have focused most of their attention on the world economy have tended to emphasize the monopolistic aspects.

NOTES ON FURTHER READING

The capitalist state

For a general comparative treatment along similar lines to this chapter, see Cole *et al.*, 1983, chapter 10. This, or Giddens, 1981, chapter 9, could usefully be read alongside the present chapter.

Clear statements of the subjective preference view of the state can be found in Friedman, 1962; Friedman and Friedman, 1980. On views of aid from the same 'stable', see Bauer, 1981; Bauer and Yamey, 1981.

The best sources for a cost-of-production view of the state are the various writings of Galbraith – see especially 1975, 1977 – and David Owen's *Face the Future*, 1981, written by the current leader of the Social Democratic Party (SDP) in Britain. For views which are similar in conclusion to those of Galbraith and Owen, but which emanate from the realms of 'political sociology', see Dahrendorf, 1959; Durkheim, 1957. Social democratic views of the institutional changes required at the international level can be found in the two reports of the Brandt Commission, 1980, 1983.

As stated earlier, there are a number of robust criticisms of the first Brandt Report. Two, from the left, which explicitly attack the Brandt theory of the state are the review article by Diane Elson, 1982, and Third World First's *Beyond Brandt*, 1982.

For systematic, but quite abstract discussions of the Marxist view of the capitalist state, I have found the best sources to be Miliband, in Miliband and Saville 1965, and Avineri, 1980, especially chapters 1 and 2. Another good source is David Fernbach's introduction to Marx, 1976. For the views of Marx (and Engels), look at the *Manifesto of the Communist Party*: Marx and Engels, 1975. If, after these, you still have the interest in pursuing the topic at a high level of abstraction, go to the debate between Miliband and Poulantzas, in Blackburn, 1976. Then, and only then, proceed either to the writings on the state of Bob Jessop: either his long and somewhat discursive article, 1977, or his book, published in 1982; or to the introductory first chapter of the book edited by John Holloway and Sol Picciotto, 1979. But better, briefer discussions can be found in Giddens, 1982, chapter 4; Lee and Newby, 1983, 161–5, and these are highly recommended.

But rather than plough on at the same level of abstraction, it is advisable to go to Marxist studies on particular states in particular periods: try 'The 18th Brumaire' of Marx, 1976, which looks at mid-nineteenth-century France; or some of the many writings on the 'post-colonial states' of the post-1945 period. On the latter, accessible starting-points are the collection of articles edited by Harry Goulbourne, 1979, the discussion of Gunder Frank, 1981b, 234–40, and the articles by Colin Leys in the *Review of African Political Economy* (RAPE), 1976, and Sklar in the *Journal of Modern African Studies*, 1979. For a concise discussion of the different views (from the 'left') of the Indian state, see John Harriss's 'Indian industrialisation and the state', 1982.

Imperialism

As will have been evident from the brief section in this chapter, most of the writings on imperialism have come from self-confessed (or self-avowed) Marxists. There was a flurry of writings in and around the First World War, the most notable of which were those of Bukharin, 1972, Hilferding, 1981, Lenin, 1970, and Luxemburg, 1963. I have found Bukharin's *Imperialism and World Economy*, 1972, especially readable and stimulating. For an excellent view of these and others, see Brewer, 1980. Warren's dual definition of imperialism can be found in his 1973 article.

In practice, the two aspects of imperialism that Warren identified are not easy to distinguish. But for writings which fall more within the first aspect – the alleged holding back of non-socialist development in the Third World – see Frank, 1981a; Girvan, 1976; Hayter, 1982. See also Kiernan, 1981, and the collection of articles edited by Robert Rhodes, 1970. For the role of aid and loans in allegedly perpetuating the dominance of the major capitalist nations (and particularly the USA), see Hayter, 1971; Payer, 1974, 1982; Lappe *et al.*, 1981; Sampson's *The Money-Lenders*, 1982, chapters 2, 5, 6 and 10; Open University, 1983, case study 9; LAB, 1983.

For writings on imperialism when the concept is used in Warren's second sense of attacks on socialist movements, see Jenny Pearce's *Under the Eagle*, 1982, which deals with the history of American intervention in the Caribbean Basin: see the studies on the relationship between the IMF and Jamaica referred to at the end of chapter 7. For an analysis of the fall of the Allendé government in Chile and the role of the US government in helping to create and maintain the Pinochet regime, and the parallels between 'Chile's experience of 1970–73, and the possible future experiences of the left in Europe', see Roxborough *et al.*, 1977, especially their concluding chapter.

For the view that imperialism is a hangover from a pre-capitalist age, see Schumpeter, 1951. For a wide-ranging, but very uneven review of a number of imperialist theories, see Stretton, 1969, chapter 4. The argument that imperialism has its 'taproot' in distribution, or rather 'maldistribution', is clearly set out in Hobson, 1961; some elements of the same 'underconsumptionist' approach can be found in Rosa Luxemburg's *The Accumulation of Capital*, 1963. For those wanting to look in more detail at the much-neglected world of weapons and the military, the following provide useful starting-points: Kidron and Smith, 1983; Kaldor, 1982; SIPRI, 1982; Smith and Smith, 1983.

Socialism and the Soviet state

Refer to Friedman, 1962; Friedman and Friedman, 1980, for an exposition of the subjective preference view of socialism and of the Soviet state. Galbraith's views on socialism are those of a cost-of-production theorist: 1975, 1977; as are those of Owen 1981; Lange, in Nove and Nuti, 1972; Nove, 1983. For Marx's views, 'The critique of the Gotha programme' is indispensable: see Marx, 1974; for a good discussion of Marx's views on socialism, see the chapter headed 'New society', in Avineri, 1980. For recent discussion, within the European left, of the problems and prospects of moving towards socialism, see Gorz, 1982; Kitching, 1983; Bahro, 1982; Hill and Scannell, 1983.

If you want to go further back to look at nineteenth-century theories about 'socialism', you might refer to Lichtheim, 1978, but better sources are the *Manifesto of the Communist Party*: Marx and Engels, 1975; and Edmund Wilson's *To the Finland Station*: Wilson, 1967. The latter takes the reader, as the title suggests, up to April 1917 and Lenin's return from exile to the Finland Station in Petrograd (Leningrad).

The immediate events of the Russian Revolution are graphically depicted in Reed's *Ten Days that Shook the World*, 1966. Various concise views of the history of the USSR since 1917 can be obtained from Carr, 1980; Nettl, 1973, and, in atlas form, from Gilbert, 1972; Fullard, 1972. Deutscher's biographies of Trotsky, 1970, and Stalin, 1976, are also highly readable, as is Frankland's *Krushchev*, 1966.

Then, if you have an appetite for more, read the contrasting pieces by Cliff, 1974; Nove, 1982; and somewhat less easily accessible, Schiffer, 1977. For Trotsky's views, see his *History of the Russian Revolution*, 1932–3, and for his views on the nature of the Soviet state (written in the 1930s) see *The Revolution Betrayed*, 1972. But before reading the latter, an excellent concise overview of the various 'left' views of the Soviet state can be obtained from URPE, 1981 – see especially the six-page introduction. The latter is particularly useful if read alongside chapter 1 of David Lane's *The Socialist Industrial State*, 1976. Then if you want to pursue the issues further, look at the debates between Mandel, Harman and Kidron, in IMG, 1973; in *Monthly Review* between Mandel, 1979, and Sweezy, 1978; and the critique of the International Socialist view in the pamphlet of the BICO, 1974.

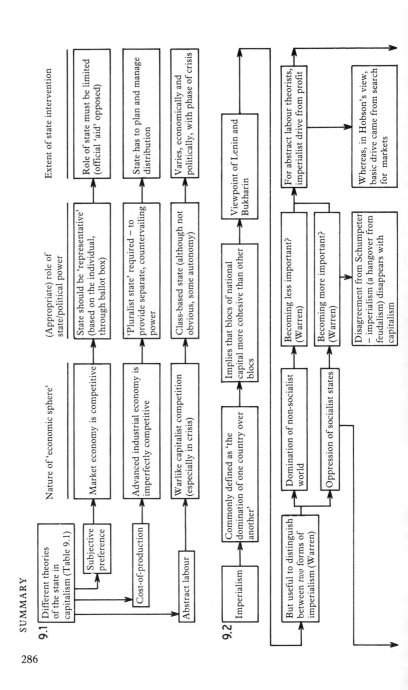

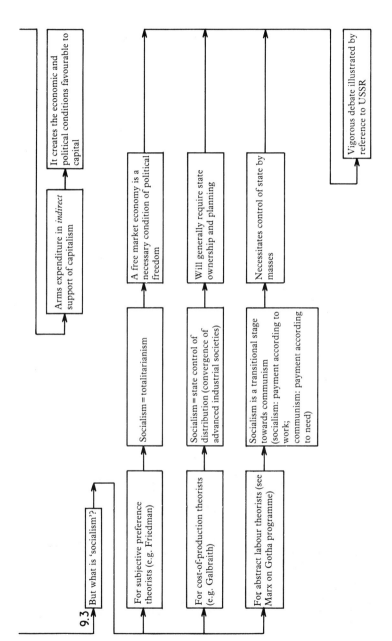

9.3 But what is 'socialism'?

For subjective preference theorists (e.g. Friedman) → Socialism = totalitarianism → A free market economy is a necessary condition of political freedom

For cost-of-production theorists (e.g. Galbraith) → Socialism = state control of distribution (convergence of advanced industrial societies) → Will generally require state ownership and planning

For abstract labour theorists (see Marx on Gotha programme) → Socialism is a transitional stage towards communism (socialism: payment according to work; communism: payment according to need) → Necessitates control of state by masses

Arms expenditure in *indirect* support of capitalism → It creates the economic and political conditions favourable to capital

Vigorous debate illustrated by reference to USSR

287

10

Summary and conclusions

The broad intent of this book has been twofold: first, to examine the determinants of the world division of labour and the role that money plays in this process; and secondly, and more narrowly, to explain and examine the theory of 'unequal exchange'.

I have argued that there is little agreement among economists about the dynamic of the world economy, and that there is no one commonly accepted theory. Given this, I think that a useful approach to understanding the various schools of economists is to examine and understand their essential differences. This comparative approach has been adopted by two colleagues and myself in a recently published book, *Why Economists Disagree* (Cole *et al.*, 1983), which disusses the various approaches to economic theory in general. Thus, to some extent, the content of this book can be viewed as an application of *Why Economists Disagree* to international economics. For here, as in *Why Economists Disagree*, three broad groups of economists have been identified. These groups are 'ideal types', identified at a high level of abstraction, but I think that such a grouping is useful. The three groups are:

1 subjective preference
2 cost-of-production
3 abstract labour

I have emphasized a number of times that this classification is at a high level of abstraction; thus you may not find it easy to neatly pigeon-hole every economist in one of these three schools. Examples of well-known 'economists' who do fit neatly into these groups are Milton Friedman in the first group, John Kenneth Galbraith in the second and Karl Marx in the third. In this book I have attempted to explain the analyses of international economic relations adopted by each of the three groups. The purpose of this final chapter is briefly to summarize and compare these approaches.

10.1 FREE TRADE IS FAIR TRADE

In Chapter 2 of this book the subjective preference approach to trade was outlined. This group of economists argues that each individual is endowed with tastes and talents which can be best expressed through a free market of voluntary contracts. Individuals' tastes are reflected (through a process of marginal utility maximization) not only in demand patterns, but also in supply patterns, because the choice between leisure and work is one of the factors determining the supply and cost of labour. Since the price of a product in the market is determined by the interaction of demand and supply, this price is ultimately determined by the tastes and talents of the world's millions of individuals.

Thus tastes and talents determine prices, and broadly prices determine the rewards of factors of production, in so far as each individual is paid according to the value of his/her production. Thus we have: *tastes/ talents* → lead to *prices* → lead to → *factor rewards*.

Once the assumption is made of a society of independent individuals each entering the market-place on an equal basis, it is hardly surprising if the outcome is said to be fair, even if (or rather especially if) the rewards (in terms of wage rates for example) are unequal. An example of precisely this reasoning can be found in the Friedmans' *Free to Choose* (see Friedman and Friedman, 1980). It is also not surprising if, at the international level, similar conclusions are reached. By this reasoning Emmanuel's 'unequal exchange' cannot possibly exist (in the unfair sense that Emmanuel meant it) in a *free* market. For the subjective preference theorists, 'free trade is fair trade'. International inequality is just as inevitable (and, if rooted in the free market, just as *desirable*), as inequality between individuals within the same national boundaries.

The subjective preference theorists argue that international trade, if free, will be determined by *comparative advantages*. The free expression of tastes and talents at the level of the national economy will generate a set of product prices in each country. But because of differences between nation-states in talents and natural resources as well as tastes, the product price ratios are likely to differ between one nation-state and another. These differences create the *potential* for profitable trade between the countries.

But it is only a potential, until the countries concerned have a competitive cost advantage in particular products. Thus a difference in pre-trade price ratios is a necessary, but not sufficient, condition for trade to take place. For trade to be attractive to profit-making merchants, a producer in a country must be able to deliver the goods at a lower price (in terms of 'international money') than competitors in other countries. In other words, that producer must have a competitive cost advantage. The question that then arises is: how does the comparative advantage get translated into a competitive advantage?

The answer to this question, say the subjective preference theorists, can be found in monetary theory. Initially, in the early stages of trade, and periodically, particular countries will have cost advantages in a number of products and will export more (in terms of international money) than they import. Assume that one of these countries is the UK. The UK will have a favourable balance of trade, and international money – say, gold – will flow into the UK from the deficit countries (say, India). On the basis of the quantity theory of money ($MV = PT$), more money (M) will be chasing the goods available (PT) in the UK, and on the assumption that the UK economy is operating at the 'natural' level of unemployment so that T (the volume of transactions or level of activity) is fixed, P (the level of prices in the UK) must rise. Thus prices in the UK (again in terms of international money) rise, while on the basis of the same quantity theory, prices in India, the deficit country, are likely to fall.

As the price level in the UK rises and that in India falls any comparative advantages held by Indian producers will be translated into competitive advantages. Merchants will find that profits can be made on a greater value of Indian exports, but on a smaller value of UK exports. The UK's surplus on its balance of trade will tend to be corrected, as will India's deficit.

Comparative advantage is then revealed in all its beneficial glory. But it is worth emphasizing that behind the smooth revelation of comparative advantage lurks the quantity theory of money. Within that theory there is the assumption that money is simply a medium of circulation; thus the velocity of circulation (the V in the $MV = PT$ equation) is assumed to be more or less constant. Money is recognized to be a store of value, but because it is finely substitutable with other assets from which income can be derived, it will not be held in more than the quantities necessary to effect exchange. Thus money will not be held (other than accidentally) *as* a store of value; it will not be hoarded.

Thus in the 'modern cash balances' version of the quantity theory, individuals and firms in the country experiencing a deficit on the balance of payments will find that their cash balances shrink as the money supply shrinks. They are then assumed to attempt to restore the *real* value of their cash balances by cutting their expenditure. And it is this drop in aggregate demand which is expected to bring about a drop in wages and prices in the deficit country (India in the earlier example). Conversely, in the country (UK in the example) which has the initial competitive advantages, and which therefore has a surplus on its external trade, there will be a tendency for aggregate demand and the price level to rise as people try to restore their 'normal' level of cash balances in the face of a rising money supply.

Thus in terms of the simple two-commodity (cloth and corn) trade model, introduced in Chapter 2, India's comparative advantage in the production of corn will be revealed as a competitive advantage as *price levels* fall in India and rise in the UK. The trade imbalances are ultimately corrected through changes in trading advantages; the trading advantages are brought about by changes in price levels; the changes in price levels are induced by changes in expenditure; the changes in expenditure are brought about by changes in money stocks; and since the latter are a result of the initial trading imbalances, the circle is completed. In terms of the quantity theory equation both V and T are fixed in the medium to long term. V is fixed by the assumption of a stable demand for money, and T is fixed by the assumption of a 'natural' level of unemployment. Thus changes in M (the money supply) must be reflected in the changes in P (the price level).

And so, the argument goes, comparative advantage will ultimately be revealed through free trade and 'sensible' monetary policies. And if, within each country, there is a free market, so that comparative advantage reflects the tastes and talents of individuals, then free international trade will in turn 'connect' these preferences. This is the essence of the Heckscher–Ohlin theory, namely that free trade will tend to compensate for restrictions on labour movements across national boundaries. In its original formulation the Heckscher–Ohlin theory argued that free trade would tend to even out factor scarcities in trading countries and, as a result, even out differences in factor rewards (that is wage rates and rates of interest). The free-marketeers argue that this tendency, arising from free trade, will be reinforced if there are free flows of money and entrepreneurship. Freedom in the world's capital markets will tend to equalize the rate of interest – the reward for abstinence; freedom in the movements of entrepreneurs will tend to equalize the rate of profit – the reward for exceptional talents; and freedom in the world's goods markets, together with adjustments in the balance of payments and money stocks, will tend to equalize relative price ratios – the reflection of tastes.

In such a world production (specialization) patterns will reflect differences in leisure preferences. Thus if the individuals in a country (say, the UK) have a high preference for abstinence, so that the rate of interest is low, not only will they tend to lend money-capital to other countries (say, India) where the rate of interest is higher but the production pattern in the UK will tend to veer towards relatively capital-intensive goods. Both these processes will tend to even out differences in the rates of interest between the UK and India. Thus in this theory, as Anwar Shaikh says:

> The underdeveloped capitalist nations . . . emerge as doubly blessed; the overwhelming productive superiority of the developed nations is manifested only in the cheapness of their exports, while their incomparably greater wealth manifests itself as a mass of capital eager and willing to go over there and help spread freedom, equality, property, and Coca-Cola.   (Shaikh, in Nell, 1980, 227)

Thus in the world of the subjective preference theorists, individuals will get rewarded fairly for their efforts, provided that a policy of free trade is followed. Policies will be judged in these terms. As Lal has expressed it in a recent book: 'The Utopian theoretical construct of perfect competition then becomes relevant as a reference point by which to judge the health of an economy, as well as the remedies suggested for its amelioration' (Lal, 1983, 15). Thus schemes of regional integration will be approved, provided that they represent a move towards free trade – that is provided that 'trade creation' outweighs 'trade diversion'. Individual projects will be evaluated according to the free trade criteria set out by Little and Mirrlees (1974). The 'cost' of protectionism will be measured in terms of its deviation from world prices (see Little *et al.*, 1970; Krueger, 1974b).

If free trade policies are followed, then all will benefit. Individuals in their different and multiple roles – as merchants, entrepreneurs, consumers, workers, rentiers and landlords – all will gain. Indeed, what is good for General Motors will not only be good for the USA, but also for the UK, France, and so on. It is not a zero-sum gain in which one person's gain is another's loss. But neither are the gains obvious; thus the battle of ideas is crucial. Indeed, development is almost *defined* through such attitudes. As Bauer puts it: 'Economic development requires modernisation of the mind. It requires revisions of the attitudes, modes of conduct and institutions adverse to material progress' (Bauer, 1976, 84).

It is claimed that 'there is one piece of policy advice that can be drawn unambiguously from the development experience of the past few decades . . . [namely] "Get the prices right"' (Lal, 1983, xi). The fewer the 'price distortions' there are in the LDCs, the faster their growth in exports and the higher their rate of economic growth (see Krueger, 1983; World Bank, 1983, section 6).

Thus free trade must be promoted wherever possible through political institutions, through the ballot box, through the maintenance of law and order, and so on. For the alternatives of communism and/or bureaucracy are bleak. If the communists win out, Soviet-style totalitarianism is the inevitable result. The left's democracy – the dictatorship of the proletariat – is, it is argued, a meaningless concept, for individuals play a variety of economic roles. The vast majority are consumers and rentiers as well as workers, and a significant minority are entrepreneurs. Communism will almost certainly mean totalitarian dictatorship by the few in the name of the many.

If, on the other hand, within a multiparty state with parliamentary democracy, the bureaucrats get their way, inflation and chaos are inevitable. Politicians are always liable to be 'captured' by particular groups of individuals, particularly in the run-up to elections, so that constitutional constraints on fiscal and monetary powers are needed 'to protect government from minorities and to preserve majority control' (see Rowley and Wiseman, 1983, 11). Thus the check on the bureaucrats can be through the ballot box; but the check on communists is likely to necessitate the use of force. There then arises the problem of using 'short-term' force to ensure long-term freedom.

10.2 UNFAIR TRADE AND UNEQUAL EXCHANGE – THE CASE FOR INSTITUTIONAL INTERVENTION

The 'free trade is fair trade' doctrine of the subjective preference theorists has been vehemently attacked by a school of economists often referred to as the neo-Ricardians. In this book I have generally referred to them much more explicitly in terms of the cost-of-production theory of value which they adopt. But it is worth nothing that the origins of this theory of value can be traced back to Ricardo, and that is why I have used the terms, cost-of-production and neo-Ricardian, interchangeably. In the rest of this chapter, for purposes of brevity, not levity, I shall refer to this school of economists as the COPs (cost-of-productionists).

The COPs have been particularly prominent in the attack on the Heckscher–Ohlin theory of comparative advantage. As pointed out in Section 2.3, the publication in 1960 of Sraffa's *Production of Commodities by Means of Commodities* stimulated an attack on the marginal productivity theory of distribution, which had been the foundation stone of the Heckscher–Ohlin structure. The Heckscher–Ohlin theory had argued that, under a regime of free trade, not only would labour-abundant countries export labour-intensive goods but also that when they did, there would be a tendency for factor prices to be equalized around the world. Thus even though equality of opportunity initially might be denied by national restrictions on labour migration, free trade would ultimately restore (in Heckscher's words) a 'harmonious state of equilibrium'. In other words, free trade in goods would substitute for the impeded movement of labour.

The COPs have taken issue with this theory of comparative advantage on both logical and empirical grounds. In Chapter 2 attention was concentrated on the attack on the Heckscher–Ohlin theory on the ground of logic. This seemed a sensible order of priorities, for if the theory is shown to be lacking in logic, there is little value (apart from the PhDs thereby obtained) in carrying out detailed empirical studies on the basis of such a theory. If there is *no* way of defining factor abundance independently of goods prices, and if there is no way of defining the labour or capital intensity of a particular good independently of factor prices, then there is no substance left in the theory. This is precisely what the COPs or neo-Ricardian attack did, namely to destroy the substance of the theory. The attack showed that *logically* there is no way in which the prices of goods can be defined independently of profits and wages, the 'prices' of capital and labour. Yet this was the foundation of the Heckscher–Ohlin theory.

Thus once the marginal productivity theory of distribution is shown to be logically flawed, we cannot say that a country has an abundance of labour relative to another. Lower wage rates in one country compared with another might signify not a relative abundance of labour, but differences in anti-union legislation, productivity or the costs of reproducing labour-power. For similar reasons, differences in rates of unemployment may give little indication of relative labour 'prices'.

Once the marginal productivity theory of distribution is shown to have no substance, the measurement of the factor intensity of a good independently of wage and profit rates is impossible. The neo-Ricardian attack showed that labour and capital cannot get, in aggregate terms, what they 'deserve', because what they each produce cannot be unambiguously identified. Yet 'they get what they produce' was the argument of the marginal productivity theory of distribution. The neo-Ricardian attack revealed the inconsistency in the theory and, in so doing, showed that comparative advantage cannot arise 'naturally', but is created by factors normally considered by the free-marketeers as 'extraeconomic'.

However, as argued in Chapter 3 and 4, there have been two identifiably separate prongs or wings to the neo-Ricardian theory. One of these I referred to as the 'Sraffian' wing; the other as the 'unequal exchange' wing.

As was shown in Section 3.2, the Sraffian wing has suggested that the gains which are so confidently predicted by the free-marketeers are by no means certain to arise, and that free trade may even generate losses for the countries concerned. The losses may arise from the devaluation of capital assets following the exposure to trade and the resulting price changes.

The arguments of this Sraffian wing have, however, attracted much less attention than those which have come from the unequal exchange group. In the late 1950s and early 1960s the unequal exchange arguments were put by W. Arthur Lewis and Raul Prebisch, but in the late 1960s the argument was restated forcefully by Arghiri Emmanuel with the publication of his *Unequal Exchange*. Emmanuel argued that labour in the Third World is paid less for the same skills and effort than labour in the north, and that it is this 'unequal exchange' which provides the foundation of the international trading system and the resulting distribution of world income.

Emmanuel's argument went beyond that of Lewis and Prebisch. Whereas the latter had argued that unequal exchange applied only to *primary product exports*, Emmanuel generalized it to *all* commodities in which the Third World traded. Emmanuel argued that labour in the south was paid less, after taking into account differences in productivity, than labour in the north because in all sectors it was less organized and had less bargaining power. Thus, he argued, the rate of exploitation of all labour in the south was higher than that in the north.

Unfortunately for the south, however, this 'superexploitation' is not reflected (Emmanuel argued) in a super-rate of profit available for re-investment in the LDCs, because of the international mobility of capital which tends to equalize the rate of profit in the world economy. Because of this mobility of capital, the higher rate of exploitation in the south may be revealed in a number of forms. Thus either it might raise the global rate of profit, or it might raise the living standards of workers in the north. And the latter might occur either as a result of lower prices of consumption goods from the south, or as a result of reduced resistance by capitalists (induced by the higher profits from the south) to higher wages. Emmanuel emphasized the benefits-to-workers effect, implying that workers in the north were a 'labour aristocracy' compared to workers in the LDCs, and that as a result there was no solidarity of interest between the workers of Detroit and those of New Delhi.

Thus for the neo-Ricardians in general, whether on the Sraffian or unequal exchange wings, empirical work which attempts to suggest that a free world trading system is rational, fair and beneficial to all concerned is less than useful. And yet that is the conclusion of the USA-based economist Bela Balassa, who has argued that 'The evidence is quite conclusive: countries applying outward-oriented development strategies had a superior performance in terms of exports, economic growth and employment whereas countries with continued inward orientation encountered increasing economic difficulties' (Balassa, 1980a, 27).

The countries to which Balassa was referring as success stories were Korea (South), Singapore and Taiwan. In view of the rapid expansion of manufactured exports from these countries, it is not surprising if, 'in the ideological battle, these [the rapidly industrializing countries of the Third World] have been the trump card of orthodox economics' (Clive Hamilton, in Limqueco and McFarlane, 1983, 137). But even if Balassa's criteria of success (exports, economic growth and manufacturing employment) are accepted, it is questionable whether the major factor in these 'successes' is the application only of outward-oriented development strategies. The orthodox literature 'implies that Singapore industrialised because Lee Kuan Yew had read Samuelson' (ibid., 140). In a useful article Hamilton goes on to argue that the development of the new industrializing countries is a *capitalist* development which 'expresses the will of capital, but not a collective will, merely the aggregation of the profit-oriented activities of many capitals' (ibid.). In Hamilton's eyes the type of approach used by Balassa is far too superficial, and Hamilton's own analysis of the development of what he calls 'the four little tigers' (Hong Kong, South Korea, Singapore and Taiwan) puts forward quite different explanations for their 'success'.

Thus the major factor in Hong Kong's success can plausibly be argued to be its special relationship with the Chinese hinterland, from which it has received a massive inflow of not only immigrant labour, but also capital (ibid., 152, 167). In the case of South Korea from which, throughout the 1960s and the first half of the 1970s, exports grew very rapidly (at an average of more than 20 per cent a year) there is substantial evidence of state intervention to promote industrial growth. Thus Stephanie Griffith-Jones argues that 'the level of imports was regulated through the rather sophisticated system of direct administrative controls, which has characterised the South Korean economy since the 1960s' (Griffith-Jones, 1982, 19), while a detailed study by Luedde-Neurath concludes that 'the Korean success occurred not *despite* but at least in part *because* of the policy of selective protectionism followed' (Luedde-Neurath, 1983). Furthermore, Hamilton points out that subsidies from the state and profitable trade arising from the war in Vietnam, played significant roles in both South Korea and Taiwan (Hamilton, in Limqueco and McFarlane, 1983, 149, 151, 160). In Singapore these factors were less important, but nevertheless played some part. But in Singapore, as in the other three little tigers, labour organization and political opposition have been severely repressed.

However, political repression may not be a sufficient condition for economic success, even in terms of Balassa's criteria of growth in exports and national income. The Chilean economy in the 1970s provides an example. For under the rule of the Pinochet junta a free market strategy has been followed, on the advice of economic advisers, who have been referred to as the 'Chicago boys', since most them were schooled at the University of Chicago, the citadel of free market economics. Although, immediately following the overthrow of the Allendé government, Chilean exports grew quite rapidly, employment fell sharply and real national income in 1977 was at about the same level as in 1973, the year of the military coup (see Griffith-Jones, 1982, 23). And since 1980 both the value of Chile's exports and its real national income have fallen (see 'The model that didn't travel', *Financial Times*, 9 March 1983).

Thus for all but the most committed of subjective preference theorists, the examples of South Korea, Singapore and Taiwan provide case studies in which trading advantages have been *created* by economic policy, rather than examples in which economic policy has capitalized on a pre-existing trading advantage. According to the COPs, the 'endowment [of factors] is itself a product of the economic development of the region, and may, therefore, be a product of past trade developments; current policies cannot, therefore, take factor endowment as given but must regard it as one of the variables which may be affected by policy' (Stewart, in Helleiner, 1976, 95).

Thus instead of prices determining wages, the COPs prefer to argue that wages (together with technology) determine prices. And whereas for the neo-classical economist the international mobility of capital is likely to increase the likelihood of factor price equalization, for the cost-of-production theorist such mobility of capital is more likely to bring about unequal exchange. For, as emphasized in Chapter 4, Emmanuel, Prebisch, Myrdal and others have argued that capital does not flow in sufficient quantities to the Third World to eliminate international inequalities because the markets are concentrated in the industrial north, and with the concentration of markets goes a concentration of technology. Thus the LDCs get the worst of all worlds. Capital flows to the LDCs in sufficient quantities to equalize rates of profit and bring about unequal exchange, but in insufficient quantities to spread the markets and technology more or less equally. To summarize the argument in another way, capital foreign to the Third World 'invades local markets, driving out local capitalists, drawing down prices and thus lowering the average rate of profit in the Third World. In this way the surplus generated in the Third World is siphoned off by foreign capital, to the detriment of the Third World' (Shaikh, in Nell, 1980). There is, in Myrdal's words, a process of 'cumulative causation', a vicious circle rather than the virtuous one suggested by the neo-classical economists.

Thus, according to the COPs, the process of unequal exchange has to be looked at dynamically. Industry has a tendency to concentrate because of external as well as internal economies of scale. In some industries the external economies reveal themselves on the side of consumption, with producers benefiting from being close to their consumers as well as to other producers (see Yeats, 1981, 137). Thus the equal availability of production techniques assumed by the Heckscher–Ohlin theory is dismissed as unrealistic by the cost-of-production theorists. Because of scale economies, external as well as internal to firms, there is a definite 'product cycle' at work (see Vernon, 1966; Hufbauer, 1966). Thus, the COPs argue, it is hardly surprising to find that north–north trade has been greater, and is growing faster than north–south trade (Stewart, in Helleiner, 1976, 94). Because of this cumulative process, not only does the Third World suffer from unequal exchange but there is no likelihood of the process being corrected by the free market. The unequal process is self-reinforcing.

This is still (or rather *particularly*) the case when the role of money is considered at the international level. For, once a Keynesian theory of money is integrated with the cost-of-production theory of trade, the unequal process is accentuated rather than reduced. For then it is likely that a debt cycle will be superimposed on the technology or product cycle to make the circle even more vicious. Then the subjective preference theorists' case for the harmony of unregulated free trade is even more open to question.

As I stressed earlier, for the free-marketeers, comparative advantage is painlessly converted into a competitive trading advantage by adjustments in the price levels of the trading countries, and these price changes are brought about by adjustments in money stocks. Thus any trade imbalances are reflected in changes in money stocks, and these changes in money stocks cause changes in the price levels. As we have seen already, the cost-of-production school rejects the theory that comparative advantage arises as a result of differences in factor endowments. They argue that comparative advantage results from differences in technology (production conditions) and wage costs (distribution). But they also argue that comparative advantages are unlikely to be smoothly translated into competitive trading advantages.

The argument was presented in Chapter 6. The example used there was of India having an initial disadvantage in traded commodities and thus running a balance-of-trade deficit. This might or might not be corrected by a devaluation of its currency (the rupee). It might not be corrected in the short run, because resources might be slow to move into the newly profitable exports and import substitutes. Thus a devaluation might be followed by a deterioration in the balance of trade – this is the J-curve effect. At the same time, the devaluation may trigger a cost–price spiral by raising import costs, so that the initial competitive advantage of the devaluation is eliminated. Thus even in the longer term the devaluation may fail to convert comparative advantages into competitive ones.

If, however, instead of the rupee being devalued, the exchange rate is maintained and the trade deficit financed by loans from overseas, then again the cost-of-production school is pessimistic that any Indian comparative advantages (even if they exist) will be revealed. The loans may come from public or private sources. If they come from multilateral sources, such as the IMF, they are likely to be accompanied with conditions that India adopts free market policies which may well lead to the J-curve and devaluation–cost–price spiral effects mentioned earlier. If they come, as in the 1970s, from private sources (commercial banks), the flow of funds is more likely to be reflected in changes in interest rates rather than directly in price changes. In Keynesian eyes money is effectively a store of value as well as a medium of circulation. Thus the velocity of circulation is not necessarily fixed, and the resulting high and fluctuating interest rates and the uncertainties generated by shorter loan periods are likely to deter investment in the industries in which India has potential trading advantages.

Thus, instead of India's comparative advantages (if any) being revealed through smooth price adjustments, India is likely to run a chronic trading deficit which is financed by short-term borrowing. And as interest is paid on the loans and as they fall due for repayment, India's situation worsens rather than improves. Thus in this view India becomes a sort of 'tributary' economy. Furthermore, the COPs argue, because the burden of international adjustment tends to fall on the deficit countries, a deflationary bias is imposed on the world economy. It is this on which the Brandt Commission's second report, *Common Crisis* (1983), focuses attention.

In those versions of cost-of-production theory further to the political left the above process is reinforced by discriminatory commercial barriers imposed by the north, and even by force exerted by the north. In this view because the north (Britannia) rules the waves, it also waives the rules. In this version the solution is for the south to cut itself off from the north as much as possible. South–south regional integration is then primarily a means to the end of better bargaining for the Third World.

In those versions of cost-of-production theory less politically inclined to the left (such as the Brandt reports) what is needed is an increase in north–south aid, capital flows and co-operation. In this view the free market needs to be managed and, for this task, stronger public or multi-lateral institutions are required. The price system should not be asked to perform the double task of allocating resources and distributing incomes. Thus income distribution needs to be managed at both the national and international levels – at the national level through incomes policies, and at the international level through aid, commodity agreements and low interest loans.

10.3 CAPITALISM AND UNEVEN DEVELOPMENT – THE CASE FOR SOCIALISM

For Marxists, cost-of-production theory is more scientific – and nearer the economic truth – than subjective preference theory. For Marx and the Marxists, the latter is simply 'vulgar'. At least the cost-of-production theorists (from Ricardo) have attempted to penetrate beneath the superficial appearances of society. Even so, they are criticized by the Marxists for not analysing capitalist economies at various levels of abstraction. Thus the COPs do not see capitalism as a historically specific mode of production, emerging in revolutionary terms from preceding modes of production, the latter being fundamentally different from capitalism in their class composition and in their methods of surplus appropriation.

Thus whereas cost-of-production theorists see the world economy as a structure of (mostly) industrialized countries, abstract labour theorists (the Marxists) see it as dominated by the capitalist mode of production. Thus, as Marx and Engels emphasized in *The Communist Manifesto*, struggles for state power have been class struggles, and the modern pattern of nation states is as much a product of the rise of capitalism as its cause (Marx and Engels 1975).

However, as pointed out in Section 5.1, even though Marx never looked in detail at the world capitalist market, he emphasized that his general approach – the abstract labour theory of value – could be used to analyse the world capitalist economy. How is it then that 'whereas Marx derives the unevenness of development *within* a capitalist nation on the basis of free competition, Marxists generally have to resort to monopoly to explain the unevenness of development *between* capitalist nations' (Shaikh, in Nell, 1980, 211)? And how is it that '"capitalism" is the system operating within the national economy, and "imperialism" is the relation between the national economy and other national economies' (Radice, 1975, 16)?

As argued in Chapters 5 and 9, a major factor in the development of this theoretical schizophrenia was the publication, during the First

World War, of Lenin's *Imperialism*. But as also argued in Chapter 5, Lenin (and to a lesser extent, Bukharin, Hilferding and Luxemburg) had emphasized the monopoly characteristics of capitalism to explain the internationally competitive struggle for colonial annexation and the subsequent war. Unfortunately it was partly due to Lenin's considerable influence among Marxists that the international operations of capitalism continued to be analysed within a framework of monopoly. And in the interwar period particularly, the abstract labour theory of value faded into obscurity.

However, with the post Second World War resurgence of Marxism, particularly since the 1960s, there has been a rebirth of Marxist methodology and a renewed interest in the abstract labour theory of value. And at the international level there have been writers (prominent examples are Brenner, 1977; Shaikh, in Nell, 1980), who have argued that the international unevenness of capitalism can best be explained by the unevenness of class struggle and by the competition, in 'civil' society, of capitalism.

Such an emphasis once more focuses on production and the labour process as the source of exploitation and surplus *value*. Such a focus is in sharp contrast to the focus of cost-of-production theorists, who emphasize the 'political' nature of conflicts over the distribution of a technologically fixed physical surplus. Thus, not surprisingly, whereas the cost-of-production theorists tend to focus politically (through social democratic parties) on the redistribution of income through political institutions and changes in ownership, the abstract labour theorists throw their political weight (through democratic socialist parties) behind measures which enhance workers' control over the means of production.

Thus, for the abstract labour theorists, both the source of exploitation and that of crisis lie *within* the operations of *capitalist production*, as does the source of crisis. Similarly, the source of inequality, between as well as within nations, lies within the 'normal' operations of capitalism. As a result, *uneven* development is not the same as *underdevelopment*. A number of writers have pointed to the way in which 'underdevelopment theory has provided a series of ad hoc positions which have had to be successively revised' (Beckman, 1981, 7). Chapter 5 outlined some of the major differences between the approaches of on the one hand the abstract labour theory, and on the other that of the underdevelopment school. Here I reiterate some of the main characteristics of abstract labour theory and re-emphasize how useful is the integration of money within the abstract theory of value in understanding the nature of economic crisis and of uneven development in the world economy.

To say that 'for Marxists as for other economists, supply and demand determine prices' may seem misleading. It is. For the Marxists, supply and demand determine only *market* prices. For them, as for the cost-of-production economists, market prices fluctuate around longer-run prices of production. But in turn the abstract labour theorists differ from the cost-of-production theorists in arguing that the prices of production are themselves a transformation of labour values. Thus the ultimate determinant of the long-run prices of production is labour-time, but not simply the labour-time spent in producing each *individual* commodity but *social* or *abstract* labour. Thus socially necessary labour-times are transformed into and expressed in money prices of production by the relentless search of capitalists for higher rates of profit and the role of money. Because of the abstracting function played by money and capital, the 'essential' role played by labour is by no means obvious.

Thus the determination and meaning of prices differs crucially in all three schools of economists. For the subjective preference theorists, individual tastes and talents determine market prices and, more crudely, prices can be said to determine wages. For the cost-of-production theorists, technology and distribution determine the prices of production, around which oscillate market prices, the latter being determined by supply and demand. While, for the Marxists, it is abstract labour which lies behind the prices of production. The latter are the form taken by value and may even coincide with market prices, when supply and demand counteract each other.

It is not surprising, then, if exploitation and the source of surplus value are hidden in capitalism. It is not surprising if interest, rent and profit-as-enterprise appear to some economists as *sources* of value, whereas for Marxist economists, they are mere *divisions* of 'pre-existing' surplus value, with the rate of interest being determined by the supply and demand for money-capital, and with rent, both differential and absolute, tending to be reduced as capitalism 'matures' (see Murray, 1977–8).

In this theory it is the rate of profit which determines whether commodities are exported, or indeed whether they are produced at all. Of course, within a particular industry the rate of profit is likely to vary between companies, but it is, nevertheless, the relative rates of profit which determine in the long term whether and where trade takes place. Capital is forced constantly to transform production and the labour process subject to the resistance of labour. This does not mean that the rate of profit will be equalized between companies in a sector any more than it will between sectors nationally or internationally. Companies within a 'sector' or 'industry' in general will vary in profitability, but the movements in the rate of profit will tend to be in the same direction with some companies going bankrupt and others expanding. Thus the uneven flow and accumulation of capital will *tend* to keep the rates of profit moving unevenly, but more or less together.

Thus capital is always on the lookout for the production locations which will give the highest rates of profit. One factor which will determine which locations meet this condition (that is give the highest rates of profit, allowing for risks and uncertainties), will be the level of labour productivity relative to the wage rate. But clearly the optimum location will also be determined by economies of concentration, transport costs and tariffs. In general, transport barriers have been eroded over the past century, but they obviously will vary in importance depending on the economies of scale in production relative to circulation for each commodity.

In general, however, transport costs will not vary according to the stage of the capitalist cycle or crisis, whereas tariffs will. Blocs of capital will have competing interests as far as transport and tariff barriers are concerned, with weaker capital generally seeking protection from stronger blocs. In so far as transport costs act like a tariff with high transport costs to some extent 'sealing off' areas of activity, weaker blocs of capital may oppose improved forms of transport. Similarly, protectionism through tariffs and quotas is likely to be supported by weaker blocs of capital. But in the case of administrative protection the pressure is likely to be much greater in times of crisis as the interests of many sections of capital (at least within a particular nation-state) coincide. For in a recession a number of capitals are likely to be weakened at the same time. Thus, in the crisis, the pressure for tariff and quota protection is likely to grow, with the likelihood of protectionist pressures being particularly strong in times of depression, as in the 1930s and late 1970s. This means that centralization tendencies are likely to intensify during downswings or crises in economic activity. Thus capitalist development is likely to be uneven not only spatially, but also over time.

The roles that money and credit are considered by the abstract labour theorists to play in a capitalist economy ensure that this unevenness through space and time is considerable. Thus if, at a particular point in time, a country (India in our earlier example) is running a deficit on the balance of trade, then what happens will depend crucially on the state of the world capitalist economy. Industrial and/or finance capital may be 'flowing' into the Indian economy at a rate sufficient to compensate for the trade deficit. Credit may be extended. Alternatively, capital flows may have dried up. Much depends on the state of the capitalist economy. If there is a financial crisis, then the credit system will be transformed into a monetary system, for in a crisis 'money alone is a commodity' (Marx, 1970, 138).

By contrast, in the upswing when capital is booming, not only will credit be extended by industrial capital but the commercial banks and financial capital, in general, will also be looking for new borrowers. But in the downswing, when money is demanded as a commodity – as the sole measure of value – then loans will only be extended (if at all) at high interest rates and the exchange rates of the economically weaker nation-states will be put under pressure. The squeeze on weaker capitals will intensify, and as they attempt to survive, increased pressure will be put on labour in the 'backward economies'. Labour will be sacked, and the 'reserve army of the unemployed' will swell, and as it does, it will weaken resistance to wage cuts and productivity increases.

As the crisis intensifies interest rates will rise most sharply in the weaker economies. This, together with rising protectionism in the rest of the world, may mean that restructuring in the weaker economies is discouraged, as the high interest rates and the protectionist uncertainties deter the relocation of production to take advantage of the higher rates of labour exploitation. Many of the blocs of capital in the weaker economies will be crying out for protection, but the government may find that a condition for obtaining loans from multilateral sources such as the IMF is to keep the economy 'open'. If the loans are obtained complete with the 'liberalization' strings, then the weaker economy may be restructured. Capital may well relocate there, and exports may well boom. Thus not only do 'the free traders remain, tirelessly selling the patient medicine of comparative costs' (Shaikh, in Nell, 1980, 230), but they can point to 'cures' which apparently result from their medicine. However, the patient's recovery is not the smooth, even and happy process which the pedlars of the medicine imply.

The reality for the abstract labour 'doctors' is quite different. The crisis is particularly severe in the backward regions whether these be within the richer nation-states or more or less whole nation-states in the Third World. The centralization-of-control process is relentless, though this is not necessarily accompanied by a process of further concentration in the workplace. But the process is uneven *not* because of monopoly in 'civil' society as implied by the underdevelopment theorists, but precisely because capitalist competition is so severe. For as Marx put it:

> In practical life we find not only competition, monopoly and the antagonism between them, but also the synthesis of the two, which is not a formula but a movement. Monopoly produces competition, but competition produces monopoly. Monopolists are made from competition; competitors become monopolists . . . the more the mass of the

proletariat grows as against the monopolists of one nation, the more desperate competition becomes between monopolists of different nations.   (Marx, 1971, 152)

But the flow of capital is not smooth. For the abstract labour theorists, the development of capitalism is uneven in the north as well as in the south. Thus the process is in constant flux, and the picture painted by Emmanuel is far too static. The limitations of his theory are most transparent, when the policy conclusions are considered. For, as argued in Section 8.4, there seems to be little possibility of many commodity cartels getting off the ground, since the obstacles are *not* limited to opposition from the richer imperialist nations. In the view of the abstract labour theorists the most important 'obstacle' is that of worldwide capitalist competition. Such an approach suggests that the rate of exploitation of labour (in the technical sense used by Marx) in the south relative to that in the north is not as great as implied by Emmanuel. This is a point that was made by Bettelheim in the appendix to *Unequal Exchange* (1972), and it is a point made by Geoffrey Kay in his *Development and Underdevelopment: A Marxist Analysis* as follows: 'In terms of value, it is more than likely that wages in the developed countries are lower than those in the underdeveloped countries' (Kay, 1975, 116).

Indeed, according to Kay: 'we have to face the unpalatable fact that capitalism has created underdevelopment not simply because it has exploited the underdeveloped countries but because it has not exploited them enough' (ibid., 55). In Kay's view the development of productive facilities in the Third World has been blocked by merchant capital, because the latter makes its profit not by revolutionizing production, but by controlling markets (ibid., 95). Thus 'The history of underdevelopment is the fullest expression we have of these contradictory tendencies of merchant capital to both stimulate and repress the development of the forces of production and to both open and block the way for the full development of capitalism' (ibid.).

Giovanni Arrighi's early 1970s analysis of development (or rather the lack of it) in tropical Africa was somewhat similar, but for him the blockage consisted of a state apparatus which supported an élite and a subélite of well-paid urban workers, which Arrighi called a labour aristocracy (see Arrighi and Saul, 1973).

Thus for both Kay and Arrighi, as for Marx a century earlier, international capital is both progressive and regressive. It is progressive inasmuch as it breaks down pre-capitalist blockages to the development of productive forces. But it also regressive inasmuch as it moulds the social relations into a capitalist framework and reinforces the hold of capital over labour.

But it is worth emphasizing that, even if the essential argument of Kay, Bettelheim and others against Emmanuel is accepted, namely that unequal exchange does not operate in the systematically 'unfair' way suggested by Emmanuel, this does not mean that unequal exchange does not exist. Unequal exchange occurs continuously within, as well as between nation-states (for Marx on this, see 1973a, 872). In other words, it exists in both the 'narrow' and the 'broad' senses implied by Emmanuel. But in the view of the abstract labour theorists it is more a somewhat accidental and random by-product of capitalism, rather than a central and systematic tendency. For the Marxists, it is more useful (for the purposes of guiding socialist action) to focus attention on the *capitalist* integration of production, distribution and exchange, rather than to focus, as Emmanuel tends to, solely on the issue of distribution.

The distributional emphasis of the COPs is rejected by the abstract labour theorists; thus, for them, the primary focus is not in terms of a north–south division. Nor does the cure to the problems of capitalism lie in the solution put forward by Keynes and latter-day COPs – namely the abolition of the rentier. For Keynes, a major problem arising from the division of ownership and control was the conflict between the speculation of the rentier and the entrepreneurship of the manager. Keynes was not the first COP to focus on this conflict; Veblen had done so three decades previously. But neither was Keynes the last; Robinson and Eatwell, from the same Keynesian stable of Cambridge, focused on this conflict in the early 1970s, in saying: 'the division of the community into idle consumers and active producers becomes a division between rentiers of all kinds (including landowners), on the one hand, and managers and workers on the other' (Robinson and Eatwell, 1973, 77).

The Marxists do not deny that there is conflict between financial and industrial capital, but they argue that it is not the *primary* conflict in a capitalist society. The primary conflict, they argue, is that between labour and capital. The identification of this as the major antagonism has important implications for labour organization. Thus they go beyond the COPs in arguing not only that trade unions are essential organizations for labour – they are for COPs as well – but that such unions must not limit themselves to struggles over the wage rates of a particular firm, industry, or even sector. For 'a rise in the price of labour . . . only means, in fact, that the length and weight of the golden chain the wage-worker has already forged for himself, allow of a relaxation of the tension of it' (Marx, 1970, 618). If the trade unions limit themselves to such guerrilla action, Marx said, they will fail. They should instead use their organized forces as a lever for the final emancipation of the working class and for the ultimate abolition of the wages system (see Marx, 1973b, 78–9).

The focus of the abstract labour theorist on the fundamentally *capitalist* aspect of the contemporary mode of production has important implications for the definition of, and strategy for, achieving socialism. The socialist image or dream of the COPs is of a society in which the 'managers of its economic activities are free to run things as they please' (F. Roosevelt, in Nell, 1980, 300). For the Marxists, it is not 'the rentier aspect of profit, as a source of wealth . . . that makes the strongest case for socialism' (Robinson, 1960, 10–11). Instead the case for socialism lies in the emancipation of individual creativity in social production.

And so the abstract labour theorists deny that the choice that we face is the stark one 'between the twin evils of property and bureaucratic domination' (Parkin, 1971, 193). The focus is on a third alternative, in which the direct producers have control over production. The achievement of this third alternative is, of course, highly problematic, and the path to it highly controversial. To go into more discussion on socialism, and the problems of getting there, is not possible within the scope of this book – I refer the reader to the references at the end of Chapter 9.

Once we move from a high level of abstraction in which the world economy is analysed in terms of dominance by a capitalist mode of production, the picture becomes much more complicated. Then the unevenness of capitalism through both space *and* time has to be recognized. Capitalism has to be recognized as a rapidly changing phenomenon, developing and decaying, with the changes being both reflected in and generating changes in nation-states and fractions of capital. Thus a particular problem for socialists 'is that while the process of capital accumulation operates on an international scale, the process of class struggle operates largely at a national level' (Elson, 1982, 120).

It is beyond the scope of this book to analyse this unevenness in capitalism over space and time in more detail. Some useful references are given at the end of this chapter. But I want to end by stressing the importance, for abstract labour theorists, of the historical analysis of the capitalist mode of production at a variety of levels of abstraction. Such analysis tends to show that even such limited democratic forms of government as parliamentary democracy are threatened continuously, but are subjected to particular threats during periods of crisis.

Similarly, the calls for a new international economic order (NIEO) are meaningless in the sense that the international economic order is always changing. Thus the British domination of the world economy in the late nineteenth century and in the early part of this century gave way, in the crisis of the 1930s, to US domination. And the latter, in the crisis of the

1980s, is being challenged by the dominance of Japanese and German capital. And now, as in the 1930s, the crisis theatens to engulf the world in a catastrophic conflict.

But the lesson that comes from a Marxist analysis is that the greatest danger of such a conflict is not perhaps between east and west, nor between north and south, but within the west. Thus in her book, *The Disintegrating West*, Mary Kaldor argues that the Soviet threat, the threat from the east, has been overstated by the US government since the end of the Second World War in order to ensure the division of Europe (Kaldor, 1978, chapter 1). It is a major theme of her book 'that the global struggle between the US and the Soviet Union has been a kind of necessary ritual, masking real social conflicts that both super powers faced within their own spheres of influence' (ibid., 207). A similar emphasis on the importance of economic conflicts between advanced capitalist countries in the postwar period can be found in Riccardo Parboni's book (1981).

Mary Kaldor emphasizes the imminence of change in the international system, and discusses two possible forms of imperialism through which this change may express itself. The first, which she associates with the writings of Harry Magdoff and Pierre Jalee, anticipates an extension of US domination, a kind of superimperialism. The second school of thought, which she identifies with Bob Rowthorn and Ernest Mandel, envisages the rise of 'interimperial rivalry', the increased power of Japan and Europe, and a growing conflict between these nations and the USA (see Kaldor, 1978, 11, 12). Kaldor's emphasis is on the latter, but the outcome of this rivalry is not at all certain, though the number of outcomes is limited (ibid., 174, 196, 197). One possibility is that of a European Union which comes into ever sharper conflict with the USA. In this scenario the crisis of capitalism is managed uneasily by social democratic governments. A second possibility is that of a continuation of the pattern of the immediate past, with a renewed but unstable American hegemony, with the economic crisis being resolved through domestic repression, and with ideological confrontation between east and west becoming ever sharper. The third possibility, 'which is much less predictable, would involve radical changes in social structure, abandoning the fundamental principles of private enterprise, in at least some European states' (ibid., 174).

In this book I have identified three schools of economic thought and have attempted to present their analyses of trade, money and crisis, and the international policies which they each advocate. The alternative scenarios put forward by Mary Kaldor for this fragmented world would tend to be favoured, in each case, by a particular school of thought.

Thus I hope that this book has not only helped the reader to put the competing theories of trade, money and crisis into clearer perspective, but will also be a guide in his/her day-to-day politics.

NOTES ON FURTHER READING

Most of the references which usefully complement this chapter have been given in previous chapters. Here I merely wish to reiterate my debt to a number of particular sources. First, my major intellectual debt for the schools-of-thought structure of this book is to John Cameron and Ken Cole. The first and last chapters of the book written jointly with them, *Why Economists Disagree*, 1983, should be read alongside this chapter. Secondly, major stimuli for my thinking on money and trade have been the article by Anwar Shaikh, in Nell, 1980, and the thesis of Howard Nicholas, 1983. In addition to Shaikh's article, it may be useful to look at the article by Frank Roosevelt in the same volume, in which the economics of the Cambridge school is analysed: Roosevelt, in Nell, 1980.

In the third section of this chapter I emphasized the importance of historical analyses of capitalism to understand the unevenness of its development both spatially and through time. A useful stab at a discussion of the development of capitalism through time – a periodization of capitalism – is provided by Fine and Harris in their *Re-Reading Capital*, 1979. See also the article by Jessop, 1977. Otherwise, for the rest, go back to the 'Notes on further reading' at the end of the previous chapters.

References

Abdel-Fadil, M., Cripps, F., and Wells, J. (1977), 'A new international economic order', *Cambridge Journal of Economics*, 1 (2) (June 1977), 205–13.

Adams, F. and Behrman, J. (1982), *Commodity Exports and Economic Development: The Commodity Problem and Policy in Developing Countries*, Lexington, Mass., Lexington Books.

Aliber, R. (1980), 'The integration of the offshore and domestic banking system', *Journal of Monetary Economics*, 6 (1980), 509–26.

Altman, E. and Sametz, A. (eds) (1977), *Financial Crises: Institutions and Markets in a Fragile Environment*, New York, Wiley.

Amin, S. (1972), 'Underdevelopment and dependence in Black Africa: origins and contemporary forms', *Journal of Modern African Studies*, 10 (4) (December), 503–24.

Amin, S. (1973), *L'Echange inégal et la loi de la valeur: la fin d'un débat, avec une contribution de J. C. Saigal*, Paris, Editions Anthropos–Idep; English trans., excluding Saigal's contribution, in Amin, S., *Imperialism and Unequal Development*, Brighton, Harvester Press; New York, Monthly Review Press, 1977.

Amin, S. (1976), *Unequal Development*, Brighton, Harvester Press; New York, Monthly Review Press.

Amin, S. (1977), 'Self-reliance and the new international economic order', *Monthly Review*, 29 (3) (July–August), 1–21.

Amin, S., Arrighi, G., Frank, A. G., and Wallerstein, I. (1982), *Dynamics of Global Crisis*, London, Macmillan.

AMPO (1977), *Free Trade Zones and the Industrialisation of Asia*, Tokyo, Pacific Asia Resources Center.

Andersson, J. O. (1971), 'Reflections on the theory of unequal exchange', International Symposium on Imperialism, Elsinor, Denmark.

Andersson, J. O. (1974), 'The law of value and unequal exchange', Institute for Social Research, Abo Akademi, series B: 33, Abo, Finland.

Andersson, J. O. (1976), 'Studies in the theory of unequal exchange between nations', Institute for Social Research, Abo Akademi, Abo, Finland.

Argy, V. (1981), *The Post-War International Money Crisis – an Analysis*, London, Allen & Unwin.

Arrighi, G. and Saul, J. (1973), *Essays on the Political Economy of Africa*, New York, Monthly Review Press.

Artis, M. and Lewis, M. (1981), *Monetary Control in the United Kingdom*, Oxford, Philip Allan.

Avineri, S. (1980), *The Social and Political Theory of Karl Marx*, Cambridge, Cambridge University Press.

Bacha, E. L. (1978), 'An interpretation of unequal exchange from Prebisch–Singer to Emmanuel', *Journal of Development Economics*, 5 (December), 319–30.

Bagchi, A. (1976), 'De-industrialisation in India in the 19th century: some theoretical implications', *Journal of Development Studies*, 12 (2) (January), 135–64.

Bahro, R. (1982), *Socialism and Survival*, New York, Heretic Books.

Balassa, B. (1971), *The Structure of Protection in Developing Countries*, Baltimore, Md, Johns Hopkins University Press.

Balassa, B. (1979), *The Changing International Division of Labour in Manufactured Goods*, Staff Working Paper No. 329, Washington, DC, World Bank.

Balassa, B. (1980a), *The Process of Industrial Development and Alternative Development Strategies*, Staff Working Paper No. 438, Washington, DC, World Bank.

Balassa, B. (1980b), *The Tokyo Round and the Developing Counties*, Staff Working Paper No. 370, Washington, DC, World Bank.

Baran, P. (1957), *The Political Economy of Growth*, New York, Monthly Review Press.

Baran, P. and Sweezy, P. (1966), *Monopoly Capital*, Harmondsworth, Penguin Books.

Barber, W. J. (1967), *A History of Economic Thought*, Harmondsworth, Penguin Books.

Bauer, P. (1976), *Dissent on Development*, London, Weidenfeld & Nicolson.

Bauer, P. (1981), *Equality, the Third World and Economic Delusion*, London, Weidenfeld & Nicolson.

Bauer, P. and Yamey, B. (1981), 'The political economy of foreign aid', *Lloyds Bank Review* (October), 1–14.

Beckman, B. (1981), 'Imperialism and the national bourgeoisie', *Review of African Political Economy* (October–December), 5–19.

Beenstock, M. (1983), *The World Economy in Transition*, London, Allen & Unwin.

Bello, W., Kinley, D., and Elinson, E. (1982), *Development Debacle: The World Bank in the Philippines*, Institute for Food Development Policy, San Francisco, Calif.

Benton, T. (1977), *Philosophical Foundations of the Three Sociologies*, London, Routledge & Kegan Paul.

Bernstein, H. and Nicholas, H. (1983), 'Pessimism of the intellect, pessimism of the will? A response to Gunder Frank', *Development and Change* (New York) 14, 609–24.

Bhagwati, J. and Eckaus, R. (eds) (1970), *Foreign Aid: Selected Readings*, Harmondsworth, Penguin Books.

BICO (1974), *The International Socialists and the Russian Revolution*, Belfast, British and Irish Communist Organization.

Bird, R. and Head, J. (eds) (1972), *Modern Fiscal Issues: Essays in Honour of Carl S. Shoup*, Toronto, University of Toronto Press.

Blackburn, R. (ed.) (1976), *Ideology in Social Science*, Glasgow, Fontana/Collins.

Bloomfield, A. (1959), *Monetary Policy under the International Gold Standard: 1880–1914*, New York Federal Reserve Bank.

Bodington, S. (1982), *The Cutting Edge of Socialism*, Nottingham, Spokesman Books.

Bogdanowicz-Bindert, C. (1983), 'Debt: beyond the quick fix', *Third World Quarterly*, 5 (4) (October), 828–38.

BP (1981), *Statistical Review of World Energy, 1981*, London, British Petroleum Company.

Bradby, B. (1975), 'The destruction of natural economy', *Economy and Society*, 4 (2) (May), 127–61.

Brandt, W. (1980), *North–South: A Programme for Survival*, Report of the Independent Commission on International Development Issues (ICIDI), chaired by Willy Brandt, London, Pan Books.

Brandt, W. (Brandt Commission) (1983), *Common Crisis: Cooperation for World Recovery*, London, Pan Books.

Braun, O. (1974), 'L'échange inégal', in Amoa, G. and Braun, O. (eds), *Echanges Internationaux et sous-développement*, Paris, Editions Anthropos-Idep.

Braun, O. (1977), *International Trade and Imperialism* (a translation into English of Braun's *Commercio Internacional e Imperialismo*), The Hague, Institute of Social Studies, rev. edn, 1980; Spanish edn: Buenos Aires, Argentina Editores, 1973.

Brenner, R. (1977), 'The origins of capitalist development: a critique of neo-Smithian Marxism', *New Left Review* (July–August), 25–92.

Brett, T., Gilliatt, S., and Pople, A. (1982), 'Planned trade, Labour Party policy, and US intervention: the successes and failures of postwar reconstruction', *History Workshop* (London), no. 13 (Spring), 130–42.

Brewer, A. (1980), *Marxist Theories of Imperialism: A Critical Survey*, London, Routledge & Kegan Paul.

Brook, E., Grilli, E., and Waelbroeck, J. (1978), *Commodity Price Stabilisation and the Developing Countries*, World Bank Reprint No. 66, Washington, DC, World Bank.

Brookfield, H. (1975), *Interdependent Development*, London, Methuen.

Brown, M. B. (1974), *Economics of Imperialism*, Harmondsworth, Penguin Books.

Brown, R. and Wright, P. (1978), *Oscar Braun's Theory of Unequal Exchange: A Critical Review*, The Hague, ISS.

Brown, W. A. (1940), *The International Gold Standard Re-Interpreted: 1914–34*, New York, National Bureau of Economic Research.

Brunner, K. (ed.) (1978), *The First World and the Third World*, New York, University of Rochester.

Bukharin, N. (1972), *Imperialism and World Economy*, London, Merlin Press.

Bullock, P. and Yaffe, D. (1975), 'Inflation, the crisis and the postwar boom', *Revolutionary Communist* (London), no. 3/4 (double issue), 5–45.

Cairncross, F. and Keeley, P. (1983), *The Guardian Guide to the Economy, Volume 2*, London, Methuen.

Cameron, J., Cole, K., and Edwards, C. (1980), 'Teaching economics principles as part of development studies', *IDS Bulletin* (June); reprinted in Livingstone, I. (eds), *Approaches to Development Studies*, London, Gower, 1982.

Cardoso, F. (1977), 'The consumption of dependency theory in the USA', *Latin America Research Review*.

Carr, E. H. (1980), *The Russian Revolution from Lenin to Stalin, 1917–1929*, London, Macmillan.

Caves, R. E. and Jones, R. W. (1977), *World Trade and Payments: An Introduction*, 2nd edn, Boston, Mass., Little, Brown.

CCP (1976), *Ugly Features of Soviet Social-Imperialism*, Chinese Communist Party, Peking, Foreign Languages Press.

Chipman, J. (1965–6), 'A survey of the theory of international trade', *Econometrica* – 'Part 1: the classical theory', 33 (July 1965); 'Part 2: the neo-classical theory', 33 (October 1965); 'Part 3: the modern theory', 34 (January 1966).

Christian Aid (1977), *The North–South Map*, London, Christian Aid.

Clairmonte, F. (1960), *Economic Liberalism and Underdevelopment*, Bombay, Asia Publishing House.

Clark, J. B. (1965), *The Distribution of Wealth*, New York, Kelley; first published in 1899.

Cliff, Tony (1964), *Russia: A Marxist Analysis*, London, International Socialism.

Cliff, Tony (1974), *State Capitalism in Russia*, London, Pluto Press.

Cline, W. R. (1983), *International Debt and the Stability of the World Economy*, Washington, DC, Institute for International Economics, September.

Coakley, J. and Harris, L. (1983), *The City of Capital*, Oxford, Blackwell.

Cole, K., Cameron, J., and Edwards, C. (1983), *Why Economists Disagree: The Political Economy of Economics*, London, Longman.

Colman, D. and Nixson, F. (1978), *Economics of Change in Less Developed Countries*, Oxford, Philip Allan.

Commonwealth Secretariat (1975), *Terms of Trade Policy for Primary Commodities*, Commonwealth Economic Papers No. 4, London.

Connolly, M. and Swoboda, A. (eds) (1973), *International Trade and Money: The Geneva Essays*, Toronto, University of Toronto Press.

Cooper, R. (ed.) (1969), *International Finance*, Harmondsworth, Penguin Books.

Cooper, R. (1972), 'Economic interdependence and foreign policy in the 1970s', *World Politics*, 24 January 1972.

Coppock, J. (1962), *International Economic Instability*, New York, McGraw-Hill.

Corden, W. M. (1971), *The Theory of Protection*, Oxford, Clarendon Press.

Corden, W. M. (1974), *Trade Policy and Economic Welfare*, Oxford, Oxford University Press.

Crockett, A. (1980), *International Money*, London, Nelson.

Cuddy, J. (1980), 'Impact of the integrated program for commodities in selected mining economies', Reprint No. 8, UNCTAD, New York.

Currie, D. (1979), 'The EEC: what it's done for Britain and can we get out?', *Marxism Today* (London), 23 (4) (April), 111–18.

Cypher, J. (1979), 'The internationalisation of capital and the transformation of social formations: a critique of the Monthly Review school', *Review of Radical Political Economics*, 11 (4), 33–49.

Dahrendorf, R. (1959), *Class and Class Conflict in Industrial Society*, Stanford, Calif., Stanford University Press.

Dale, R. (1983), 'Basle Concordat: lessons from Ambrosiano', *The Banker*, 133 (691) (September), 55–60.

Davidson, P. (1982), *International Money and the Real World*, London, Macmillan.

Davies, A. and Wright, C. (1981), 'The changing world of interest rates', *Barclays Bank Review*, LVI (August), 51–6.

Deane, P. (1978), *The Evolution of Economic Ideas*, Cambridge, Cambridge University Press.

Dell, S. (1981), *On Being Grandmotherly: The Evolution of IMF Conditionality*, Essays in International Finance No. 144, Princeton University, Princeton, NJ, October.

Department of Trade and Industry (DTI) (1981), *British Business*, London, DTI, 4 September.

Deutscher, I. (1970), *Trotsky: A Biography*, 3 vols, Oxford, Oxford University Press.

Deutscher, I. (1976), *Stalin*, Harmondsworth, Penguin Books; first published in 1949.

Dobb, M. (1973), *Theories of Value and Distribution since Adam Smith*, Cambridge, Cambridge University Press.

Dos Santos, T. (1970), 'The structure of dependence', *American Economic Review, Papers and Proceedings*, 60 (2), 231–6.

Droucopoulos, V. (1981), 'The non-American challenge: a report on the size and growth of the world's largest firms', *Capital and Class*, no. 14 (September), 36–46.

Duignan, P. and Rabushka, A. (eds) (1980), *The US in the 1980s*, Stanford, Calif., Hoover Institution.

Dunning, J. (1981), *International Production and the Multinational Enterprise*, London, Allen & Unwin.

Durkheim, E. (1957), *Professional Ethics and Civic Morals*, London, Routledge & Kegan Paul.

The Economist (1979), *The World Economy*, London, The Economist Newspaper.

The Economist (1982), *Money and Finance*, London, The Economist Newspaper.

Edwards, C. (1975), 'Protection, profits and policy: industrialisation in Malaysia', PhD thesis, University of East Anglia, Norwich.

Edwards, C. (1980), 'Do the NICs represent a NIDL?', *Jurnal Ekonomi Malaysia* (Universiti Kebangsaan), no. 2 (December), 116–23.

Ellis, H. and Metzler, L. (eds) (1950), *Readings in the Theory of International Trade*, London, Allen & Unwin/American Economic Association.

Elson, D. (1982), 'The Brandt Report; a programme for survival?', *Capital and Class*, no. 16 (Spring), 110–26.

Eltis, W. and Sinclair, P. (eds) (1981), *The Money Supply and the Exchange Rate*, Oxford, Clarendon Press.

Emmanuel, A. (1972), *Unequal Exchange – a Study of the Imperialism of Trade*, London, New Left Books.

Emmanuel, A. (1974), 'Current myths of development', *New Left Review*, no. 85 (May–June), 61–82.

Engels, F. (1975), *Socialism: Utopian and Scientific*, Peking, Foreign Languages Press; first published in 1880.

Erdman, P. (1973), *The Billion Dollar Killing*, London, Hutchinson.

Evans, D. (1976), 'Unequal exchange and economic policies: some implications of the neo-Ricardian critique of the theory of comparative advantage', *Economic and Political Weekly*, annual number, XI (5, 6, 7), 143–58; reprinted in Livingstone, I. (ed.), *Development Economics and Policy: Readings*, London, Allen & Unwin, 1981; first published in *IDS Bulletin* (Brighton), 6 (4) (March 1975), 28–52.

Evans, D. (1979), 'International commodity policy: UNCTAD and NIEO in search of a rationale', *World Development*, 7 (3), 259–79.

Evans, D. (1981a), 'Monopoly power and imperialism: Oscar Braun's theory of unequal exchange', *Development and Change* (London) 12, 601–10.

Evans, D. (1981b), 'A critical discussion of neo-Marxian trade theories', Discussion Paper No. 12, La Trobe University, Melbourne, Australia.

Evans, D. and Jairath, J. (1977), 'Terms of trade and unequal exchange: annotated readings and references with a summary of some terms of trade movements, 1970–75', Institute of Development Studies, Brighton, mimeo.

Evans, P. (1979), *Dependent Development – the Alliance of Multinational, State, and Local Capital in Brazil*, Princeton, NJ, Princeton University Press.

FCO (1979), *The NICs and the Adjustment Problem*, London, Foreign and Commonwealth Office, July.

FCO (1980), *The Brandt Commission Report*, memorandum prepared by Foreign and Commonwealth Office for the Overseas Development Subcommittee of Foreign Affairs Committee, London, FCO, July.

Findlay, R. (1970), *Trade and Specialisation*, Harmondsworth, Penguin Books.

Fine, B. (1975), *Marx's Capital*, London, Macmillan.

Fine, B. (1982), *Theories of the Capitalist Economy*, London, Edward Arnold.

Fine, B. and Harris, L. (1979), *Re-Reading Capital*, London, Macmillan.

Frank, A. G. (1967), *Capitalism and Underdevelopment in Latin America*, New York, Monthly Review Press.

Frank, A. G. (1972), *Lumpenbourgeoisie and Lumpendevelopment. Dependency, Class and Politics in Latin America*, New York, Monthly Review Press.

Frank, A. G. (1978), *Dependent Accumulation and Underdevelopment*, London, Macmillan.

Frank, A. G. (1980), *Crisis in the World Economy*, London, Heinemann.

Frank, A. G. (1981a), *Reflections on the World Economic Crisis*, London, Hutchinson.

Frank, A. G. (1981b), *Crisis in the Third World*, London, Heinemann Educational.

Frankland, M. (1966), *Krushchev*, Harmondsworth, Penguin Books.

Frenkel, J. and Johnson, H. (eds) (1976), *The Monetary Approach to the Balance of Payments*, London, Allen & Unwin.

Friedman, M. (1955), 'Theory and measurement of long-run costs', in *Business Concentration and Price Policy*, Princeton, NJ, National Bureau for Economic Research/Princeton University Press.

Friedman, M. (1962), *Capitalism and Freedom*, Chicago, University of Chicago Press.

Friedman, M. (1977), *Inflation and Unemployment*, London, Institute of Economic Affairs.

Friedman, M. and Friedman, R. (1980), *Free to Choose*, Harmondsworth, Penguin Books.

Friedman, M. and Schwartz, A. (1963), *A Monetary History of the United States, 1867–1960*, Princeton, NJ, Princeton University Press.

Frobel, F., Heinrichs, J., and Kreye, O. (1980), *The New International Division of Labour*, Cambridge, Cambridge University Press.

Fullard, H. (ed.) (1972), *Soviet Union in Maps*, London, George Philip.

Galbraith, J. K. (1975), *Economics and the Public Purpose*, Harmondsworth, Penguin Books.

Galbraith, J. K. (1977), *The New Industrial State*, Harmondsworth, Penguin Books.

Gardner, R. (1969), *Sterling–Dollar Diplomacy*, Oxford, Oxford University Press.

Gemmill, G. (ed.) (1981), *Commodities Yearbook 1980/81*, London, International Commodities Clearing House.

Gibson, B. (1980), 'Unequal exchange', *Review of Radical Political Economics*, 12 (3), 15–35.

Giddens, A. (1981), *A Contemporary Critique of Historical Materialism*, London, Macmillan.

Giddens, A. (1982), *Sociology: A Brief but Critical Introduction*, London, Macmillan.

Gilbert, M. (1972), *Soviet History Atlas*, London, Routledge & Kegan Paul.

Girvan, N. (1976), *Corporate Imperialism: Conflict and Expropriation*, New York, Monthly Review Press.

Glyn, A. and Harrison, J. (1980), *The British Economic Disaster*, London, Pluto Press.

Gorz, A. (1982), *Farewell to the Working Class: An Essay on Post-Industrial Socialism*, London, Pluto Press; first published in France as *Adieux au Prolétariat*, Paris, Editions Galilee, 1980.

Goulbourne, H. (ed.) (1979), *Politics and State in the Third World*, London, Macmillan.

Green, F. and Nore, P. (eds) (1977), *Economics: An Anti-Text*, London, Martin Robertson.

Greenaway, D. and Milner, C. (1979), *Protectionism Again . . .?*, Hobart Paper No. 84, London, Institute of Economic Affairs.

Griffin, K. (1971), *Underdevelopment in Spanish America*, London, Allen & Unwin.

Griffith-Jones, S. (1982), *Adjustment Experience in the 1970s*, Discussion Paper No. 173, Brighton, Institute of Development Studies, May.

Grubel, H. (1977), 'The case against the new international economic order', *Weltwirtschaftliches Archiv*, 113, 284–307.

Grubel, H. (1978), *The International Monetary System*, Harmondsworth, Penguin Books.

Grubel, H. (1982), 'Towards a theory of free economic zones', *Weltwirtschaftliches Archiv*, 118, 39–61.

Grubel, H. and Johnson, H. (eds) (1971), *Effective Tariff Protection*, Geneva, GATT.

Hahn, F. (1972), *The Share of Wages in the National Income: An Enquiry into the Theory of Distribution*, London, Weidenfeld & Nicolson.

Hallwood, P. (1979), *Stabilisation of International Commodity Markets*, Greenwich, Conn., JAI Press.

Harcourt, G. (1972), *Some Cambridge Controversies in the Theory of Capital*, Cambridge, Cambridge University Press.

Hardwick, P. Khan, B., and Langmead, J. (1982), *An Introduction to Modern Economics*, London, Longman.

Hargreaves-Heap, S. (1980/1), 'World profitability crisis in the 1970s: some empirical evidence', *Capital and Class*, no. 12 (Winter), 66–84.

Harris, N. (1983), *Of Bread and Guns – the World Economy in Crisis*, Harmondsworth, Penguin Books.

Harris, N. and Hallas, D. (1981), *Why Import Controls Won't Save Jobs*, London, Socialist Workers Party.

Harris, S., Salmon, M., and Smith, B. (1978), *Analysis of Commodity Markets for Policy Purposes*, London, Trade Policy Research Centre.

Harrison, J. (1978), *Marxist Economics for Socialists: A Critique of Reformism*, London, Pluto Press.

Harriss, J. (1982), 'Indian industrialisation and the state', School of Development Studies, University of East Anglia, Norwich, mimeo.

Havrylyshyn, O. (1982), 'From cooperation to liberalisation', *Far Eastern Economic Review*, 24 December, 36–7.

Hayek, F. A. (1975), *Full Employment at Any Price?*, Occasional Paper No. 45, London, Institute of Economic Affairs.

Hayter, T. (1971), *Aid as Imperialism*, Harmondsworth, Penguin Books.

Hayter, T. (1982), *Creation of World Poverty*, London, Pluto Press.

Heckscher, E. (1919), 'The effect of foreign trade on the distribution of income', *Ekonomisk Tidskrift*, XXI; reprinted in Ellis, H. and Metzler, L. (eds), *Readings in the Theory of International Trade*, London, Allen & Unwin/American Economic Association, 1950.

Helleiner, G. K. (1972), *International Trade and Economic Development*, Harmondsworth, Penguin Books.

Helleiner, G. K. (1973), 'Manufactured exports from less-developed countries and multinational firms', *Economic Journal*, 83 (March), 21–47.

Helleiner, G. K. (ed.) (1976), *A World Divided*, Cambridge, Cambridge University Press.

Helleiner, G. K. (1978), 'A bad case: Grubel on the new international economic order', *Weltwirtschaftliches Archiv*, 114, 160–71.

Helleiner, G. K. (1981), *Intra-Firm Trade and the Developing Countries*, London, Macmillan.

Hilferding, R. (1981), *Finance Capital*, London, Routledge & Kegan Paul; originally published in German, 1910.

Hill, J. and Scannell, H. (1983), *Due South: Socialists and World Development*, London, Pluto Press.

Hirschman, A. (1958), *The Strategy of Economic Development*, New Haven, Conn., Yale University Press.

Hobson, J. (1961), *Imperialism: A Study*, 3rd edn, London, Allen & Unwin; first published in 1902.

Holloway, J. and Picciotto, S. (eds) (1979), *State and Capital: A Marxist Debate*, London, Edward Arnold.

Hood, N. and Young, S. (1979), *The Economics of Multinational Enterprise*, London, Longman.

Horowitz, I. (1966), *Three Worlds of Development*, London, Oxford University Press.

Horsefield, J. K. (1969); *The International Monetary Fund: 1945–65*, Washington, DC, IMF.

Howard, M. and King, J. (1975), *The Political Economy of Marx*, London, Longman.

Hufbauer, G. (1966), *Synthetic Materials and the Theory of International Trade*, London, Duckworth.

Illich, I. (1971), *Deschooling Society*, Harmondsworth, Penguin Books.

Ingham, B. and Simmons, C. (1981), 'The two world wars and economic development: editors' introduction', *World Development*, 9 (8), 701–5.

International Marxist Group (IMG) (1973), *Readings on 'State Capitalism'*, London, IMG.

International Monetary Fund (IMF) (1981), *Balance of Payments Yearbook, 1981*, Washington, DC, IMF.

International Monetary Fund (IMF) (1982), *World Economic Outlook, 1982*, Washington, DC, IMF.

International Monetary Fund (IMF) (1983), *World Economic Outlook, 1983*, Washington, DC, IMF.

Jenkins, R. (1983), *Transnational Corporations and Industrial Transformation in Latin America*, London, Macmillan.

Jessop, Bob (1977), 'Recent theories of the capitalist state', *Cambridge Journal of Economics*, 353–73.

Jessop, Bob (1982), *The Capitalist State*, London, Martin Robertson.

Jha, P. (1980), *India: A Political Economy of Stagnation*, Bombay, Oxford University Press.

Johnson, H. (1967), *Economic Policies Towards Less Developed Countries*, London, Allen & Unwin.

Kaldor, M. (1978), *The Disintegrating West*, Harmondsworth, Penguin Books.

Kaldor, M. (1982), *The Baroque Arsenal*, London, Deutsch.

Kaldor, N. (1976), 'Inflation and recession in the world economy', *Economic Journal*, 86 (December), 703–14.

Kaldor, N. (1980), 'Monetarism and UK monetary policy', *Cambridge Journal of Economics*, 4, 293–318.

Kaldor, N. (1982), *The Scourge of Monetarism*, Oxford, Oxford University Press.

Kalecki, M. (1976), *Essays on Developing Economies*, Brighton, Harvester Press.

Kautsky, K. (1915), 'Zwei Schrifte zum Umlernen', *Neue Zeit*, XXXIII (1914–15), 107–16.

Kautsky, K. (1970), 'Ultra-imperialism', *New Left Review*, 59 (January–February), 41–6; originally published in German, 1914.

Kay, G. (1975), *Development and Underdevelopment: A Marxist Analysis*, London, Macmillan.

Kay, G. (1979), *The Economic Theory of the Working Class*, London, Macmillan.

Keynes, J. M. (1976), *The General Theory of Employment, Interest and Money*, London, Macmillan; first published in 1936.

Kidron, M. (1970), *Western Capitalism since the War*, Harmondsworth, Penguin Books.

Kidron, M. and Segal, R. (1981), *The State of the World Atlas*, London, Pluto Press.

Kidron, M. and Smith, D. (1983), *The War Atlas*, London, Pan Books.

Kiernan, V. (1981), *America: The New Imperialism – from White Settlement to World Hegemony*, London, Zed Press.

Killick, T. (ed.) (1984a), *The Quest for Economic Stabilisation: The IMF and the Third World*, London, Heinemann.

Killick, T. (ed.) (1984b), *The IMF and Stabilisation: Developing Country Experiences*, London, Heinemann.

Kindleberger, C. (1981), *Manias, Panics and Crashes*, London, Macmillan.

Kitching, G. (1978), *The Marxist Theory of Imperialism and the Historical Study of Underdevelopment*, Centre for Development Studies, Swansea, mimeo.

Kitching, G. (1982), *Development and Underdevelopment in Historical Perspective*, London, Methuen.

Kitching, G. (1983), *Rethinking Socialism: A Theory for a Better Practice*, London, Methuen.

Krueger, A. (1974a), 'The political economy of the rent-seeking society', *American Economic Review*, 64 (3), 291–303.

Krueger, A. (1974b), *Foreign Trade Regimes and Economic Development: Turkey*, New York, National Bureau of Economic Research.

Krueger, A. (1983), 'The effects of trade strategies on growth', *Finance and Development*, Washington, DC, World Bank, 6–8.

Kurian, G. (1978), *Encyclopaedia of the Third World*, 2 vols, New York, Facts on File.

Labour Party (1977), *International Big Business: Labour's Policy on the Multinationals*, London, The Labour Party, October.

Labour Research Department (1977), *Inequality in Britain Today*, London, LRD.

Labour Research Department (1981), 'The press gang', in *Labour Research*, 7 (2), 34–6.

Laclau, E. (1977), *Politics and Ideology in Marxist Theory*, London, New Left Books.

Lal, D. (1983), *The Poverty of 'Development Economics'*, London, Institute of Economic Affairs.

Lall, S. (1980a), *The Multinational Corporation: Nine Essays*, London, Macmillan.

Lall, S. (1980b), 'Export manufacturing by NICs', *Economic and Political Weekly* (Bombay), XV (49) (6 December), 2057–62; XV (50) (13 December), 2103–12.

Lancaster, K. (1974), *Introduction to Modern Micro Economics*, 2nd edn, Chicago, Rand McNally.

Landsberg, M. (1979), 'Export-led industrialisation in the Third World: manufacturing imperialism', *Review of Radical Political Economics*, 11 (4), 50–63.

Lane, D. (1976), *The Socialist Industrial State*, London, Allen & Unwin.

Lappe, F. M., Collins, J., and Kinley, D. (1981), *Aid as Obstacle*, San Francisco, Calif., Institute for Food and Development Policy.

Latin American Bureau (LAB) (1983), *The Poverty Brokers: The IMF and Latin America*, London, LAB.

Laursen, K. (1978), 'The integrated programme for commodities', *World Development*, 6, 423–35.

Lavigne, M. (1974), *The Socialist Economies of the Soviet Union and Europe*, London, Martin Robertson.

Lee, D. and Newby, H. (1983), *The Problem of Sociology*, London, Hutchinson.

Leijonhufvud, A. (1971), *Keynes and the Classics*, Occasional Paper No. 30, Institute of Economic Affairs, London.

Lenin, V. (1970), *Imperialism, the Highest Stage of Capitalism*, Moscow, Progress Publishers.

Leontief, W. (1953), 'Domestic production and foreign trade: the American capital position re-examined', *Proceedings of American Philosophical Society*, 97 (4); reprinted in Leontief, W., *Input–Output Economics*, Oxford, Oxford University Press, 1966.

Lewis, W. (1954), 'Economic development with unlimited supplies of labour', *Manchester School*, 22 (2), 139–91; reprinted in Agarwala, A. and Singh, S. (eds), *Economics of Underdevelopment*, New Delhi, Oxford University Press, 1958.

Lewis, W. (1958), 'Unlimited labour: further notes', *Manchester School*, 26 (1), 1–32.

Leys, C. (1976), 'The "overdeveloped" post-colonial state: a re-evaluation', *Review of African Political Economy*, no. 5 (January–April), 39–48.

Lichtheim, G. (1978), *A Short History of Socialism*, London, Collins.

Limqueco, P. and McFarlane, B. (eds) (1983), *Neo-Marxist Theories of Development*, London, Croom Helm.

Linder, S. B. (1961), *An Essay on Trade and Transformation*, New York, Wiley.

Lindert, P. (1969), *Key Currencies and Gold, 1900–1913*, Princeton Studies in International Finance No. 24, Princeton, NJ, Princeton University Press.

Little, I. and Mirrlees, J. (1974), *Project Appraisal and Planning for Developing Countries*, London, Heinemann.

Little, I., Scitovsky, T., and Scott, M. (1970), *Industry and Trade in Some Developing Countries*, Oxford, Oxford University Press/OECD Development Centre.

Lomax, D. and Gutmann, P. (1981), *The Euromarkets and International Financial Policies*, London, Macmillan.

Luedde-Neurath, R. (1983), 'Import policy in South Korea, 1962–82: a reassessment', Institute of Development Studies, Brighton.

Lutz, E. and Bale, M. (1980), *Agricultural Protectionism in Industrialised Countries and its Global Effects: A Survey of Issues*, Reprint No. 174, Washington, DC, World Bank.

Luxemburg, R. (1963), *The Accumulation of Capital*, London, Routledge & Kegan Paul; first published in 1913.

MacAvoy, P. (1976), *Economic Perspective on the Politics of International Commodity Agreements*, Tucson, University of Arizona, mimeo.

MacBean, A. (1966), *Export Instability and Economic Development*, Cambridge, Mass., Harvard University Press.

McLellan, D. (1976), *Karl Marx: His Life and Thought*, London, Paladin Books.

McLellan, D. (1980), *The Thought of Karl Marx*, London, Macmillan.

McKenzie, G. (1981), 'Regulating the euro-markets', *Journal of Banking and Finance*, 5, 109–134.

McMichael, P., Petras, J., and Rhodes, R. (1974), 'Imperialism and the contradictions of development', *New Left Review*, no 85, (May–June), 83–104.

Magee, S. (1980), *International Trade*, London, Addison-Wesley.

Mandel, E. (1968), *Marxist Economic Theory*, London, Merlin Press.

Mandel, E. (1978), *Late Capitalism*, London, Verso.

Mandel, E. (1979), 'Why the Soviet bureaucracy is not a ruling class', *Monthly Review*, 31 (3) (July–August), 63–76.

Marx, K. (1967), *Capital. Volume 2*, ed. F. Engels, London, Lawrence & Wishart; first published in German, 1885.

Marx, K. (1970), *Capital. Volume 1*, London, Lawrence & Wishart;

London, first published in German, 1867.

Marx, K. (1971), *The Poverty of Philosophy*, New York, International Publishers; written in 1846–7.

Marx, K. (1972), *Capital. Volume 3*, ed. F. Engels, London, Lawrence & Wishart; first published in German, 1894.

Marx, K. (1973a), *Grundrisse (Introduction to the Critique of Political Economy)*, Harmondsworth, Penguin Books.

Marx, K. (1973b), *Wages, Price and Profit*, Peking, Foreign Languages Press; written in 1865, first published in English, 1898.

Marx, K. (1974), *The First International and After*, ed. and intro. by David Fernbach, Harmondsworth, Penguin Books.

Marx, K. (1975), *Early Writings*, Harmondsworth, Penguin Books.

Marx, K. (1976), *Surveys from Exile*, ed. and intro. by David Fernbach, Harmondsworth, Penguin Books.

Marx, K. (1977), *A Contribution to the Critique of Political Economy*, Moscow, Progress Publishers.

Marx, K. and Engels, F. (1974), *The German Ideology*, intro by C. J. Arthur, London, Lawrence & Wishart; written in 1845–6.

Marx, K. and Engels, F. (1975), *Manifesto of the Communist Party*, Peking, Foreign Languages Press; first published in German, 1848.

Marx, K. and Engels, F. (1976), *On Colonialism*, Moscow, Progress Publishers.

Mayer, M. (1974), *The Bankers*, New York, Ballantine.

Mayer, M. (1980), *The Fate of the Dollar*, New York, Times Books.

Mazrui, A. (1980), *The African Condition*, London, Heinemann.

Meade, J. E. (1982), *Stagflation. Volume 1, Wage Fixing*, London, Allen & Unwin.

Meek, R. (1961), 'Mr Sraffa's rehabilitation of classical economics', *Scottish Journal of Political Economy*, 8; reprinted in Meek, R., *Economic Ideology and Other Essays*, London, Chapman & Hall, 1967.

van Meerhaeghe, M. (1971), *International Economic Institutions*, 2nd edn, London, Longman.

Meier, G. (1968), *The International Economics of Development*, New York and London, Harper & Row.

Miliband, R. (1969), *The State in Capitalist Society*, London, Weidenfeld & Nicolson.

Miliband, R. and Saville, J. (eds) (1965), *Socialist Register*, London, Merlin Press.

Miller, M. (1981), 'Monetary control in the UK', *Cambridge Journal of Economics*, 5, 71–9.

Miller, R. (1981), 'Latin American manufacturing and the First World War: an exploratory essay', *World Development*, 9 (8), 707–16.

Milner, C. and Greenaway, D. (1979), *An Introduction to International Economics*, London, Longman.

Mitchell, B. (1982), *International Historical Statistics: Africa and Asia*, London, Macmillan.

Moore, J. B. (1966), *Social Origins of Dictatorship and Democracy*, Harmondsworth, Penguin Books.

Morgan Guaranty Trust (various dates), *World Financial Markets* (New York).

Morton, K. and Tulloch, P. (1977), *Trade and Developing Countries*, London, Croom Helm.

Mundell, R. (1962), *The Appropriate Use of Monetary and Fiscal Policy for Internal and External Stability*, International Monetary Fund Staff Papers, Washington, DC, IMF, March.

Murray, R. (1973), *The Internationalisation of Capital*, Nottingham, Spokesman Books.

Murray, R. (1977–8), 'Value and theory of rent' (in two parts), *Capital and Class*, no. 3 (Autumn 1977), 100–22, and no. 4 (Spring 1978), 11–33.

Murray, R. (ed.) (1981), *Multinationals beyond the Market*, Brighton, Harvester Press.

Myint, H. (1958), 'The "classical" theory of international trade and the underdeveloped countries', *Economic Journal*, LXVIII (June), 317–37.

Myrdal, G. (1956a), *An International Economy*, London, Harper.

Myrdal, G. (1956b), 'Development and underdevelopment', National Bank of Egypt, fiftieth anniversary commemoration lectures, Cairo; excerpts in Meier, G. (ed.), *Leading Issues in Economic Development*, Oxford, Oxford University Press, 1976.

Myrdal, G. (1957), *Economic Theory and Underdeveloped Regions*, London, Duckworth.

Nell, E. J. (ed.) (1980), *Growth, Profits and Property*, Cambridge, Cambridge University Press.

Nelson, D. R. (1981), *The Political Structure of the New Protectionism*, Staff Working Paper No. 471, Washington, DC, World Bank, July.

Nettl, J. (1973), *The Soviet Achievement*, London, Thames & Hudson.

New Internationalist (Oxford) (various dates).

Nicholas, H. (1983), 'Money and world market crises', PhD thesis, University of East Anglia, Norwich.

Nichols, T. (ed.) (1980), *Capital and Labour*, London, Fontana.

Nove, A. (1982), *An Economic History of the USSR*, Harmondsworth, Penguin Books.

Nove, A. (1983), *The Economics of Feasible Socialism*, London, Allen & Unwin.

Nove, A. and Nuti, M. (eds) (1972), *Socialist Economics: Readings*, Harmondsworth, Penguin Books.

Nowzad, B. (1978), *The Rise in Protectionism*, Pamphlet No. 24, Washington, DC, IMF.

Nurkse, R. (1944), *International Currency Experience*, Geneva, League of Nations.

OECD (1978) *Economic Outlook*, Paris, OECD, December.

OECD (1979a), *Balance of Payments of OECD Countries*, Paris, OECD, January.

OECD (1979b), *The Impact of the NICs on Production and Trade in Manufactures*, Paris, OECD.

OECD (1982a), *OECD Observer*, Paris, OECD, March.

OECD (1982b), *Economic Outlook*, Paris, OECD, July.

OECD (1983a), *Historical Statistics, 1960–81*, Paris, OECD.

OECD (1983b), *Economic Outlook*, Paris, OECD, July.

Ohlin, B. (1967), *Interregional and International Trade*, Cambridge, Mass., Harvard University Press; first published in 1933.

Open University (1976), *Inequalities Between Nations*, Milton Keynes, Open University.

Open University (1983), *Third World Studies*, U204 course material, Milton Keynes, Open University.

Overseas Development Institute (ODI) (1983), *Developing Country Bank Debt: Crisis Management and Beyond*, Briefing Paper No. 2, London, ODI, March.

Owen, D. (1981), *Face the Future*, London, Cape.

Oxaal, I., Barnett, T., and Booth, D. (eds) (1975), *Beyond the Sociology of Development*, London, Routledge & Kegan Paul.

Palma, G. (1978), 'Dependency: a formal theory of underdevelopment or a methodology for the analysis of concrete situations of underdevelopment?', *World Development*, 6 (7/8), 881–924.

Parboni, R. (1981), *The Dollar and Its Rivals*, London, New Left Books.

Parkin, M. (1971), *Class Inequality and Political Order*, London, MacGibbon & Kee.

Parkin, M. (1974), 'Inflation: a world problem', paper presented at 1974–5 session of Manchester Statistical Society, 12 November 1974.

Payer, C. (1974), *The Debt Trap: The IMF and the Third World*, Harmondsworth, Penguin Books.

Payer, C. (ed.) (1975), *Commodity Trade of the Third World*, London, Macmillan.

Payer, C. (1982), *The World Bank: A Critical Analysis*, New York, Monthly Review Press.

Pearce, I. (1970), *International Trade*, London, Macmillan.

Pearce, J. (1982), *Under the Eagle*, London, Latin America Bureau.

Pearson, L. (commission report, chairman Pearson) (1969), *Partners in Development*, New York, Praeger.

Phillips, A. (1958), 'The relation between unemployment and the rate of change of money wage rates in the UK, 1861–1957', *Economica*, XXV (100), 283–99.

Pillay, V. (1981), 'The international economic crisis', in Currie, D. and Smith, R. (eds), *Socialist Economic Review*, London, Merlin.

Polanyi, K. (1944), *The Great Transformation*, Boston, Mass., Beacon Press.

Power, J. (1979), *Migrant Workers in Western Europe and the United States*, Oxford, Pergamon.

Prebisch, R. (1959), 'Commercial policy in the underdeveloped countries', *American Economic Review. Papers and Proceedings*, XLIX (2), 251–73.

Prebisch, R. (1962), 'The economic development of Latin America and its principal problems', *Economic Bulletin for Latin America* (United Nations Commission for Latin America), 7 (1) (February), 1–22.

Prebisch, R. (1964), *Towards a New Trade Policy for Development*, New York, United Nations.

Radice, H. (ed.) (1975), *International Firms and Modern Imperialism*, Harmondsworth, Penguin Books.

Rangarajan, L. (1978), *Commodity Conflict*, London, Croom Helm.

Raj, K. (1973), 'The politics and economics of "intermediate regimes"', *Economic and Political Weekly* (Bombay), 8 (27) (7 July), 1189–98.

Ray, G. (1977), 'The "real" price of primary products', *National Institute Economic Review*, no. 81 (August), 72–6.

Reed, J. (1966), *Ten Days that Shook the World*, Harmondsworth, Penguin Books; first published in England, 1926.

Reid, M. (1982), *The Secondary Banking Crisis: 1973–75*, London, Macmillan.

Reubens, E. (ed.) (1981), *The Challenge of the NIEO*, Boulder, Colo., Westview Press.

Revell, J. (1980), *Costs and Margins in Banking, an International Survey*, Paris, OECD.

Rey, P. (1971), *Colonialisme, neo-colonialisme et transition au capitalisme*, Paris, Maspero.

Rey, P. (1973), *Les Alliances de classes*, Paris, Maspero.

Rhoades, S. (1983), 'Concentration of world banking and the role of US banks among the 100 largest, 1956–80', *Journal of Banking and Finance*, 7, 427–37.

Rhodes, R. (ed.) (1970), *Imperialism and Underdevelopment*, New York, Monthly Review Press.

Ricardo, D. (1971), *On the Principles of Political Economy and Taxation*, Harmondsworth, Penguin Books.

Riddell, A. (1979), *Restructuring British Industry: The Third World Dimension*, London, Catholic Institute for International Relations.

Rimmer, D. (1973), *Macromancy*, Hobart Paper No. 55, London, Institute of Economic Affairs.

Robinson, J. (1960), *Collected Economic Papers*, Vol. II, Oxford, Blackwell.

Robinson, J. (1968), *Economic Philosophy*, Harmondsworth, Penguin Books.

Robinson, J. (1971), 'The measure of capital: the end of the controversy', *Economic Journal*, 81 (September), 597–602.

Robinson, J. and Eatwell, J. (1973), *An Introduction to Modern Economics*, London, McGraw-Hill.

Robson, P. (1980), *The Economics of International Integration*, London, Allen & Unwin.

Rodney, W. (1972), *How Europe Underdeveloped Africa*, London, Bogle-L'Ouverture Publications; Dar es Salaam, Tanzania Publishing House.

Roemer, J. (1982), *A General Theory of Exploitation and Class*, Cambridge, Mass., Harvard University Press.

Rosdolsky, R. (1980), *The Making of Marx's Capital*, London, Pluto Press.

Ross, A. (1976), 'Emmanuel on unequal exchange: a Marxist contribution on trade relations between rich and poor, *Journal of Economic Studies*, 3 (1), 42–58.

Ross, J. (1983), *Thatcher and Friends – the Anatomy of the Tory Party*, London, Pluto Press.

Routh, G. (1980), *Occupation and Pay in Great Britain, 1906–79*, London, Macmillan.

Rowley, C. and Wiseman, J. (1983), 'Inflation versus unemployment: is the government important?', *National Westminster Bank Review* (February).

Rowthorn, B. (1980), *Capitalism, Conflict and Inflation*, London, Lawrence & Wishart.

Rowthorn, B. and Grahl, J. (1982), 'Europe . . . or bust', *New Socialist* (London), (May–June).

Roxborough, I. (1979), *Theories of Underdevelopment*, London, Macmillan.

Roxborough, I., O'Brien, P., and Roddick, J. (1977), *Chile, the State and Revolution*, London, Macmillan.

Rybczynski, T. (1978), 'Structural changes in the world economy', *Three Banks Review*, no. 120 (December), 21–35.

Sachs, J. (1980), 'The changing cyclical behaviour of wages and prices; 1890–1976', *American Economic Review*, LXX (1), 78–90.

Salvadori, N. (1981), 'Falling rate of profit with a constant real wage: an example', *Cambridge Journal of Economics*, 5 (1), 59–66.

Sampson, A. (1982), *The Money-Lenders*, London, Coronet Books.

Scammell, W. M. (1980), *The International Economy since 1945*, London, Macmillan.

Schiffer, J. (1977), 'The Russian industrialisation debate of the 1920s, *Problems of Communism* (British and Irish Communist Organization, Belfast), no. 8, 7–40.

Schiffer, J. (1981), 'The changing post-war pattern of development: the accumulated wisdom of Samir Amin', *World Development*, 9 (6), 515–37.

Schumacher, E. F. (1973), *Small Is Beautiful*, London, Sphere Books.

Schumpeter, J. (1951), *Imperialism and Social Classes*, trans. H. Norden and ed. P. Sweezy, Oxford, Blackwell.

Schwartz, A. (1984), 'Taming Leviathan', *The Banker*, 134 (696), 130.

Seers, D. (ed.) (1981), *Dependency Theory: A Critical Reassessment*, London, Pinter.

Sengupta, A. (ed.) (1980), *Commodities, Finance and Trade*, London, Pinter.

Shaikh, A. (1978), 'Political economy of capitalism: notes on Dobb's theory of crisis', *Cambridge Journal of Economics*, 2 (2), 233–51.

Shaikh, A. (1979), 'Foreign trade and the law of value: part 1', *Science and Society*, 43 (Fall), 281–302.

Shaikh, A. (1979–80), 'Foreign trade and the law of value: part II', *Science and Society*, 44 (Winter), 27–57.

Shone, R. (1972), *The Pure Theory of International Trade*, London, Macmillan.

Singer, H. (1950), 'US foreign investment in underdeveloped areas: the distribution of gains between investing and borrowing countries', *American Economic Review: Papers and Proceedings*, 40 (2), 473–85.

Singer, H. (1975), 'The distribution of gains from trade and investment revisited', *Journal of Development Studies*, II (4), 376–82.

Sklar, R. (1979), 'The nature of class domination in Africa', *Journal of Modern African Studies*, 17 (4), 531–52.

Smith, D. and Smith, R. (1983), *The Economics of Militarism*, London, Pluto Press.

Smith, S. (1980), 'The ideas of Samir Amin: theory or tautology?', *Journal of Development Studies*, 17 (1), 5–21.

Smith, S. and Toye, J. (eds) (1979), *Trade and Poor Economies*, London, Cass.

Sodersten, B. (1980), *International Economics*, London, Macmillan.

South (London) (various dates).

Spraos, J. (1980), 'The statistical debate on the net barter terms of trade between primary commodities and manufactures', *Economic Journal*, 90 (March), 107–28.

Spuler, B. (1977), *Rulers and Governments of the World. Vol. 3, 1930–1975*, London and New York, Bowker.

Sraffa, P. (1960), *Production of Commodities by Means of Commodities*, Cambridge, Cambridge University Press.

Stead, C. (1938), *House of All Nations*, New York, Simon & Schuster.

Steedman, I. (ed.) (1979a), *Fundamental Issues in Trade Theory*, London, Macmillan.

Steedman, I. (1979b), *Trade amongst Growing Economies*, Cambridge, Cambridge University Press.

Stockholm International Peace Research Institute (SIPRI) (1982), *The Arms Race and Arms Control*, Stockholm, SIPRI.

Stopford, J., Dunning, J., and Haberich, K. (1980), *The World Directory of Multinational Enterprises*, London, Macmillan.

Streeten, P. (ed.) (1969), *Unfashionable Economics*, London, Weidenfeld & Nicolson.

Streeten, P. (ed.) (1973), *Trade Strategies for Development*, London, Macmillan.

Stretton, H. (1969), *The Political Sciences*, London, Routledge & Kegan Paul.

Sunkel, O. (1972), 'Big business and dependency', *Foreign Affairs*, 24 (1), 517–31.

Sutcliffe, Bob (1983), *Hard Times – the World Economy in Turmoil*, London, Pluto Press.

Sweezy, P. (1968), *The Theory of Capitalist Development*, New York, Monthly Review Press; first published in 1942.

Sweezy, P. (1978), 'Is there a ruling class in the USSR?', *Monthly Review*, 30 (5), 1–17.

Sweezy, P. and Bettelheim, C. (1971), *On the Transition to Socialism*, New York, Monthly Review Press.

Tew, B. (1982), *The Evolution of the International Monetary System, 1945–81*, London, Hutchinson.

Theberge, J. (ed.) (1968), *Economics of Trade and Development*, London and New York, Wiley.

Third World First (1982), *Beyond Brandt*, Oxford, Third World First.

Thoburn, J. (1977), *Primary Commodity Exports and Economic Development*, London and New York, Wiley.

Thomson, D. and Larson, R. (1978), *Where Were You, Brother? An Account of Trade Union Imperialism*, London, War on Want.

Tobin, J. (1981), 'The monetarist counter-revolution today: an appraisal', *Economic Journal*, 91 (March), 29–42.

Travis, W. (1964), *The Theory of Trade and Protection*, Cambridge, Mass., Harvard University Press.

Trevithick, J. (1980), *Inflation*, Harmondsworth, Penguin Books.

Triffin, R. (1947), *National Central Banking and the International Economy*, International Monetary Policies No. 7, Board of Governors of the Federal Reserve System, New York.

Trotsky, L. (1932–3), *History of the Russian Revolution*, 3 vols, London, Gollancz.

Trotsky, L. (1972), *The Revolution Betrayed*, New York, Pathfinder Press; written in 1936.

UN (1976), *World Energy Supplies, 1950–74*, Statistical Papers, series J, No. 19, New York, United Nations.

UN (1978), *Transnational Corporations in World Development: A Re-examination*, New York, United Nations.

UN (1981), *Yearbook of World Energy Statistics*, Statistical Papers, series J, No. 24; New York, United Nations.

UNCTAD (1978), *The Role of Transnational Corporations in the Marketing and Distribution of Exports and Imports of Developing Countries*, Geneva, UNCTAD, February.

UNCTAD (1981), *Trade and Development Report, 1981*, Geneva, UNCTAD.

UNCTAD (1983a), *Export Processing Free Zones in Developing Countries: Implications for Trade and Industrialisation Policies*, Geneva, UNCTAD Trade and Development Board, January.

UNCTAD (1983b), *Economic Cooperation among Developing Countries*, Geneva, UNCTAD Trade and Development Board, October.

UNCTC (1979), *Transnational Corporations in Advertising*, New York, United Nations Centre for Transnational Corporations.

UNCTC (1981), *Transnational Banks: Operations, Strategies and Their Effects in Developing Countries*, New York, UNCTC.

UNCTC (1983), *Transnational Corporations in World Development – Third Survey*, New York, United Nations.

UNIDO (1981), *A Statistical Review of the World Industrial Situation, 1980*, Vienna, United Nations Industrial Development Organization.

URPE (1978), *US Capitalism in Crisis*, New York, Union for Radical Political Economics.

URPE (1981), *The Review of Radical Political Economics: Special Issue on the Soviet Union*, New York, URPE, Spring.

US Government (1981), *Economic Report of the President*, Washington, DC, January.

US Government (1982), *Economic Report of the President*, Washington, DC, February.

US Government (1983), *Economic Report of the President*, Washington, DC.

Vaitsos, C. (1974), *Intercountry Income Distribution and Transnational Enterprise*, Oxford, Clarendon Press.

Vaitsos, C. (1978), 'Crisis in regional economic cooperation (integration) among developing countries; a survey', *World Development*, 6 (6), 719–69.

Veil, E. (1982), 'The world current account discrepancy', *Economic Outlook. Occasional Studies*, (June), 46–63.

Vernon, R. (1966), 'International investment and international trade in the product cycle', *Quarterly Journal of Economics*, 80 (May), 190–207.

Viner, J. (1950), *The Customs Union Issue*, New York, Carnegie Endowment for International Peace.

Wallerstein, I. (1974), *The Modern World System*, New York, Academic Press.

Warren, B. (1973), 'Imperialism and capitalist industrialization', *New Left Review*, no. 81 (September–October), 3–44.

Warren, B. (1980), *Imperialism: Pioneer of Capitalism*, London, New Left Books/Verso.

Weeks, J. (1981), *Capital and Exploitation*, London, Edward Arnold.

Weeks, J. (1982), 'Equilibrium, uneven development, and the tendency of the rate of profit to fall', *Capital and Class*, no. 16 (Spring).

Williamson, J. (1977), *The Failure of World Monetary Reform: 1971–1974*, London, Nelson.

Wilson, E. (1967), *To the Finland Station*, London, Fontana; first published in 1940.

Wionczek, M. (1978), 'Can the broken humpty-dumpty be put together again and by whom? Comments on the Vaitsos survey', *World Development*, 6, 779–82.

Wolpe, H. (1972), 'Capitalism and cheap labour power in South Africa:

from segregation to apartheid', *Economy and Society*, 1 (4), 424–55.

World Bank (1981a), *Commodity Trade and Price Trends*, Baltimore, Md, Johns Hopkins University Press/World Bank, August.

World Bank (1981b), *World Development Report, 1981*, Washington, DC, World Bank.

World Bank (1983), *World Development Report, 1983*, Washington, DC, World Bank.

Worsley, P. (1978), *The Third World*, London, Weidenfeld & Nicolson.

Yeager, L. B. (1976), *International Monetary Relations*, New York, Harper & Row.

Yeats, A. J. (1981), *Trade and Development Policies*, London, Macmillan.

Young, K., Wolkowitz, C., and McCullagh, R. (eds) (1981), *Of Marriage and the Market*, London, CSE.

Zarembka, P. (ed.) (1977), *Research in Political Economy*, Greenwich, Conn., JAI Press.

Zis, G. (1975), 'Political origins of the international monetary crisis', *National Westminster Bank Review* (August), 28–43.

Index

absorption (income) effect, 130
abstract labour theory of value, 6, 14, 78, 89, 92, 95–6, 108–10, 125–6, 134, 136–7, 152, 155–6, 158–9, 166–7, 184, 202, 224, 252, 254, 261, 263–7, 271–2, 274, 276, 288, 300–2, 305–7
accumulation: capitalist, 65, 152; cumulative, 105; historical, 126; of capital, 73, 76–7, 93, 104–5, 126, 134, 136, 153, 158, 166–7, 184, 200, 203, 211, 267, 303, 307; primitive, 92; process, 153, 155, 265, 274, 303; renewed, 156
Accumulation of Capital, the (Luxemburg), 94, 104
Adams, F., 242
advertising, 104, 200
agrarian reform, 104
aid: and Emmanuel's thesis, 82, 246; and loans, 81, 172; and technical assistance, 80; and the state, 268; economic and military, 20–1, 173, 261; multilateral, 172
Aid as Imperialism (Hayter), 268
Algeria, 235
Aliber, R., 179–80
Alternative Economic Strategy, 217
Amin, Samir, 54, 77–8, 94, 97, 101, 103–10, 112
Anderson, Otto, 73, 105
Andean Pact, 202, 231
Angola, 233

Argentina, 98, 187, 189, 213, 219
Argy, V., 181
Arrighi, Giovanni, 94, 97, 305
Artis, M., 185
Association of South-East Asian Nations (ASEAN), 229
Australia, 5, 98

Bagchi, A., 71
Bahamas, the, 179
balance of payments, 58, 132, 151, 168, 171–2, 200, 222; adjustments, 123, 129, 132, 149–50, 168, 299; constraints, 212; deficits, 127–8, 132–3, 142, 150–1, 173, 181, 290, 298; surplus, 173
Balassa, B., 218, 295–7
Bale, M., 241
Bank of International Settlements (BIS), 175, 188
Baran, P., 20, 54, 77, 103–4, 107–10, 112, 268, 273–4
Bauer, Peter, 9, 20, 200, 261, 263, 292
Beckman, B., 301
Behrman, J., 242
Belgium, 144, 175
Bettelheim, Charles, 14, 76–7, 109, 111, 280, 305–6
Bhagwati, J. N., 4, 19–20, 261
big business, 47
Bird, R., 229

Bogdanowicz-Bindert, C., 188, 192
Bolivia, 231
bourgeois(ie), 90, 136, 264, 267, 271;
    and workers, 101; dependent, 106;
    lumpen, 106–7, 110; modes of
    production, 90, 279; national, 270;
    production, 190; small industrial,
    208
Brandt, Willy, 9, 77–81, 201, 241,
    263
Brandt Commission, 9, 14, 201–2,
    299; Report, 9, 45, 47, 77, 79–81,
    108, 235, 263, 299
Braun, Oscar, 72–3, 105
Brazil, 107, 187, 189, 195–7, 202,
    219, 241, 267
Brenner, R., 108–11, 202, 301
Brett, T., 173
Bretton Woods agreement, *see*
    International Monetary Fund
    (IMF)
Brewer, A., 97, 105, 109, 269–70,
    272
Britain, *see* UK
Brookfield, H., 108
Brown, M. B., 24, 62, 99, 212
Brown, William, 169–70
Brunner, K., 141–4
Bukharin, Nicolai, 98, 100–1,
    269–70, 272, 301
bureaucracy, sociological theories of,
    47, 277, 293; and the USSR,
    278–80
Burma, 21

Cairncross, F., 75
Cambodia, 278
Cameron, John, 6, 7, 46, 96, 288
Canada, 79, 98, 140, 144, 175, 197
capital, 135, 186, 190–1, 252, 269,
    274, 304–5, 307; banking or
    financial, 98, 136, 183, 264, 267,
    304; bargaining, 156, 217, 306;
    composition of, 154; constant, 65,
    68, 96, 154–5; cost of, 35, 37;

debate on definition of, 33–9,
    48–9, 167; depreciation of, 155–7;
    export of, 100, 281; factor of
    production, 23, 25–7, 31–7, 48,
    124; finance, 98, 267, 269; foreign,
    267–8, 297; 'fractions' of, 268–9,
    307; heterogeneous, 33;
    homogeneous, 39; human, 38;
    industrial, 98, 166, 186, 194, 264,
    267, 306; interest-bearing, 93;
    marginal productivity of, 35, 37;
    mobility of, 63, 69, 73–4, 124–5,
    182–4, 297; realization of, 157;
    restructuring of, 153, 157; short-
    term, 151; total, 153; value of,
    34–5, 37, 39, 49; variable, 65,
    67–8, 96, 153–4
Capital (Marx), 65, 89, 92, 134, 155
capital controversy, the, 32–40, 48–9,
    74, 124
capitalism, 14, 17, 64, 76–8, 82, 93,
    95–6, 98, 101, 102, 135–7, 140,
    152–5, 166–7, 192, 203, 224, 252,
    254, 264–5, 268–70, 273–4, 278,
    280, 300–1; and its reproduction,
    64, 94, 166–7; and its reformation,
    47; and the capitalist class, 52, 64,
    95–6, 126, 131, 146, 265–6; as a
    social relationship in a particular
    historical context, 65, 88–90, 92–5,
    97, 110, 302; competitive, 281–2;
    crises in, 92, 135–7, 140, 152–3,
    155–6, 158, 161, 168, 192–3, 198,
    308; international, 100, 103–4,
    106, 108–9, 111, 135–6, 170, 231,
    270; 'monopoly', 263–4, 268, 281;
    national, 224, 230, 272; scientific
    analysis of, 88–9; sexist and racist
    divisions within, 77
*Capitalism and Underdevelopment in
    Latin America* (Frank), 110
capital-output ratios, 154–5, 157
Caribbean Community (CARICOM),
    the, 224
Caves, R. E., 25–6, 39, 141
Cayman Islands, the, 179

Uganda, 21, 231
UK, 9, 20–32, 38, 99, 102, 124,
    127–8, 130, 132, 134, 144, 155,
    157, 159, 161, 174–5, 179–80, 183,
    186, 194–9, 202, 263, 290–2;
    abolition of wheat imports into, 45;
    and Emmanuel's thesis, 65, 67, 69,
    71–2, 75, 77; and terms of trade, 54
'ultra-imperialism', theory of, 100,
    269, 271
UNCTAD, 73, 80, 156, 175, 182,
    201, 228, 232–3, 238, 240, 243,
    245, 250–1, 254
'underconsumption', 274
underdeveloped countries, *see*
    developing countries
underdevelopment, 4, 5, 78, 101–2,
    231, 261, 301, 304–5; theory,
    103–12, 301
Underdevelopment in Spanish America
    (Griffin), 50
unemployment, 37–8, 96, 139, 145,
    148, 150, 158; average level, 139,
    149; growing rate, 145; natural
    level, 139, 149; rate, 146
unequal exchange, theories of, 46, 48,
    53–82, 105, 124–5, 246, 288–9,
    295, 297–8, 306; and the neo-
    Ricardian school, 47–8, 53–82,
    124–5, 288–9, 306
Unequal Exchange (Emmanuel), 61,
    63–4, 68, 76–7, 82, 101, 111, 115,
    235, 295, 305
United Arab Emirates (UAE), 235
United Nations, 9, 79–81, 195, 198,
    208, 232–3, 235, 238; and public
    education, 81
United Nations Centre on
    Transnational Corporations
    (UNCTC), 195, 198, 200
United Nations Industrial
    Development Organization
    (UNIDO), 218–19
USA, 5, 9, 98, 126, 139–40, 142,
    144, 148, 151, 154–5, 157, 159,
    167, 172–6, 178–81, 185–6, 191,
193–6, 200, 211, 213, 221, 230,
    251, 262, 273–4, 292, 307–8; and
    the Bretton Woods agreement,
    171–2, 180–1; and the 'communist
    threat' in Europe, 173; and the
    Leontief paradox, 38; and the war
    in Vietnam, 141; emigration into,
    29; restrictions on capital flows,
    178; restrictions on immigration,
    24, 75
USSR, 5, 19, 24, 100, 150, 178, 187,
    198, 273, 275, 278–82, 308; and
    the Communist Party of the Soviet
    Union (CPSU), 279
utility, 17, 247; a metaphysical
    concept, 18; and maximizing
    individuals, 17, 39; marginal, 289;
    maximization of, 17–18, 289

Vaitsos, C., 224, 230–1
value(s), 135, 154, 302; commodity's,
    65; deviation of prices from, 65, 67,
    253, *see also* 'transformation
    problem'; embodied, 136;
    exchange, 65, 95, 253; form, 77,
    95; surpluses, 65, 67, 280; theories
    of, 78, 123, 137, 260, 280; use, 95,
    253
value composition of capital, 154; *see
    also* organic composition of capital
Veblen, T. B., 44, 306
Venezuela, 187, 189, 235
Vernon, Raymond, 31, 38, 298
Vietnam, 141, 173, 233, 273
Viner, Jacob, 228

wage(s), 23, 28–9, 35–6, 39, 45, 51,
    57, 60, 68, 73, 75–8, 96, 124, 131,
    147, 154, 183, 252, 292, 294, 298,
    303, 305; adjustments, 129; and
    distribution, 44, 78; and the 'real
    wage resistance', 147; average, 64;
    bargaining, 22, 53, 57–8, 63, 82,
    124, 126, 152, 304; costs, 145;
    depression of, 155; equalization,
    125; fixed, 45; goods, 65, 154, 158;

DEVELOPMENT AND UNDERDEVELOPMENT

Series editors: Ray Bromley and Gavin Kitching

Tho

In the same series

Already published:

Development and Underdevelopment in Historical Perspective:
Populism, nationalism and industrialization
Gavin Kitching

Development Projects as Policy Experiments:
An adaptive approach to development administration
Dennis A. Rondinelli

Development and the Environmental Crisis:
Red or green alternatives?
Michael Redclift

Regions in Question:
Space, development theory and regional policy
Charles Gore

Forthcoming:

Multinational Corporations
Rhys Jenkins

Latin American Development Theories:
Structuralism, internal colonialism, marginality and dependency
Cristóbal Kay